Philo of Alexandria's Exposition of the Tenth Commandment

Society of Biblical Literature

Studia Philonica Monographs

General Editor
Thomas H. Tobin, S.J.

Number 6
Philo of Alexandria's Exposition
of the Tenth Commandment

PHILO OF ALEXANDRIA'S EXPOSITION OF THE TENTH COMMANDMENT

Hans Svebakken

Society of Biblical Literature
Atlanta

Copyright © 2012 by the Society of Biblical Literature

All rights reserved. No part of this work may be reproduced or transmitted in any form or by any means, electronic or mechanical, including photocopying and recording, or by means of any information storage or retrieval system, except as may be expressly permitted by the 1976 Copyright Act or in writing from the publisher. Requests for permission should be addressed in writing to the Rights and Permissions Office, Society of Biblical Literature, 825 Houston Mill Road, Atlanta, GA 30329, USA.

Library of Congress Cataloging-in-Publication Data

Philo, of Alexandria.
  [De Decalogo. Selections. English]
  Philo of Alexandria's exposition on the Tenth Commandment / by Hans Svebakken.
     pages. cm. — (Studia philonica monographs ; 6)
  ISBN 978-1-58983-618-1 (paper binding : alk. paper)
  1. Ten commandments—Covetousness—Early works to 1800. I. Svebakken, Hans. II. Title.
  BV4710.P4513 2012
  296.3'6—dc23
                                            2012034228

Printed on acid-free, recycled paper conforming to
ANSI/NISO Z39.48-1992 (R1997) and ISO 9706:1994
standards for paper permanence.

STUDIA PHILONICA MONOGRAPHS

Studies In Hellenistic Judaism

Editor
Thomas H. Tobin, S.J.

Advisory Board
Ellen Birnbaum, *Cambridge, Mass.*
Jacques Cazeaux, *CNRS, University of Lyon*
Lester Grabbe, *University of Hull*
Annewies van den Hoek, *Harvard Divinity School*
Pieter W. van der Horst, *Zeist, The Netherlands*
Alan Mendelson, *McMaster University*
Robert Radice, *Sacred Heart University, Milan*
Jean Riaud, *Catholic University, Angers*
James R. Royse, *Claremont, Calif.*
David T. Runia, *Queen's College, University of Melbourne*
Gregory E. Sterling, *Yale Divinity School*
David Winston, *Berkeley*

The Studia Philonica Monographs series accepts monographs in the area of Hellenistic Judaism, with special emphasis on Philo and his *Umwelt*. Proposals for books in this series should be sent to the Editor: Prof. Thomas H. Tobin, S.J., Theology Department, Loyola University Chicago, 1032 W. Sheridan Road, Chicago IL 60660-1537, U.S.A; Email: ttobin@luc.edu.

Written with the financial support of the Netherlands Organization for
Scientific Research (N.W.O.)

Published with the financial support of the
Prof. dr. C. J. de Vogel Foundation

Behold me daring, not only to read the sacred messages of Moses, but also in my love of knowledge to peer into each of them and unfold and reveal what is not known to the multitude.

Philo of Alexandria, *De specialibus legibus* 3.6

TABLE OF CONTENTS

Acknowledgements	xii
List of Tables	xiv
List of Abbreviations	xv

Chapter One:
INTRODUCTION

Philo's Commentary on Mosaic Legislation	2
Philo's Exposition of the Tenth Commandment	8
The Value of Philo's Exposition	11
History of Research	15
Harry A. Wolfson	16
Kathy L. Gaca	20
Plan of the Monograph	31

Chapter Two:
PHILO ON DESIRE (ΕΠΙΘΥΜΙΑ)

Introduction	33
Philo's Middle-Platonic Contemporaries	33
"Irrational" and "Non-Rational" in Moral Psychology	37
Platonic Foundations	38
Bipartition in Middle Platonism	40
Reason over against Ἐπιθυμία /Θυμός	40
Reason over against Appetite (ὄρεξις)	41
Reason over against Impulse (ὁρμή)	44
Reason over against Emotion (πάθος)	47
Summary	49
Bipartition in Philo's Writings	50
Reason over against Ἐπιθυμία /Θυμός	50
Reason over against Appetite (ὄρεξις)	51
Reason over against Impulse (ὁρμή)	53

Reason over against Emotion (πάθος) 56
Reason over against Sense-Perception (αἴσθησις) 60
Reason over against "Stoic" Non-Rational Soul 62
Summary 64
Problematic Malfunctions of Desire 65
Passionate Desire (πλεονάζουσα [ἄμετρος] ἐπιθυμία) 65
Tyrannical Desire (ἔρως) 71
Ἔρως as Advanced Grade of Desire 72
Negative Impact of Ἔρως 75
Conclusion 79

Chapter Three:
PHILO ON SELF-CONTROL (ΕΓΚΡΑΤΕΙΑ) AND PRACTICE (ΑΣΚΗΣΙΣ)

Introduction 81
The Nature of Ἐγκράτεια 82
Ἐγκράτεια – *Victory of Rational over Non-Rational* 82
Ἐγκράτεια – *Curtailing Excessive Impulse* 88
Ἐγκράτεια – *Predominance of Rational Motivation* 94
Summary 97
The Acquisition of Ἐγκράτεια 98
Ἐγκράτεια *through* Ἄσκησις 98
Ἐγκράτεια *through Ascetic Precepts* 103
Conclusion 108

Chapter Four:
PHILO'S EXPOSITION OF THE TENTH COMMANDMENT: TRANSLATION AND COMMENTARY

Philo's Expository Agenda 109
Traditional Interpretations of Clean and Unclean Animals 110
Contemporary Genres of Philosophical Literature 113
Structure of Philo's Exposition 118
Translation and Commentary 119
I. *Introduction (§78b)* 119
§78b: Introduction 119
II. *Diagnosis (Κρίσις) (§§79–94)* 120
§79: Problem: Every Passion 120
§79 Excursus: Parallel Material in Decal. 142–45 122

§§80 – 83: Overview of Tyrannical Desire............................	124
§§80 – 83 Excursus: Parallel Material in Decal. 146–50...............	129
§§84 – 91: Tyrannical Desire as "Source of All Evils"................	133
§§84 – 91 Excursus: Parallel Material in Decal. 151–53..............	137
§§92 – 94: Location of Ἐπιθυμία	138
III. Treatment (Ἄσκησις) (§§95–130)..	141
§§95 – 97: Overview of Moses' "Paradigmatic Instruction".............	141
§§98 – 99: First Fruits	145
§§100 – 102. Introduction to Clean and Unclean Animals..............	147
§§103 – 109: Land Animals	154
§§110 – 112: Aquatic Animals	163
§§113 – 115: "Reptiles"	165
§§116 – 117: Birds	169
§118: Conclusion of Clean and Unclean Animals.......................	171
§§119 – 121: Animals Killed by Predators or Natural Causes..........	172
§§122 – 125: Blood and Fat..	175
§§126 – 131: Conclusion	178

CHAPTER FIVE:
SUMMARY AND LINES OF FURTHER RESEARCH

Summary	184
Lines of Further Research..	186
Bibliography	189
Indices	210

ACKNOWLEDGEMENTS

This study grew out of a doctoral seminar in Hellenistic Judaism offered by Thomas Tobin, S.J., at Loyola University Chicago. In that seminar, he sparked my interest in Philo—then he helped to shape some of the ensuing ideas into a dissertation, completed in 2009 under his direction and appearing here in a revised and updated form. At every critical juncture of this extensive project, his expert guidance steered me toward a better outcome. My debt of gratitude has now come full circle, since he became the editor of Studia Philonica Monographs shortly after this volume was accepted for publication, helping me to finish at last the study he helped to begin.

Of course, I have many others to thank for helping me with this project. The faculties of Classical Studies and Theology at Loyola generously gave me years of support, training, and encouragement. In particular, I want to thank Robert Di Vito (Theology) and James Keenan (Classical Studies), readers of my dissertation, along with two professors no longer at Loyola, David E. Aune and John L. White. Among Loyola's staff, I want to thank the theology department's Catherine Wolf and Marianne Wolfe, along with the staff at Cudahy Library's interlibrary loan office. Gregory Sterling of Yale Divinity School first read my dissertation on behalf of Studia Philonica Monographs. I want to thank him for his encouraging remarks, for his helpful suggestions and corrigenda, and for recommending my work for publication. In addition, I want to thank both Leigh Andersen, Managing Editor of SBL Publications, for her friendly and accommodating supervision of this project, and Gonni Runia, for formatting the manuscript for publication. In the final stages before publication, Joseph Latham and Cambry Pardee provided valuable assistance (with the indexing and proofreading respectively), and I owe both of them a word of thanks. Finally, I want to thank the Arthur J. Schmitt Foundation for funding my first year of dissertation research through the Schmitt Dissertation Fellowship.

I have a large extended family, and each member—in his or her own way—deserves a personal word of thanks, but for brevity's sake I'll mention here only my family of origin. My brother, Pete, and sister, Khris, never questioned my choice of a meandering academic career, and I appreciate their confidence. My father, Gene, gave me invaluable support in my student days and encouraged me with his questions about Philo. My mother, Kay, gave me a gift of love that continues to shape my life. Although she did not live to see this fruit of my graduate school labors, I can well imagine her happy words and congratulations.

Three people inspire everything that I do. My wife, Mary Jane, graciously welcomed Philo into our lives and supported this project in every possible way. I cannot begin to express the value of her unfailing encouragement. Our son, Elias, arrived as I was completing chapter four of the dissertation. Our daughter, Annabeth, arrived as I was preparing this manuscript for publication. They have brought us extraordinary joy, and I hope that they know (if they happen to be reading this someday) just how much they are loved.

This has been a long journey, and I consider its completion a great blessing. Unsure of how to express my deepest sense of gratitude, I'll let Philo have the last word, in honor of our many hours together: "It is for God to give benefits and for mortals to give thanks, since they have nothing else to give in return" (*Plant.* 130).

LIST OF TABLES

1. Variations of Bipartition in Middle Platonism 49
2. Variations of Bipartition in Philo's Writings 64

LIST OF ABBREVIATIONS

Abbreviations of primary sources are those of *The SBL Handbook of Style* (ed. Patrick H. Alexander et al.; Peabody, Mass.: Hendrickson, 1999), with the following exceptions:

Primary Sources

Colson	English trans. of *Spec.* 4 by F. H. Colson in vol. 8 of *Philo*. Translated by F. H. Colson et al. 12 vols. Loeb Classical Library. Cambridge: Harvard University Press, 1929–1962.
Didask.	*Didaskalikos* by Alcinous. English trans. cited by ch. and sec. in *The Handbook of Platonism*. Translated with intro. and comm. by John Dillon. Oxford: Clarendon, 1993. Gk. text cited in brackets by p. [ed. Hermann, 1853] and line in *Enseignement des doctrines de Platon*. Edited with intro. and comm. by John Whittaker. Translated by Pierre Louis. 2d ed. Paris: Belles Lettres, 2002 (e.g., *Didask.* 32.4 [186.14–18]).
DL	Diogenes Laertius, *Lives of Eminent Philosophers*. Translated by R. D. Hicks. 2 vols. Loeb Classical Library. Cambridge: Harvard University Press, 1925.
Eclog.	*Eclogae Physicae et Ethicae* by Ioannes Stobaeus. Cited by p. and line in vol. 2 of Ioannes Stobaeus. *Anthologii libri duo priores*. 2 vols. Edited by Curt Wachsmuth. Berlin: Weidmann, 1884.
ESE	*Epitome of Stoic Ethics* by Arius Didymus. Cited by sec. in *Epitome of Stoic Ethics*. Edited by Arthur J. Pomeroy. Texts and Translations 44. Greco-Roman Series 14. Atlanta: Society of Biblical Literature, 1999.
Heinemann	German trans. of *Spec.* 4 by Isaak Heinemann in vol. 2 of *Philo von Alexandria: Die Werke in deutscher Übersetzung*. Edited by L. Cohn, I. Heinemann, et al. 7 vols. Breslau, Berlin 1909–1964.
LS	A. A. Long and D. N. Sedley. *The Hellenistic Philosophers*. 2 vols. Cambridge: Cambridge University Press, 1987. Cited by section number and text letter (e.g., 25B).
Mazz.	Claudio Mazzarelli, "Raccolta e interpretazione delle testimonianze e dei frammenti del medioplatonico Eudoro di

	Alessandria: Parte prima: Testo e traduzione delle testimonianze e dei frammenti sicuri," *Rivista di filosofia neo-scolastica* 77 (1985): 197–209. Cited by fragment number and line (e.g., 1.10).
Mosès	French trans. of *Spec.* 4 by André Mosès in vol. 25 of *Les œuvres de Philon d'Alexandrie.* Edited by R. Arnaldez, J. Pouilloux, C. Mondésert. Paris, 1961–92.
PAPM	*Les œuvres de Philon d'Alexandrie.* French translation under the general editorship of R. Arnaldez, J. Pouilloux, C. Mondésert. Paris, 1961–92.
PCH	*Philo von Alexandria: Die Werke in deutscher Übersetzung.* Edited by L. Cohn, I. Heinemann, et al. 7 vols. Breslau, Berlin 1909–1964.
PCW	*Philonis Alexandrini opera quae supersunt.* Edited by L. Cohn, P. Wendland, S. Reiter. 6 vols. Berlin ,1896–1915.
Petit	*Philon d'Alexandrie: Quæstiones: Fragmenta Græca.* Edited and translated by Françoise Petit. Les œvres de Philon d'Alexandrie 33. Paris: Cerf, 1978.
PHP	*De Placitis Hippocratis et Platonis* by Galen. Cited by bk., ch., and sec. in *On the Doctrines of Hippocrates and Plato.* Edited and trans. with comm. by Phillip De Lacy. 3 vols. 2d ed. Corpus Medicorum Graecorum 5.4.1.2. Berlin: Akademie-Verlag, 1980–84.
PLCL	*Philo in Ten Volumes (and Two Supplementary Volumes).* Translated by F. H. Colson, G. H. Whitaker (and R. Marcus). 12 vols. Loeb Classical Library. Cambridge: Harvard University Press, 1929–1962.
Ps.-Andr.	Pseudo-Andronicus, Περὶ παθῶν. Cited by p. and line in A. Gilbert-Thirry. *Pseudo-Andronicus de Rhodes «ΠΕΡΙ ΠΑΘΩΝ»: Edition critique du texte grec et de la traduction latine médiévale.* Corpus latinum commentariorum in Aristotelem graecorum. Supp. 2. Leiden: Brill, 1977.
Ps.-Arch.	Pseudo-Archytas, *On Moral Education.* Cited by p. [ed. Thesleff, 1965] and line in *Pseudopythagorica Ethica: I trattati morali di Archita, Metopo, Teage, Eurifamo.* Edited and translated by Bruno Centrone. Elenchos 17. Naples: Bibliopolis, 1990.

Ps.-Metop.	Pseudo-Metopus, *On Virtue*. Cited by p. [ed. Thesleff, 1965] and line in *Pseudopythagorica Ethica: I trattati morali di Archita, Metopo, Teage, Eurifamo*. Edited and translated by Bruno Centrone. Elenchos 17. Naples: Bibliopolis, 1990.
Ps.-Theag.	Pseudo-Theages, *On Virtue*. Cited by p. [ed. Thesleff, 1965] and line in *Pseudopythagorica Ethica: I trattati morali di Archita, Metopo, Teage, Eurifamo*. Edited and translated by Bruno Centrone. Elenchos 17. Naples: Bibliopolis, 1990.
SVF	*Stoicorum veterum fragmenta*. H. von Arnim. 4 vols. Leipzig, 1903–1924. Cited by vol., p., and line (e.g., III 113, 15).
TL	Timaeus of Locri, *On the Nature of the World and the Soul*. Cited by paragraph in *Timaios of Locri*, On the Nature of the World and the Soul. Edited and trans. with notes by Thomas H. Tobin. Texts and Translations 26. Greco-Roman Religion Series 8. Chico, Calif.: Scholars Press, 1985.
Troph.[B]	Περὶ τροφῆς[B] by Musonius Rufus. Cited by p. and line in Cora E. Lutz. *Musonius Rufus: The Roman Socrates*. Yale Classical Studies 10. New Haven: Yale University Press, 1947.

Secondary Sources

AB	Anchor Bible
ABD	*Anchor Bible Dictionary*. Edited by D. N. Freedman. 6 vols. New York, 1992.
ACPQ	*American Catholic Philosophical Quarterly*
AJP	*American Journal of Philology*
ALGHJ	Arbeiten zur Literatur und Geschichte des hellenistischen Judentums
AMMTC	Ancient Mediterranean and Medieval Texts and Contexts
AMP	Ancient and Medieval Philosophy
ANRW	*Aufstieg und Niedergang der römischen Welt: Geschichte und Kultur Roms im Spiegel der neueren Forschung*. Edited by H. Temporini and W. Haase. Berlin, 1972—
AP	*Ancient Philosophy*
ARGU	Arbeiten zur Religion und Geschichte des Urchristentums
ASE	*Annali di storia dell'esegesi*
ASNSP	*Annali della Scuola Normale Superiore di Pisa*
ASR	*Annali di scienze religiose*

LIST OF ABBREVIATIONS

BBB	Bonner biblische Beiträge
BEATAJ	Beiträge zur Erforschung des Alten Testaments und des antiken Judentum
BEHE	Bibliotheque de l'Ecole des hautes études
BICSSup	Bulletin of the Institute of Classical Studies: Supplements
BJS	Brown Judaic Studies
BThSt	Biblisch-Theologische Studien
BU	Biblische Untersuchungen
BZAW	Beihefte zur Zeitschrift für die alttestamentliche Wissenschaft
CBQ	*Catholic Biblical Quarterly*
CBQMS	Catholic Biblical Quarterly Monograph Series
CCWJCW	Cambridge Commentaries on Writings of the Jewish and Christian World 200 BC to AD 200
CEC	Collection d'études classiques
CJA	Christianity and Judaism in Antiquity
CQ	*Classical Quarterly*
CR	*Classical Review*
CRINT	Compendia Rerum Iudaicarum ad Novum Testamentum
CS	Collected Studies
CSCP	Cornell Studies in Classical Philology
CSP	Cornell Studies in Philosophy
CUAPS	Catholic University of America Patristic Studies
CWS	Classics of Western Spirituality. New York, 1978—
DCLY	Deuterocanonical and Cognate Literature Yearbook
ELA	Études de littérature ancienne
EP	Études platoniciennes
EPM	Études de philosophie médiévale
ETL	*Ephemerides Theologicae Lovanienses*
ETR	*Études théologiques et religieuses*
EUSLR	Emory University Studies in Law and Religion
FIOTL	Formation and Interpretation of Old Testament Literature
FJCD	Forschungen zum jüdisch-christlichen Dialog
GRBS	*Greek, Roman, and Byzantine Studies*
GRRS	Greco-Roman Religion Series
HBS	Herders Biblische Studien
HCS	Hellenistic Culture and Society. Anthony W. Bulloch, Erich S. Gruen, A. A. Long, and Andrew F. Stewart, general editors.
HPhQ	*History of Philosophy Quarterly*
HSCP	*Harvard Studies in Classical Philology*
HTR	*Harvard Theological Review*

JACE	Jahrbuch für Antike und Christentum, Ergänzungsband
JBL	*Journal of Biblical Literature*
JHS	*Journal of Hellenic Studies*
JJML	*Journal of Jewish Music and Liturgy*
JJS	*Journal of Jewish Studies*
JLAS	Jewish Law Association Studies
JSH	*Journal of Sport History*
JSHRZ	*Jüdische Schriften aus hellenistisch-römischer Zeit*
JSNT	*Journal for the Study of the New Testament*
JSPSup	Journal for the Study of the Pseudepigrapha: Supplement Series
JTS	*Journal of Theological Studies*
LTE	Library of Theological Ethics
MCL	Martin Classical Lectures
MScRel	*Mélanges de science religieuse*
MdB	*Le monde de la Bible*
MP	*Museum Patavinum*
NAWG	*Nachrichten von der Akademie der Wissenschaften in Göttingen*
NovT	*Novum Testamentum*
NovTSup	Supplements to Novum Testamentum
NTOA	Novum Testamentum et Orbis Antiquus
OBO	Orbis biblicus et orientalis
OPM	Oxford Philosophical Monographs
OTM	Oxford Theological Monographs
PA	Philosophia Antiqua
PASSV	*Proceedings of the Aristotelian Society Supplementary Volume*
PBACAP	*Proceedings of the Boston Area Colloquium in Ancient Philosophy*
Ph&PhenR	*Philosophy and Phenomenological Research*
PhilSup	*Philologus: Supplementband*
PHR	*Problèmes d'histoire des religions*
REG	*Revue des études grecques*
REL	*Revue des études latines*
RKAM	Religion und Kultur der alten Mittelmeerwelt in Parallel forschungen
RM	*Review of Metaphysics*
RMCS	Routledge Monographs in Classical Studies
RSR	*Recherches de science religieuse*
RTL	*Revue théologique de Louvain*
SA	Studia Anselmiana
SAP	Studien zur antiken Philosophie
SBLTT	Society of Biblical Literature Texts and Translations

SBS	Stuttgarter Bibelstudien
ScEs	*Science et esprit*
SCHNT	Studia ad corpus hellenisticum Novi Testamenti
ScrTh	*Scripta Theologica*
SF	*Studi filosofici*
SJLA	Studies in Judaism in Late Antiquity
SJPh	*Southern Journal of Philosophy*
SNTSMS	Society for New Testament Studies Monograph Series
SO	*Symbolae Osloenses*
SPh	*Studia Philonica*
SPhA	*Studia Philonica Annual*
SPhA	Studies in Philo of Alexandria
SPhAMA	Studies in Philo of Alexandria and Mediterranean Antiquity
SSEJC	Studies in Scripture in Early Judaism and Christianity
STA	Studia et Testimonia Antiqua
SUNT	Studien zur Umwelt des Neuen Testaments
TDNT	*Theological Dictionary of the New Testament.* Edited by G. Kittel and G. Friedrich. Translated by G. W. Bromily. 10 vols. Grand Rapids, 1964–1976.
TSAJ	Texte und Studien zum antiken Judentum
TSHP	New Synthese Historical Library: Texts and Studies in the History of Philosophy
TSP	Trivium: Special Publications
TUGAL	Texte und Untersuchungen zur Geschichte der altchristlichen Literatur
VC	*Vigiliae Christianae*
VCSup	Supplements to Vigiliae Christianae
VTSup	Supplements to Vetus Testamentum
WMANT	Wissenschaftliche Monographien zum Alten und Neuen Testament
WS	*Wiener Studien: Zeitschrift für Klassische Philologie und Patristik*
WS	World Spirituality: An Encyclopedic History of the Religious Quest
WTS	Wijsgerige Teksten en Studies
WUNT	Wissenschaftliche Untersuchungen zum Neuen Testament
ZNW	*Zeitschrift für die neutestamentliche Wissenschaft und die Kunde der älteren Kirche*

CHAPTER ONE

INTRODUCTION

The Septuagint version of Exodus 20:17, translated literally, reads as follows:

> You shall not desire your neighbor's wife. You shall not desire your neighbor's house, nor his field, nor his male servant, nor his female servant, nor his ox, nor his beast of burden, nor any of his flock, nor anything that is your neighbor's.[1]

This is the last of the Ten Commandments,[2] and although Philo of Alexandria (ca. 20 B.C.E.–50 C.E.) must have known the full biblical version,[3] he cites the Tenth Commandment simply as "You shall not desire" (οὐκ ἐπιθυμήσεις), indicating that in his view the principle concern of this Commandment is desire itself (ἐπιθυμία), not desire's object.[4]

---

[1] My translation of LXX Exod 20:17 [=LXX Deut 5:21 verbatim]: οὐκ ἐπιθυμήσεις τὴν γυναῖκα τοῦ πλησίον σου. οὐκ ἐπιθυμήσεις τὴν οἰκίαν τοῦ πλησίον σου οὔτε τὸν ἀγρὸν αὐτοῦ οὔτε τὸν παῖδα αὐτοῦ οὔτε τὴν παιδίσκην αὐτοῦ οὔτε τοῦ βοὸς αὐτοῦ οὔτε τοῦ ὑποζυγίου αὐτοῦ οὔτε παντὸς κτήνους αὐτοῦ οὔτε ὅσα τῷ πλησίον σού ἐστιν. For details on the text of Exod 20:17, including ancient versions, see Innocent Himbaza, *Le Décalogue et l'histoire du texte: Etudes des formes textuelles du Décalogue et leurs implications dans l'histoire du texte de l'Ancien Testament* (OBO 207; Fribourg: Academic Press, 2004), 155–65 (cf. 68–72).
[2] The Ten Commandments appear first in Exod 20:1–17 (cf. Deut 5:1–21) *spoken* by God and so become known as the "ten words," or in modern usage the "Decalogue" (N.B. LXX Deut 10:4: τοὺς δέκα λόγους). Philo often refers to them as οἱ δέκα λόγοι (e.g., *Decal.* 154, *Spec.* 1.1) or δέκα λόγια (e.g., *Decal.* 36, *Spec.* 3.7).
[3] Philo used the LXX, not the Hebrew Bible (see Valentin Nikiprowetzky, *Le commentaire de l'écriture chez Philon d'Alexandrie: Son caractère et sa portée, observations philologiques* [ALGHJ 11; Leiden: Brill, 1977], 50–96, esp. 51–52). No evidence for an abbreviated version of the Tenth Commandment exists in the MS tradition of the LXX. On the LXX Pentateuch, see the introductory essays in *Le Pentateuque d'Alexandrie: Text grec et traduction* (ed. Cécile Dogniez and Marguerite Harl; Bible d'Alexandrie; Paris: Cerf, 2001), 31–130, including David Runia, "Philon d'Alexandrie devant le Pentateuque," 99–105.
[4] In *Spec.* 4.78, Philo cites the Tenth Commandment as an abbreviated, two-word prohibition: "Let us turn now to the last of the Ten Words (δέκα λογίων) ... 'You shall not desire' (οὐκ ἐπιθυμήσεις)" (my translation; unless otherwise noted, all translations of Philo's writings are from PLCL.) In *Decal.* 142, he clearly has this abbreviated version in mind: "Finally, he places a prohibition on desiring (τελευταῖον δ'ἐπιθυμεῖν ἀπαγορεύει), knowing that desire (τὴν ἐπιθυμίαν) is crafty and treacherous (νεωτεροποιὸν καὶ ἐπίβουλον)" (my translation). (Cf. *Decal.* 173: πέμπτον [of the second tablet] δὲ τὸ ἀνεῖργον τὴν τῶν ἀδικημάτων πηγήν, ἐπιθυμίαν; *Her.* 173: ἡ δ'ἑτέρα πεντάς ἐστιν ἀπαγόρευσις μοιχείας, ἀνδροφονίας, κλοπῆς, ψευδομαρτυρίας, ἐπιθυμίας.) In his discussion of the Tenth Commandment (*Decal.* 142–153, 173–174; *Spec.* 4.78b–131), Philo mentions none

This monograph explains in detail Philo's exposition of the Tenth Commandment. As an introduction, this chapter (1) situates Philo's exposition within his larger corpus of works, (2) summarizes the nature and content of the exposition, (3) explains the value of the exposition, (4) reviews prior research, and (5) outlines the plan of the monograph.

Philo's Commentary on Mosaic Legislation

Philo describes the contents of the Pentateuch as a sequence of three topics: creation, history, and legislation.[5] In a series of works known collectively as the Exposition of the Law, he offers an exegesis of the Pentateuch using these topics as his basic outline.[6] The Exposition begins with a treatise on the creation of the world (*De opificio mundi*), continues with a set of

---

of the prohibited objects of desire listed in the LXX version (οἰκία, ἀγρός, παῖς, παιδίσκη, βοῦς, ὑποζύγιον, κτῆνος), with the exception of γυνή, which appears once in a list that includes also "reputation" (δόξα) and categorically "anything else that produces pleasure" (τινος ἄλλου τῶν ἡδονὴν ἀπεργαζομένων) (*Decal.* 151). Similarly, πλησίος, an essential element of the LXX version (τοῦ πλησίον σου ... ὅσα τῷ πλησίον σού ἐστιν), appears only once (*Spec.* 4.93), and there it involves Platonic psychology: the θυμός, or spirited part of the soul, is a "neighbor" to the λόγος, or rational part.

[5] "The oracles delivered through the prophet Moses are of three kinds (τρεῖς ἰδέας). The first deals with the creation of the world (τὴν μὲν περὶ κοσμοποιίας), the second with history (τὴν δὲ ἱστορικήν) and the third with legislation (τὴν δὲ τρίτην νομοθετικήν)" (*Praem.* 1). The same classification appears in *Mos.* 2.46–47, although Philo initially identifies only *two* parts: (1) the historical part (ἱστορικὸν μέρος), which he subdivides into two sections dealing respectively with the creation of the world (κόσμου γενέσεως) and genealogy (γενεαλογικοῦ), and (2) the part dealing with commands and prohibitions (περὶ προστάξεις καὶ ἀπαγορεύσεις). The part dealing with commands and prohibitions corresponds to the third topic in *Praem.* 1, while the subdivisions of the first part correspond to the first two topics in *Praem.*1. (On the relation between γενεαλογικός and ἱστορικός, see F. H. Colson's note on *Mos.* 2.47 in PLCL 6, 606; also PLCL 8, 313, n. a.) On the correlation of *Praem.* 1 and *Mos.* 2.46–47, see also Peder Borgen, "Philo of Alexandria," in *Jewish Writings of the Second Temple Period* (ed. M. E. Stone; vol. 2 of *The Literature of the Jewish People in the Period of the Second Temple and the Talmud*; CRINT 2; Assen: Van Gorcum, 1984), 233–82, 234, n. 5; Richard Hecht, "Preliminary Issues in the Analysis of Philo's *De Specialibus Legibus*," *SPh* 5 (1978): 1–55, 3; Leopold Cohn, "Einteilung und Chronologie der Schriften Philos," *PhilSup* 7 (1899): 387–436, 405–06.

[6] On the Exposition of the Law see Peder Borgen, "Philo of Alexandria—A Systematic Philosopher or an Eclectic Editor? An Examination of his *Exposition of the Laws of Moses*," *SO* 71 (1996): 115–34; also Jenny Morris, "The Jewish Philosopher Philo," in Emil Schürer, *The History of the Jewish People in the Age of Jesus Christ (175 B.C.–A.D. 135): A New English Version Revised and Edited by Geza Vermes, Fergus Millar, and Martin Goodman* (vol. 3, part 2; Edinburgh: T&T Clark, 1987), 809–89, 840–54.

treatises on the patriarchs (*De Abrahamo* and *De Iosepho*),[7] and ends with a set of treatises on Mosaic legislation (*De decalogo, De specialibus legibus* 1–4, and *De virtutibus*).[8] This last set dealing with legislation consists thematically of only two parts, despite its formal division into six treatises: the first comprises *De decalogo* and practically all of *De specialibus legibus* (1.1–4.132), the second comprises the remainder of *De specialibus legibus* (4.133–238) and *De virtutibus*.[9] In both parts, Philo cites then analyzes laws, noting mostly their literal bearing on practical and ethical matters.[10] But the real

---

[7] See Cristina Termini, "The Historical Part of the Pentateuch According to Philo of Alexandria: Biography, Genealogy, and the Philosophical Meaning of the Patriarchal Lives," in *History and Identity: How Israel's Later Authors Viewed Its Earlier History* (ed. Núria Calduch-Benages and Jan Liesen; DCLY 2006; Berlin: de Gruyter, 2006), 265–95. Originally, the set included treatises also on Isaac and Jacob (see *Ios.* 1), which are now lost. Most assign these treatises to the "history" portion of the creation-history-legislation triad of *Praem.* 1 (e.g., Borgen, "Philo," 237–38). Some, however, assign them to the legislative portion, based on Philo's claim that the patriarchs themselves represent unwritten counterparts to the written laws he begins to consider in *De decalogo* (see *Abr.* 3–4). The historical portion, in this configuration, consists of Philo's Allegorical Commentary, a separate series of treatises covering most of Genesis (on which see Borgen, "Philo," 243–44; Morris, "Philo," 830–40). Valentin Nikiprowetzky, for example, holds this view: see PAPM 23, 13, and *Commentaire*, 234–35, n. 217. But if the correlation of *Praem.* 1 and *Mos.* 2.46–47 is correct, the legislative portion mentioned in *Praem.* 1 corresponds explicitly to "commands and prohibitions" in *Mos.* 2.46 and cannot reasonably include the lives of the patriarchs. For other problems with this view, see Cohn, "Einteilung und Chronologie," 406, n. 23; cf. Morris, "Philo," 845–46, n. 134.

[8] Another treatise, *De praemiis et poenis*, immediately follows *De virtutibus* and concludes the Exposition. In *Praem.* 2–3, Philo states that he has fully discussed (i.e., finished) the legislative section in the preceding treatises and is moving on to a new topic: "the rewards and punishments which the good and the bad have respectively to expect." *De praemiis et poenis* thus forms a fitting conclusion to the Exposition, insofar as the stipulated rewards and punishments are contingent on observance of the laws. But it does not form part of the legislative section proper, because it does not deal with the laws themselves. Philo's treatise on Moses, *De vita Mosis* 1–2, is closely connected with, but not part of, the Exposition (see Erwin R. Goodenough, "Philo's Exposition of the Law and His *De Vita Mosis*," *HTR* 26 [1933]: 109–25).

[9] Philo makes an explicit transition from one major topic to another in *Spec.* 4.132–34. For division of the same material into the same two parts, see points B and C on Peder Borgen's outline of the Exposition ("Philosopher or Editor," 118).

[10] In *Decal.* 1 Philo announces that his investigation of the written laws will not neglect allegorical interpretations, when they are warranted, and indeed it does not (e.g., *Spec.* 2.29–31). Nevertheless, Philo's legal commentary tends to avoid allegory, in some instances offering only a literal treatment of laws read allegorically in the Allegorical Commentary (see Colson, PLCL 7, xiii, n. c, and Isaak Heinemann, PCH 2, 4, n. 1, for examples, such as *Ebr.* 14–95 vs. *Spec.* 2.232 on Deut 21:18–21). Samuel Sandmel ("Philo Judaeus: An Introduction to the Man, His Writings, and His Significance," *ANRW* 21.1:3–46, 10) thus goes too far in saying: "The treatises in [the 'Exposition of the Law'] are no less allegorical than those in the 'Allegory of the Law.'"

commentary on Mosaic legislation in Philo's Exposition is the first part (*Decal.* 1–*Spec.* 4.132), which he frames as a unified, systematic, and comprehensive exposition of Mosaic commands and prohibitions, using an organizational scheme based on the Ten Commandments.[11]

For Philo, the Ten Commandments are absolutely preeminent, and *their* arrangement and content determine the overall arrangement and content of his legal commentary in *Decal.* 1–*Spec.* 4.132.[12] To establish their importance, Philo begins his systematic study of Mosaic legislation with a distinction between two categories of law:

> I will proceed to describe the laws (τοὺς νόμους) themselves in order, with this necessary statement by way of introduction, that some of them (οὓς μέν) God judged fit to deliver in His own person alone without employing any other, and some (οὓς δέ) through His prophet Moses whom He chose as of all men the best suited to be the revealer of verities. Now we find that those

---

[11] *Praem.* 2 suggests that part one (*Decal.* 1–*Spec.* 4.132) represents, from Philo's perspective, the Pentateuch's "legislative part" proper (thus Borgen, "Philosopher or Editor," 132–33; cf. Borgen, "Philo," 239–40). Part two (*Spec.* 4.133–238 and *Virt.*) has a different organizational scheme (categorization by *virtues*, not *Commandments* [see *Spec.* 4.133–35]) and is secondary to part one in terms of both length and design. Part one is roughly three times as large (ca. 277 vs. ca. 95 pages in PCW); but, more importantly, part one represents Philo's principal effort to organize all Mosaic precepts into a single logical system (on which see esp. Yehoshua Amir, "The Decalogue According to Philo," in *The Ten Commandments in History and Tradition* [ed. B.-Z. Segal and G. Levi; Jerusalem: Magnes Press, 1990], 121–60, 128–30; idem, "Philon und die jüdische Wirklichkeit seiner Zeit," in *Die hellenistische Gestalt des Judentums bei Philon von Alexandrien* [FJCD 5; Neukirchen-Vluyn: Neukirchener Verlag, 1983], 3–51, esp. 42–44 [="Das System der Gebote"]). In this respect, part two serves as a catchall, accommodating laws that do not fit neatly into Philo's primary scheme (see Amir, "Decalogue," 127; Morris, "Philo," 851).

[12] On the Decalogue in Philo, see esp. Amir, "Decalogue"; also Ulrich Kellermann, "Der Dekalog in den Schriften des Frühjudentums: Ein Überblick," in *Weisheit, Ethos, und Gebot* (ed. H. G. Reventlow; BThSt 43; Neukirchen-Vluyn: Neukirchener, 2001), 147–226, esp. 161–70 [="Philo von Alexandria und der Dekalog"]; Paul Kuntz, "Philo Judaeus: A Decalogue in the Balance," in *The Ten Commandments in History: Mosaic Paradigms for a Well-Ordered Society* (ed. Thomas d'Evelyn; EUSLR; Grand Rapids: Eerdmans, 2004), 11–26; Miguel Lluch Baixauli, "El tratado de Filón sobre el Decálogo," *ScrTh* 29 (1997): 415–41; André Myre, "La loi et le Pentateuque selon Philon d'Alexandrie," *ScEs* 25 (1973): 209–25, 222–24; Samuel Sandmel, "Confrontation of Greek and Jewish Ethics: Philo: *De Decalogo*," in *Judaism and Ethics* (ed. Daniel J. Silver; New York: Ktav, 1970), 163–76. On the Decalogue as an organizational scheme, see Hecht, "Preliminary Issues," 3–17; for the scheme's presence in *Decal.* and *Spec.* see Borgen, "Philosopher or Editor," 123–28; for details of the scheme see Daniel Jastram, "Philo's Concept of Generic Virtue" (Ph.D. diss., University of Wisconsin—Madison, 1989), 30–35, and Cristina Termini, "Taxonomy of Biblical Laws and φιλοτεχνία in Philo: A Comparison with Josephus and Cicero," *SPhA* 16 (2004): 1–29, esp. 1–10.

which He gave in His own person and by His own mouth alone are[13] (συμβέβηκε) both laws and heads summarizing the particular laws (καὶ νόμους ... καὶ νόμων τῶν ἐν μέρει κεφάλαια), but those in which He spoke through the prophet all belong to the former class. (*Decal.* 18–19)

Two key traits set the Ten Commandments apart. First, God delivered them personally to the Israelites without a human mediator.[14] Second, each of the Ten Commandments has a unique dual significance: like any law, it stands on its own as a distinct ethical imperative, but it also functions as the "head" (κεφάλαιον) or "summary" of an entire category of particular laws (νόμων τῶν ἐν μέρει).[15]

In Philo's view, God delivered each of the Ten Commandments "in the form of a summary,"[16] stating succinctly what Moses spells out at length by means of additional laws found elsewhere in the Pentateuch.[17] These other laws form a distinct set of subsidiary precepts, which—despite their

---

[13] Substituting "are" (συμβέβηκε) for Colson's "include," which does not properly emphasize the dual nature of each Commandment. Cf. Nikiprowetzky, PAPM 23 ("sont non seulement des lois, mais aussi les principes qui commandent le détail des lois particulières"); Treitel, PCH 1 ("sind zugleich Gesetze und Grundprinzipien"); Francesca Calabi, *Filone di Alessandria,* De Decalogo (Philosophica 24; Pisa: ETS, 2005) ("sono leggi e principi delle leggi particolari").

[14] E.g., *Spec.* 2.189. Philo rejects an anthropomorphic concept of God speaking to the Israelites, developing instead the notion of a miraculous "divine voice" created especially for the occasion (*Decal.* 32–35; for analysis see Amir, "Decalogue," 135–48; also Reinhard Weber, *Das "Gesetz" bei Philon von Alexandrien und Flavius Josephus: Studien zum Verständnis und zur Funktion der Thora bei den beiden Hauptzeugen des hellenistischen Judentums* (ARGU 11; Frankfurt am Main: Lang, 2001), 68–77.

[15] E.g., *Decal.* 154: "[W]e must not forget that the Ten Words (οἱ δέκα λόγοι) are summaries of the special laws (κεφάλαια νόμων εἰσὶ τῶν ἐν εἴδει) which are recorded in the Sacred Books and run through the whole of the legislation" (substituting "Words" [λόγοι] for Colson's "Covenants"). Thus the title of *De decalogo*: περὶ τῶν δέκα λόγων, οἵ κεφάλαια νόμων εἰσίν. On κεφάλαιον, see Termini, "Taxonomy," 5–6.

[16] κεφαλαιώδει τύπῳ (*Spec.* 4.78; also *Decal.* 168); cf. *Gaius* 178–79: "We determined to give Gaius a document, presenting in a summarized form (κεφαλαιώδη τύπον) the story of our sufferings and our claims. This document was practically an epitome (ἐπιτομή) of a longer supplication which we had sent to him a short time before through the hands of King Agrippa."

[17] E.g., *Decal.* 175: "For it was in accordance with His nature that the pronouncements in which the special laws were summed up (κεφάλαια μὲν τῶν ἐν εἴδει νόμων) should be given by Him in His own person, but the particular laws (νόμους δὲ τοὺς ἐν τῷ μέρει) by the mouth of the most perfect of the prophets whom He selected for his merits and having filled him with the divine spirit, chose him to be the interpreter of His sacred utterances." Cf. *Congr.* 120, where these ten are "general heads (γενικὰ κεφάλαια), embracing the vast multitude of particular laws (τῶν κατὰ μέρος ἀπείρων νόμων), the roots (ῥίζαι), the sources (ἀρχαί), the perennial fountains of ordinances (πηγαὶ ἀέναοι διαταγμάτων) containing commandments positive and prohibitive (προστάξεις καὶ ἀπαγορεύσεις περιεχόντων) for the profit of those who follow them."

individual variety—all express in some way the moral essence of their respective summary Commandment. Philo characterizes this unique relationship of particular law(s) to summary Commandment in a variety of ways. In terms of status, the particular laws are all subordinate to their respective "heads," as Philo's use of ὑπό ("under") and related compounds clearly indicates.[18] In terms of function, they all "refer to" (ἀναφέρεσθαι; ἀναφορὰν λαμβάνειν) a single summary command, serving or promoting its moral purpose in some way.[19] But in abstract terms, Philo envisions the relationship between summary Commandment and particular law(s) as that of genus to species.[20]

The treatises *De decalogo* and *De specialibus legibus* represent, at least in part, Philo's painstaking and systematic attempt to illustrate this genus-species relationship. His treatise on the Ten Commandments deals with the ten genera, expounding each of the Commandments in sequence (*Decal.* 50–153) and introducing the idea of their summary function (*Decal.* 154–75).[21] His treatise on the particular laws (*De specialibus legibus*) again expounds the ten genera, in even greater depth, but goes on to identify and comment on their respective species. The Pentateuch itself never uses a genus-species taxonomy to organize precepts systematically, so Philo must

---

[18] For the particular laws as simply "under" (ὑπό) their respective heads, see *Decal.* 170; as "arranged under" (ὑποτάσσεσθαι), see *Decal.* 168, 171; as "falling under" (ὑποπίπτειν), see *Decal.* 174 (cf. ὑποστέλλειν in *Decal.* 157, *Spec.* 4.1, and *Spec.* 4.132).

[19] E.g., *Spec.* 2.223: "I have now completed the discussion of the number seven [i.e., the fourth "head" (cf. *Spec.* 2.39)] and of matters connected with days and months and years that have reference to that number (τῶν εἰς αὐτὴν ἀναφερομένων)." *Spec.* 2.242: "I have gone through the five heads of laws (κεφάλαια νόμων) that belong to the first table, along with whatever particular laws have reference to each of them (ὅσα τῶν κατὰ μέρος εἰς ἕκαστον ἐλάμβανε τὴν ἀναφοράν)" (my translation). Cf. *Leg.* 2.102: "This is practically the summation (τὸ κεφάλαιον) of the whole Song [of Moses], to which every other part refers (ἐφ'ὃ τὰ ἄλλα πάντα ἀναφέρεται)" (my translation). In *Hist. eccl.* 2.18.5, Eusebius refers to *De specialibus legibus* as Περὶ τῶν ἀναφερομένων ἐν εἴδει νόμων εἰς τὰ συντείνοντα κεφάλαια τῶν δέκα λόγων α β γ δ.

[20] The δέκα λόγοι are τά ... γένη τῶν ἐν εἴδει νόμων (*Spec.* 1.1; *Spec.* 3.125: τὰ γένη τῶν ἐν εἴδει νόμων) and thus "generic" (*Congr.* 120: γενικὰ κεφάλαια; *Her.* 167: τῶν γενικῶν δέκα νόμων; *Her.* 173: γενικοί ... κανόνες). On this as a *legal* taxonomy in Philo, see esp. Jastram, "Generic Virtue," 30–35. Jastram's remarks situate the legal taxonomy in the context of Philo's broader application(s) of the genus-species concept (see his chapter one, "Theory of Genus, Species, and Particular," 10–72). Termini, "Taxonomy," argues that Philo's application of a genus-species taxonomy to Mosaic legislation is radically innovative, although his interest in the systematic organization of legal materials reflects contemporary trends in Roman jurisprudence.

[21] Philo first treats introductory questions such as why God delivered the Ten Commandments in the desert (§§2–17), why there were ten (§§20–31), what voice announced the Commandments (§§32–35), and why the form of address was second-person singular (§§36–43).

construct the system himself. In other words, *Philo* must match species with genera, indicating which laws belong with which of the Ten Commandments.[22] When his work is finished, he leaves no doubt as to his purpose:

> For if we are right in describing the main heads delivered by the voice of God as generic laws (κεφάλαια γένη νόμων), and all particular laws of which Moses was the spokesman as dependent species (εἴδη), for accurate apprehension free from confusion scientific study was needed, with the aid of which I have assigned and attached to each of the genera what was appropriate to them throughout the whole legislation (ἑκάστῳ τῶν γενῶν ἐξ ἁπάσης τῆς νομοθεσίας τὰ οἰκεῖα προσένειμα καὶ προσέφυσα). (*Spec.* 4.132)[23]

The scope of Philo's project is immense: considering each of the generic summaries in turn, he has scoured the Pentateuch in search of corresponding specific precepts. In this respect, *De specialibus legibus* complements *De decalogo* by presenting for each Commandment subsidiary laws that reflect its moral essence.[24]

---

[22] Despite disagreement over the originality of Philo's use of the Decalogue as a comprehensive taxonomic framework, consensus holds that Philo at least did the work of matching species with genera, justifying the study of *Philo's* view of the Tenth Commandment. In other words, it seems that *Philo* decided which laws logically pertain to the Tenth Commandment, according to *his* understanding of that Commandment. For a minimalist position, which concedes the originality of Philo's genus-species matching but otherwise attributes his basic taxonomy to traditional (rabbinic) Judaism, see Naomi Cohen, *Philo Judaeus: His Universe of Discourse* (BEATAJ 24; Frankfurt am Main: Peter Lang, 1995), 72–85, esp. 84–85. (On Philo's understanding of the Decalogue in relation to rabbinic tradition, see esp. Hecht, "Preliminary Issues," 3–17.) For a more generous position, which sees Philo as an innovator not only in his assignment of species to genus but also in his granting of a special inclusive status to the Decalogue, see Termini, "Taxonomy." Borgen, "Philosopher or Editor," 126, has an intermediate position, which nevertheless approximates Cohen's: "Philo seems to develop in a more systematic fashion a notion also found in Palestinian tradition, that the Decalogue contained *in nuce* all the commandments of the Mosaic laws. Thus, Philo has a Jewish concept as organizing principle, but he has developed it into a broader systematic rewriting than found elsewhere in the contemporary Jewish sources."

[23] Substituting "genera" (γενῶν) for Colson's "heads." On this passage, see also Termini, "Taxonomy," 8. Cf. *Spec.* 3.7: "Since out of the ten oracles which God gave forth Himself without a spokesman or interpreter, we have spoken of five, namely those graven on the first table, and also of all the particular laws which had reference to these, and our present duty is to couple them with those of the second table as well as we can, I will again endeavour to fit the special laws into each of the genera (πειράσομαι πάλιν καθ'ἕκαστον τῶν γενῶν ἐφαρμόζειν τοὺς ἐν εἴδει νόμους)" (substituting "genera" [γενῶν] for Colson's "heads").

[24] Cf. Morris on *De specialibus legibus* ("Philo," 847–48): "In this work Philo makes an extremely interesting attempt to bring the Mosaic special laws into a systematic arrangement according to the ten rubrics of the Decalogue."

8   CHAPTER ONE

For the most part, Philo follows a rigid ten-point outline in both *De decalogo* and *De specialibus legibus*, introducing each Commandment, saying what he wants to say, then moving on to the next.[25] As a result, both treatises contain a series of self-contained text units, each devoted essentially to *one* of the Ten Commandments. So Philo's commentary on a particular Commandment consists of the material from two complementary text units—one in *De decalogo* and a corresponding unit in *De specialibus legibus*—dealing with both the Commandment itself (the genus) and the subordinate laws (the species).[26]

Philo's Exposition of the Tenth Commandment

Decal. 142–53 and *Spec.* 4.78b–131 contain Philo's commentary on the Tenth Commandment, which he reads as a two-word prohibition, οὐκ ἐπιθυμήσεις.[27] Philo abbreviates the Septuagint version, which lists various objects of desire: a neighbor's wife, house, field, etc.[28] Although he never explains or justifies this abbreviation, it makes good sense in light of his overall treatment of the Ten Commandments, especially his view of the last five as a pentad of basic prohibitions governing human affairs.[29] Superficially, the abbreviation accomplishes a stylistic leveling, bringing the Tenth Commandment into line with the four other basic prohibitions: οὐ μοιχεύσεις, οὐ κλέψεις, οὐ φονεύσεις, and οὐ ψευδομαρτυρήσεις—the last of which is itself an abbreviation of the Ninth Commandment.[30] More

---

[25] Structural outlines of the treatises reveal Philo's straightforward sequential movement through the list of Ten Commandments. For an outline of *De decalogo*, see Borgen, "Philosopher or Editor," 124–25. For an outline of the four books of *De specialibus legibus*, see Heinemann, PCH 2, 8–13 (although, as Heinemann's outline indicates, Philo in effect treats the First and Second Commandments as a single unit).

[26] For a schematic correlation of material from *De decalogo* and *De specialibus legibus*, see the outline of the Sixth through Tenth Commandments in André Mosès, PAPM 25, 15–16.

[27] On οὐκ ἐπιθυμήσεις as Philo's version of the Tenth Commandment, see above, n. 4.

[28] LXX Exod 20:17 [=LXX Deut 5:21], on which see above, n. 1.

[29] E.g., *Decal.* 121: ἀπαγορεύσεις τῶν πρὸς ἀνθρώπους. In Philo's view, these five prohibitions are comprehensive: "These are general rules forbidding practically all sins (οὗτοι γενικοὶ σχεδὸν πάντων ἁμαρτημάτων εἰσὶ κανόνες), and to them the specific sins may in each case be referred (ἐφ'οὓς ἕκαστον ἀναφέρεσθαι τῶν ἐν εἴδει συμβέβηκεν)" (*Her* 173). For the division of the Ten Commandments into pentads, see esp. *Decal.* 50–51 (also *Her.* 168).

[30] N.B. Philo's citation of οὐ ψευδομαρτυρήσεις (*Spec.* 4.41; cf. *Decal* 172: τέταρτον δὲ [κεφάλαιον] τὸ περὶ τοῦ μὴ ψευδομαρτυρεῖν) compared with Exod 20:16 [=Deut 5:20]: οὐ ψευδομαρτυρήσεις κατὰ τοῦ πλησίον σου μαρτυρίαν ψευδῆ. For the other prohibitions, whose simple two-word expressions Philo adopts verbatim, see Exod 20:13–15 [=Deut

importantly, however, a *specific* formulation of the Tenth Commandment would contradict Philo's claim that the Commandments are comprehensive, generic summaries—or, as with οὐκ ἐπιθυμήσεις, generic *prohibitions*. In his system of thought, limiting the scope of the Tenth Commandment to specific objects would blur the distinction between genus and species. Rather than a summary, the Commandment would read more like a short list of "particular laws."[31] Philo does consider various objects of desire, but only as concrete illustrations of the nature and function of desire *itself*, not restrictions on the Commandment's proscriptive *range* of objects.[32]

The first unit of commentary, *Decal.* 142–53, is the last installment in his initial survey of the Ten Commandments (*Decal.* 50–153). Focusing on what the prohibition entails, this unit contains a sketch of the nature, mechanics, and potentially disastrous effects of desire, framed initially (§§142–46) as a review of the four cardinal πάθη: pleasure (ἡδονή), grief (λύπη), fear (φόβος), and desire (ἐπιθυμία).[33] (*Decal.* 173–74 briefly restates the ill effects

---

5:17–19]. Cf. Rom 13:9 (Codex Sinaiticus): οὐ μοιχεύσεις, οὐ φονεύσεις, οὐ κλέψεις, οὐ ψευδομαρτυρήσεις, οὐκ ἐπιθυμήσεις.

[31] Although the LXX version does include a general prohibition of ὅσα τῷ πλησίον σού ἐστιν, it never loses the fundamental specification τοῦ πλησίον σου. In its full LXX formulation, the Commandment does not proscribe, for example, the desire for a house per se, only the desire for a specific *type* of house—viz., the house of a neighbor.

[32] For example, in *Spec.* 4.86–91 Philo wants to illustrate how desire "produces a change for the worse in all which it attacks" (§86) by listing various aims of desire and the respective vices associated with those aims. The aims are all quite general: "money" (χρήματα), "reputation" (δόξα), "power" (ἀρχή), "physical beauty" (σώματος κάλλος), "the tongue" (γλῶττα) (i.e., desire to speak or keep silent), "the belly" (γαστήρ) (i.e., desire for food and drink).

[33] On πάθος as a philosophical term, see in general F. E. Peters, *Greek Philosophical Terms: A Historical Lexicon* (New York: New York University Press, 1967), 152–55. The term πάθος essentially denotes something that happens *to* someone (i.e., an experience one undergoes), so "passion" bears literally the sense of its cognate "passive" despite its often active sense. (For an ancient [Platonic] discussion of active and passive connotations of πάθος, see Galen, *PHP* VI 1.5–23; cf. Martin Elsky [trans.], "Erich Auerbach, '*Passio* as Passion' ['*Passio* als Leidenschaft']" *Criticism* 43 [2001]: 288–308.) As a term of moral psychology, πάθος refers to an experience undergone in one's soul; for example, the experience ("passion," "feeling," "emotion") of fear. Ancient moral philosophers proposed various definitions for both πάθος per se and the individual πάθη, along with various strategies for how best to manage passion(s). On management, see, for example, Martha Nussbaum, *The Therapy of Desire: Theory and Practice in Hellenistic Ethics* (3d ed.; Princeton: Princeton University Press, 2009). On the four cardinal πάθη see Simo Knuuttila and Juha Sihvola, "How the Philosophical Analysis of the Emotions Was Introduced," in *The Emotions in Hellenistic Philosophy* (ed. J. Sihvola and T. Engberg-Pedersen; TSHP 46; Dordrecht: Kluwer, 1998), 1–19, esp. 14–16. For an explanation of the Stoic view of πάθος over against the Platonic-Aristotelian view, see Michael Frede, "The Stoic Doctrine of the Affections of the Soul," in *The Norms of Nature: Studies in Hellenistic Ethics* (ed. Malcolm Schofield and Gisela Striker; Cambridge: Cambridge

of desire, then previews *De specialibus legibus* by noting the existence of "many ordinances which come under this head," without identifying any of those ordinances.) The second unit of commentary, *Spec.* 4.78b–131, represents the exposition proper, since it contains Philo's comprehensive treatment of *both* οὐκ ἐπιθυμήσεις *and* the corresponding subordinate laws.[34] Again he covers the nature, mechanics, and effects of desire, as in the first unit, but in much greater depth (*Spec.* 4.78b–94). Then, in keeping with his overarching program for *De decalogo* and *De specialibus legibus*, Philo cites and expounds the Mosaic dietary laws, which he considers the "particular laws" belonging under the rubric οὐκ ἐπιθυμήσεις (*Spec.* 4.95–131). The two units of commentary together amount to 351 lines of Greek text in PCW, with the exposition proper (*Spec.* 4.78b–131) amounting to 298 lines, all devoted to Philo's understanding of the Tenth Commandment. In sheer quantity, Philo's exposition of οὐκ ἐπιθυμήσεις stands on a par with some of

---

University Press, 1986), 93–110. On Philo's concept of emotion(s), see David Charles Aune, "Mastery of the Passions: Philo, 4 Maccabees and Earliest Christianity," in *Hellenization Revisited: Shaping a Christian Response within the Greco-Roman World* (ed. Wendy E. Helleman; Lanham, Md.: University Press of America, 1994), 125-58, esp. 125–34; John Dillon, *The Middle Platonists: 80 B.C. to A.D. 220* (rev. ed.; Ithaca, N.Y.: Cornell University Press, 1996), 151–52; Petra von Gemünden, "La culture des passions à l'époque du Nouveau Testament: Une contribution théologique et psychologique," *ETR* 70 (1995): 335–48, esp. 339–42; Margaret Graver, "Philo of Alexandria and the Origins of the Stoic ΠΡΟΠΑΘΕΙΑΙ," in *Philo of Alexandria and Post-Aristotelian Philosophy* (ed. Francesca Alesse; SPhA 5; Leiden: Brill, 2008), 197–221; repr. from *Phronesis* 44 (1999): 300–25; Carlos Lévy, "Philon d'Alexandrie et les passions," in *Réceptions antiques: Lecture, transmission, appropriation intellectuelle* (ed. Lætitia Ciccolini et al.; ELA 16; Paris: Éditions Rue d'Ulm, 2006), 27–41; idem, "Philo's Ethics," in *The Cambridge Companion to Philo* (Cambridge: Cambridge University Press, 2009), 146–71, esp. 154–64 [="The Passions"]; Salvatore Lilla, *Clement of Alexandria: A Study in Christian Platonism and Gnosticism* (OTM; London: Oxford University Press, 1971), 84–92, esp. 92; Max Pohlenz, *Philon von Alexandreia* (*NAWG* 5; Göttingen: Vandenhoeck & Ruprecht, 1942), 457–61; David Runia, *Philo of Alexandria and the* Timaeus *of Plato* (PA 44 ; Leiden: Brill, 1986), 299–301; Helmut Schmidt, *Die Anthropologie Philons von Alexandreia* (Würzburg: Konrad Triltsch, 1933), 86–101 [="Die Lehre vom Pathos"]; Michel Spanneut, "*Apatheia* ancienne, *apatheia* chrétienne. Ière partie: *L'apatheia* ancienne," *ANRW* 36.7: 4641–4717, 4701–04; Walther Völker, *Fortschritt und Vollendung bei Philo von Alexandrien: Eine Studie zur Geschichte der Frömmigkeit* (TUGAL 49.1; Leipzig: J. C. Hinrich, 1938), 80–95; David Winston, "Philo's Ethical Theory," *ANRW* 21.1:372–416, 400–05; idem, "Philo of Alexandria on the Rational and Irrational Emotions," in *Passions and Moral Progress in Greco-Roman Thought* (ed. John T. Fitzgerald; RMCS; New York: Routledge, 2008), 201–20.

[34] Because it amounts to a self-contained treatise, the unit *Spec.* 4.79–135 receives its own title "*De concupiscentia*" in some MSS (see PCW 5, xiv, xxvi), and, as Colson notes (PLCL 8, 56, n. 1), Cohn "here begins a fresh numeration of chapters." Older studies sometimes refer to *Spec.* 4.79–135 using the Latin title and Cohn's fresh numeration (e.g., Emile Bréhier, *Les idées philosophiques et religieuses de Philon d'Alexandrie* [EPM 8; 3d ed.; Paris: J. Vrin, 1950], 253).

his independent treatises—for example, *De gigantibus* (320 lines in PCW). The importance of this exposition, however, lies in the material itself, first in its own right but also in its relation to other first-century treatments of the Tenth Commandment and key topics in Philo's ethical theory.

The Value of Philo's Exposition

As a substantive, detailed analysis of the Tenth Commandment from arguably the best representative of Hellenistic Judaism in antiquity, Philo's exposition of οὐκ ἐπιθυμήσεις deserves a complete study in and of itself. In his exposition, he considers in depth both the Tenth Commandment and the dietary laws that for him reflect its moral essence, so a careful reading should answer two fundamental questions:

1. In Philo's view, *what* does the Tenth Commandment prohibit? (All desire? A certain type? What type?)

2. In Philo's view, *how* is the Tenth Commandment observed? (What are the mechanics of its observance? What role do the dietary laws play in its observance?)

Answering these specific questions helps to illuminate general aspects of Philo's fusion of Judaism and Hellenism. For example, how does a first-century Jew, who is also an accomplished student of Greek philosophy, make sense of the Decalogue's prohibition of *desire* (ἐπιθυμία), an emotion that Greek philosophers studied at length? And how does an obscure set of dietary regulations, which often placed observant Jews at odds with the broader culture, become the centerpiece of Moses' philosophically astute training program for managing desire?[35] Philo's exposition speaks to these and other issues.

---

[35] For general considerations of the Jewish dietary laws in Philo's day, see, for example, John M. G. Barclay, *Jews in the Mediterranean Diaspora: From Alexander to Trajan (323 BCE–117 CE)* (Edinburgh: T&T Clark, 1996), 434–37 [="Separatism at Meals"]; Christoph Heil, *Die Ablehnung der Speisegebote durch Paulus: Zur Frage nach der Stellung des Apostels zum Gesetz* (BBB 96; Weinheim: Beltz Athenäum, 1994), 23–123, esp. 39–99 [="Die Speisegebote im Frühjudentum"]; Hermut Löhr, "Speisenfrage und Tora im Judentum des Zweiten Tempels und im entstehenden Christentum," *ZNW* 94 (2003): 17–37; E. P. Sanders, "Purity, Food and Offerings in the Greek-Speaking Diaspora," in *Jewish Law from Jesus to the Mishnah: Five Studies* (London: SCM Press, 1990), 255–308, 272–83 [="Food"]. On Philo and the dietary laws, see Mireille Hadas-Lebel, *Philon d'Alexandrie: Un penseur en diaspora* (Paris: Fayard, 2003), 159–62 [="Les lois alimentaires"]; Richard D. Hecht, "Patterns of Exegesis in Philo's Interpretation of Leviticus," *SPh* 6 (1979–1980): 77–155,

But Philo's work also bears importance for the comparative assessment of a broader first-century interest in the Tenth Commandment attested elsewhere by two of Philo's contemporaries, Paul and the author of 4 Maccabees.[36] All three authors cite abbreviated Greek versions of the Tenth Commandment and consider its moral significance.[37] Such an interest in οὐκ ἐπιθυμήσεις makes sense in light of a number of ancient perspectives on ἐπιθυμία: for example, Judeo-Christian speculations regarding ἐπιθυμία as the root of all sin.[38] But it also makes sense in light of

---

esp. 108–15; Isaak Heinemann, *Philons griechische und jüdische Bildung: Kulturvergleichende Untersuchungen zu Philons Darstellung der jüdischen Gesetze* (Breslau: Marcus, 1932; repr. Darmstadt: Wissenschaftliche Buchgesellschaft, 1962), 155–66; Walter Houston, "Towards an Integrated Reading of the Dietary Laws of Leviticus," in *The Book of Leviticus: Composition and Reception* (ed. R. Rendtorff and R. Kugler; VTSup 93; FIOTL 3; Leiden: Brill, 2003), 142–61, esp. 144–47; Alan Mendelson, *Philo's Jewish Identity* (BJS 161; Atlanta: Scholars Press, 1988), 67–71 [="Dietary Laws"]; James N. Rhodes, "Diet and Desire: The Logic of the Dietary Laws according to Philo," *ETL* 79 (2003): 122–33; Cristina Termini, "Philo's Thought within the Context of Middle Judaism," in *The Cambridge Companion to Philo* (ed. Adam Kamesar; Cambridge: Cambridge University Press, 2009), 95–123, esp. 119–21 [="The Dietary Laws"] (cf. Katell Berthelot, "L'interprétation symbolique des lois alimentaires dans la *Lettre d'Aristée*. Une influence pythagoricienne," *JJS* 52 [2001]: 253–68; Robert M. Grant, "Dietary Laws among Pythagoreans, Jews, and Christians," *HTR* 73 [1980]: 299–310; James N. Rhodes, "Diet as Morality: Tracing an Exegetical Tradition" [M. A. thesis; Catholic University of America, 2000]; Abraham Terian, "Some Stock Arguments for the Magnanimity of the Law in Hellenistic Jewish Apologetics," *JLAS* 1 [1985]: 141–49; Giovanni Maria Vian, "Purità e culto nell'esegesi giudaico-ellenistica," *ASE* 13 [1996]: 67–84, esp. 78–80). On Philo's commitment to literal observance of Mosaic legislation (including dietary laws), see *Migr.* 89–93.

[36] See Romans 7:7–25 and 4 Maccabees 2:4–6. Although the exact dates of the relevant texts cannot be determined, their sequence *can*. The absolute terminus ad quem for Philo's exposition is his death, which by general consensus is hardly later than 50 C.E. (Peder Borgen, "Philo of Alexandria," *ABD* 5:333–42, 333). Paul's letter to the Romans dates from between 55 and 60 C.E. (Joseph Fitzmyer, *Romans: A New Translation with Introduction and Commentary* [AB 33; New York: Doubleday, 1993], 85–88). 4 Maccabees dates from near the end of the first century C.E. (Hans-Josef Klauck, *4. Makkabäerbuch* [*JSHRZ* 3.1; Gütersloh: Gerd Mohn, 1989], 668–69).

[37] Paul's version, like Philo's, is οὐκ ἐπιθυμήσεις (Rom 7:7; cf. Rom 13:9). 4 Maccabees has a longer, more specific version, οὐκ ἐπιθυμήσεις τὴν γυναῖκα τοῦ πλησίον σου οὐδὲ ὅσα τῷ πλησίον σού ἐστιν (2:5), but the context suggests a comprehensive scope (N.B. πάσης ἐπιθυμίας in 2:4; and esp. μὴ ἐπιθυμεῖν εἴρηκεν ἡμᾶς ὁ νόμος in 2:6).

[38] E.g., *Apoc. Mos.* 19.3: ἐπιθυμία γάρ ἐστι πάσης ἁμαρτίας (ed. Jan Dochhorn, *Die Apokalypse des Mose: Text, Übersetzung, Kommentar* [TSAJ 106; Tübingen: Mohr Siebeck, 2005]; some MSS: ἐπιθυμία γάρ ἐστι κεφαλὴ πάσης ἁμαρτίας [idem, 331]); Jas 1:14–15: esp. ἡ ἐπιθυμία συλλαβοῦσα τίκτει ἁμαρτίαν; Philo himself identifies ἐπιθυμία as the source of all evils (ἁπάντων πηγὴ τῶν κακῶν) in *Spec.* 4.84–85 (cf. *Decal.* 173: τὴν τῶν ἀδικημάτων πηγήν, ἐπιθυμίαν). For consideration of such texts and their relation to exegetical traditions construing the disobedience of Adam and Eve as a violation of the Tenth Commandment, see Jan Dochhorn, "Röm 7,7 und das zehnte Gebot: Ein Beitrag

Greco-Roman *philosophical* speculations regarding the function and malfunction of ἐπιθυμία, one of the four cardinal πάθη, whose ill effects are counteracted by ἐγκράτεια.[39] In any case, a full comparative assessment of these three treatments of the Tenth Commandment and their relation to broader trends in biblical exegesis and ethical reflection requires a proper understanding of *Philo's* treatment—which is by far the most elaborate of the three.

Finally, a comprehensive investigation of Philo's exposition of the Tenth Commandment promises a better understanding of key topics in Philo's ethical theory, which can in turn illuminate broader trends in Middle-Platonic ethical theory.[40] For example, Philo grounds his exposition in

---

zur Schriftauslegung und zur jüdischen Vorgeschichte des Paulus," *ZNW* 100 (2009): 59–77, esp. 63–65. On such texts considered as a possible basis for Paul's reflection on οὐκ ἐπιθυμήσεις, see J. A. Ziesler, "The Role of the Tenth Commandment in Romans 7," *JSNT* 33 (1988): 41–56, 47. Regardless of the knowledge Philo had of traditions construing ἐπιθυμία as the root of all sin, he frames his discourse on ἐπιθυμία in distinctly *philosophical* terms. Although he considers ἐπιθυμία a source of wrongdoing (*Spec.* 4.84–85; *Decal.* 173), he does *not* think in terms of "sin" (the term ἁμαρτία appears nowhere in his exposition). Instead, he thinks in terms of πάθος (e.g., *Spec.* 4.79), choosing a technical term from moral philosophy.

[39] On considerations of the Tenth Commandment in light of *philosophical* concerns, see esp. Thomas H. Tobin, *Paul's Rhetoric in Its Contexts: The Argument of Romans* (Peabody, Mass.: Hendrickson, 2004), 229–32. Tobin concludes that Philo, Paul, and the author of 4 Maccabees reflect "broader discussions within Hellenistic Judaism about the function of the law in relation to theories about the nature of the passions, particularly desire, in Greco-Roman philosophy" (232); see also Petra von Gemünden, "Der Affekt der ἐπιθυμία und der νόμος: Affektkontrolle und soziale Identitätsbildung im 4. Makkabäerbuch mit einem Ausblick auf den Römerbrief," in *Das Gesetz im frühen Judentum und im Neuen Testament: Festschrift für Christoph Burchard zum 75. Geburtstag* (ed. Dieter Sänger and Matthias Konradt; NTOA / SUNT 57; Göttingen: Vandenhoeck & Ruprecht; Fribourg: Academic Press, 2006), 55–74; Stanley Stowers, "Paul and Self-Mastery," in *Paul in the Greco-Roman World: A Handbook* (ed. J. Paul Sampley; Harrisburg, Pa.: Trinity Press International, 2003), 524–50, 531–34 [="Judaism as a School for Self-Mastery"] (cf. Stanley Stowers, *A Rereading of Romans: Justice, Jews, and Gentiles* [New Haven: Yale University Press, 1994], 58–65); Emma Wasserman, *The Death of the Soul in Romans 7: Sin, Death, and the Law in Light of Hellenistic Moral Psychology* (WUNT 256; Tübingen: Mohr Siebeck, 2008), 105–06.

[40] On the fundamentally Platonic orientation of Philo's thought, see esp. Thomas H. Billings, *The Platonism of Philo Judaeus* (Chicago: University of Chicago Press, 1919; repr., New York: Garland, 1979), made more useful by A. C. Geljon and D. T. Runia, "An *Index Locorum* to Billings," *SPhA* 7 (1995): 169–85. On Philo as a *Middle* Platonist, see esp. Dillon, *Middle Platonists*, 139–83; also "Special Section: Philo and Middle Platonism," *SPhA* 5 (1993): 95–155. In terms of contemporary Middle-Platonic moral psychology, Philo's exposition of the Tenth Commandment qualifies him as a "*de facto* Middle Platonist," one of the six positions outlined in David Runia's typological spectrum ("Was Philo a Middle Platonist? A Difficult Question Revisited," *SPhA* [1993]:

theoretical overviews of the πάθη, using a variety of technical terms and concepts.[41] He clearly intends to establish first a working model of ἐπιθυμία as πάθος and then use it to inform his discussion of the prohibition οὐκ ἐπιθυμήσεις. Because Philo is a Middle Platonist, his exposition offers valuable insight into the elements of a Middle-Platonic theory of the "passions," insofar as it deals with *passionate desire*.[42] The concept of self-control (ἐγκράτεια) also bears directly on Philo's understanding of the Tenth Commandment.[43] When he begins his survey of the "particular laws," *species* of the genus οὐκ ἐπιθυμήσεις, Philo cites the law of first fruits (Exod 23:19; Deut 18:4), which in his view exists "for the practice of self-control" (πρὸς ἄσκησιν ... ἐγκρατείας).[44] This phrase suggests not only the importance of

---

112–140, 125): "he does not belong to the school, but has a philosophical stance which is fundamentally Platonist and might well make him welcome in such circles."

[41] See esp. *Decal.* 142–46; *Spec.* 4.79.

[42] Simply put, Philo's exposition reflects a Middle-Platonic theory of the passions, insofar as it combines a fundamentally Platonic psychology (esp. *Spec.* 4.92–94) with Stoic technical definitions of passion(s) (esp. *Spec.* 4.79; cf. *Decal.* 142)—a combination evident in other Middle-Platonic texts (e.g., *Didask.* 32.1 [185.26]: κίνησις ἄλογος ψυχῆς [cf. DL 7.110]). Middle Platonists rework these Stoic definitions, enabling them to describe psychological phenomena whose existence "orthodox" (i.e., Chrysippean) Stoicism would deny (e.g., non-rational parts of the soul in conflict with a rational part). Evidence in Philo's exposition for this sort of reinvention exists but has not been properly assessed. For example, Philo in *Spec.* 4.79 adds to the Stoic definition of passion as "excessive impulse" (πλεονάζουσα ὁρμή; e.g., DL 7.110 [=*SVF* I 50, 23]; *ESE* 10 [=*SVF* III 92, 11]; *PHP* IV 2.8 [=*SVF* III 113, 15]) the qualifier "unmeasured" (ἄμετρος), which is unattested in the Stoic sources and indicates a failure to limit the *quantitative* force of a non-rational impulse—a notion incompatible with the Stoic understanding of impulse as a form of rational assent (on which see Brad Inwood, *Ethics and Human Action in Early Stoicism* [Oxford: Clarendon, 1985], esp. chs. 3 and 5, N.B. 167–68 on "excessive impulse": "no aspect of the theory [Stoic psychology] ... admits of the sort of variation of degree which would be needed for a more familiar quantitative sense of 'excessive'.").

[43] For the term, see *Spec.* 4.97, 99, 101, 112 [bis], 124. For explicit connection of ἐγκράτεια with the Tenth Commandment, see, for example, vol. 2 of Harry Austryn Wolfson, *Philo: Foundations of Religious Philosophy in Judaism, Christianity, and Islam* (2 vols; 2d rev. print.; Cambridge, Mass.: Harvard University Press, 1948), 235–36; also Stowers, "Paul and Self-Mastery," 532. For general considerations of ἐγκράτεια in Philo, see esp. Maren Niehoff, *Philo on Jewish Identity and Culture* (TSAJ 86; Tübingen: Mohr Siebeck, 2001), 75–110 [="Jewish Values: Religion and Self-Restraint"], esp. 94–110; also Stowers, "Paul and Self-Mastery," 531–34 (cf. Stowers, *Romans*, 58–65).

[44] *Spec.* 4.99. Philo twice lists ἐγκράτεια as one of many different kinds of ἄσκησις (*Leg.* 3.18; *Her.* 253). Pierre Hadot uses Philo's two lists as a basis for his discussion of different "spiritual" exercises in antiquity, by which he means exercises of Greco-Roman philosophers pertaining to the soul, not exercises practiced in a religious setting (Pierre Hadot, "Spiritual Exercises," in *Philosophy as a Way of Life: Spiritual Exercises from Socrates to Foucault* [ed., intro. Arnold I. Davidson; trans. Michael Case; Malden, Mass.: Blackwell, 1995], 81–125, 84).

ἐγκράτεια, but also the relevance of another ethical concept, ἄσκησις—specifically, how Mosaic laws regarding food and drink function as *practice* in the cultivation of self-control.[45] Understanding Philo's exposition involves the clarification of these and other topics.

Even an introductory survey of the nature and content of Philo's exposition of the Tenth Commandment commends it to further study, and Philo facilitates such study by neatly packaging his material: the structural layout of his broader Exposition of the Law makes his exposition of οὐκ ἐπιθυμήσεις a complete text in and of itself. Earlier studies of Philo have touched on this text in a variety of ways, from a variety of perspectives, with a variety of results.

History of Research

Had Philo chosen to publish his exposition of the Tenth Commandment as an independent work, it surely by now would have received more attention. But to date no comprehensive study of this important treatise exists, one that deals exclusively with Philo's view of the Tenth Commandment in light of *his* agenda *his* interests, *his* organization of the material, and *his* understanding of the relevant topics—one that clearly and adequately answers the two fundamental questions of *what* οὐκ ἐπιθυμήσεις actually prohibits and *how* to observe the injunction. Translators of the relevant units (*Decal.* 142–53, 173–74 and *Spec.* 4.78b–131) offer general remarks on Philo's interpretation of the Tenth Commandment, along with commentary on specific passages, but the scope of their work is too broad and too sketchy to treat those units—especially the exposition proper (*Spec.* 4.78b–131)—in sufficient depth.[46] Similarly, a number of works whose aims

---

[45] In regard to Philo's usage, the term ἄσκησις has little to do with modern terms such as "ascetic" or "asceticism," whose connotations derive mostly from Christian monasticism. The Greek term has no intrinsic association with religious practice (see Hermigild Dressler, *The Usage of Ἀσκέω and Its Cognates in Greek Documents to 100 A.D.* [CUAPS 78; Washington: Catholic University of America Press, 1947]). For Philo, ἄσκησις pertains mainly to moral philosophy, as one of three ways to acquire virtue: nature, instruction, and *practice* (e.g., *Abr.* 52); see Ellen Birnbaum, "Exegetical Building Blocks in Philo's Interpretation of the Patriarchs," in *From Judaism to Christianity: Tradition and Transition: A Festschrift for Thomas H. Tobin, S.J., on the Occasion of His Sixty-fifth Birthday* (ed. Patricia Walters; NovTSup 136; Leiden: Brill, 2010), 69–92.

[46] For translations of the *De decalogo* units (§§142–53, §§173–74), see Leopold Treitel, PCH 1 (1909); F. H. Colson, PLCL 7 (1937); Valentin Nikiprowetzky, PAPM 23 (1965); Francesca Calabi, *Filone*, Decalogo (2005); cf. Ronald Williamson, *Jews in the Hellenistic World: Philo* (CCWJCW 1.2; Cambridge: Cambridge University Press, 1989), 255–78. For the exposition proper (*Spec.* 4.78b–131), see Isaak Heinemann, PCH 2 (1910); F. H. Colson, PLCL 8 (1939); and André Mosès, PAPM 25 (1970).

lie elsewhere offer incidental, often helpful, remarks on Philo's view of the Tenth Commandment, but never in an effort to explain it in full.[47] In fact, only two works offer sustained treatments of the Tenth Commandment in Philo, and neither satisfies the need for a comprehensive study.

Harry A. Wolfson

In an extensive work on Philo, Harry Wolfson devotes part of a chapter on ethics to a study of the Tenth Commandment.[48] The title of his brief analysis, "The Virtue of the Control of Desire," reflects a broader aim on Wolfson's part to explore the relationship between law and virtue, especially *where* and *how* Philo's understanding of Mosaic law incorporates terms and concepts derived from Greek ethical theory.[49] He does not intend to provide a comprehensive analysis of the contents of Philo's

---

[47] For example, Amir, "Decalogue," 158–59; Klaus Berger, *Die Gesetzesauslegung Jesu* (WMANT 40.1; Neukirchen-Vluyn: Neukirchener Verlag, 1972), 346–48; Erwin Goodenough, *The Jurisprudence of the Jewish Courts in Egypt* (New Haven: Yale University Press, 1929), 207–08; Houston, "Dietary Laws," 144–47; Kellermann, "Dekalog," 168; Hermann Lichtenberger, *Das Ich Adams und das Ich der Menschheit: Studien zum Menschenbild in Römer 7* (WUNT 164; Tübingen: Mohr Siebeck, 2004), 246–50; Lluch Baixauli, "Decálogo," 436–38; William Loader, "The Decalogue" in *The Septuagint, Sexuality, and the New Testament* (Grand Rapids: Eerdmans, 2004), 5–25, 12-1-4; Anita Méasson, *Du char ailé de Zeus à l'Arche d'Alliance: Images et mythes platoniciens chez Philon d'Alexandrie* (Paris: Études Augustiniennes, 1987), 154; Thomas E. Phillips, "Revisiting Philo: Discussions of Wealth and Poverty in Philo's Ethical Discourse," *JSNT* 83 (2001): 111–21, 114–15; Alexander Rofé, "The Tenth Commandment in the Light of Four Deuteronomic Laws," in *The Ten Commandments in History and Tradition* (ed. B.-Z. Segal and G. Levi; Jerusalem: Magnes Press, 1990), 45–65, 48–49; Torrey Seland, "The Moderate Life of the Christian *paroikoi*: A Philonic Reading of 1 Pet 2:11," in *Philo und das Neue Testament* (WUNT 172; Tübingen: Mohr Siebeck, 2004), 241–64, 259–63; Stowers, "Paul and Self-Mastery," 531–34 (cf. Stowers, *Romans*, 58–65); Tobin, *Paul's Rhetoric*, 231–32; Wasserman, *Death of the Soul*, 105–06.

[48] Wolfson, *Philo*, 2:225–37.

[49] Before his discussion of the Tenth Commandment, Wolfson deals with the topics "'Under the Law' and 'In Accordance with Nature'" (165–200) and "Commandments and Virtues" (200–225). In his discussion of the Tenth Commandment, Wolfson also considers relevant material from "native Jewish literature" (226), including the topics of regulating emotion (226–29) and the evil *yetser* (230–31). Despite arguable (and isolated) rabbinic parallels adduced by Wolfson (cf. Joel Marcus, "The Evil Inclination in the Epistle of James," *CBQ* 44 [1982]: 606–21, 613–15), the moral theory informing Philo's exposition of οὐκ ἐπιθυμήσεις—*taken as a whole*—undoubtedly derives from Greek philosophy. On the regulation of desire in Rabbinic Judaism, see esp. Jonathan Wyn Schofer, *The Making of a Sage: A Study in Rabbinic Ethics* (Madison: University of Wisconsin Press, 2005); also Bernard S. Jackson, "Liability for Mere Intention in Early Jewish Law," in *Essays in Jewish and Comparative Legal History* (ed. Jacob Neusner; SJLA 10; Leiden: Brill, 1975), 202–34.

exposition. Instead, as part of a sweeping effort to reconstruct Philo's system of thought, he considers the significance within that system of a moral imperative aimed not at action(s) but at "pure emotion."[50] Although limited, Wolfson's treatment nevertheless includes substantive claims about Philo's interpretation of οὐκ ἐπιθυμήσεις.

Wofson's most valuable contribution comes at the end of his analysis, where he recognizes the central importance of ἐγκράτεια in Philo's overall understanding of the Tenth Commandment.[51] In particular, he recognizes that "[t]he negative tenth commandment is ... a command to control one's desire."[52] In other words, the negative prohibition implies a positive command to cultivate the virtue of ἐγκράτεια, which—as Wolfson notes—is "the positive term ... by which the control of excessive desire is to be described."[53] But because his interests lie elsewhere, he only considers *that* this is true, not *how* this is true. He never answers the basic question of how someone observes the Tenth Commandment or how it in fact promotes ἐγκράτεια. Wolfson also realizes that, for Philo, *other* Mosaic laws work along with the Tenth Commandment to promote ἐγκράτεια.[54] But he never mentions the dietary laws, let alone explains how—in Philo's view—they pertain to οὐκ ἐπιθυμήσεις. In this respect Wolfson's treatment, even where it does correctly characterize Philo's view of the Tenth Commandment, remains sketchy.

Although valuable for its emphasis on ἐγκράτεια, Wolfson's study misconstrues Philo's view of what the Commandment prohibits. He makes the unfounded assumption that Philo, with the Septuagint version in mind, understands the Tenth Commandment to be a prohibition *only* of desire for what belongs to another person.[55] Wolfson does not acknowledge the generalizing effect of Philo's abbreviated οὐκ ἐπιθυμήσεις, choosing instead to retain the Septuagint version's specification "of your neighbor" (τοῦ πλησίον σου).[56] He admits that this specification does not appear in Philo's commentary but assumes it nevertheless:

---

[50] Wolfson, *Philo*, 2:225.
[51] Stowers (e.g., "Paul and Self-Mastery," 532) similarly notes the importance of ἐγκράτεια for Philo's understanding of the Tenth Commandment.
[52] Wolfson, *Philo*, 2:235.
[53] Wolfson, *Philo*, 2:235. Wolfson refers to the concept of ἐγκράτεια found in *Eth. eud.* 1223 b 11–14) (e.g., ἐγκρατεύεται δ'ὅταν πράττῃ παρὰ τὴν ἐπιθυμίαν κατὰ τὸν λογισμόν).
[54] "It is the virtue of 'continence' ... that is taught by the tenth commandment as well as by all those special laws of which the purpose, as seen by [Philo], is to teach the control of desire" (Wolfson, *Philo*, 2:236).
[55] Wolfson, *Philo*, 2:228–29.
[56] Wolfson takes this in its most general sense of ὅσα τῷ πλησίον σού ἐστιν, as the LXX version stipulates. He cites and disagrees with Colson, whose assessment is correct:

> Though Philo speaks of desire in general, that is, of a desire for what we have not, and not of a desire for that which belongs to somebody else, still his discussion, in so far as it is a commentary upon the commandment, implies that the desire of which he speaks is that desire which the commandment explicitly describes as a desire for that which belongs to another person. (Wolfson, *Philo*, 2:228)[57]

The only evidence Wolfson offers in support of this view involves Philo's first example of an object of desire, money (χρήματα).[58] He argues that, although Philo does not specify the money's source:

> the subsequent statement that a desire for money leads to robbery and purse-cutting and house-breaking makes it quite evident that the desire for money spoken of was not a desire for money in general but rather for the money in the pocket or the purse or the house of one particular person. (Wolfson, *Philo*, 2:228)

But Wolfson fails to cite the entire passage, which goes on to associate the desire for money also with, for example, receiving bribes (δωροδοκίαις), which clearly involves greed per se and not desire for the money "of one particular person." Moreover, the other objects of desire on Philo's list, none of which Wolfson mentions, hardly make sense when construed strictly as belonging to another person. This is especially true in the case of desires for food and drink, which are, for Philo, governed by the Tenth Commandment's particular laws.[59]

Wolfson's study suffers also from an outdated conception of Philo's relationship to Greek philosophy. As he investigates select details of Philo's "homily on the evils of desire," Wolfson considers Philo an eclectic who adopts any number of different philosophical positions ad hoc. Wolfson suggests that in most of his analysis of ἐπιθυμία Philo chooses a Stoic

---

"The words 'thy neighbour's,' which are repeated so emphatically in the tenth commandment, as we have it and Philo also had it in the LXX, receive little attention from him" (PLCL 8, x).

[57] Also 2:229: "It is exactly the latter kind of desire, the desire for that which belongs to somebody else, that the tenth commandment as a law, and not a mere moral maxim, legally prohibits, according to Philo ...." Ibid.: "In his discussion of the legal prohibition not to desire that which belongs to one's neighbor, a prohibition, as we have said, of a mere desire for that which belongs to one's neighbor."

[58] *Spec.* 4.87: "If the desire is directed to money it makes men thieves and cut-purses, footpads, burglars, guilty of defaulting to their creditors, repudiating deposits, receiving bribes, robbing temples and of all similar actions."

[59] On Philo's association of the Tenth Commandment with dietary laws, Amir notes: "This association of ideas is possible only if the Commandment is shorn of its concluding words, 'anything that is your neighbor's.' For after all, kashrut has nothing to do with issues of ownership, of 'mine and thine.' An animal is not forbidden as food because it is stolen goods" ("Decalogue," 159).

position, but "[w]henever forced by certain native Jewish presuppositions, he departs from the Stoics and follows some other philosopher or presents a new view of his own."[60] Wolfson is correct, generally speaking, when he matches various terms and concepts in Philo's commentary with the same terms and concepts in sources known to be, for example, Stoic.[61] But he gives the misleading impression that Philo freely vacillates from one philosophical *opinion* to another with no underlying commitment to one philosophical *orientation* over another. Philo's "eclectic" philosophical mix is instead best understood as a reflection of his Middle Platonism—without this insight, Wolfson's study cannot provide an adequate understanding of Philo's philosophical perspective.[62]

In sum, Wolfson offers a substantial discussion of the Tenth Commandment in Philo, but one whose breadth and depth are severely limited due to the relatively minor role it plays within a much larger and more broadly oriented work. His answer to the question of *what*, in Philo's view, the Tenth Commandment prohibits is incorrect, since he limits the scope of ἐπιθυμία to only desire for what belongs to another person. Nor does he answer the question of *how* someone observes the Tenth Commandment, although he provides the proper context for an answer—namely, the acquisition, development, and exercise of ἐγκράτεια. Finally, his comments on the nature and function of ἐπιθυμία, although helpful at times, do not represent Philo's relationship with Greek philosophy properly.

---

[60] Wolfson, *Philo*, 2:231. Wolfson initially emphasizes Stoic provenance: e.g., 2:230: "It is the Stoics ... whom Philo follows here in the external formulation of his views." Ibid.: "He similarly follows the Stoics ...."

[61] E.g., Wolfson cites *SVF* for definitions of emotion comparable to *Spec.* 4.79, but he fails to note the significance of the non-Stoic ἄμετρος in Philo's definition (see above, n. 42).

[62] Cf. Dillon, *Middle Platonists*, 182: "My chief thesis (as against such an authority as H. A. Wolfson, for example) is that Philo was not so much constructing for himself an eclectic synthesis of all Greek philosophy, from the Presocratics to Posidonius, as essentially adapting contemporary Alexandrian Platonism, which was itself heavily influenced by Stoicism and Pythagoreanism, to his own exegetical purposes." For a fuller, yet still concise, statement of this position, in which Dillon rejects the misconceptions of (1) Philo as an "eclectic" who (2) merely uses philosophical *language* to serve exegetical aims, see his preface to *Philo of Alexandria:* The Contemplative Life, The Giants, *and Selections* (trans. and intro. David Winston; CWS; Mahwah, N.J.: Paulist, 1981), xii–xiii. See also David Winston's introduction (idem, 1–37), in which he accepts Philo's views as "Middle Platonist, that is, a highly Stoicized form of Platonism, streaked with Neopythagorean concerns" (3). In general, see John M. Dillon and A. A. Long, eds., *The Question of "Eclecticism": Studies in Later Greek Philosophy* (HCS 3; Berkeley: University of California Press, 1988).

20   CHAPTER ONE

Kathy L. Gaca

In *The Making of Fornication*, Kathy Gaca includes a chapter on Philo that deals in part with his understanding of the abbreviated Tenth Commandment.[63] While the broad scope of her work precludes an exhaustive treatment of Philo's exposition, Gaca nevertheless presents a sustained and virtually self-contained study of Philo's interpretation of οὐκ ἐπιθυμήσεις, offering summary conclusions and a bold thesis about Philo's notion of forbidden desire.[64] Taking all three of the relevant text units into account (*Decal.* 142–53, 173–74; *Spec.* 4.78b–131), she addresses not only the question of *what*, in Philo's view, the Commandment prohibits, but also *how* someone observes the Commandment, including an explanation of how the dietary laws promote its observance.[65] In one important general respect Gaca's work breaks new ground and sets a worthy standard: in her consideration of Philo's view of οὐκ ἐπιθυμήσεις, she takes seriously the idea that he is a Middle Platonist, consistently bearing in mind his debt to Plato and his acceptance of Platonic doctrines pertinent to an analysis of ἐπιθυμία.[66] But in her analysis of Philo's view, Gaca misconstrues the

---

[63] Chapter seven, "Philo's Reproductive City of God," in *The Making of Fornication: Eros, Ethics, and Political Reform in Greek Philosophy and Early Christianity* (HCS 40; Berkeley: University of California Press, 2003), 190–217. Pages 193–99 deal directly with the Tenth Commandment.

[64] See esp. her section titled "Philo's Revolutionary Conception of Forbidden Desire" (Gaca, *Making of Fornication*, 194–204). The aim of her book is "to resolve an important philosophical and historical problem about the making of sexual morality in Western culture: Do the patristic sexual rules of second-century Christianity differ notably from the Greek philosophical sexual principles that the patristic writers used to help formulate their own? Alternatively, are these Christian rules in unison with the Greek philosophical basis that they claim to have" (1). Her interest in Philo lies mainly in his contribution to the sexual ethics of "Christian Platonism" (see 193–94, along with her study of Clement of Alexandria in 247–72).

[65] Gaca does not quote Philo at length, but she does refer to passages from all three units of his exposition, indicating her awareness of the extent of his treatment. Her references take into account esp. *Decal.* 142, 173–174 and *Spec.* 4.78, 85, 87–96, 100–118.

[66] On Gaca's concept of Philo as a "Jewish Middle Platonist," see *Making of Fornication*, 191, n. 2. Although her *conclusions* are problematic, Gaca's *approach* is commendable in several respects. For example, she brings a Platonic psychological model to bear on the textual data of Philo's exposition, relating his discussion of ἐπιθυμία to Plato's theory that there is in the soul a distinct, non-rational source of ἐπιθυμία—i.e., [τὸ] ἀλόγιστόν τε καὶ ἐπιθυμητικόν [εἶδος] (*Resp.* 439 D; N.B. *Spec.* 4.92–94 [cf. *Tim.* 70 D–E]). Moreover, she notes key implications of Plato's theory, such as the moral agent's inability to remove appetitive ἐπιθυμία entirely and the consequent importance of *moderation* (e.g., *Making of Fornication*, 197). Gaca also understands that Philo's Middle Platonism involves the reinvention of Stoic terms and definitions: "The Stoic definitions of the passions that Philo uses are thus like a label that at first glance looks Stoic,

textual data, misreading a number of passages and failing to mention others that would readily disprove her claims.[67] For this reason, and because her study proposes a definitive—but incorrect—account of how Philo understands the Tenth Commandment, it deserves a detailed review.

Stated in its broadest terms, Gaca's thesis is that Philo's explanation of the abbreviated Tenth Commandment combines two elements into one innovative "Jewish Middle Platonist notion of forbidden desire"—namely, (1) "the Hellenistic Jewish concern about the desire (ἐπιθυμία) to disobey God's laws" and (2) "the Middle Platonist problem of excessive physical appetites (ἐπιθυμίαι) for the pleasures of food, drink, and especially sexual activity, contrary to reason's judicious sense of moderation."[68] What this means is that Philo follows a broader exegetical trend within Hellenistic Judaism to treat the Tenth Commandment as an abbreviated, two-word prohibition (οὐκ ἐπιθυμήσεις), but he does *not* follow the standard line of interpretation, which takes the prohibition to mean "that it is wrong or sinful even to desire to act contrary to God's will."[69] Instead, Philo follows

---

but the contents have changed" (201). Gaca's understanding of exactly *how* Philo changes the contents is problematic, but this statement as such is correct.

[67] Cf. David Runia's review of *The Making of Fornication* in *SPhA* 17 (2005): 237–43, esp. 241–43. Runia's summary assessment of Gaca's study includes a caveat: "[B]ecause its method of analyzing and interpreting texts is flawed, it is to be used with caution" (243).

[68] See Gaca, *Making of Fornication*, 194–95. Stated differently: "He reinterprets Platonic appetition—and sexual desire foremost—in light of the Hellenistic Jewish prohibition against the desire (ἐπιθυμία) to disobey God's will" (197). Gaca frames her thesis as a matter of sexual ethics: "Philo's sexual principles are part of an innovative agenda for social order that borrows from Plato and the Pentateuch, makes sense only in relation to both, and yet represents neither without noteworthy transformation. This is especially true for Philo's reinterpretation of the problems Plato sees with sexual desire, which Philo presents in his take on the aphoristic version of the Tenth Commandment: 'You will not desire' (οὐκ ἐπιθυμήσεις). In Philo's synthesis, forbidden desire (ἐπιθυμία) in the Hellenistic Jewish sense, which signifies any inclination to defy God's will, becomes primarily sexual in light of Plato's conviction that uncontrolled desire (ἐπιθυμία) for sexual pleasure is the single biggest source of individual and social corruption" (Gaca, *Making of Fornication*, 193).

[69] Gaca, *Making of Fornication*, 153. See 153–54 for Gaca's idea of a "Hellenistic Jewish variant on the Septuagint Tenth Commandment." In her discussion of Philo, Gaca speaks of "the Hellenistic Jewish Tenth Commandment in its two more traditional forms," by which she means (a) the LXX version itself (Exod 20:17 [=Deut 5:21]) and (b) the abbreviated version οὐκ ἐπιθυμήσεις, which omits the list of direct objects (198). She believes that Paul and Philo's citations of οὐκ ἐπιθυμήσεις serve as evidence for a hypothetical *tertium quid*—namely, an exegetical tradition that *influenced* these two authors. Her supposition involves first the claim that prior to Philo, who in fact offers the earliest extant citation of οὐκ ἐπιθυμήσεις (see above, n. 36), one or more unidentified Hellenistic Jewish exegetes chose to make an abbreviated Tenth Commandment

Plato's conviction that uncontrolled appetitive desire, especially sexual desire, corrupts individuals and societies, and for this reason he interprets οὐκ ἐπιθυμήσεις as a divine injunction to control appetitive, especially sexual, desire.

This last idea, that Philo's Tenth Commandment deals especially with sexual desire, deserves careful attention, since it in effect answers the question of *what* the Commandment prohibits. Ultimately, this idea derives from a reasonable but false assumption on Gaca's part that Philo imports without modification a certain concept of desire found in Plato's writings—a concept she outlines in an earlier chapter of her study.[70] Taken for granted, this assumption drives an almost syllogistic logic that informs much of what Gaca has to say about Philo's view of the Tenth Commandment: (a) when Plato thinks of ἐπιθυμία and its dangerous propensity for excess, he has in mind physical appetites, *especially* the sexual appetite; (b) when Philo thinks of the Commandment οὐκ ἐπιθυμήσεις, he has in mind Plato's concept of ἐπιθυμία and its dangerous propensity for excess, therefore (c) Philo has in mind physical appetites, *especially* the sexual appetite. A number of sweeping claims ensue:

> Philo reinterprets this commandment in a Platonic spirit that is very much in keeping with "nothing in excess," as though οὐκ ἐπιθυμήσεις meant "you will restrain your physical appetites from becoming excessive," the sexual

---

their object of inquiry. This is of course plausible, but the alternate supposition that Philo himself was the first to cite and interpret οὐκ ἐπιθυμήσεις is equally plausible and less speculative. After all, his is the most extensive extant commentary on the abbreviated version and—contingent on unknown facts regarding the publication of his Exposition of the Law—is as likely as any to have been the seminal work. Be that as it may, Gaca goes on to attribute a standard line of interpretation to this already hypothetical exegetical tradition. Οὐκ ἐπιθυμήσεις, the "newer prohibition" offered by the tradition, means "that it is wrong or sinful even to desire to act contrary to God's will" (153). Gaca's view problematically requires Philo to creatively modify a tradition for which no evidence exists, at least in terms of an extant text that cites οὐκ ἐπιθυμήσεις, then explicitly offers the interpretive conclusion "that it is wrong or sinful even to desire to act contrary to God's will." (On 152 Gaca cites "a broader Hellenistic Jewish and early Christian trend that stresses the danger of rebellious impulses very stringently"; but this broader trend—even if it did exist—does not constitute evidence for the exegetical trend that Gaca posits.)

[70] See Gaca, *Making of Fornication*, 26–41, esp. 32–33. The accuracy of Gaca's reading of Plato on this point bears less importance than the question of what *Philo* has to say about desire in his exposition of the Tenth Commandment. Even if she has correctly understood Plato's concept of appetitive desire, this concept must not serve *automatically* as the interpretive lens for Philo's understanding of οὐκ ἐπιθυμήσεις, without proof that Philo too is employing the same concept. This is especially true if Philo, as Gaca admits, is a Middle Platonist, which implies that he would have employed "Platonic" concepts that had been modified in significant respects in light of philosophical developments postdating Plato.

INTRODUCTION   23

appetite especially. By οὐκ ἐπιθυμήσεις in this sense, God too teaches the Platonic doctrine that depravity is grounded primarily in the unrestrained sexual appetite and its progeny of vices. (Gaca, *Making of Fornication*, 196)

Or similarly:

In God's social order these iniquities would become a thing of the past, so long as the people heed the commandment οὐκ ἐπιθυμήσεις by getting their appetitive urges under control, especially sexual desire. (Ibid.)[71]

Gaca frames these statements carefully, avoiding the claim that οὐκ ἐπιθυμήσεις deals *exclusively* with sexual desire. She does, after all, understand that the basic operation of the Platonic ἐπιθυμητικόν involves desires also for food and drink.[72] But in some instances there is no clear acknowledgement of the relevance of non-sexual desire(s) within the Commandment's purview: "Philo's Tenth Commandment is innovative as a Decalogue rule because it valorizes sexual desire as the main source of all wickedness."[73] In other instances, particularly in concluding summaries of her argument, there is no indication that anything *but* sexual desire lies within the proscriptive range of οὐκ ἐπιθυμήσεις:

Though Philo supports Plato's argument that uncontrolled sexual desire is the primary and most incorrigible source of all vices, he identifies the Hellenistic Jewish notion of desiring to disobey God (ἐπιθυμία) *with the Platonic sexual appetite* (ἐπιθυμία). (Gaca, *Making of Fornication*, 297; emphasis added)[74]

---

[71] The "iniquities" Gaca has in mind appear in *Republic* 575 B. In her view, Philo cites this passage in *Spec.* 4.87 (certainly an allusion, but Philo's χρεωκοπίαις τε καὶ παρακαταθηκῶν ἀρνήσεσι has no parallel in the *Republic* passage) to illustrate "proliferating vices that he attributes to breaking his version of the Tenth Commandment" (196). But in *Spec.* 4.87, Philo explicitly considers desire directed at "money" (χρήματα), not sexual or even appetitive desire per se. Plato *does* consider χρήματα an object of appetitive desire (see *Resp.* 580 E), but Philo's inclusion of other objects of ἐπιθυμία, like "reputation" (δόξα), which Plato does *not* associate with appetitive desire, proves that ἐπιθυμία in his exposition must be conceived more broadly.

[72] E.g., Plato cites thirst to illustrate the distinction between rational and appetitive elements within the soul (see *Resp.* 439 A–E; cf. 437 D: "'[S]hall we say that the desires (ἐπιθυμιῶν) constitute a class and that the most conspicuous members of that class are what we call thirst and hunger?' 'We shall,' said he" [trans. Paul Shorey; unless otherwise noted, all translations of Plato's writings are from LCL]).

[73] Gaca, *Making of Fornication*, 198. Also: " Philo's version of οὐκ ἐπιθυμήσεις, however, prohibits unrestrained sexual desire as the primary religious defiance and corruption in the city of God" (ibid.).

[74] Cf. idem, 216, where Philo is said to identify "*the Platonic notion of sexual desire* (ἐπιθυμία) with the Hellenistic Jewish concern about the inherently wrongful impulse (ἐπιθυμία) to transgress God's laws. He makes this identification most notably through his Jewish Middle Platonist explanation of the commandment against forbidden desire (οὐκ ἐπιθυμήσεις)" (emphasis added). Also idem, 23: "[Plato] would have needed an

Gaca clearly has an answer to the question of what Philo's Tenth Commandment prohibits. Although she ostensibly points to "excessive appetitive desire," she in fact has *sexual* desire in mind.[75]

But the idea that Philo's concept of desire in his exposition is exclusively—or even primarily—sexual is incorrect, since Philo associates οὐκ ἐπιθυμήσεις with a generic desire involving any number of different objects, none of which figures more prominently than another in the Commandment's theoretically limitless proscriptive range.[76] In fact, the idea that οὐκ ἐπιθυμήσεις deals with a *specific* desire of any type undermines Philo's concept of the Ten Commandments as generic summaries.[77] Philo's commentary consistently reflects his underlying belief in a prohibition of desire able to subsume any and all specific types. For example, in *Spec.* 4.80 Philo identifies this most troublesome passion simply as "desire of what we have not" (ἐπιθυμία τῶν ἀπόντων).[78] When Philo goes on to

interpreter to understand how the problems that he associates with uncontrolled sexual desire were written into the Tenth Commandment that Philo and Clement produced."
[75] This exclusive focus is confirmed by Gaca's construal of the Mosaic dietary laws, which in her view do not ultimately regulate appetitive desires for food and drink, but instead target the Tenth Commandment's real concern—*sexual* desire: "Philo regards Moses' dietary laws as the one sure regimen that reduces sexual desire and thereby subdues its offspring of vices" (*Making of Fornication*, 196).
[76] On this point commentators generally agree, with the exception of Gaca. For example, Colson (PLCL 7, 76, n. c): "Philo extends the meaning of the word from covetousness of what is another's to desire in general"; Mosès (PAPM 25, 17, n.1): Philo's version of the Tenth Commandment "n'admet pas de contenu veritable, puisque le désir est lui-même coupe de tout objet précis"; Williamson (*Philo*, 267): "Philo ... extends the meaning of a desire to include its most general sense." Even Wolfson (*Philo*, 2:228), who needlessly specifies "desire for that which belongs to another person," nevertheless acknowledges that "Philo speaks of desire in general, that is, of a desire for what we have not." On the concept of generic desire, note esp. *Migr.* 155: "It is this mixed multitude which takes delight not in a few species of desire only (μὴ μόνον ὀλίγοις εἴδεσιν ἐπιθυμίας), but claims to leave out nothing at all, that it may follow after desire's entire genus (ὅλον δι'ὅλων τὸ γένος), including all its species" (substituting "desire" [ἐπιθυμία] and "desire's" [ἐπιθυμίας] for Colson's "lusting" and "lust's").
[77] N.B. *Spec.* 4.78b: "Let us move on to the last of the Ten Words (δέκα λογίων), delivered like each of the others in the form of a summary (κεφαλαιώδει τύπῳ καθάπερ καὶ τῶν ἄλλων ἕκαστον): 'You shall not desire' (οὐκ ἐπιθυμήσεις)" (my translation). Note also the following descriptions of the Ten Commandments: *Her.* 167: τῶν γενικῶν δέκα νόμων; *Her.* 173: γενικοί ... κανόνες; *Congr.* 120: γενικὰ κεφάλαια.
[78] Philo's immediate specification of "things which seem good, though they are not truly good" (ὅσα τῷ δοκεῖν ἀγαθῶν, πρὸς ἀλήθειαν οὐκ ὄντων) mitigates the generic sense of ἐπιθυμία somewhat but still allows for most any particular ostensible "good" (cf. *Decal.* 146: ἔννοιαν ἀγαθοῦ μὴ παρόντος). When Philo turns to the Tenth Commandment's particular laws (dietary laws) he singles out the desire for food and drink, but in a *paradigmatic* (not absolute) sense (see *Spec.* 4.96).

associate this desire with specific aims, he is merely illustrating its troublesome nature, noting that it creates a savage hunger and thirst in people, "but not for something to fill the void in their bellies—they hunger for money, fame, power, shapely bodies, or any of the countless other things that seem to them enviable and worth a struggle" (*Spec.* 4.82; my translation).[79] As this list indicates, sexual desire is not foremost in Philo's mind, nor even appetitive desire per se.[80] At most, sexual desire forms a part, but only a small part, of Philo's overall concept of desire with respect to the Tenth Commandment.[81] Not only do Philo's words fail to support the claim that οὐκ ἐπιθυμήσεις targets sexual desire—they positively refute it.

---

[79] Cf. *Spec.* 4.86–91.

[80] In fact, Gaca's proposal that ἐπιθυμία in Philo's exposition refers specifically to Platonic appetitive desire (a function of τὸ ἐπιθυμητικόν) collapses with the mention in *Spec.* 4.82 of δόξα (cf. §88) and ἡγεμονία (cf. ἀρχή in §89)—which Plato identifies as ambitions of the *spirited* part of the soul, τὸ θυμοειδές; e.g., *Resp.* 581 A–B: "'[D]o we not say that [τὸ θυμοειδές] is wholly set on predominance (τὸ κρατεῖν) and victory (νικᾶν) and good repute (εὐδοκιμεῖν)?' 'Yes indeed.' 'And might we not appropriately designate it as the ambitious part (φιλόνικον) and that which is covetous of honour (φιλότιμον)?' 'Most appropriately.'" (On τὸ θυμοειδές see John M. Cooper, "Plato's Theory of Human Motivation," in *Reason and Emotion: Essays on Ancient Moral Psychology and Ethical Theory* [Princeton: Princeton University Press, 1999], 118–37, esp. 130–36; repr. from *HPhQ* 1 [1984].) On Philo's concept of desire, Schmidt, *Anthropologie*, 92–93, notes: "Als Gegenstand des Begehrens werden fast durchweg die Strebungen, die Platon von dem zweiten und dritten Sellenteil aussagt, zusammengefaßt." This conflation of τὸ ἐπιθυμητικόν and τὸ θυμοειδές makes sense in light of Middle-Platonic moral psychology, which was influenced by Aristotle's concept of ἐπιθυμία and θυμός as two types of ὄρεξις, both belonging to a single faculty of the soul, the ὀρεκτικόν (see P. A. Vander Waerdt: "The Peripatetic Interpretation of Plato's Tripartite Psychology," *GRBS* 26 [1985]: 283–302 and "Peripatetic Soul-Division, Posidonius, and Middle Platonic Moral Psychology," *GRBS* 26 [1985]: 373–94; cf. Charles Kahn, "Plato's Theory of Desire," *RM* 41 [1987]: 77–103, 78–80).

[81] The passage in Philo's exposition that pertains to sexual desire appears in *Spec.* 4.89: "If the object [of desire] is bodily beauty they are seducers (φθορεῖς), adulterers (μοιχούς), pederasts (παιδεραστάς), cultivators of incontinence and lewdness (ἀκολασίας καὶ λαγνείας), as though these worst of evils were the best of blessings." In *Decal.* 168–69, Philo has in mind the very same types of immoral sexual behavior, but he is commenting on a different Commandment, the κεφάλαιον τὸ κατὰ μοιχῶν, "under which come many enactments against seducers (φθορέων) and pederasty (παιδεραστῶν), against dissolute living (τῶν λαγνίστερον βιούντων) and indulgence in lawless and licentious forms of intercourse (ὁμιλίαις τε καὶ μίξεσιν ἐκνόμοις καὶ ἀκολάστοις)." The lack of commentary on sexual matters in Philo's exposition of the Tenth Commandment is best explained by his having already dealt with such matters in his exposition of the Sixth Commandment, which governs the obviously sexual transgression of adultery. The preeminence of the Sixth Commandment, not the Tenth, in Philo's consideration of sexual ethics is correctly noted by Baudouin Decharneux, "Interdits sexuels dans l'œuvre de Philon d'Alexandrie dit 'Le Juif,'" *Religion et tabou*

So where and how does Gaca find textual support for her idea that the desire proscribed by Philo's Tenth Commandment is primarily sexual? She asserts that "Philo accepts Plato's theory of the irrational physical appetites *as well as his position that the sexual appetite is the most domineering and recalcitrant of the lot*" (emphasis added), citing *Spec.* 4.92–94 to support her claim:[82]

> Finally, they determined that desire must reside in the area around the navel known as the "diaphragm" (ἐπιθυμίᾳ δὲ [ἀπένειμαν] τὸν περὶ τὸν ὀμφαλὸν καὶ τὸ καλούμενον διάφραγμα χῶρον). Since desire has the least to do with reason (λογισμοῦ), it clearly must reside as far as possible from reason's royal domain—practically at the outskirts. Naturally, the pasture of this most insatiable and licentious of beasts (ἀπληστότατον καὶ ἀκολαστότατον ... θρεμμάτων) is the area of the body associated with primal drives for food and sex (τροφαί τε καὶ ὀχεῖαι). (*Spec.* 4.93–94)[83]

Philo clearly marks in this passage the Platonic ἐπιθυμητικόν as the seat of primal drives for food and sex, but this is ultimately nothing more than an endorsement of Plato's tripartite psychology.[84] By itself, this passage does not prove that Philo saw οὐκ ἐπιθυμήσεις primarily as a restriction of sexual desire. In fact, not one of the passages Gaca cites reflects a special emphasis on *sexual* appetite in Philo's exposition. She claims that "Philo fully agrees with Plato" that:

> The combined sexual appetite and reproductive urge, when fattened and left to their own devices, are the main root of depraved minds and social mores because they stimulate a proliferation of other passions. (Gaca, *Making of Fornication*, 195)

To support this claim, she cites *Spec.* 4.85 as follows: "Sexual eros is 'the passion at the origin of wrongdoing' (ἀρχέκακον πάθος) (*Spec* 4.85)."[85] But a fuller citation shows that Gaca misreads Philo's statement:

---

sexuel (ed. Jacques Marx; *PHR* 1; Bruxelles: Editions de l'Université de Bruxelles, 1990), 17–31, esp. 18–25.

[82] See Gaca, *Making of Fornication*, 195. Presumably, *Spec.* 4.92–94 is the textual evidence Gaca has in mind, since it is the only passage she cites in the paragraph other than *Decal* 173–74, which proves only that "appetites are an unavoidable part of our human and animal nature."

[83] My translation. Cf. *Tim.* 70 D–71 A; on the relation of *Spec.* 4.92–94 to the *Timaeus* passage, see Runia, *Philo and the* Timaeus, 304.

[84] N.B. λόγος, θυμός, and ἐπιθυμία in *Spec.* 4.92. Gaca rightly suggests Philo's endorsement here of "Plato's theory of the irrational physical appetites" (Gaca, *Making of Fornication*, 195), but Philo says nothing about "[Plato's] position that the sexual appetite is the most domineering and recalcitrant of the lot." Gaca assumes that a reference to the Platonic ἐπιθυμητικόν and its characteristic appetites proves ipso facto that Philo holds a highly sexualized concept of ἐπιθυμία throughout his exposition.

[85] Gaca, *Making of Fornication*, 195.

For the passion to which the name of originator of evil can truly be given is desire (τό ... ἀρχέκακον πάθος ἐστιν ἐπιθυμία), of which one and that the smallest fruit the passion of love (ἧς ἓν τὸ βραχύτατον ἔγγονον, ἔρως) has not only once but often in the past filled the whole world with countless calamities (ἀμυθήτων ... συμφορῶν) .... (*Spec.* 4.85)

The ἀρχέκακον πάθος in this passage is clearly ἐπιθυμία (desire involving *any* object), not "sexual eros" as Gaca states.[86] Philo does identify ἔρως as an "offspring" (ἔγγονον) of ἐπιθυμία, but nothing in the passage requires even *this* word to have a sexual connotation.[87] Gaca also misconstrues the phrase ἁπάντων πηγὴ τῶν κακῶν (*Spec.* 4.84), which she cites four times. Here Philo does indeed identify ἐπιθυμία as "the fountain of all evils," but in light of *Spec.* 4.82 (esp. ἄλλων ἀμυθήτων) it *must* be understood as desire involving any number of possible objects—*not* sexual desire, or even appetitive desire per se. Gaca first misunderstands the sense when she states that "physical appetition in general" (ἐπιθυμία) is "the origin of all wrongdoing,"[88] then she provides in each subsequent reference to *Spec.* 4.84 a different rendering of ἐπιθυμία:

---

[86] Cf. Méasson, *Char ailé*, 154: "Philon analyse d'abord le désir en lui-même et, *sans référence à aucun objet*, le définit: ἀρχέκακον πάθος, «la passion qui est le principe du mal» (§ 85)" (emphasis added).

[87] *Spec.* 4.85 in its entirety shows that the "calamities" (συμφορῶν) Philo has in mind mainly involve warfare, which of course *can* result from sexual ἔρως (e.g., the Trojan war, noted by Colson in regard to *Spec.* 4.85 [PLCL 8, 61, n. b]), but obviously *need* not. *Decal.* 152–53 also mentions "calamities" (συμφορῶν) involving warfare and attributes all wars (πόλεμοι πάντες) to *desire* (ἐπιθυμία): for money (χρημάτων), glory (δόξης), or pleasure (ἡδονῆς) (cf. esp. *Phaed.* 66 C). In general, Gaca fails to note that ἔρως in Philo's exposition is not inherently sexual (e.g., *Decal.* 151: χρημάτων ἔρως). Gaca seems to limit the scope of ἔρως, by definition, to sexual desire alone: "Uncontrolled sexual desire, or eros, is especially problematic for Philo and his predecessor Plato" (Gaca, *Making of Fornication*, 195). This is surprising, since Gaca in an earlier chapter on Platonic desire emphatically notes the difference between "sexual appetite" and "Platonic eros" (see *Making of Fornication*, 36–39). On ἔρως in Plato, including its orientation in theory toward *any* object, see David M. Halperin, "Platonic *Erôs* and What Men Call Love," *AP* 5 (1985): 161–204. Gaca faults Halperin's study for "diminish[ing] the opposition" between eros and sexual desire (*Making of Fornication*, 38, n. 53), when in fact he clearly and carefully notes the difference (Halperin, "Platonic *Erôs*," 170–76). Her citation of Halperin, intended to prove his conflation of eros and *sexual* appetite for *sexual* pleasure, fails to take into account his explicit distinction between the terms "appetite" and "desire" (see Halperin, "Platonic *Erôs*," 170). For the generic Platonic notion of ἔρως, see esp. *Symp.* 205 D, which defines ἔρως as πᾶσα ἡ τῶν ἀγαθῶν ἐπιθυμία.

[88] Gaca, *Making of Fornication*, 198.

- "sexual and other appetition" (ἐπιθυμία) is "the origin of all wrongdoing"[89]
- "innate sexual desire" (ἐπιθυμία) is "the origin of wrongdoing"[90]
- "eros" (ἐπιθυμία) is "the origin of wrongdoing"[91]

The same word, from the same passage, receives a progressively more sexual connotation in the course of Gaca's study, without justification or explanation. Gaca can produce no clear evidence for an especially sexual connotation of ἐπιθυμία in Philo's exposition because no such evidence exists. Moreover, the principal evidence she cites (three times) from elsewhere in Philo's writings, *Opif.* 151–52, is inconclusive.[92] Although this passage does deal with sexual attraction, it has little to say about the kind of ἐπιθυμία Philo envisions when commenting on the Tenth Commandment.[93] In fact, this passage does not even contain the word ἐπιθυμία, contrary to Gaca's original citation:

> "The irrational appetite" (ἐπιθυμία), and the sexual appetite in particular, "is the beginning of wrongs and violations of the Law" (*Opif* 151–2).[94]

The relevant section reads in full:

> And this desire begat likewise bodily pleasure (ὁ δὲ πόθος οὗτος καὶ τὴν τῶν σωμάτων ἡδονὴν ἐγέννησεν), that pleasure which is the beginning of wrongs and violation[s] of law (ἥτις ἐστὶν ἀδικημάτων καὶ παρανομημάτων ἀρχή) .... (*Opif.* 152)[95]

Clearly, the passage states that "bodily pleasure" (τὴν τῶν σωμάτων ἡδονήν), and not "irrational appetite" (ἐπιθυμία), is ἀδικημάτων καὶ παρανομημάτων

---

[89] Gaca, *Making of Fornication*, 198: "Philo, however, differs dramatically from Plato by insisting that sexual and other appetition is a 'great and excessive wickedness, truly the origin of all wrongdoing'" (*Spec* 4.84).

[90] Gaca, *Making of Fornication*, 200: "For Philo, however, the 'origin of wrongdoing' and 'of violation of the Law' (*Spec* 4.84, *Opif* 151–2) is innate sexual desire and its tendency to excessive pleasure ...."

[91] Gaca, *Making of Fornication*, 216: "In support of Plato's political theory, Philo formulates a distinctively Jewish Platonist position that sexual desire is the primary root of rebellion against God. As he phrases this idea, eros is the 'origin of wrongdoing' and 'of violation of the Law'" (*Spec* 4.84, *Opif* 151–2).

[92] See Gaca, *Making of Fornication*, 198, 200, and 216.

[93] As part of his commentary on Genesis 1–3, Philo considers the nature and consequences of sexual ἔρως between Adam and Eve.

[94] Gaca, *Making of Fornication*, 198.

[95] The "desire" mentioned here is πόθος, which—like ἔρως, also in *Opif.* 152—need not have a sexual connotation, although it clearly does in this case (cf. *Opif.* 5: ἔρωτι καὶ πόθῳ σοφίας; *Ebr.* 21: πόθος ἀρετῆς; *Fug.* 164: πόθον ἐπιστήμης; *Decal.* 148: πόθῳ τοῦ τρανωθῆναι ταῖς ἀκοαῖς τὸν ἦχον).

ἀρχή.⁹⁶ The pleasure (ἡδονή) mentioned here arguably involves sexual ἐπιθυμία, but the word ἐπιθυμία simply does not appear, and applying this passage to Philo's commentary on the Tenth Commandment is unwarranted. Gaca is unable, with this or any other passage, to demonstrate that Philo sees οὐκ ἐπιθυμήσεις mainly as a proscription of sexual desire, or that he anywhere in his exposition singles out sexual desire as especially problematic over against any other type.

Because her study misidentifies *what* the Commandment prohibits, its explanation of *how* someone observes the Commandment, particularly the role played by the dietary laws, is also incorrect. According to Gaca, and in keeping with her overall emphasis, the dietary laws for Philo ultimately target sexual desire.⁹⁷ Since a dangerous causal link exists between unrestrained eating and unrestrained sexual desire (which in turn causes a proliferation of other vices), dietary laws that restrict food intake restrict also sexual desire and thus limit the vice associated with sexual excess.⁹⁸ But nowhere in Philo's discussion of the dietary laws (*Spec.* 4.96–131) is sexual desire mentioned, much less cited as the ultimate concern. This again calls into question Gaca's treatment of Philo's text—*what* does she claim to find

---

⁹⁶ Philo's comments in this passage reflect a much broader consideration, attested throughout his works, of pleasure (ἡδονή) as a moral danger. On Philo's view of pleasure, see esp. Alain Le Boulluec, "La place des concepts philosophiques dans la réflexion de Philon sur le plaisir," in *Philon d'Alexandrie et le langage de la philosophie: Actes du colloque international organisé par le Centre d'études sur la philosophie hellénistique et romaine de l'Université de Paris XII-Val de Marne, Créteil, Fontenay, Paris, 26–28 octobre 1995* (ed. Carlos Lévy; Turnhout: Brepolis, 1998), 129–52; also Peter Booth, "The Voice of the Serpent: Philo's Epicureanism," in *Hellenization Revisited: Shaping a Christian Response within the Greco-Roman World* (ed. Wendy E. Helleman; Lanham, Md.: University Press of America, 1994), 159–72; Francesca Calabi, "Il serpente e il cavaliere: Piacere e 'sophrosyne' in Filone di Alessandria" *ASR* 8 (2003): 199–215; Schmidt, *Anthropologie*, 92–93; Graziano Ranocchia, "Moses against the Egyptian: The Anti-Epicurean Polemic in Philo," in *Philo of Alexandria and Post-Aristotelian Philosophy* (ed. Francesca Alesse; SPhA 5; Leiden: Brill, 2008), 75–102, esp. 88–100; Winston, "Philo on the Emotions," 206.

⁹⁷ "Restricting diet is an important part of taming sexual desire for both Philo and Plato. Philo regards Moses' dietary laws as the one sure regimen that reduces sexual desire and thereby subdues its offspring of vices" (Gaca, *Making of Fornication*, 196).

⁹⁸ Gaca elsewhere makes the connection between food and sexual desire without explicitly mentioning dietary laws: "Human beings must keep their appetites under rational guard by curbing their wild sexual desire through restricting the intake of food and drink" (*Making of Fornication*, 195). Also: "Sexual eros on Plato's view comes into its own as a raging tyrant once surplus nutriment fuels its voracity. The combined sexual appetite and reproductive urge, when fattened and left to their own devices, are the main root of depraved minds and social mores because they stimulate a proliferation of other passions. Philo fully agrees with Plato on this matter" (ibid.).

30   CHAPTER ONE

and *where*. She refers to *Spec.* 4.96, where Philo states the rationale of the dietary laws from Moses' perspective, but she misinterprets his statement:

> Moses thus "began to train and chastise the appetite centered on the belly" (*Spec* 4.96), because he knew God's people needed to put their "love-mad" sexual behavior on the right kind of diet (*Spec* 3.9–10).[99]

According to *Philo*, the reason Moses focused on training the desire "whose field of activity is the belly" (τὴν περὶ γαστέρα πραγματευομένην ἐπιθυμίαν) is so that "the other forms (τὰς ἄλλας) will cease to run riot as before and will be restrained by having learnt that their senior and as it were the leader of their company (τὴν πρεσβυτάτην καὶ ὡς ἡγεμονίδα) is obedient to the laws of temperance" (*Spec.* 4.96). The desire for food and drink is preeminent and serves as a "paradigmatic instruction" (παραδειγματικῇ διδασκαλίᾳ in *Spec.* 4.96), whose training applies to *any other form of desire*, including—but certainly neither limited nor especially pertinent to—sexual desire. Gaca omits the second half of Philo's sentence in *Spec.* 4.96, which contains *his* understanding of the rationale for training dietary desires, and substitutes a different rationale based on a passage from a different treatise, which has no direct application to Philo's discussion of the Tenth Commandment.[100] As for prohibited animals, Gaca understands Philo to say that Moses "knew that the prohibited types of animal flesh, such as pork, are particularly laced with an aphrodisiac surplus (*Spec* 4.100–18)."[101] But Philo says nothing of the sort in *Spec.* 4.100–18. He does say that Moses prohibited animals "whose flesh is the finest and fattest, thus titillating and exciting the malignant foe pleasure (τὴν ἐπίβουλον ἡδονήν) ... knowing that they set a trap for the most slavish of the senses, the taste (γεῦσιν), and produce gluttony, an evil very dangerous both to soul and body" (*Spec.* 4.100).[102] Without exploring here the full import of this statement for Philo's understanding of the dietary laws, it is enough to note that the sensory pleasure involved is gustatory, not sexual.[103] Gaca notes also Philo's

---

[99] Gaca, *Making of Fornication*, 196.
[100] Philo's comments in *Spec.* 3.9–10 pertain, as he explicitly states, to the *Sixth* Commandment (not the Tenth), the first in the second table (see *Spec.* 3.7–8).
[101] Gaca, *Making of Fornication*, 196. Gaca essentially considers only Philo's discussion of prohibited animals (*Spec.* 4.100–18), leaving out *Spec.* 4.119–31, which also treats particular laws falling under the rubric οὐκ ἐπιθυμήσεις.
[102] Presumably, this is the passage Gaca has in mind, since Philo immediately gives the example of pork in *Spec.* 4.101 and Gaca mentions pork explicitly when citing this passage.
[103] In any case, the context suggests that Philo's interest is in Moses' proscriptive cultivation of self-control (N.B. *Spec.* 4.101: πρός ... ἐγκράτειαν), not the avoidance of "aphrodisiac surplus." Isaak Heinemann, commenting on this passage, correctly notes

summary statement concerning Moses' prohibition of various animals, that "by this as by the withdrawal of fuel from a fire he creates an extinguisher to desire (σβέσιν τῆς ἐπιθυμίας)" (*Spec.* 4.118).[104] But this has no explicit bearing on sexual desire, unless the term ἐπιθυμία is presumed to have an especially sexual connotation in *Spec.* 4.96–131, which it does not. In fact, due to an overemphasis on sexual desire, Gaca overlooks the fundamental role of the dietary laws from Philo's perspective, which is to promote self-control (ἐγκράτεια) initially with respect to desire(s) for food and drink, but ultimately with respect to desires of any type.[105]

Despite their respective contributions, the studies of Wolfson and Gaca, along with other shorter, incidental treatments of οὐκ ἐπιθυμήσεις, fail to answer with sufficient depth or accuracy the fundamental questions surrounding Philo's exposition of the Tenth Commandment. As a result, this important element of Philo's thought remains obscure.

Plan of the Monograph

Chapters two and three of this monograph do not deal directly with Philo's exposition of the Tenth Commandment. Instead, they offer an introductory survey of terms and concepts that Philo uses in that exposition, situating his moral psychology within the philosophical context of Middle Platonism.[106] Chapter two treats Philo's concept of desire (ἐπιθυμία), including explanations of its source, nature, function, and problematic *malfunction*. Chapter three treats Philo's concept of self-

---

this interest on Philo's part: "Nach SpL. IV 100 ff. will Moses durch seine Speisegesetze vor allem zur Selbstbeherrschung anregen; daher sind gerade besonders wohlschmeckende Tiere verboten, wie das Schwein" (*Bildung*, 163).

[104] Gaca, *Making of Fornication*, 196.

[105] Other considerations of Philo and the dietary laws emphasize the importance of ἐγκράτεια to various extents without finding any special concern with *sexual* desire: e.g., Norman Bentwich, *Philo-Judaeus of Alexandria* (Philadelphia: Jewish Publication Society of America, 1910), 123–24; Peder Borgen, *Philo of Alexandria: An Exegete for His Time* (NovTSup 86; Leiden: Brill, 1997), 168–69; Hadas-Lebel, *Philon*, 159–62; Hecht, "Patterns of Exegesis," 108–15; Heinemann, *Bildung*, 155–66; Houston, "Dietary Laws," 144–47; Mendelson, *Philo's Jewish Identity*, 67–71; Niehoff, *Philo on Jewish Identity*, 105–06; Rhodes, "Diet and Desire"; Karl Olav Sandnes, *Belly and Body in the Pauline Epistles* (SNTSMS 120; Cambridge: Cambridge University Press, 2002), 128–29; Termini, "Philo's Thought," 119–21; Vian, "Purità e culto," 78–80.

[106] Without assuming or suggesting that Philo intends to write as a systematic philosopher, chapters two and three nevertheless demonstrate the existence of coherent strands of thought running throughout his works. Multiple attestation confirms the reliability of these strands as accurate representations of Philo's Middle-Platonic convictions regarding ἐπιθυμία and other concepts.

control (ἐγκράτεια), including explanations of its nature, its acquisition through ἄσκησις, and its role in the proper management of desire. With this conceptual backdrop in place, Philo's exposition of οὐκ ἐπιθυμήσεις emerges more clearly as a coherent, representative statement of his ethical theory.

Chapter four focuses on *Spec.* 4.78b–131, Philo's exposition of the Tenth Commandment (although *Decal.* 142–53 and *Decal.* 173–74 receive consideration in connection with relevant sections of the exposition proper). Along with introductory matters, an outline of Philo's exposition, a fresh translation of the PCW text, and notes on select passages, chapter four comments on each distinct unit of text. This commentary, however, does not treat all aspects of the text equally and so does not serve as a commentary in the traditional sense. Instead, it is focused and thematic, explaining how Philo uses the conceptual nexus of ἐπιθυμία, ἐγκράτεια, and ἄσκησις as an overarching expository agenda for his work.

Chapter five summarizes the results of the monograph by providing direct, concise answers to the basic questions regarding Philo's exposition:

> 1. In Philo's view, *what* does the Tenth Commandment prohibit? (All desire? A certain type? What type?)
>
> 2. In Philo's view, *how* is the Tenth Commandment observed? (What are the mechanics of its observance? What role do the dietary laws play in its observance?)

Chapter five also suggests lines of further research based on the results of this study.

CHAPTER TWO

PHILO ON DESIRE (ΕΠΙΘΥΜΙΑ)

Introduction

Understanding Philo's exposition of οὐκ ἐπιθυμήσεις depends on a clear understanding of his concept of ἐπιθυμία, including its source, nature, function, and problematic *malfunction*. Philo's concept of ἐπιθυμία depends in turn on his concept of the soul, in particular his *moral psychology*—his understanding of how various elements of the soul's structure and function relate to questions of morality. This chapter begins with a survey of the basic moral psychology of Philo's Middle-Platonic contemporaries, especially their concept of a fundamental bipartition between rational and non-rational components within the soul and their concept of various non-rational capacities whose normal operation includes instances of ἐπιθυμία. Next comes a survey of *Philo's* moral psychology, with a special emphasis on the correspondence between contemporary Middle-Platonic views and his own understanding of both bipartition and the various capacities involved with ἐπιθυμία. The chapter ends with a consideration of how Philo views the *malfunction* of ἐπιθυμία in the soul, identifying two grades of problematic desire—passionate and tyrannical desire—both analyzed in light of contemporary Middle Platonism.

Philo's Middle-Platonic Contemporaries

As a *de facto* Middle Platonist, Philo reflects the views of his Middle-Platonic contemporaries, in particular Eudorus of Alexandria (fl. ca. 25 B.C.E.) and his associates.[1] As representatives of a movement known for its renewed

---

[1] On the notion of a "*de facto* Middle Platonist," see above, p. 13, n. 40. In the afterword to his 1996, revised edition of *The Middle Platonists*, John Dillon reviews his position on the relation between Philo and Eudorus: "Despite my cautionary remarks, I have been repeatedly accused (or worse, commended), for presenting Philo as a pupil of Eudorus, and as a Middle Platonist. Let me make it clear once again that I wish to make neither claim. There is no evidence that Philo had ever heard of Eudorus (though I regard it as very probable that he did). All I would claim is that *Philo shows the influence of a brand of Platonism that is in many ways close to that of Eudorus, and that he constitutes good evidence for prevailing trends in contemporary Platonism.*" (*Middle Platonists*, 438–39; emphasis added). On the relation between Philo and the Alexandrian Platonism of Eudorus, see also Mauro Bonazzi, "Towards Transcendence: Philo and the Renewal of Platonism in the Early Imperial Age," in *Philo of Alexandria and Post-*

interest in the doctrines of Plato, Middle Platonists naturally derived fundamental convictions from the writings of Plato himself, but to rely solely on Plato and project his views onto later Platonists without qualification ignores centuries of philosophical activity postdating Plato.[2] For this

---

Aristotelian Philosophy (ed. Francesca Alesse; SPhA 5; Leiden: Brill, 2008), 233–51; M. R. Niehoff, "Philo's Role as a Platonist in Alexandria," in *Philon d'Alexandrie* (ed. Jean-François Pradeau; EP 7; Paris: Belles Lettres, 2010), 35–62. On Eudorus himself, see John Dillon, *Middle Platonists*, 115–35, 436–39; also Heinrich Dörrie, "Der Platoniker Eudorus von Alexandreia," in *Platonica Minora* (STA 8; München: W. Fink, 1976), 297–309; Mauro Bonazzi, "Eudorus of Alexandria and Early Imperial Platonism, " in *Greek and Roman Philosophy 100 BC–200 AD* (ed. Richard Sorabji and Robert W. Sharples; 2 vols.; BICSSup 94; London: Institute of Classical Studies, 2007), 365–77. For fragments of the work of Eudorus, see esp. Mazz.

[2] For example, Middle Platonists adapted Stoic technical terms, infusing them with new meaning for use within their fundamentally different system of thought, and a failure to appreciate this leads to a false impression of their incoherent *adoption* of the Stoic principles underlying those terms. When Eudorus expounded a dogmatic Platonism in the first century B.C.E. (after the Academy's skeptical phase), an elaborate lexicon of Stoic terms and definitions, with an accompanying conceptual vocabulary, had already been systematically formulated. Rather than creating *de novo* an alternative system, with its own terms, definitions, etc., Middle Platonists chose to revise the system at hand, creating distinctively *Platonic* understandings of *Stoic* philosophical language. (Cf. Mauro Bonazzi, "Eudorus' Psychology and Stoic Ethics," in *Platonic Stoicism–Stoic Platonism: The Dialogue between Platonism and Stoicism in Antiquity* [ed. Mauro Bonazzi and Christoph Helmig; AMP 39; Leuven: Leuven University Press, 2007], 126–27: "The use of terms taken from Stoic philosophy implies neither adherence to Stoicism nor a constructive conciliatory attitude. Rather it displays a subtler plan: an operation that could be dubbed 'polemic resemantization', where terms are reclaimed and then employed in other contexts.") Such revision occurred especially in the field of ethics (e.g., the topic of "passions" [πάθη], including ἐπιθυμία) and moral psychology. On this aspect of Middle-Platonic ethics, note Dörrie, "Eudorus," 301–03 (e.g., 302: "Der Platonismus konnte hier [Ethik] nirgends aus dem Vollen schöpfen wie in der Physik und der Theologie"; 303: "Die bloße Einteilung der Ethik konnte niemanden befriedigen—jetzt galt es, den neuen platonischen Inhalt in diese alte Form zu gießen"); also Giovanni Reale, *The Schools of the Imperial Age* (ed. and trans. John R. Catan; vol. 4 of *A History of Ancient Philosophy*; Albany: State University of New York Press, 1990), 233: "The eclectic character of Middle Platonic ethics has frequently been emphasized, for in addition to Platonic tenets Middle Platonists saw no difficulty in accepting Aristotelian as well as Stoic doctrines. A great deal of evidence could be brought forward as proof of this assertion. Nevertheless, *that the Middle Platonists only rarely accepted the results after Plato which are opposed to the Platonic spirit has not been adequately appreciated*. In fact, in the great majority of cases they reinterpret and ground again the new results according to the Platonic spirit" (original emphasis); Inwood, *Ethics and Human Action*, 132: "so many of the innovators who looked back beyond Stoic monism to the psychological observations made by Plato and Aristotle continued to use the terminology of the Stoic theory in setting forth their own doctrines"; John Whittaker, "Platonic Philosophy in the Early Centuries of the Empire," *ANRW* 36.1: 81–123, 116: "We may in fact conclude that the Stoic element in Middle Platonism, both in the

reason, Middle-Platonic evidence must act as a guide—confirming, supplementing, and modifying what can be otherwise known from the Platonic dialogues. Enough evidence exists to reconstruct the basic moral psychology and corresponding concept of ἐπιθυμία held by Alexandrian Middle Platonists of Philo's day, based—in addition to the extant fragments from Eudorus himself (Mazz.)—on the following sources:

> ARIUS DIDYMUS[3] (b. ca. 75 B.C.E.): Arius was a Stoic philosopher, probably a native of Alexandria and personal acquaintance of Eudorus.[4] He composed surveys of contemporary philosophical views, including Eudorus and certain "Platonic philosophers" (οἱ κατὰ Πλάτωνα φιλοσοφοῦντες [*Eclog.* 38.14–15]). Information on this *group* of philosophers in *Eclog.* 37.18–38.15 bears special importance, since it most likely depicts contemporary Alexandrian (Middle-) Platonists, summarizing principal tenets of their moral psychology and providing crucial evidence for an otherwise unattested aspect of Eudoran Middle Platonism.[5]
>
> PSEUDO-TIMAEUS,[6] *On the Nature of the World and the Soul* [=TL]: Probably composed in the late first century B.C.E. or the first century C.E., this treatise arguably represents Eudoran Middle Platonism, based on its distinct profile of agreements with Eudorus on a number of points.[7] Purportedly written by Timaeus of Locri (of Plato's *Timaeus*), in an affected Doric dialect, the

---

'Didaskalikos' and elsewhere, is generally of a superficial nature and indicates rather a generous disposition toward Stoic concepts and terminology than a whole-hearted attempt to accommodate Platonism to a Stoic mould."

[3] See David E. Hahm, "The Ethical Doxography of Arius Didymus," *ANRW* 36.4: 2935–3055, 3234–43 (indices).

[4] Hahm, "Arius Didymus," 3035–41.

[5] Arius presents the definitions *currently* held by his contemporaries: οὕτως μὲν οὖν οἱ κατὰ Πλάτωνα φιλοσοφοῦντες ὁρίζονται (*Eclog.* 38.14–15). His familiarity with one particular Middle-Platonic philosopher from first-century B.C.E. Alexandria (Eudorus) implies some familiarity with other "Platonic philosophers" from the same milieu (whose views he presumably cites in *Eclog.* 37.18–38.15). The doxographical nature of Arius's report on the moral psychology of these "Platonic philosophers" suggests that the attested views were standard, which in turn suggests that these would have been the views of Eudorus. Without considering the question of Eudorus, P. A. Vander Waerdt nevertheless holds that *Eclog.* 37.18–38.15 represents good evidence for Middle Platonism (see "Moral Psychology," 378).

[6] See *Timaios of Locri*, On the Nature of the World and the Soul (text, trans., notes, Thomas H. Tobin; SBLTT 26; GRRS 8; Chico, Calif.: Scholars Press, 1985); also the commentary of Matthias Baltes, *Timaios Lokros*, Über die Natur des Kosmos und der Seele (PA 21; Leiden: Brill, 1972).

[7] On the date of TL, see Tobin, *Timaios of Locri*, 3–7. On the agreements between TL and Eudorus, see Baltes, *Timaios Lokros*, 22–26. Baltes does not believe that Eudorus himself composed TL, but that the work is more likely "ein Produkt aus der Schule des Eudor" (25). Tobin notes some problems with Baltes's position (*Timaios of Locri*, 6) but nevertheless affirms the likelihood of some connection between TL and Eudorus: "One can probably say that the TL came after Eudorus and that the author of the TL was aware of his work" (7).

treatise generally reads like an epitome of *Timaeus* 27 C–92 C, although it offers scholastic Middle-Platonic elaborations on key topics.

PSEUDO-METOPUS,[8] *On Virtue* [=Ps.-Metop.]: This treatise, probably composed in the first century B.C.E., in a Doric similar to TL, is one of many Pseudo-Pythagorean ethical writings that arguably reflect Eudoran Middle Platonism.[9] The clearly didactic aim of *On Virtue* suggests a handbook, which in turn suggests conventional ethical doctrines.[10]

PLUTARCH (b. ca. 45 C.E.): Plutarch was a Middle Platonist who knew the works of Eudorus.[11] Furthermore, Plutarch's teacher Ammonius was both a contemporary of Philo and a native of Alexandria.[12] Assuming Plutarch did not radically depart from his teacher on basic ethical theory, his views—especially insofar as they corroborate the testimony of Arius, Ps.-Timaeus, and Ps.-Metopus—reflect standard views among Philo's Middle-Platonic contemporaries.[13]

---

[8] See *Pseudopythagorica Ethica: I trattati morali di Archita, Metopo, Teage, Eurifamo* (text, trans., comm., Bruno Centrone; Elenchos 17; Naples: Bibliopolis, 1990), esp. 87–94 (text), 193–216 (comm.).
[9] On the date of Ps.-Metopus, see Centrone, *Pseudopythagorica Ethica*, 41–44; on the connection with Eudorus, see idem, 17, n. 10. Centrone suggests that Philo made use of these Pseudo-Pythagorean ethical writings (idem, 30–34, 43–44); cf. David Runia, "Why Does Clement Call Philo 'The Pythagorean'?," in *Philo and the Church Fathers: A Collection of Papers* (VCSup 32; Leiden: Brill, 1995), 54–76; repr. from *VC* 49 (1995): 1–22.
[10] Cf. Centrone, *Pseudopythagorica Ethica*, 193: "Il trattato di Metopo sulla virtù presenta, in forma sintetica e condensate, una serie di *loci* classici della dossografia etica, amalgamate in maniera più o meno felice."
[11] On Plutarch as a Middle Platonist, see Dillon, *Middle Platonists*, 184–230. Plutarch cites Eudorus by name in *De animae procreatione in Timaeo* (*An. procr.*) 1013 B, 1019 E, and 1020 C.
[12] On Ammonius see C. P. Jones, "The Teacher of Plutarch," *HSCP* 71 (1967), 205–13; also Dillon, *Middle Platonists*, 189–92; Jan Opsomer, "M. Annius Ammonius, A Philosophical Profile," in *The Origins of the Platonic System: Platonisms of the Early Empire and their Philosophical Contexts* (ed. Mauro Bonazzi and Jan Opsomer; CEC 23; Louvain: Peeters, 2009), 123–86. Jones suggests approximate dates for Ammonius of 20 to 70–80 C.E. ("Teacher of Plutarch," 208; cf. Dillon, *Middle Platonists*, 191: "Ammonius was probably dead by about A.D. 80"). Dillon calls Ammonius "a product of Alexandrian Platonism" (*Middle Platonists*, 190), although he taught and died in Athens. John Glucker believes, concerning Ammonius's career as a "personal teacher" (καθηγητής) and his arrival in Athens, that "[w]hatever philosophy he knew he had already learnt in Egypt" (*Antiochus and the Late Academy* [Hypomnemata 56; Göttingen: Vandenhoeck & Ruprecht, 1978], 133). Jean Daniélou suggests that Philo and *Plutarch* have a similar "platonisme éclectique" because Philo and *Ammonius* were educated in the same Alexandrian philosophical environment (*Philon d'Alexandrie* [Paris: A. Fayard, 1958], 58–59).
[13] Among Plutarch's works, *De virtute morali* bears special significance, because of its summary representation of a Middle-Platonic (over against Stoic) stance on moral psychology and passion(s). Moreover, the moral psychology of *De virtute morali* reflects Plutarch's broader commitment to a fundamentally Platonic understanding of the soul, such as he elaborates in *An. procr.* (see Jan Opsomer, "L'âme du monde et l'âme de l'homme chez Plutarque," in *Estudios sobre Plutarco: Ideas religiosas: Actas del III Simposio*

For the most part, the identification of this material with Eudorus rests on reasonable conjecture, not demonstrable fact. But in any case, this material *does* represent Middle-Platonic thought, as general consensus and corroborating evidence from, for example, Alcinous's doctrinal handbook the *Didaskalikos* attest.[14] Therefore, while the comparison of Philo to Arius Didymus, Ps.-Timaeus, Ps.-Metopus, and Plutarch *probably* illustrates his relation to Eudoran Middle Platonism, it *certainly* illustrates Philo's relation to general trends in Middle-Platonic thought.

"Irrational" and "Non-Rational" in Moral Psychology

The most fundamental question to ask concerning ἐπιθυμία in Middle-Platonic moral psychology involves the Greek word ἄλογος, which has two radically different meanings. On the one hand, ἄλογος can mean "non-rational," indicating the absence of a capacity for reason. On the other hand, ἄλογος can mean "irrational," indicating the corruption or malfunction of a capacity for reason that nevertheless exists. In a treatise that defends a Platonic view of the passions over against the Stoic view of Chrysippus, Galen explains the distinction:

> [S]ometimes the α negates the meaning of the word to which it is prefixed, and sometimes it does not. And I find the word ἄλογον used in this way by all the ancients and by men of today. When a person says that a fish or a crab is ἄλογον, he completely negates the meaning of the word logos; but when men criticize a particular statement of a particular person by saying that it is ἄλογον, they do not give it this name because it has no logos, but because it is blameworthy and faulty. (*PHP* IV 4.13–15)[15]

Philo understands the same distinction just as clearly:

> There are two ways of understanding the absence of reason (τὸ ἄλογον): it means either defying the dictates of reason, as when people call the sense-

---

Internacional sobre Plutarco: Oviedo 30 de abril a 2 de mayo de 1992 [ed. Manuela García Valdés; Madrid: Ediciones Clásicas, 1994], 33–49). Also important are five ethical treatises—*De curiositate, De cohibenda ira, De garrulitate, De vitioso pudore*, and *De laude ipsius*—that pertain directly to moral virtue, in particular the role of "practice" (ἄσκησις) in management of the passions (see Heinz Gerd Ingenkamp, *Plutarchs Schriften über die Heilung der Seele* [Hypomnemata 34; Göttingen: Vandenhoeck & Ruprecht, 1971]).

[14] On which see *Alcinous: The Handbook of Platonism* (trans., comm. John Dillon; Oxford: Clarendon, 1993); *Alcinoos: Enseignement des doctrines de Platon* (ed., comm. John Whittaker; trans. Pierre Louis; 2d ed.; Paris: Belles Lettres, 2002).

[15] Trans. De Lacey (slightly modified).

less man "irrational" (ἄλογον), or having no reason at all, as with the non-rational animals (ὡς τῶν ζῴων τὰ μὴ λογικά). (*Sacr.* 46)[16]

Do Philo and his Middle-Platonic contemporaries see ἐπιθυμία as an "irrational" (ἄλογος) or a "non-rational" (ἄλογος) function of the soul? Plato himself offers the best place to begin answering this critical question.

Platonic Foundations

Plato believed that the human soul has three essential components: one rational (τὸ λογιστικόν), one assertive (τὸ θυμοειδές),[17] and one intensely desirous (τὸ ἐπιθυμητικόν).[18] Among these three, the most antagonistic relation exists between reason and desire. In fact, Plato establishes the independence of desire from reason by noting its capacity for diametric and simultaneous opposition to reason as a distinct source of motivation in the soul along with reason.[19] If the ἐπιθυμητικόν exists in contradistinction to

---

[16] My translation. In *De animalibus*, Philo argues at length that beasts are non-rational (see §§77–100), a position he consistently holds throughout his works: e.g., ζῷα ἄλογα (*Opif.* 73, *Spec.* 2.89, *Virt.* 160) or simply ἄλογα (*Spec.* 1.260).

[17] "Assertive" captures the essence of this component of the soul; cf. John Cooper, "Human Motivation," 133–34: "the motivations that Plato classifies under the heading of spirit are to be understood as having their root in competitiveness and the desire for self-esteem and (as a normal presupposition of this) esteem by others."

[18] *Resp.* 580 D–E: "But the third part, owing to its manifold forms (διὰ πολυειδίαν), we could not easily designate by any one distinctive name, but gave it the name of its chief and strongest element (ὃ μέγιστον καὶ ἰσχυρότατον); for we called it the appetitive part (ἐπιθυμητικόν) because of the intensity of its appetites concerned with food and drink and love (διὰ σφοδρότητα τῶν περὶ τὴν ἐδωδὴν ἐπιθυμιῶν καὶ πόσιν καὶ ἀφροδίσια) and their accompaniments (καὶ ὅσα ἄλλα τούτοις ἀκόλουθα), and likewise the money-loving part (φιλοχρήματον), because money is the chief instrument for the gratification of such desires (διὰ χρημάτων μάλιστα ἀποτελοῦνται αἱ τοιαῦται ἐπιθυμίαι)." On Platonic tripartition, see Cooper, "Human Motivation." On Plato's general theory of desire, see Charles Kahn, "Plato's Theory of Desire." On *appetitive* desire, see esp. Hendrik Lorenz, *The Brute Within: Appetitive Desire in Plato and Aristotle* (OPM; Oxford: Clarendon, 2006). Lorenz outlines the basic model of ἐπιθυμία developed by Plato and appropriated in large part by Aristotle. This basic model was formative in Middle-Platonic moral psychology and helps to explain many aspects of Philo's thought.

[19] In the *Republic* (436 B), Plato posits an axiom that shapes his moral psychology, considering it obvious (δῆλον) that "the same thing (ταὐτόν) will never do or suffer opposites (τἀναντία ποιεῖν ἢ πάσχειν) in the same respect (κατὰ ταὐτόν) in relation to the same thing (πρὸς ταὐτόν) and at the same time (ἅμα). So that if ever we find these contradictions in the functions of the soul (ἐν αὐτοῖς ταῦτα γιγνόμενα) we shall know that it was not the same thing functioning (οὐ ταὐτόν) but a plurality (πλείω)" (substituting "soul" for Shorey's "mind" [N.B. ψυχῇ earlier in 436 B]). In *Resp.* 439 A–D, Plato argues that the human soul has a λογιστικόν element ᾧ λογίζεται and a *separate* ἀλόγιστόν τε καὶ ἐπιθυμητικόν element ᾧ ἐρᾷ τε καὶ πεινῇ καὶ διψῇ, since it is otherwise

reason, it must also operate apart from reason, so Platonic ἐπιθυμία must be "non-rational" (ἄλογος).[20] Without rational calculation, without deliberating on the *best* course of action, ἐπιθυμία reflexively pursues pleasure (ἡδονή) as its ultimate aim (notably via food, drink, and sex) whenever stimulated by the appropriate thought or sensory impression.[21] Reason's task is to manage desire, as a rational human being would manage a non-rational animal, ensuring that desire's myopic pursuits *serve*, rather than *subvert*, the greater good: the rational pursuit of the best overall course of life.[22]

---

impossible to explain an agent who at the same time desires a drink (via the ἐπιθυμητικόν) but for whatever reason counteracts that desire and abstains from drinking (via the λογιστικόν). (On the argument for tripartition and the axiomatic "Principle of Opposites," see Lorenz, *Brute Within*, 18–34.) Middle Platonists continued to assert the probative force of this axiom as well as the validity of Plato's proof (e.g., Plutarch *Virt. mor.* 442 A, esp. [Πλάτων] ἀποδείκνυσι δὲ τὴν διαφοράν etc.; also *Didask.* 24 [176.43–177.3]; cf. Galen, *PHP* V 7.1–33).

[20] *Resp.* 439 D: ἀλόγιστόν τε καὶ ἐπιθυμητικόν; *Tim.* 71 D: λόγου καὶ φρονήσεως οὐ μετεῖχε [τὸ ἐπιθυμητικὸν τῆς ψυχῆς]. For a full explanation of ἐπιθυμία as a non-rational phenomenon, see Lorenz, *Brute Within*, e.g. 9: "The notion of a part of the soul that is incapable of reasoning, but capable of giving rise to episodes of behaviour, even to episodes of human behaviour, sets the scene for the book's central theme: the idea, shared by Plato and Aristotle, that while reason can, all by itself, motivate a person to act, parts or aspects of the soul other than reason are equipped with non-rational cognitive resources that are sufficient for the generation of fully formed motivating conditions." For explanations of how desire manages to operate *without* the capacity for reason, see esp. Lorenz, *Brute Within*, 55–95 [="Belief and Appearance in Plato"] and 113–86 [="*Phantasia* and Non-Rational Desire in Aristotle"], esp. 119–73; also John Cooper, "Reason, Moral Virtue, and Moral Value," in *Reason and Emotion*, 253–280, esp. 255–64 [="Non-Rational Desires"]; repr. from *Rationality in Greek Thought* (ed. M. Frede and G. Striker; Oxford: Clarendon, 1996), 81–114; and idem, "Some Remarks on Aristotle's Moral Psychology," in *Reason and Emotion*, 237–52, esp. 241–44; repr. from *SJPh* 27 supp. (1988): 25–42; cf. the discussion of "sense-appetite" in N. J. H. Dent, "Varieties of Desire," *PASSV* 50 (1976): 153–75, esp. 154–58.

[21] On the connection between ἐπιθυμία and ἡδονή, see e.g. *Resp.* 439 D: τό ... ἀλόγιστόν τε καὶ ἐπιθυμητικόν ... ἡδονῶν ἑταῖρος; *Phaedr.* 238 A: ἐπιθυμίας δὲ ἀλόγως ἑλκούσης ἐπὶ ἡδονάς. Cf. Cooper, "Human Motivation," 126–30; idem, "Reason, Virtue, Value," 253–70; David Halperin, "Platonic *Erôs*," 172; Lorenz, *Brute Within*, passim, e.g. 2: "Appetite's stubborn and inflexible attachment to whatever happens to give a person pleasure renders psychological conflict ineliminable.... Appetite's attachment to what in fact gives us pleasure is unreformable." Later philosophers recognized this association in Plato's writings and stated it precisely (e.g., Aristotle, *De an.* 414 b 5–6: ἡ ἐπιθυμία· τοῦ γὰρ ἡδέος ὄρεξις αὕτη; Galen, *PHP* V 5.8: πρός ... τὴν ἡδονὴν διὰ τὸ ἐπιθυμητικόν).

[22] The Platonic view of ἐπιθυμία as a non-rational (ἄλογος) force facilitates its comparison to a non-rational animal, explaining the Platonic imagery of desire as "beast"; see esp. *Tim.* 70 D–E: ἐπιθυμητικόν ... ὡς θρέμμα ἄγριον; *Resp.* 588 B–591 A (passim): θηρίον, θρέμμα (cf. Urs Dierauer, *Tier und Mensch im Denken der Antike: Studien zur Tierpsychologie, Anthropologie und Ethik* [SAP 6; Amsterdam: Grüner, 1977], 66–89 [="Hinweise auf Tiere

Bipartition in Middle Platonism

Reason over against Ἐπιθυμία / Θυμός

Like other Middle Platonists, Ps.-Timaeus endorses Platonic tripartition, but in a distinctly modified version:

> With regard to human souls (ἀνθρωπίνας ψυχᾶς), one part is reasonable and intelligent (τὸ μὲν λογικόν ἐστι καὶ νοερόν),[23] but the other part is without reason and foolish (τὸ δ'ἄλογον καὶ ἄφρον).... Of the non-rational part (τῶ δ'ἀλόγω μέρεος), the irascible element is located around the heart (τὸ μὲν θυμοειδὲς περὶ τὰν καρδίαν) and the appetitive element around the liver (τὸ δ'ἐπιθυματικὸν περὶ τὸ ἧπαρ). (TL 46)[24]

Although he clearly identifies each of Plato's three "parts," including its respective location in the body, Ps.-Timaeus frames this tripartition in dualistic terms: the soul, it seems, has only two parts—the rational and the non-rational (τὸ μὲν λογικόν ... τὸ δ'ἄλογον).[25] This *bipartite* conception of Platonic tripartition subsumes the spirited and desiderative parts under a single "non-rational part" (ἄλογον μέρος), coordinating them as one pair that stands over against reason. Plato did not formulate tripartition in this way.[26] *Aristotle*, to facilitate his discussion of ethics, endorsed a simple dichotomy in the soul between "rational" (τὸ λόγον ἔχον) and "non-rational" (τὸ

---

in der Anthropologie und Ethik Platons"]). This comparison of the ἐπιθυμητικόν (ἐπιθυμία) to a beast appears also in Middle Platonism, see, e.g., *Didask.* 23 [176.22]: ἄγριον θρέμμα; Plutarch, *Virt. mor.* 447 C: τὸ θηρίον (cf. Julia Annas, "Humans and Beasts: Moral Theory and Moral Psychology," in *Platonic Ethics, Old and New* [CSCP 57; Ithaca: Cornell University Press, 1999], 117–36, esp. 134–36).

[23] On τὸ μὲν λογικόν ἐστι καὶ νοερόν, cf. John Whittaker, "The Terminology of the Rational Soul in the Writings of Philo of Alexandria," *SPhA* (1996): 1–20.

[24] Cf. TL 82: "Music and philosophy, its guide, which were established by the gods and the laws for the correction of the soul, accustom, persuade, and sometimes even coerce the non-rational part to obey reason (τὸ μὲν ἄλογον τῷ λογισμῷ πείθεσθαι), the irascible part of the non-rational soul (τῶ δ'ἀλόγω θυμὸν μέν) to be tame, and the appetitive part (ἐπιθυμίαν δέ) to remain quiet when the mind summons it either to action or to enjoyment." (Unless otherwise noted, all translations of TL are from Tobin, *Timaios of Locri*.)

[25] Arius Didymus provides evidence for bipartite psychology among the "Platonic philosophers" of his day: *Eclog.* 38.3–4: τοῦ ἀλόγου μέρους τῆς ψυχῆς ... τῷ λόγῳ; *Eclog.* 38.5–6: ἄλογον μέρος τῆς ψυχῆς ... τῷ λόγῳ; *Eclog.* 38.12–13: ψυχῆς τοῦ ἀλόγου μέρους ... τῷ λογικῷ.

[26] First, Plato never uses the terminology λόγος – ἄλογος in reference to a bipartite division of the soul (see Vander Waerdt, "Peripatetic Interpretation," 283–86). Second, Plato's tripartition often views reason and τὸ θυμοειδές as a united pair over against τὸ ἐπιθυμητικόν (e.g., *Resp.* 441 A; *Phaedr.* 253 D–254 E). But the absence of a *particular formulation* of tripartition as bipartition does not mean that Plato never ascribes bipartition to the soul (see e.g. D. A. Rees, "Bipartition of the Soul in the Early Academy," *JHS* 77 [1957]: 112–18).

ἄλογον) (*Eth. nic.* 1102 a 29–30), but he did not use this dichotomy as a frame for Platonic tripartition.[27] Instead, this formulation derives from an early and highly influential Peripatetic rendering of Plato's tripartite psychology, first attested in the *Magna Moralia*.[28] Peripatetic philosophers superimposed Aristotle's dichotomy onto Platonic tripartition, making his rational part (τὸ λόγον ἔχον) equivalent to Plato's λογιστικόν, while his non-rational part (τὸ ἄλογον) was taken to comprise Plato's θυμοειδές (or θυμικόν, θυμός)[29] and ἐπιθυμητικόν (or ἐπιθυμία). This hybrid version of Platonic tripartition, which pits rational against non-rational, became a standard model for moral psychology among Middle Platonists.[30]

Reason over against Appetite (ὄρεξις)

Although Middle-Platonic bipartition appears only to reconfigure Plato's three soul parts and thus leave Plato's conception of those parts intact, it actually owes much to *Aristotle's* theory of desire, which differed from Plato's in significant respects.[31] Unlike Plato, who envisioned three distinct soul parts, each with its own sorts of desires (ἐπιθυμίαι), Aristotle acknowledged just *one* appetitive faculty of the soul, which generates three

---

[27] Vander Waerdt, "Peripatetic Interpretation," esp. 286–87. Cf. idem, "Aristotle's Criticism of Soul-Division," *AJP* 108 (1987): 627–43.
[28] Vander Waerdt, "Peripatetic Interpretation." On the appropriation of this Peripatetic rendering in Middle Platonism, see Vander Waerdt, "Moral Psychology." On the use of Aristotle's writings among Platonic philosophers, see, for example, George E. Karamanolis, *Plato and Aristotle in Agreement? Platonists on Aristotle from Antiochus to Porphyry* (OPM; Oxford: Clarendon, 2006).
[29] Plato's term for the assertive part is θυμοειδές (e.g., *Resp.* 441 A: ἐν ψυχῇ τρίτον τοῦτό ἐστι τὸ θυμοειδές [εἶδος]). Middle Platonists often used the Aristotelian term θυμικός instead of θυμοειδές (cf. *Leg.* 1.70–72, *Leg.* 3.124; also θυμός [e.g., *Conf.* 21; *Spec.* 4.92]). See Whittaker, *Alcinoos*, 87, n. 73 (N.B. his citation of *Leg.* 3.115); Vander Waerdt, "Peripatetic Interpretation," 286, n. 9; also Jean Bouffartigue, "La structure de l'âme chez Philon: Terminologie scolastique et metaphors," in *Philon d'Alexandrie et le langage de la philosophie*, 59–75, 60, n. 3 (on *Leg.* 3.115).
[30] Vander Waerdt, "Moral Psychology," 378–81, notes six representative examples of Middle-Platonic sources that "harmonize bipartition and tripartition in accordance with Peripatetic doctrine by collapsing the θυμικόν and ἐπιθυμητικόν into a single ἄλογον and by opposing this to a reasoning faculty" (377): Arius Didymus's epitome, the *Didaskalikos*, Apuleius, Plutarch, Philo, and Clement. To this list may be added TL 46, 82, and Ps.-Metop. 118.1–5: τὰς ψυχὰς δύο μέρεα, τὸ μὲν λογιστικὸν τὸ δὲ ἄλογον, ... τῶ δὲ ἀλόγω τὸ μὲν θυμοειδές τὸ δ᾽ἐπιθυματικόν.
[31] On the fundamental revision of Plato's theory of desire resulting from a bipartite conception of tripartition, see Vander Waerdt, "Peripatetic Interpretation," esp. 286–87 and 291–301. Ultimately the "attribution of the division ἄλογον/λόγον ἔχον to Plato is based upon an interpretation of tripartition in the terms of Aristotle's doctrine of ὄρεξις" (286).

different sorts of appetite (ὄρεξις): ἐπιθυμία, θυμός, and βούλησις.[32] Of these, ἐπιθυμία and θυμός are non-rational ὀρέξεις analogous to the motivations generated by Plato's ἐπιθυμητικόν and θυμοειδές.[33] For example, Aristotle understood θυμός to be the sort of non-rational motivation at work when people get angry, mirroring Plato's concept of the θυμοειδές, which is—among other things—the seat of anger in the soul.[34] In addition, Aristotle associated ἐπιθυμία with "bodily" desires for food, drink, and sex—the three desires that characterize Plato's ἐπιθυμητικόν.[35] But in two key respects, the Aristotelian conception of θυμός and ἐπιθυμία underlying Middle-Platonic bipartition differs from that of Plato. First, what for Plato are acquisitive aims of the θυμοειδές—such as victory, honor, and fame—

---

[32] See, for example, *Resp.* 580 D and *De an.* 414 b 2. On Aristotle's theory of desire, see esp. Cooper's essays "Aristotle's Moral Psychology" and "Reason, Virtue, Value." Ὄρεξις in Aristotle serves as the generic term for "appetite," of which there are several specific types. Plato, who had no corresponding notion of "generic appetite," never uses the term ὄρεξις. (The term itself derives from ὀρέγω: *reach, stretch* [LSJ, s.v.], which Plato *does* use in the context of moral psychology: e.g., *Resp.* 439 B: τούτου ὀρέγεται.) Because ὄρεξις only becomes a term of moral psychology with *Aristotle*, its use among Middle Platonists demonstrates their appropriation of terms and concepts postdating Plato.

[33] On ἐπιθυμία and θυμός in Aristotle, see Cooper, "Reason, Virtue, Value," esp. 255–64. N.B. 257: "Aristotle seems throughout his career to have accepted from Plato's account of the human soul in the *Republic* the division of our non-rational desires into two types, appetitive and spirited (*epithumia* and *thumos*)."

[34] Plato, in fact, argues for the distinct function of the θυμοειδές over against the ἐπιθυμητικόν by citing the story of Leontius, whose anger *against* his own repugnant desire to view corpses demonstrates the separation of θυμός and ἐπιθυμία within the soul (see *Resp.* 439 E–440 A, esp. 440 A: τὴν ὀργὴν πολεμεῖν ἐνίοτε ταῖς ἐπιθυμίαις ὡς ἄλλο ὂν ἄλλῳ). On the role of the θυμοειδές in Plato's writings, see Cooper, "Human Motivation," esp. 130–36.

[35] E.g., *Eth. nic.* 1147 b 25–29. N.B. ἀναγκαῖα [τῶν ποιούντων ἡδονήν] ... τὰ σωματικά (1147 b 25–26) (cf. *Resp.* 558 C-E; 559 A-D). On Plato's ἐπιθυμητικόν, note *Resp.* 437 D, where of all ἐπιθυμίαι, δίψα (ἐπιθυμία ποτοῦ) and πεῖνα (ἐπιθυμία ἐδωδῆς) are the "most obvious" (ἐναργεστάτας); also *Tim.* 70 D: τὸ δὲ δὴ σίτων τε καὶ ποτῶν ἐπιθυμητικόν τῆς ψυχῆς καὶ ὅσων ἔνδειαν διὰ τὴν τοῦ σώματος ἴσχει φύσιν. In *Spec.* 4.96–97 Philo acknowledges as chief of all desires τὴν περὶ γαστέρα πραγματευομένην ἐπιθυμίαν, which concerns ἐδωδὴ καὶ πόσις (cf. Plato, *Leg.* 782 E: ἐδωδή ... καὶ πόσις). In *Leg.* 1.86, ἐπιθυμία (τὸ ἐπιθυμητικόν [see *Leg.* 1.70–71]) compels one toward σιτία καὶ ποτά (cf. *Leg.* 3.147). Cf. δίψα and πεῖνα as "harsh mistresses" in *Mos.* 1.191, *Spec.* 4.82, *Virt.* 130, *Contempl.* 37. The desire for sexual pleasure is another basic function of τὸ ἐπιθυμητικόν (e.g., *Resp.* 580 E [cf. 436 A–B]). In fact, desires for food, drink, and sex often appear together as the primal triumvirate of appetites (e.g., *Leg.* 782 E; *Phaed.* 81 B). Although closely tied to bodily requirements and conditions, the desires for food, drink, and sex properly belong to the *soul* (viz. τὸ ἐπιθυμητικόν)—there are, for Plato, no desires *of the body*, only "bodily desires," desires *of the soul* bearing a unique connection to the body (R. Hackforth, *Plato's Examination of Pleasure* [Cambridge: Cambridge University Press, 1945], 61; cf. 79, n. 4; 112, n. 2; 140, n. 2).

lose all association with "assertive appetite" (θυμός) and become simply additional objects of "acquisitive appetite" (ἐπιθυμία), along with food, drink, and sex.[36] In other words, Aristotle followed Plato in viewing ἐπιθυμία as a non-rational desire for pleasure, but he expanded the scope of ἐπιθυμία to include the intangible—but nevertheless *pleasurable*—objects of victory, honor, and fame.[37] This broader concept of ἐπιθυμία strips θυμός of its acquisitive aims, leaving it associated primarily with *anger* and *aggression* in Middle-Platonic thought.[38] In other words, Middle Platonists continued to associate ἐπιθυμία with a particular component of the Platonic soul, but they conceived it more broadly as the *one* source for *all* non-rational appetites, pursuing its aim of pleasure through any number of possible objects. Second, since Aristotle assigned both θυμός and ἐπιθυμία to a single ὀρεκτικόν faculty of the soul, and since θυμός and ἐπιθυμία constitute the soul's ἄλογον μέρος in the bipartite version of Platonic tripartition, ὀρεκτικόν and ἄλογον μέρος become interchangeable in Middle-Platonic moral psychology. Attesting this trend, Arius Didymus lists τὸ ὀρεκτικὸν μέρος τῆς ψυχῆς (*Eclog.* 38.8) as a variant Middle-Platonic designation for the soul's non-rational part over against its rational part.[39] In fact, Middle-Platonic ethical theory in general, which considers reason's management of non-rational forces in the soul and systematically conceptualizes the nature and function of those non-rational forces, takes full advantage of

---

[36] Cf. Cooper, "Reason, Virtue, Value," 263: "In the *Republic* Plato gives this intermediate kind of desire [sc. θυμός] its own special object of pursuit, victory, and/or esteem or honor (*timē*), corresponding to appetite's [sc. ἐπιθυμία] pursuit of pleasure. As we have already seen, Aristotle rejects this identification: according to him, akratic lovers of honor and victory are incontinently pursuing a pleasure and so are inappropriately subject not to spirited desire but to certain appetites, appetites for victory and honor."

[37] *De an.* 414 b 5–6: ἡ ἐπιθυμία· τοῦ γὰρ ἡδέος ὄρεξις αὕτη (cf. *Eth. nic.* 1119 b 6–8).

[38] In Plato's *Republic* (548 C–550 B), the man ruled by τὸ θυμοειδές is not constantly angry: he is rather φίλαρχος and φιλότιμος (549 A)—he *wants* power and honor. The Middle-Platonic conception (following Aristotle) would identify a φίλαρχος or φιλότιμος as one ruled by ἐπιθυμία (sc. τὸ ἐπιθυμητικόν), while someone ruled by θυμός (τὸ θυμοειδές) *would* in fact be irascible. When Ps.-Timaeus considers training of the soul (TL 82), in particular the obedience of the non-rational part to reason (τὸ μὲν ἄλογον τῷ λογισμῷ πείθεσθαι), the ideal for θυμός, which constitutes the non-rational part along with ἐπιθυμία, is that it be "tame" (τῷ δ'ἀλόγῳ θυμὸν μὲν πρᾶον εἶμεν)—in other words, Ps.-Timaeus envisions θυμός *primarily* as an irascible element (also Philo: e.g., *Leg.* 3.123; Plutarch: e.g., *De cohibenda ira*, although he sometimes retains the strictly Platonic role for τὸ θυμοειδές [see Tim Duff, *Plutarch's Lives: Exploring Virtue and Vice* (Oxford: Clarendon, 1999), 83–89]).

[39] Cf. Ps.-Metop.117.9–10: ἁ μὲν ὦν διάνοια ἀπὸ τῶ λογικῶ μέρεός ἐντι τᾶς ψυχᾶς, ἁ δὲ ὄρεξις ἀπὸ τῶ ἀλόγω (cf. Ps.-Theag. 193.13–14: ἁ δ'ὄρεξις τῶ ἀλόγω); *Didask.* 29.2 [182.33–35]: τεταγμένως καὶ εὐπειθῶς ἔχουσιν αἱ ὀρέξεις πρὸς τὸ φύσει δεσποτικόν, τουτέστι τὸ λογιστικόν (cf. Plutarch, *Virt. mor.* 450 E–F).

ἄλογον μέρος as a heuristic device, making it the locus not only of appetite (ὄρεξις) but also of impulse (ὁρμή) and emotion (πάθος).

Reason over against Impulse (ὁρμή)

"Appetite" (ὄρεξις), generally speaking, bears a close relation to "impulse" (ὁρμή), so Middle-Platonic moral psychology, which placed ὄρεξις in the soul's non-rational part, naturally placed ὁρμή there as well.[40] The term ὁρμή denotes above all directed *movement* within the soul.[41] Thus ὄρεξις, as a type of impulse, denotes directed movement *toward* something, and ἐπιθυμία, more specifically, denotes movement *toward* pleasure (a *pursuit*), with other types of impulses denoting other types of directed movement.[42] The issue dividing Stoics and Middle Platonists was not how to describe the phenomenon of impulse, since both could acknowledge the experience of directed movement within the soul. They disagreed over *where* in the soul (in theory) impulse occurred and what role reason played in the generation of impulse. Arius Didymus notes that "Platonic philosophers" (οἱ κατὰ Πλάτωνα φιλοσοφοῦντες) associated ὁρμή with the non-rational part of the soul (ἄλογον μέρος τῆς ψυχῆς) over against the rational part (τῷ λογικῷ).[43]

---

[40] On the topic of impulse (ὁρμή), see Inwood, *Ethics and Human Action* (cf. Tad Brennan, "Stoic Moral Psychology," in *The Cambridge Companion to the Stoics* [ed. Brad Inwood; Cambridge: Cambridge University Press, 2003], 265–69). Inwood considers primarily the Stoic view (esp. 42–101 [="The Psychology of Action"]), but also the less technical views of Plato and Aristotle (see 242–49 [="*Hormê* in Plato, Aristotle, and the *Magna Moralia*"]). Plato uses neither ὁρμή nor ὄρεξις as a technical term (the latter does not appear in his writings), so their precise relation cannot be determined. For Aristotle, the terms were more or less interchangeable, which allowed for their conflation among later philosophers, as Inwood notes: "For although one was the central theoretical term for the Stoa [ὁρμή] and the other for Aristotle [ὄρεξις], they could be blended together by those who were not interested in or did not understand the difference between the two psychological theories. This process continued to the point where ... the desiderative part of the soul could be called *to hormêtikon* rather than *to orektikon*" (245). For the Stoics, ὄρεξις was a *type* of impulse: namely, a rational impulse toward the apparent good (see Inwood, *Ethics and Human Action*, 235–37; cf. 114–15, 227–28).

[41] Stoics defined impulse generically (κατὰ τὸ γένος) as "a motion of the soul toward something"—e.g., *ESE* 9: λέγουσιν ... ὁρμὴν εἶναι φορὰν ψυχῆς ἐπί τι (Cf. Inwood, *Ethics and Human Action*, 32: "In most of our sources impulse is explicitly defined as a kind of change, movement or activity of the soul"). Stoics considered this definition broad enough to apply both to rational animals (human beings) and non-rational animals (*ESE* 9: ταύτης δ'ἐν εἴδει θεωρεῖσθαι τήν τε ἐν τοῖς λογικοῖς γιγνομένην ὁρμὴν καὶ τὴν ἐν τοῖς ἀλόγοις ζῴοις).

[42] Pleasure (ἡδονή), for example, as an impulse denotes directed movement *upward*—an "elevation" (ἔπαρσις) of the soul (*ESE* 10b; DL 7.114).

[43] *Eclog.* 38.10–14 (citing various equivalent definitions of ἠθική): ὁρμὴ ψυχῆς πρακτική ... ἣ [=] ψυχῆς τοῦ ἀλόγου μέρους ποιότης ... δυναμένη τῷ λογικῷ ἐπακολουθεῖν. In *Eclog.*

This same association appears in other writings with "Eudoran" affinities (Ps.-Timaeus, Ps.-Metopus, Plutarch) and arguably in the extant fragments of Eudorus himself.[44] By locating impulse in the non-rational part of the soul, which stands *over against* reason, Middle Platonists affirmed the existence of non-rational impulses in adult human beings. For them, impulses capable of motivating human action could arise, subsist, and desist wholly apart from reason, without reason's assent or authorization.[45] Such impulses are thus capable of genuinely opposing, or even usurping, reason. In sharp contrast, the Stoics flatly denied the existence of non-rational impulse in adult human beings.[46] For them, impulse (ὁρμή) *always* involves

---

117.11–12, Arius notes the explicit identification of ἄλογον μέρος with ὁρμητικόν by *Peripatetic* philosophers: τῆς γὰρ ψυχῆς τὸ μὲν εἶναι λογικόν, τὸ δ'ἄλογον· λογικὸν μὲν τὸ κριτικόν, ἄλογον δὲ τὸ ὁρμητικόν (N.B. Vander Waerdt, "Peripatetic Interpretation," 294, n. 29: "Arius' description of the ἄλογον as ὁρμητικόν contravenes Stoic doctrine and appears to represent a Peripatetic adaptation of the Stoic theory of ὁρμή"). Middle Platonists surely made the same identification, given their readiness to adopt Peripatetic models in moral psychology (e.g., tripartition as bipartition). But even without an *explicit* identification of ἄλογον μέρος with ὁρμητικόν in Middle-Platonic sources, the *association* of ἄλογον μέρος with ὁρμή unmistakably appears.

[44] See esp. Bonazzi, "Eudorus' Psychology." On the basis of a distinction between θεωρία and ὁρμή in *Eclog.* 42.13–23 [=Mazz. 1.4–10], Bonazzi convincingly argues for Eudorus's acknowledgement of *non-rational impulse* in the context of a Platonic bipartition between rational and non-rational parts of the soul. The association between ὁρμή and ἄλογον μέρος appears explicitly in Ps.-Metop. 117.12–14: τῶν μερέων τᾶς ψυχᾶς δύο τὰ πρᾶτα, τὸ μὲν λογιστικὸν τὸ δ'ἄλογον· καὶ λογιστικὸν μέν, ᾧ κρίνομες καὶ θεωρέομες· ἄλογον δέ, ᾧ ὁρμῶμες [ὁρμή] καὶ ὀρεγόμεθα [ὄρεξις] (cited also by Bonazzi, "Eudorus' Psychology," 125). Ps.-Timaeus has the association, but not as clearly: e.g., TL 71, which considers diseases affecting various faculties of the soul (ἄλλαι [νόσοι] δ'ἄλλων δυναμίων ἐντί), lists the soul's hormetic faculty (ὁρματικᾶς) *separately* from its rational faculty (λογικᾶς), ascribing it a *non-rational* function. See also Plutarch, *Virt. mor.* 450 E–F: προσήκει ... τὸν λογισμὸν ἡγεῖσθαι καὶ ἄρχειν τοῦ ἀλόγου, with αἱ ὁρμαὶ πρὸς τὰ σωματικά then implicitly associated with τοῦ ἀλόγου (cf. Bonazzi, "Eudorus' Psychology," 125–26).

[45] Just as non-rational animals, who have no capacity for reason, nevertheless operate according to impulse. For an explanation of the role of impulse in animal behavior, see Inwood, *Ethics and Human Action*, 66–91, esp. 72–82.

[46] See, for example, Inwood, *Ethics and Human Action*, 224–42 [=Appendix 2: "The Kinds of Impulse"], esp. 225. Commenting on Arius Didymus's detailed summary of the Stoic classification of impulse (see *Eclog.* 86.17–88.7), Inwood notes the Stoic attribution of non-rational impulse to *non-rational animals*, while noting also that for *rational animals* (i.e., human beings) the concept of non-rational impulse simply does not apply (225). Cf. Julia Annas, *Hellenistic Philosophy of Mind* (HCS 8. Berkeley: University of California Press, 1992), 106: "Our normal talk of 'irrational' impulses suggests that they are not rational at all; but for the Stoics ordinary language is just wrong here, for there can be no such thing as a totally nonrational impulse, at least not in undefective humans. We grasp the phenomenon, but it is not what we think it is, namely, reason versus something devoid of reason, but rather good reason versus bad, inadequate reason."

46   CHAPTER TWO

rational assent (συγκατάθεσις) and thus *always* denotes an activity of the mind (ἡγεμονικόν).[47] Stoics, in other words, considered impulse a *rational* function, precluding on theoretical grounds the idea of impulse *opposing*, much less *usurping*, reason.[48] The Middle-Platonic discussion of impulse certainly owed much to the Stoics, insofar as the Stoics brought the topic into prominence by emphasizing the role of impulse in moral theory, but the difference in their respective understandings of the origin and nature of impulse could not be starker. Simply put, the Stoics conceived impulse as an exclusively rational function, while Middle Platonists conceived impulse as a *non*-rational function, appropriately located in the soul's *non*-rational part.[49]

---

[47] The relation between impulse and assent forms part of the broader Stoic psychology of action (see Inwood, *Ethics and Human Action*, 42–101). The translation of ἡγεμονικόν as "mind" follows Inwood (*Ethics and Human Action*, 28; also A. A. Long, "Stoic Psychology," in *The Cambridge History of Hellenistic Psychology* [ed. Keimpe Algra et al.; Cambridge: Cambridge University Press, 1999], 560–84, esp. 572–83 [="Rationality and the faculties of the mind"]). Technically, ἡγεμονικόν refers to the "governing" *part* of the human soul (ψυχή), which commands the operation of strictly instrumental non-rational parts such as the five senses (αἰσθήσεις), the faculty of speech, and the faculty of reproduction—thus in Stoic theory, the soul has eight parts (see Inwood, *Ethics and Human Action*, 27–41; cf. Long, "Stoic Psychology," esp. 560–72). The mind itself has four powers—"impression" (φαντασία), "impulse" (ὁρμή), "assent" (συγκατάθεσις), and "reason" (λόγος)—of which the first two have non-rational analogues in non-rational animals (on the mind's powers, see esp. Long, "Stoic Psychology," 572–83). The presence of reason in human beings, however, influences the operation of the entire mind, making all of its functions distinctly rational: "[O]ur sources are correct, but misleading, when they say that the mind or 'governing part' of the human *psuchē* has the four faculties, impression, assent, impulse, reason. The Stoics' model of the mind would be better rendered by saying that there are three mental faculties—rational impression, rational impulse, and rational assent. Reason is not something over and above the other three. It is the mind in its entirety. Hence reason (*logos*), mind (*nous*), and thought (*dianoia*) are all terms that refer to the distinctive nature of a human being's *psuchē*" (Long, "Stoic Psychology," 575).

[48] For the Stoics, a moment of rational assent is always the direct cause of human behavior, whether or not the agent is consciously aware of that moment. The idea of an internal, non-rational force *causing* or *determining* behavior clearly and flatly contradicts the Stoic theory of human action. (Cf. Inwood, *Ethics and Human Action*, 139: "[A]t no time do we experience impulses or passions which are produced independently of our assenting reason or which conflict with and resist it.") This reflects the Stoic "monistic" psychology, which holds that the human psyche stands united under *one* arbiter—reason. Thus no psychic power other than reason (i.e., no non-rational power) can ultimately determine the course of human action, which *always* proceeds on the basis of an autonomous agent's rational decision. As Inwood explains (idem, 33), Stoic monism did not preclude the existence of soul parts (μέρη), only the possibility of opposition *among* those parts.

[49] The acknowledgement of non-rational impulses (ἄλογοι ὁρμαί) in adult human beings serves *in itself* as a criterion for distinguishing Middle-Platonic from Stoic moral

Reason over against Emotion (πάθος)

Along with ὄρεξις and ὁρμή, Middle Platonists placed also emotion (πάθος) in the non-rational part of the soul: *feelings* of dejection, fear, elation and desire can all arise, subsist, and desist *apart from* the rational faculty.[50] Arius Didymus confirms that "Platonic philosophers" (*Eclog.* 38.14–15) considered the soul's non-rational part to be also its "emotional part" (παθητικὸν μέρος), thus indicating that emotions are essentially non-rational phenomena.[51] Similarly, in TL 71 Ps.-Timaeus lists the soul's "emotional faculty" (παθητικᾶς [δυνάμιος]) as something *other than* its rational faculty (λογικᾶς [δυνάμιος]), indicating that emotions occur apart from reason. Along with the Stoics, Middle Platonists acknowledged four cardinal πάθη: grief (λύπη), fear (φόβος), pleasure (ἡδονή), and desire (ἐπιθυμία).[52] But

---

psychology, *including* the moral psychology of the Stoic Posidonius (ca. 130–50 B.C.E.). While Posidonius *did* acknowledge non-rational forces in the soul analogous to Platonic ἐπιθυμία and θυμός, he did *not* count these non-rational "affective movements" (παθετικαὶ κινήσεις [see *PHP* V 5.28]) as impulses (ὁρμαί)—although they could influence the character of (always rational) impulses (see esp. John Cooper, "Posidonius on Emotions," in *Reason and Emotion*, 449–84, esp. 467–68, 474–75; repr. from pages 71–111 in *The Emotions in Hellenistic Philosophy* [ed. J. Sihvola and T. Engberg-Pedersen; TSHP 46; Dordrecht: Kluwer, 1998]). In other words, Posidonius should not be allowed to muddle the clear and radical difference between Middle Platonists (including Philo) and Stoics on the question of non-rational impulses in adult human beings—*or*, for that matter, on the question of πάθη, which both groups analyzed ultimately as a type of impulse: for Middle Platonists a type of *non-rational* impulse, for Stoics a type of (*ir*)*rational* impulse.

[50] The term πάθος bears various translations, and a comparison of Middle-Platonic over against Stoic ethical theory demands the subtle yet crucial distinction between "emotion" (πάθος) and "passion" (πάθος): *emotion* (πάθος) as a strictly amoral function of normal human life and *passion* (πάθος) as an immoral function of abnormal human life. These different connotations led to semantic confusion and charges of equivocation (see Plutarch, *Virt. mor.* 449 A–C).

[51] *Eclog.* 38.5–7: ἄλογον μέρος τῆς ψυχῆς εἰθισμένον ὑπακούειν τῷ λόγῳ· ἢ πάθος ἢ παθητικὸν μέρος τῆς ψυχῆς εἰθισμένον ὑπακούειν τῷ λογικῷ. Cf. Plutarch, *Virt. mor.* 442 A: [ἡ τ'ἀνθρώπου ψυχὴ] ἕτερον μὲν ἔχει τὸ νοερὸν καὶ λογιστικόν, ... ἕτερον δὲ τὸ παθητικὸν καὶ ἄλογον (*Virt. mor.* represents in large part Plutarch's polemic against the Stoics, who refuse to acknowledge that passions are something *different from* reason, not—as they claim—aberrant manifestations *of* reason; see 441 C [the Stoic view], 443 B, 446 F–447 C, 448 D); also *Didask.* 5.2 [156.35–37]: τέμνομεν τὴν ψυχὴν εἴς τε τὸ λογικὸν καὶ εἰς τὸ παθητικόν, καὶ αὖ πάλιν τὸ παθητικὸν εἴς τε τὸ θυμικὸν καὶ τὸ ἐπιθυμητικόν (cf. 17.4 [173.11–15]). Lilla (*Clement of Alexandria*, 87) suggests that a general tenet of the Middle-Platonic doctrine of πάθος is "the tendency to consider it as produced by the irrational [non-rational] parts of the soul."

[52] On the four cardinal passions, see Inwood, *Ethics and Human Action*, 144–45. The four appear also in Middle Platonism, e.g. TL 72: ἀρχαὶ δὲ κακίας ἁδοναὶ καὶ λῦπαι ἐπιθυμίαι τε καὶ φόβοι; Philo, *Her.* 269–70: τὰς τῶν τεττάρων παθῶν δυνάμεις ... ἡδονῆς ... ἐπιθυμία ... λύπης ... φόβου (cf. Schmidt, *Anthropologie*, 88, n. 92). Baltes, *Timaios Lokros*,

agreement between the two groups essentially ends with this taxonomy. In the first place, Stoics considered these four passions to be expressions *of the mind*, albeit aberrant expressions (i.e., "irrational" [ἄλογος]).[53] This follows from the Stoic conviction that (a) passions are a type of impulse and (b) *every* impulse derives from reason. By claiming that passions arise *apart from* the rational faculty, Middle Platonists reject Stoic theory unequivocally.[54] In addition, Stoics considered these four πάθη to be always and inherently bad—thus *passions* and not just *emotions*. Middle Platonists, by contrast, considered the cardinal πάθη an amoral part of normal human existence: their non-rational energy provides essential motivation for human activity, including *virtuous* human activity, and they become problematic only when they overstep the dictates of reason.[55] So Middle Platonists endorsed as an ethical norm the *moderation* of emotion.[56] This emphasis on moderation

---

199, suggests that the doctrine of four cardinal passions attested in TL 72 formed (for Middle Platonists) part of "ein neues ethisches Lehrgebäude."

[53] *ESE* 10: εἶναι δὲ πάθη πάντα τοῦ ἡγεμονικοῦ τῆς ψυχῆς; cf. Plutarch, *Virt. mor.* 446 F–447 A: ἔνιοι δέ φασιν οὐχ ἕτερον εἶναι τοῦ λόγου τὸ πάθος ... καὶ γὰρ ἐπιθυμίαν καὶ ὀργὴν καὶ φόβον καὶ τὰ τοιαῦτα πάντα δόξας εἶναι καὶ κρίσεις πονηράς, οὐ περὶ ἕν τι γινομένας τῆς ψυχῆς μέρος, ἀλλ᾽ ὅλου τοῦ ἡγεμονικοῦ ῥοπὰς καὶ εἴξεις καὶ συγκαταθέσεις καὶ ὁρμάς.

[54] In other words, they side with the Platonic-Aristotelian tradition over against the Stoic. For a discussion of the radical difference between the Platonic-Aristotelian concept of πάθος (as non-rational) and the Stoic concept (as [ir]rational), see Frede, "Stoic Affections," esp. 94–100.

[55] E.g., Ps.-Metop. 121.10–12: οὐκ ἀφελὲν ὧν δεῖ τὰ πάθεα τὰς ψυχᾶς, οὔτε γὰρ ὠφέλιμον αὐτὰ ἀφελέν, ἀλλὰ συναρμόσασθαι ποτὶ τὸ λόγον ἔχον τῶ δέοντος καὶ τῶ μετρίω; Plutarch, *Virt. mor.* 443 C: οὐ βουλομένου [τοῦ λόγου] τὸ πάθος ἐξαιρεῖν παντάπασιν (οὔτε γὰρ δυνατὸν οὔτ᾽ ἄμεινον), ἀλλ᾽ ὅρον τινὰ καὶ τάξιν ἐπιτιθέντος αὐτῷ; 451 C: μέτεστιν οὖν αὐτῷ [ὁ ἄνθρωπος] καὶ τοῦ ἀλόγου, καὶ σύμφυτον ἔχει τὴν τοῦ πάθους ἀρχήν, οὐκ ἐπεισόδιον ἀλλ᾽ ἀναγκαίαν οὖσαν, οὐδ᾽ ἀναιρετέαν παντάπασιν ἀλλὰ θεραπείας καὶ παιδαγωγίας δεομένην; *Didask.* 32.4 [186.14–18]: τῶν δὲ παθῶν τὰ μέν ἐστιν ἄγρια, τὰ δὲ ἥμερα (cf. TL 71: ἄγρια πάθεα)· καὶ ἥμερα μὲν ὅσα κατὰ φύσιν ὑπάρχει τῷ ἀνθρώπῳ ἀναγκαῖά τε καὶ οἰκεῖα· οὕτως δ᾽ ἔχει ἕως ἂν σύμμετρα ὑπάρχῃ, προσελθούσης δὲ αὐτοῖς ἀμετρίας ἡμαρτημένα ὑπάρξει. For Middle Platonists, emotions are in fact an essential *component* of moral virtue (ἠθικὴ ἀρετή): TL 73: τὸ πῶς ἔχεν ποτὶ τὰ πάθεα ἀρχά τε καὶ πέρας ἀρετᾶς καὶ κακίας ἐστί· τὸ γὰρ πλεονάζεν ἐν ταύταις ἢ κάρρον αὐτᾶν εἶμεν εὖ ἢ κακῶς ἀμὲ διατίθητι (on which see Baltes, *Timaios Lokros*, 206: "[W]ie bei Platon ... sind die Affekte an sich noch nicht schlecht, sie werden es erst durch Übermaß und Unkontrolliertheit"); Arius Didymus (*Eclog.* 38.6–7): [defining ἠθικὴ ἀρετή]: πάθος ἢ παθητικὸν μέρος τῆς ψυχῆς εἰθισμένον ὑπακούειν τῷ λογικῷ; Ps.-Metop. 119.8: τὰ δὲ πάθεα τᾶς ἀρετᾶς ὕλα; 121.7: γίνεται γὰρ ἐκ τῶν παθέων ἁ ἀρετά; Plutarch, *Virt. mor.* 440 D: [on ἠθικὴ ἀρετή] τὸ μὲν πάθος ὕλην ἔχειν τὸν δὲ λόγον εἶδος.

[56] Ps.-Metop. 120.24: μεσότατα τῶν παθέων (cf. Ps.-Arch. 41.16: ἀσκητέον ... μετριοπάθειαν); Plutarch, *Virt. mor.* 443 D: παθῶν ... μεσότητας; 444 C: τοῦτ᾽ οὖν τοῦ πρακτικοῦ λόγου κατὰ φύσιν ἔργον ἐστί, τὸ ἐξαιρεῖν τὰς ἀμετρίας τῶν παθῶν καὶ πλημμελείας; 445 A: εἰς τὸ μέτριον ... καθιστᾶσα τῶν παθῶν ἕκαστον; cf. TL 72: ἀδοναὶ ἄμετροι. Cf. Claudio Moreschini, "Considerazioni sulla dottrina del pathos nel Medioplatonismo, *SF* 8–9

derives from the Middle-Platonic insistence that a non-rational component of the soul exists *inherently* as the locus of emotion, and its existence calls for active management on the part of reason.[57]

Summary

According to Alexandrian Middle Platonism, the human soul consists of two essentially different parts: a rational part and a non-rational part. Although the non-rational part consists in theory of a composite of Platonic θυμός and ἐπιθυμία, the representation of tripartition as bipartition involves significant modifications of Plato's views. Along with expanding the scope of acquisitive desire (ἐπιθυμία), it facilitates a unitary conception of the soul's non-rational part as the locus of appetite (ὄρεξις), impulse (ὁρμή), and emotion (πάθος)—all conceived as non-rational capacities due to their non-rational origin. In sum, Middle Platonists understand "rational" over against "non-rational" to be the *one* overarching paradigm for moral psychology, although that paradigm accommodates a number of different conceptual models:

Table One: Variations of Bipartition in Middle Platonism

	TRIPARTITION	APPETITE (ὄρεξις)	IMPULSE (ὁρμή)	EMOTION (πάθος)
RATIONAL λογικὸν μέρος	λογικὸν μέρος	λογικὸν μέρος	λογικὸν μέρος	λογικὸν μέρος
NON-RATIONAL ἄλογον μέρος	θυμός/ἐπιθυμία	ὀρεκτικὸν μέρος	ὁρμητικὸν μέρος	παθητικὸν μέρος

The various models naturally allow for variant conceptions of desire (ἐπιθυμία). For Middle Platonists, the term ἐπιθυμία can denote either an

---

(1985–86), 23–33, 24: "il medioplatonismo ... sostiene l'eccellenza della dottrina della *metriopatheia*." See also Lilla, *Clement of Alexandria*, 92–103; John Dillon, "'*Metriopatheia* and *Apatheia*': Some Reflections on a Controversy in Later Greek Ethics," in *Essays in Ancient Greek Philosophy II* (ed. John Anton and Anthony Preus; Albany: SUNY Press, 1983), 508–17; repr. in *The Golden Chain: Studies in the Development of Platonism and Christianity*; CS 333; Aldershot: Variorum, 1990.

[57] Cf. Dillon, "*Metriopatheia* and *Apatheia*," 515: "the controversy about *metriopatheia* and *apatheia*, which generated such heat in later Greek philosophy, is properly one between the concept of a bipartite or tripartite soul, in which the lower part [or] parts can never be eradicated—at least while the soul is in the body—but must constantly be chastised, and that of a unitary one."

enduring "part" of the soul or an intermittent *function* of some "part" (ὀρεκτικόν, ὁρμητικόν, παθητικόν). In any case, ἐπιθυμία represents a non-rational force within the soul in need of reason's management.

Bipartition in Philo's Writings

Reason over against Ἐπιθυμία / Θυμός

Philo consistently maintains the bipartite model of the soul held by his Middle-Platonic contemporaries:[58]

---

[58] Studies commonly identify the bipartition of rational and non-rational (often "irrational") as Philo's persistent, overarching concept of the soul: e.g., Billings, *Platonism of Philo*, 52: "The one distinction which persists throughout is the one ... between the rational and the irrational parts of the soul"; Dillon, *Middle Platonists*, 174–75: "[F]or Philo each of these divisions expresses some aspect of the truth, but the most basic truth remains the division into rational and irrational" (175) [cf. idem, "Philo of Alexandria and Platonist Psychology," in *Philon d'Alexandrie* (ed. Jean-François Pradeau; EP 7; Paris: Belles Lettres, 2010), 163–69, esp. 164–65] ; Runia, *Philo and the Timaeus*, 468: "Philo regarded the main thrust of Plato's psychology as tending towards a *bipartition* of the soul into a rational and an irrational part" [cf. 304–05]); Schmidt, *Anthropologie*, 50: "Trotzdem Philon zwischen den verschiedenen Einteilungen ... hin- und herschwankt ..., dominiert doch entsprechend seiner dualisischen Grundhaltung die Zweiteilung der Seele"; Winston, "Philo on the Emotions," 202. On the bipartite schema λογικόν-ἄλογον, Hermann S. Schibli notes: "This was the working model for Philo of Alexandria in the first century A.D., probably following Eudorus" ("Xenocrates' Daemons and the Irrational Soul," *CQ* 43 [1993]: 143–67, 161). For a helpful collection of Philonic material on the soul, in outline form and arranged under rubrics relevant to moral psychology, see Gretchen Reydams-Schils, "Philo of Alexandria on Stoic and Platonist Psycho-Physiology: The Socratic Higher Ground," in *Philo of Alexandria and Post-Aristotelian Philosophy* (ed. Francesca Alesse; SPhA 5; Leiden: Brill, 2008), 169–95; repr. from *AP* 22 (2002): 125–47. In addition to assembling and collating data (175–87 [="Philo's Psychology, Nuts and Bolts"]), Reydams-Schils considers "which psychological model Philo prefers in his analysis of rational behavior and the passions" (169–70) and so seeks to *explain* the data (see esp. 169–75, 187–95). She concludes that Philo—despite skepticism regarding the *precise* nature of the soul—consistently maintains an overarching "Socratic" notion of soul-body opposition able to accommodate psychological models of both Platonic *and* Stoic provenance, which he can then deploy in various forms according to exegetical need (esp. 190: "A return to the Socratic position of a struggle between soul and body" etc.). Her thesis, however, does not address the question of whether or not Philo holds a consistent view of the *soul itself*, since in the end a "soul-body" dichotomy only affirms the existence of a soul over against the body, which both Platonists and Stoics acknowledged. The bipartition espoused by Middle Platonists (rational over against non-rational) accommodates all of Reydams-Schils's data within one working model of the *soul* and so provides what the soul-body dichotomy cannot: an overarching paradigm for *moral psychology*. The soul-body dichotomy belongs not so much to Philo's moral psychology as to his moral *rhetoric*, in which the body (esp. the belly) serves as a foil for loftier pursuits of the soul (see Sandnes, *Belly*

Since our soul is bipartite (τῆς γὰρ ψυχῆς ἡμῶν διμεροῦς ὑπαρχούσης), having one rational part (τὸ μὲν λογικόν) and one non-rational part (τὸ δὲ ἄλογον ἐχούσης), there is a virtue associated with each part .... (*Congr.* 26)[59]

Furthermore, Philo uses this bipartite model to accommodate Platonic tripartition, again in agreement with contemporary Middle Platonism:

[Esau] was wild and indocile, brimful of fierce temper and desire (θυμοῦ γέμοντα καὶ ἐπιθυμίας),[60] who to sum him up armed the non-rational part of the soul to war against the rational part (τὸ τῆς ψυχῆς ἄλογον μέρος ἐπιτετειχικότα τῷ λογικῷ). (*Praem.* 59)[61]

Reflecting the full range of variant models endorsed by Middle Platonists, Philo also locates appetite (ὄρεξις), impulse (ὁρμή), and emotion (πάθος) within the non-rational part of the soul.

Reason over against Appetite (ὄρεξις)

In agreement with his Middle-Platonic contemporaries, Philo locates ὄρεξις in the non-rational part of the soul:

Our soul is tripartite (τριμερῆ): one part is rational (μέρος μὲν ἓν λογιστικόν), a second is assertive (δεύτερον δὲ θυμικόν), and a third is desiderative (τρίτον δὲ ἐπιθυμητικόν) .... To the desiderative part [philosophers have assigned] the area around the abdomen and belly, since that is the dwelling

---

and Body, esp. 35–60 [="The belly in ancient moral philosophy"], 97–107 [="The belly-*topos* in Jewish-Hellenistic sources"], and 108–35 [="The belly in Philo's writings"]). On Philo's various formulations of the soul (along with a proposal of νοῦς-αἴσθησις as the one overarching model subsuming the rest), see Bouffartigue, "La structure de l'âme chez Philon," 59–75; also Schmidt, *Anthropologie,* 49–67.

[59] My translation. Also *Leg.* 2.2: ἐγὼ πολλά εἰμι, ψυχὴ σῶμα, καὶ ψυχῆς ἄλογον λογικόν; *Conf.* 111: ἑκάστας τῶν ἐν ψυχῇ δυνάμεων ... τὰς μὲν λογικῇ, τὰς δὲ ἀλόγῳ μερίδι; *Her.* 132: τὴν μὲν ψυχὴν εἰς λογικὸν καὶ ἄλογον; *Her.* 167: δύο εἰσὶν ἰσάριθμοι τοῖς τῆς ψυχῆς μέρεσι, λογικῷ καὶ ἀλόγῳ; *Spec.* 1.66: ἀγγέλους, ἀσωμάτους ψυχάς, οὐ κράματα ἐκ λογικῆς καὶ ἀλόγου φύσεως, οἵας τὰς ἡμετέρας; *Spec.* 1.201: δυοῖν δ'ὄντων, ἐξ ὧν ἡ ἡμετέρα ψυχὴ συνέστη, λογικοῦ τε καὶ ἀλόγου; *Spec.* 1.333: τὴν ὅλην ψυχὴν ἐκ λογικοῦ καὶ ἀλόγου μέρους συνεστῶσαν.

[60] Philo does use the term ἐπιθυμητικόν to refer to the desiderative element of the tripartite soul in, for example, *Leg.* 1.70–72 and *Leg.* 3.115, but he elsewhere uses the term ἐπιθυμία (cf. θυμός for θυμοειδές), as Ioannes Leisegang notes (*Indices ad Philonis Alexandrini Opera* [= vol. 7 of PCW], s.v. at no. 1, "tertia pars animae"), citing *Conf.* 21; *Spec.* 4.92; *Spec.* 1.146–50, cf. 206 ff.; *Virt.* 13; *Migr.* 67; *Her.* 64; *Spec.* 4.10; *Praem.* 59; *Migr.* 66 ff.; *Spec.* 4.93.

[61] Substituting "desire" for Colson's "lust"; "non–rational" for "unreasoning." Cf. *Leg.* 3.116: ὁ θυμὸς καὶ ἡ ἐπιθυμία, μέρη τοῦ ἀλόγου; *Migr.* 66: τῆς ἐπιθυμίας ... τὸν θυμόν ... ὅλον τὸ τῆς ψυχῆς ἄλογον... μέρος; *Her.* 64: τοῦ ἑτέρου ψυχῆς τμήματος, ὅπερ ἄλογον ὑπάρχον ... θυμοὺς ζέοντας καὶ πεπυρωμένας ἐπιθυμίας ἀναφλέγον (also *QG* 4.216).

place of desire (ἐνταῦθα γὰρ κατοικεῖ ἐπιθυμία), non-rational appetite (ὄρεξις ἄλογος). (*Leg.* 3.115)[62]

Philo indicates in *Leg.* 3.116 that he views this tripartite Platonic model in Middle-Platonic terms, as a *bipartite* dichotomy: ὁ λόγος over against ὁ θυμός and ἡ ἐπιθυμία, with the latter pair identified as μέρη τοῦ ἀλόγου. If Philo places ἐπιθυμία in the soul's non-rational part, then his equation of ἐπιθυμία with ὄρεξις ἄλογος clearly places ὄρεξις there as well. So Philo, in good Middle-Platonic fashion, sees ὄρεξις operating *apart* from reason as a *non-rational* force deriving from a distinct, non-rational part of the soul. This flatly contradicts the Stoics, who themselves defined ἐπιθυμία as ὄρεξις ἄλογος but unequivocally meant "*irrational* appetite," a malfunction *of* the rational faculty.[63]

Philo's identification of ἐπιθυμία as ὄρεξις ἄλογος derives ultimately from Aristotle, and Philo's *overall* use of the term ὄρεξις further reflects the Aristotelian modifications of Platonic theory inherent in Middle-Platonic bipartition. Plato had understood pleasure (ἡδονή) to be the ultimate aim of ἐπιθυμία, and Aristotle added technical precision to this idea by defining ἐπιθυμία as an ὄρεξις τοῦ ἡδέος, or appetite *for the pleasant*.[64] Philo likewise associates ἐπιθυμία with ὀρέξεις ... ἡδονῶν (*Leg.* 3.138).[65] He can speak of

---

[62] My translation. Cf. *Post.* 26: ἐπιθυμία δὲ ἀλόγους ἐμποιοῦσα ὀρέξεις.
[63] E.g., DL 7.113: ἡ δ'ἐπιθυμία ἐστὶν ἄλογος ὄρεξις [=*SVF* III 96, 22]. Galen understands both the ambiguity of ἄλογος and the clear intention of Chrysippus to mean "irrational" in his definition of ἐπιθυμία: "[I]n his definition of desire (τὸν τῆς ἐπιθυμίας ὅρον), which he calls ὄρεξιν ἄλογον, he touches in a way, verbally at least, on the non-rational power in the soul (τῆς ἀλόγου κατὰ τὴν ψυχὴν δυνάμεως); but here too he departs from it in his explanation, since even the appetite (ἡ ὄρεξις) that he includes in the definition belongs to the rational power (τῆς λογικῆς ἐστι δυνάμεως). Thus he defines appetite as 'rational impulse' (ὁρμὴν λογικήν) ... " (*PHP* IV 2.2–3; trans. De Lacey, slightly modified). Schmidt, *Anthropologie*, 89, citing *Leg.* 3.115 (see 162, n. 126), recognizes that the definition of ἐπιθυμία as ὄρεξις ἄλογος is "aus der Stoa wörtlich übernommene," but also that the words by themselves mean very little ("inhaltlich recht leere"). The meaning must be supplied, either through explicit commentary or through clear contextual cues, such as Philo provides using the framework of Platonic tripartition, in which ἐπιθυμία explicitly resides apart from the reasoning faculty and is thus non-rational.
[64] E.g., *De an.* 414 b 5–6; *Eth. nic.* 1119 b 6–8.
[65] "We have already mentioned that pleasure goes not only on its breast (ἐπὶ τῷ στήθει) but also on its belly (τῇ κοιλίᾳ), and pointed out that the stomach (γαστέρα) is a place most appropriate to pleasure, for we may almost describe it as a reservoir of all the pleasures (σχεδὸν γὰρ ἀγγεῖον τῶν ἡδονῶν ἁπασῶν). For when the belly has been filled, cravings after the other pleasures also become vehement (ὀρέξεις καὶ τῶν ἄλλων ἡδονῶν γίνονται σύντονοι), but when it has been emptied, these are quieted and become more still" (N.B. κοιλία in Philo's allegory stands for ἐπιθυμία, i.e., τὸ ἐπιθυμητικόν). Cf. *Post.* 71, where Philo similarly implies that *desire* (τῆς ἐπιθυμίας) consists of an *appetite* (τῶν

the typical varieties of Platonic ἐπιθυμία (for food, drink, sex) i[n] ὄρεξις, as did Aristotle.[66] But more importantly, his concept o[f] rational appetite for pleasure expands to include, as it did for Aristotle, objects that Plato had associated with the soul's *assertive* function, not its *appetitive* function—objects like victory, honor, and fame.[67] So for Philo, as for other Middle Platonists, ἐπιθυμία encompassed the objects of *both* of Plato's inferior soul parts (τὸ ἐπιθυμητικόν, τὸ θυμοειδές) in its pursuit of pleasure.[68] This "expansion" of the role of ἐπιθυμία in turn casts θυμός more exclusively as the non-rational source of anger.[69] Philo does not use the term ὄρεξις often, but (when he does) his use reflects standard trends within Middle-Platonic moral psychology.[70]

Reason over against Impulse (ὁρμή)

Siding with his Middle-Platonic contemporaries against the Stoics, Philo believes that the soul's non-rational part can generate non-rational impulses (ὁρμαί), whose independent origin allows them genuinely to oppose, or even usurp, reason.[71] Philo's acceptance of non-rational impulse as a factor

ὀρέξεων) for *pleasure* (ἡδονῶν); also *Abr.* 96: τάς ... ἐφ'ἡδονὴν ἀγούσας ὀρέξεις (cf. *Praem.* 71: ἐπιθυμήσῃ τινὸς ἡδέος).
[66] E.g., *Det.* 113: ταῖς πρὸς συνουσίαν ὀρέξεσιν; *Gig.* 35: μὴ πρὸς πάντα οὖν τὰ τῇ σαρκὶ φίλα αἱ ὀρέξεις ἀνηρεθίσθωσαν; *Ebr.* 214: τὰς ὀρέξεις ἀναρρηγνύντα [earlier: σιτίων, ὄψου, ποτῶν]; *Decal.* 123: τὰς ὀρέξεις (of the adulterer); *Virt.* 136: τῆς ὑπερφυοῦς γαστριμαργίας ὀρέξεις.
[67] Philo attests this view *explicitly* only in *Post.* 116, but the passage is telling. Philo has in mind people whose appetites are engaged (ταῖς ἀορίστοις αὐτῶν ὀρέξεσιν)—appetites involving not only "bodily pleasures" (σωματικὰς ἡδονάς) but also objects typically associated with Plato's θυμοειδές, such as fame (N.B. φιλοδόξους).
[68] E.g., *Opif.* 79: αἱ δόξης ἢ χρημάτων ἢ ἀρχῆς ἐπιθυμίαι; *Leg.* 2.107: τὰ γοῦν ποιητικὰ [ἡδονῆς] ..., χρυσὸς ἄργυρος δόξα τιμαὶ ἀρχαί, αἱ ὗλαι τῶν αἰσθητῶν; *Ios.* 70: ἀρχῆς ἐπιθυμία. Schmidt, *Anthropologie*, recognized this tendency, without noting the historical developments in moral psychology that account for it: "Als Gegenstand des Begehrens werden fast durchweg die Strebungen, die Platon von dem zweiten und dritten Sellenteil aussagt, zusammengefaßt" (92–93).
[69] *Leg.* 3.123: οὐ πέφυκε γὰρ ὁ θυμὸς σαφηνείας εἶναι φίλος· τῶν γοῦν ὀργιζομένων ... ; *Leg.* 3.130: τοῦ θυμοῦ ... τοῦ πολεμικοῦ μέρους; *Migr.* 67: τὸν πολεμικὸν θυμόν; *Migr.* 210: τὸ θυμοῦ καὶ ὀργῆς πάθος. Cf. Méasson, *Char ailé*, 158–60 [="Le «thumos» chez Platon et chez Philon"].
[70] Compare the instances of ὄρεξις (15) and ἐπιθυμία (218) (see Peder Borgen, Kåre Fuglseth, and Roald Skarsten, *The Philo Index: A Complete Greek Word Index to the Writings of Philo of Alexandria* [Grand Rapids: Eerdmans, 2000], s.v.). Because the two terms are virtually equivalent (ἐπιθυμία = [ἄλογος] ὄρεξις), Philo's preference for ἐπιθυμία over ὄρεξις may come from a conviction that ὄρεξις in most cases amounts to needless technical jargon.
[71] Philo acknowledges also *rational* impulses in human beings (e.g., *Migr.* 67: τὸ λοιπὸν μέρος καὶ ἄμεινον τῆς ψυχῆς, τὸ λογικόν, ... χρήσηται πρὸς τὰ καλὰ πάντα ὁρμαῖς; *Praem.*

54   CHAPTER TWO

in *human* moral psychology derives from broader convictions about the relation between animal and human souls. Following standard formulations of the *scala naturae*, which ranks various forms of existence according to natural endowment, Philo recognizes impulse (ὁρμή) as a capacity possessed by non-rational animals.[72] Because animals are non-rational (ἄλογος), their impulses are likewise non-rational (ἄλογος), generated by a reflexive mechanism whenever an appropriate stimulus appears, *without the authorization or assent of reason*.[73] Occupying a higher rank on the scale, human beings have not only the capacity for impulse (ὁρμή), but also the endowment of reason (λόγος), which distinguishes them as a more advanced type of soul. But in Stoic theory, reason is not just one additional endowment among others. In other words, a human soul in no way amounts to simply the capacities of an animal soul, *as they function in animals* (i.e., non-rationally), with reason added on as a distinct new element.[74] Reason transforms the very nature of the human soul, making its capacities thoroughly rational. So human beings, for the Stoics, experience only *rational* impulses. In Philo's view, by contrast, the capacities of the animal soul, *as they function in animals* (i.e., non-rationally), remain intact within the human soul, coexisting with reason in what amounts to an animal soul superintended by reason:

> Each one of us ... is two in number (ἀριθμῷ δύο εἶναι), an animal and a man (ζῷόν τε καὶ ἄνθρωπον). To each of these has been allotted an inner power akin to the qualities of their respective life-principles (συγγενὴς δύναμις τῶν κατὰ ψυχήν), to one the power of vitality (ἡ ζωτική), in virtue of which we are alive, to the other the power of reasoning (ἡ λογική), in virtue of which we are reasoning beings. Of the power of vitality the non-rational creatures (τὰ ἄλογα) partake with us .... (*Det.* 82)[75]

104: τὰς ὁρμὰς τῆς διανοίας). But the issue is not whether the mind can generate impulses or not (it can), but whether or not there are *also* non-rational parts of the soul capable of generating non-rational impulses. Previous studies of Philo's concept of emotion(s) (see above, p. 9, n. 33) do not fully account for the role of non-rational impulse, which in itself proves the fundamentally Platonic (*not* Stoic) orientation of Philo's perspective (see above, p. 46, n. 49). On ὁρμή in Philo's writings, including rational ὁρμή, see Schmidt, *Anthropologie*, 86–87.

[72] E.g., *Leg.* 2.23: ψυχὴ δέ ἐστι φύσις προσειληφυῖα φαντασίαν καὶ ὁρμήν· αὕτη κοινὴ καὶ τῶν ἀλόγων ἐστίν (cf. *Leg.* 1.30; *Deus* 41). On the *scala naturae*, see Inwood, *Ethics and Human Action*, 18–27 [="The Place of Man in Nature"].

[73] For a discussion of how impulse works in non-rational animals, see Inwood, *Ethics and Human Action*, 66–91 [="Human and Animal Action"].

[74] See Long, "Stoic Psychology," esp. 574–75.

[75] Substituting "each" for Colson's "either"; "non-rational" for Colson's "irrational." For Philo, ἡ ζωτικὴ δύναμις (the life power of the ζῷον) includes ὁρμή: e.g., *Leg.* 1.30: τὸ γὰρ ζῷον τοῦ μὴ ζῴου δυσὶ προὔχει, φαντασίᾳ καὶ ὁρμῇ (cf. *Leg.* 2.23; *Deus* 41). Furthermore, Philo states that ἡ ζωτικὴ δύναμις, including ὁρμή, retains its distinct

This Middle-Platonic understanding of the *scala naturae* gives Plato's image of the "beast within" a more sophisticated theoretical basis—one that has profound implications for Philo's moral psychology. In particular, Philo considers the same mechanism of non-rational impulse found in animals to operate also in human beings. Just like non-rational animals, human beings experience non-rational impulses (ἄλογοι ὁρμαί).[76]

In his description of Moses, Philo presents an idealized portrait of reason's management of non-rational impulse(s):

> He did not ... allow the desires of adolescence (τὰς μειρακιώδεις ἐπιθυμίας) to go unbridled, ... But he kept a tight hold on them with the reins, as it

---

nature within the human soul, functioning for human beings as it does for non-rational animals (e.g., *Sacr.* 47: τὰς δὲ καθ'ἑτέραν ἐκδοχὴν ἀλόγους [δυνάμεις], οὐχ αἳ παρὰ τὸν ὀρθὸν λόγον εἰσὶν ἀλλ'ὅσαι μὴ λογικαί, ὧν καὶ τὰ ἄλογα ζῷα κοινωνεῖ; *Spec.* 3.99: τὸ τῆς ψυχῆς φαυλότερον εἶδος ... ἐν τῷ σώματι, τὸ ἄλογον, οὗ καὶ τὰ θηρία μετέσχηκεν); cf. Wolfson, *Philo*, 1:385–89 [="Animals and the Irrational Soul of Man"].

[76] In *QG* 1.55 (Petit), Philo acknowledges the reflexive generation of impulse (ὁρμή) at the mere *appearance* of something (ὅταν ... προσπέσῃ τινὸς φαντασία), i.e., without rational assent. In other words, he describes a mechanism of non-rational impulse *in human beings*. Commenting on the Armenian version of this passage, Margaret Graver correctly notes: "Here the 'impulse ... of which the appearance is the cause' cannot be the usual Stoic ὁρμή, since in adult humans ὁρμή is always caused by assent, never by the presentation itself" ("Stoic ΠΡΟΠΑΘΕΙΑΙ," 207, n. 19). She then suggests, however, that Philo, "using the term ὁρμή loosely," has in mind the Stoic technical term προπάθεια. But Philo more likely speaks with precision: he refers in this case to a *non-rational* ὁρμή (neither the rational ὁρμή of the Stoics, nor a προπάθεια). The suggestion that προπάθειαι played a meaningful role in Philo's theory of the passions presumes that rational *assent* (συγκατάθεσις) played a meaningful role as well: "Philo ... assumes that προπάθειαι can be called upon to explain away apparent exceptions to the posited incompatibility of virtue and emotion, taking advantage of a theoretical time-lag between impression and assent" (idem, 200–01); "Philo employs [the appeal to the προπάθειαι] only where there is some textual warrant for positing a time-lag between impression and assent" (205–06; cf. 208: "the gap between impression and assent"). Philo, however, in keeping with his Middle-Platonic affinities, nowhere brings συγκατάθεσις into his discussion of πάθος (cf. Pohlenz, *Philon*, 456, n. 1). He would have had precedent for his view of non-rational impulse in the Academic tradition, since Arcesilaus (ca. 316–240 B.C.E.), in dispute with the Stoics and using Stoic terminology, claimed that *in human beings* impulses reflexively occur in response to the appropriate sensory impression. See, e.g., LS 53S [=Plutarch, *Stoic. rep.* 1057 A (=SVF III 42, 22–27)]: οἰκείας φαντασίας γενομένης εὐθὺς ὁρμᾶν μὴ εἴξαντας μηδὲ συγκαταθεμένους; cf. LS 69A and commentary: "In effect, Arcesilaus applies to human action the Stoics' account of non-rational animal behaviour" (LS 1:456) (see also Inwood, *Ethics and Human Action*, 86–88). For the terminology of ἄλογοι ὁρμαί, see, e.g., *Leg.* 3.185: ἄλογος ὁρμή; *Ebr.* 98: ἐν ἡμῖν αἱ ἄλογοι ὁρμαί; *Ebr.* 111: πάθους ἀλόγοις ὁρμαῖς (cf. *Det.* 5: τὰς ψυχῆς ἀλόγους φοράς; *Agr.* 41: τῆς ἀνθρώπων ἁπάντων ἀλόγου φορᾶς; *Spec.* 3.129: ἀλόγῳ φορᾷ). Elsewhere Philo indicates ἄλογοι ὁρμαί by using the term ὁρμή when he means ἐπιθυμία (ἄλογος ὄρεξις: non-rational appetite), referring to basic desires for food, drink, and sex (esp. *Spec.* 1.101: ταῖς πρὸς συνουσίαν ὁρμαῖς; *Spec.* 1.193: ἐπιστομίζοντας τὰς ἐφ'ἡδονὴν ὁρμάς).

were, of temperance and self-control, and forcibly pulled them back from their forward course (τὴν εἰς τὸ πρόσω φορὰν ἀνεχαίτιζε βίᾳ). And each of the other emotions (τῶν ἄλλων μέντοι παθῶν ἕκαστον), which rage so furiously if left to themselves, he tamed and assuaged and reduced to mildness; ... and in general he watched *the first directions and impulses of the soul* (τὰς πρώτας τῆς ψυχῆς ἐπιβολάς τε καὶ ὁρμάς) as one would a restive horse (ὡς ἀφηνιαστὴν ἵππον), in fear *lest they should run away with the reason which ought to rein them in* (μὴ προεκδραμοῦσαι τοῦ ἡνιοχεῖν ὀφείλοντος λογισμοῦ), and thus cause universal chaos. For it is these impulses (αὗται) which cause both good and bad (εἰσιν αἱ ἀγαθῶν αἴτιαι καὶ κακῶν)—good when they obey the guidance of reason (ὅταν ἡγεμόνι λόγῳ πειθαρχῶσι), bad when they turn from their regular course into anarchy. (*Mos.* 1.25–26; emphasis added)[77]

The characterization here of reason's *relation* to impulse illustrates the Middle-Platonic perspective evident throughout Philo's writings.[78] The "primary impulses" (πρῶται ὁρμαί) clearly arise apart from reason, since reason must act *upon* them, actively managing them as a rational human being would manage a non-rational animal (ἀφηνιαστὴν ἵππον).[79] Although quite dangerous when left to themselves, these impulses are not inherently bad. Their moral import lies entirely in their relation to reason—viz., whether or not they obey its commanding authority (ἡγεμόνι λόγῳ πειθαρχῶσι).

In this passage, Philo does not name the source of the impulses, but clearly desire (ἐπιθυμία) and the "other emotions" (πάθη) derive from the same source. This grouping of ὁρμή, ἐπιθυμία, and πάθος over against reason reflects the Middle-Platonic dichotomy between "rational part" (λογικὸν μέρος) and "non-rational part" (ἄλογον μέρος) evident among Philo's contemporaries. In particular, the placement of *emotion* within the soul's non-rational part bears special significance for Philo's moral theory.

Reason over against Emotion (πάθος)

Philo agrees with his Middle-Platonic contemporaries, against the Stoics, when he locates emotion (πάθος) *outside of* the rational faculty *within* the

---

[77] Substituting "desires" for Colson's "lusts"; "emotions" for Colson's "passions."
[78] Along with τὰς πρώτας ... ὁρμάς, the phrase τὴν εἰς τὸ πρόσω φοράν denotes impulse as well (cf. *Deus* 149: τὴν εἰς τὸ πρόσω ... ὁρμήν). On the essential synonymy of ὁρμή and φορά, note the generic Stoic definition of impulse: τὴν δὲ ὁρμὴν εἶναι φορὰν ψυχῆς ἐπί τι κατὰ τὸ γένος (*ESE* 9). On "primary impulse," see Inwood, *Ethics and Human Action*, 184–94, 218–23.
[79] Cf. *Spec.* 2.142: ἐὰν λογισμῷ τὰς πρώτας ἡνιοχῶμεν ὁρμὰς μὴ ἐπιτρέποντες αὐταῖς ἀφηνιάζειν καὶ ἀνασκιρτᾶν τρόπον θρεμμάτων ἀγελάρχην οὐκ ἐχόντων; *Spec.* 3.79: οἳ ταῖς πρώταις εὐθὺς ὁρμαῖς ἐνδιδόντες, ὁποῖαί περ ἂν οὖσαι τυγχάνωσιν, ἃς ἡνιοχεῖν δέον ἀχαλινώτους ἐῶσιν.

non-rational part of the soul.[80] In *Leg.* 3.114–16, Philo identifies the two non-rational "parts" of the Platonic soul (θυμός and ἐπιθυμία) as the locus of emotion (πάθος):[81]

> If, therefore, O mind, thou art ever inquiring what quarter pleasure (ἡδονή) has for her portion, do not consider the place occupied by the head, where the reasoning faculty resides (ὅπου τὸ λογιστικόν), *for thou wilt assuredly not find it there*, since reason is at war with emotion (μάχεται ὁ λόγος τῷ πάθει), and cannot remain in the same place with it (ἐν ταὐτῷ μένειν οὐ δύναται).... But look for it in the breast and belly, where high spirit (ὁ θυμός) and desire (ἡ ἐπιθυμία) are, portions of the non-rational (μέρη τοῦ ἀλόγου); for in the non-rational part of the soul (ἐν αὐτῷ) are found both our "judgment" (κρίσις) and the resulting emotions (τὰ πάθη). (*Leg.* 3.116)[82]

In this passage, the "judgment" (κρίσις) Philo places within the non-rational part of the soul must refer to the non-rational *discernment* exercised by sense-perception (αἴσθησις), which can result in non-rational emotion, *not* the mind's irrational "judgments" (κρίσεις), which Stoics equated with emotion.[83] In fact, Philo elsewhere explicitly rejects the Stoic view:

---

[80] E.g., *QG* 2.59 (Gk. Petit): περὶ σάρκα δὲ ἡ αἴσθησις καὶ τὸ πάθος, οὐχ ὁ νοῦς καὶ ὁ λογισμός (cf. Pohlenz, *Philon*, 458); cf. *Migr.* 25–26, which pits ὁ νοῦς against non-rational emotion (πάθους ἀλόγου). Schmidt (*Anthropologie*, 88) correctly notes Philo's assignment of emotion to the non-rational part of the soul, but he incorrectly associates this view with Posidonius: "Er weist in Übereinstimmung mit Poseidonios die Affekte dem unvernünftigen Seelenteile zu und lehnt ausdrücklich ihren Platz im Kopf, d.h. am Sitz des vernünftigen Seelenteils, ab, während sie nach stoischer Anschauung sich gerade im Hegemonikon vollziehen sollen." On Posidonius's adherence to the Stoic conviction that emotion per se derives *from the mind*, despite the involvement of non-rational factors, see Cooper, "Posidonius on Emotions."

[81] Philo's remarks on the locus of emotion appear in the context of an allegorical interpretation of the serpent's curse in Gen 3:14: "Ἐπὶ τῷ στήθει σου καὶ τῇ κοιλίᾳ πορεύσῃ." Since for him the serpent stands for pleasure (ἡδονή), he immediately frames his interpretation in terms of πάθος: περὶ γὰρ ταῦτα φωλεύει τὰ μέρη τὸ πάθος, τά τε στέρνα καὶ τὴν γαστέρα (*Leg.* 3.114). On θυμός and ἐπιθυμία as emotion, note esp. *Agr.* 78: θυμοῦ ... καὶ ἐπιθυμίας καὶ συνόλως ἁπάντων παθῶν.

[82] Emphasis added; substituting "emotion" for Colson's "passion" and "non-rational" for "irrational"; my translation of the final phrase: ἐν αὐτῷ γὰρ εὑρίσκεται καὶ ἡ κρίσις ἡ ἡμετέρα καὶ τὰ πάθη. On this passage, see also Lévy, "Philon et les passions," 33–34, and Winston, "Philo on the Emotions," 208–09. Although helpful in many respects, the studies of Lévy ("Philon et les passions"; cf. "Philo's Ethics," 154–64) and Winston ("Philo on the Emotions") do not appreciate the crucial significance of Philo's acknowledgement (*against* the Stoics, *including* Posidonius) of non-rational impulse in adult human beings (see above, p. 46, n. 49).

[83] DL 7.111: "They hold the emotions to be judgments (δοκεῖ δ'αὐτοῖς τὰ πάθη κρίσεις εἶναι), as is stated by Chrysippus in his treatise *On the Passions* (Περὶ παθῶν)" (trans. R.D. Hicks). Construing κρίσις in *Leg.* 3.116 as "the discernment exercised by sense-perception" makes sense for at least three reasons. First, by distinguishing it *from* τὸ λογιστικόν and aligning it *with* the soul's non-rational (ἄλογος) component, Philo

The non-rational part of the soul consists of sense-perception and its offspring the emotions, which are also non-rational—*especially* if they are not our "judgments" (κρίσεις). (*Leg.* 2.6)[84]

As part of the non-rational equipment of the soul, emotions are an endowment of human nature.[85] In this respect, emotions are akin to a natural

---

implies a non-rational mode of operation for κρίσις in this case. Second, Philo elsewhere uses κρίσις in reference to the function of sense-perception (αἴσθησις)—e.g., *Somn.* 1.28: "Sound (φωνή), too, does not entirely elude our discernment (τὴν ἡμετέραν κρίσιν)" (cf. *Congr.* 21: κρίνει δὲ τὸ αἰσθητὸν αἴσθησις). Third, Philo elsewhere couples αἴσθησις and πάθος (e.g., *Leg.* 2.50: τὴν παθῶν αἰτίαν αἴσθησιν), so his coupling of κρίσις (as function of non-rational αἴσθησις) and πάθος in this passage fits within that broader association. As a translation, the phrase "both our 'judgment' (κρίσις) and the resulting emotions (τὰ πάθη)" interprets Philo's remarks as both an *allusion* to the Stoic concept and a clever *rejection* of it: i.e., Middle Platonists—along with the Stoics—acknowledge a connection between κρίσις and πάθος, but they radically relocate that connection, and its essential character, from the soul's *rational* part to its *non-rational* part. In addition, the translation suggests the sort of connection Philo envisions between αἴσθησις and πάθος (i.e., "resulting").

[84] τὸ δὲ ἄλογον αἴσθησίς ἐστι καὶ τὰ ταύτης ἔκγονα πάθη, καὶ μάλιστα εἰ μὴ κρίσεις εἰσὶν ἡμέτεραι. The translation (my own) freely interprets the Greek, but the obscurity of the construction calls for it. Despite Philo's wording, his *meaning* is clear, given the broader context of the passage (*Leg.* 2.1–8). In the course of his allegorical exegesis of Gen 2:8, Philo establishes the following points: the soul is divided into rational (λογικόν) and non-rational (ἄλογον) parts (*Leg.* 2.2); to assist the mind (νοῦς [rational part]), God *separately* fashioned sense-perception (αἴσθησις) and emotions (πάθη) as "helpers" (*Leg.* 2.5); the rational "ruling part" of the soul (τὸ ἡγεμονικὸν τῆς ψυχῆς) holds preeminence over the non-rational part (τὸ ἄλογον), which consists of the "helpers" sense-perception and emotion, which in turn represent a distinct, inferior order of creation (*Leg.* 2.6); mind, sense-perception, and the emotions are distinct "parts" (μέρη) of one soul (ψυχή) (*Leg.* 2.8). Philo *clearly* affirms Middle-Platonic bipartition in this passage: λογικὸν μέρος over against ἄλογον μέρος. He *clearly* assigns the πάθη to the soul's non-rational part, identifying them as something *other than* reason and therefore not *functions* of reason. There cannot be any real question in Philo's mind as to whether or not the passions are judgments, because he repeatedly and unmistakably claims that they are not, insofar as he identifies them as something distinctly *other than* the rational faculty. By using the term κρίσεις in connection with πάθη, Philo undoubtedly alludes to the Stoic doctrine, which he cites only to reject. Commentators who understand *Leg.* 2.6 in this way include Bréhier, *Idées philosophiques et religieuses*, 263; Le Boulluec, "Philon sur le plaisir," 137; Pohlenz, *Philon*, 458–59; Schmidt, *Anthropologie*, 88. Alcinous, in his Middle-Platonic treatment of the passions, similarly cites *and rejects* the Stoic view that passions are judgments (κρίσεις) (*Didask.* 32.1 [185.24–42]). Lilla not only understands Philo to reject the idea of passions as judgments in *Leg.* 2.6 (*Clement of Alexandria*, 92) but also more generally identifies the "refusal to regard [πάθος] as a wrong judgement of reason" as one of three principal tenets in the Middle-Platonic doctrine of πάθος (idem, 87); cf. Le Boulluec, "Philon sur le plaisir," 131: "Une altération sensible consiste à dissocier «passion» ... et capacité intellectuelle."

[85] They are also, for that matter, an endowment of *animal* nature. Just as human beings have within them a mechanism of non-rational impulse analogous to the mechanism within non-rational animals, they also have within them a mechanism of

faculty (δύναμις) and comparable to other faculties, such as sense-perception.[86] Philo acknowledges the natural occurrence of non-rational πάθη most clearly in *Congr.* 81, where he notes that before the onset of mature rational calculation (λογισμός) children have only their emotions (πάθη) to guide them.[87]

Because they are not intrinsically immoral, these emotions can provide non-rational motivation for perfectly natural, ethically appropriate behavior.[88] Philo accordingly asserts that *God created the emotions* as "helpers" (βοηθοί) for the human race:

> Moreover, there are, as I have said, helpers of another kind (ἕτερον εἶδος βοηθῶν), namely the emotions (τὰ πάθη). For pleasure (ἡδονή) and desire (ἐπιθυμία) contribute to the permanence of our kind: pain (λύπη) and fear (φόβος) are like bites or stings warning the soul to treat nothing carelessly: anger (ὀργή) is a weapon of defense, which has conferred great boons on many (μεγάλα πολλοὺς ὠφέλησε): and so with the other emotions (καὶ τᾶλλα ταύτῃ). (*Leg.* 2.8)[89]

The emotion of ἐπιθυμία, for example, can be especially useful, and in fact *necessary*, as a non-rational motivator for the procurement of food and

---

emotion (which consists of non-rational impulses) analogous to the emotional mechanism of non-rational animals. For a consideration of the nature of *animal* emotion, see Juha Sihvola, "Emotional Animals: Do Aristotelian Emotions Require Beliefs?," in *Psychology and Ethics* (ed. Lloyd P. Gerson; vol. 3 of *Aristotle: Critical Assessments*; London: Routledge, 1999), 50–82.

[86] E.g., *Abr.* 236: τὰς ἐν ἡμῖν τῶν τεττάρων παθῶν δυνάμεις, ἡδονῆς, ἐπιθυμίας, φόβου, λύπης.

[87] See esp. *Congr.* 81–82, on which Le Boulluec ("Philon sur le plaisir," 131) notes: "Prises en elles-mêmes, les quatre «passions» principales, chagrin, peur, désir, plaisir, semblent selon Philon moralement neutres"; cf. Lévy, "Philon et les passions,"; idem, "Philo's Ethics," 158.

[88] Cf. Williamson, *Philo*, 203–04.

[89] Substituting "emotion" for Colson's "passion." Philo's allegorical exegesis of Gen 2:19 (see *Leg.* 2.9) equates the πάθη with the "beasts" (τὰ θηρία) God created then presented to Adam as "helpers." Because he considers the emotions morally dangerous, Philo qualifies this identification (see *Leg.* 2.10–11), but he never denies it outright. In *Plant.* 43, he similarly equates θηρία with πάθη, acknowledging their ferocity but nevertheless admitting that they are a necessary component of life in the body (N.B. ἐξ ἀνάγκης; cf. *Praem.* 88). On Philo's allegorical equation of beasts with emotions, see Carl Siegfried, *Philo von Alexandria als Ausleger des Alten Testaments* (Jena: Hermann Dufft, 1875), 182–84, esp. 182: "Die Thiere, *insofern sie vernunftlose Wesen sind*, werden Symbole der Leidenschaften, welche ebenfalls das ἄλογον im Menschen darstellen" (emphasis added). A similar Middle-Platonic understanding of the emotions appears in *Didask.* 32.4 [186.14–29], where Alcinous discusses "wild" and "tame" emotions: τῶν δὲ παθῶν τὰ μέν ἐστιν ἄγρια, τὰ δὲ ἥμερα [186.14–15]. "Tame" emotions are ὅσα κατὰ φύσιν ὑπάρχει τῷ ἀνθρώπῳ ἀναγκαῖά τε καὶ οἰκεῖα [186.16–17]. These emotions only become problematic when they exhibit a lack of moderation (ἀμετρίας) [186.18].

drink, both of which are obviously necessary for survival.[90] So, for example, in the case of desire for food, virtue requires not the eradication of ἐπιθυμία but its proper management by reason. In general, Philo promotes the value of restraint by endorsing the *moderation* of emotion (μετριοπάθεια) as an ethical norm, although he admits the theoretical possibility of a perfect sage becoming free from the influence of emotion (ἀπάθεια).[91]

Reason over against Sense-Perception (αἴσθησις)

Philo holds yet another conception of the soul's bipartition between rational and non-rational—one closely related to the dichotomy of reason over against *emotion*—which despite a relative lack of attestation among his contemporaries still bears Middle-Platonic affinities: a bipartition of *mind* (νοῦς) over against *sense-perception* (αἴσθησις).[92] Xenocrates (396–314

---

[90] Plato, *Resp.* 558 D–E: "[D]esires that we cannot divert or suppress may be properly called necessary (ἀναγκαῖαι), and likewise those whose satisfaction is beneficial to us (ὠφελοῦσιν ἡμᾶς), may they not? For our nature compels us to seek their satisfaction (τῇ φύσει ἀνάγκη)." Cf. Philo, *Leg.* 1.86 (substituting "desire" for Colson's "lust"): "Mark you not that even the most self-controlled of men (οἱ ἐγκρατέστατοι) under compulsion of the mortal element in them (ἀνάγκῃ τοῦ θνητοῦ) resort to food and drink (σιτία καὶ ποτά), out of which the pleasures of the appetite develop (ἐξ ὧν αἱ γαστρὸς ἡδοναὶ συνεστᾶσιν)? So we must be content to face and fight desire as a principle (ἀντιβῆναι καὶ μαχέσασθαι τῷ γένει τῆς ἐμιθυμίας)" (cf. *Leg.* 3.147; *Ebr.* 214; *Contempl.* 37).

[91] Philo in fact endorses *both* μετριοπάθεια and ἀπάθεια, as the respective goals for intermediate and advanced stages of ethical development (see esp. Lilla, *Clement of Alexandria*, 92–106; also Lévy, "Philon et les passions," 36–37; idem, "Philo's Ethics," 160–61; Richard Sorabji, *Emotion and Peace of Mind: From Stoic Agitation to Christian Temptation: The Gifford Lectures* [Oxford: Oxford University Press, 2000], 385–86; Spanneut, "Apatheia," 4701–04; Williamson, *Philo*, 205–07; Winston, "Philo's Ethical Theory," 400–05; idem, "Philo on the Emotions," 207–11). But since ἀπάθεια presumes a sort of moral perfection, μετριοπάθεια becomes, practically speaking, the ethical ideal (e.g., *Virt.* 195: αἰδὼς καὶ ἀλήθεια μετριοπάθειά τε καὶ ἀτυφία καὶ ἀκακία τίμια; cf. Gemünden, "Culture des passions," 339–42; Williamson, *Philo*, 206). Philo's concept of ἀπάθεια differs from the *Stoic* concept of ἀπάθεια, in accordance with his rejection of Stoic monistic psychology. Whereas the Stoics envision a mind that avoids false assessments of value and thus avoids passions, Philo envisions a mind so divorced from the sensible world, and so immersed in the intelligible world, that it operates free from the influence of emotions (e.g., *Congr.* 106: τὸ ψυχικὸν Πάσχα, ἡ <ἀπὸ> παντὸς πάθους καὶ παντὸς αἰσθητοῦ διάβασις πρὸς ... ὃ δὴ νοητόν ἐστι καὶ θεῖον; cf. *Leg.* 1.103; *Ebr.* 99–103; *Fug.* 91). Plutarch promotes a similar Middle-Platonic notion of ἀπάθεια, while at the same time endorsing μετριοπάθεια, as Christopher Gill notes in his comment on *Virt. mor.* 444 C–D: "[T]here are two ideals: *apatheia* for the mind as the vehicle of abstract thought and knowledge and *metriopatheia* for the body-based emotions as regulated by practical reason" (*The Structured Self in Hellenistic and Roman Thought* [Oxford: Oxford University Press, 2006], 238).

[92] On Philo's dichotomy between mind and sense-perception in the context of Middle Platonism, see esp. Bouffartigue, "Structure de l'âme chez Philon," 62–73; also Runia,

B.C.E.), third scholarch of Plato's Academy, used the *Timaeus* to endorse a bipartition of the soul into λογικόν and αἰσθητικόν, indicating a dichotomy between parts of the soul geared respectively to the intelligible (νοητός) and sensible (αἰσθητός) realms.[93] In this view, sense-perception, a non-rational component of the soul, stems from embodiment and entails the emotions—so αἴσθησις (like πάθος) often *opposes* νοῦς (and intelligible realities) through its attachment to the sensible realm.[94] Philo affirms the non-rationality of αἴσθησις,[95] its close association with the emotions,[96] its link to the *sensible* over against *intelligible* realm,[97] and particularly its capacity to *oppose* νοῦς:

> Now the younglings that are reared among the herd are tame and docile, because they are guided by the care of the herdsman who rules them (ὑπὸ ἐπιστάτου ... βουκόλου). For those that roam at large and in liberty become wild (ἐξαγριαίνεται) for want of one to tame them, but those who are led by goatherd, neat-herd, shepherd, and the like, the herdsman, that is, who tends whatever kind of animal it may be, must needs be tame and gentle (ἡμεροῦται). So then, the senses also as a kind (τὸ αἰσθήσεων γένος) may be either wild or tame. They are wild (ἀτίθασον) when, throwing off the control of their herdsman the mind (ἀφηνιάσαν ὥσπερ βουκόλου τοῦ νοῦ), they are carried away in their unreason (ἀλόγως) into the outer sphere of

---

Philo and the Timaeus, 262–66; Thomas H. Tobin, *The Creation of Man: Philo and the History of Interpretation* (CBQMS 14; Washington: Catholic Biblical Association America, 1983), 148–49; cf. Gérard-Henry Baudry, "Le péché original chez Philon d'Alexandrie," *MScRel* 50 (1993): 99–115; Petra von Gemünden, "La femme passionnelle et l'homme rationnel? Un chapitre de psychologie historique," *Biblica* 78 (1997): 457–80, 468–70.

[93] See Schibli, "Xenocrates' Daemons," esp. 149–53. For Xenocrates, "τὸ αἰσθητικόν points to that part of the soul which links the psyche to the material, sensate world (the αἰσθητὴ οὐσία); as such it merely serves as the conduit for sensations and operates without reason. The dichotomy of τὸ αἰσθητικόν—τὸ λογικόν not only implies that the sensitive element lacks what its counterpart possesses, but it conceivably also points to the antithetical dimension of the two divisions, in so far as the sensible part may give rise to affections and passions that militate against reason, and that reason in turn must conquer" (153).

[94] See esp. *Tim.* 42 A–B (cf. *Didask.* 16.2 [172.2–19]). On αἴσθησις and embodiment, N.B. *Congr.* 21: αἴσθησις δέ, τὸ σωματοειδέστερον ψυχῆς μέρος.

[95] E.g., *Leg.* 3.50: αἴσθησις ... ἄλογος οὖσα; *Spec.* 2.89: αἴσθησις ... ἡ κοινὴ καὶ τῶν ἀλόγων ζῴων (cf. *Leg.* 1.24; *Migr.* 213; *Spec.* 4.123).

[96] E.g., *Leg.* 2.6: τὸ δὲ ἄλογον αἴσθησίς ἐστι καὶ τὰ ταύτης ἔκγονα πάθη; *Leg.* 2.50: τὴν παθῶν αἰτίαν αἴσθησιν (cf. *Abr.* 236–39).

[97] For the distinction between realms, note esp. *Her.* 75: δύο γὰρ ἔοικε συστῆναι, τὸ μὲν νοητόν, τὸ δ'αἰσθητόν. αἰσθητῶν μὲν οὖν φύσεων ὁ κόσμος οὗτος, ἀοράτων δ'ὡς ἀληθῶς ὁ νοητός (cf. *Her.* 209: τἄλλα δὲ ἐναντία ... αἰσθητὰ νοητά). For αἴσθησις as link to sensible realm, see (e.g.) *Her.* 111: νῷ γὰρ ὁ θεὸς καταλαμβάνειν τὸν μὲν νοητὸν κόσμον δι'ἑαυτοῦ, τὸν δὲ ὁρατὸν δι'αἰσθήσεως ἐφῆκεν. See also David Runia, "A Brief History of the Term *Kosmos Noetos* from Plato to Plotinus," in *Traditions of Platonism: Essays in Honour of John Dillon* (ed. John J. Cleary; Aldershot: Ashgate, 1999), 151–71.

things perceptible by them (πρὸς τά ... αἰσθητά). They are tame (ἥμερον) when they respond submissively to reflection (λογισμῷ), the ruling element in our compound nature, and accept its guidance and control. (*Sacr.* 104–05)

Here Philo casts αἴσθησις as a non-rational animal in need of a rational ruler (ἐπιστάτης), the mind (νοῦς). With the mind in charge, αἴσθησις functions like an obedient, tame creature.[98] But αἴσθησις can become "wild," rejecting the authority of reason and bringing destructive chaos to the soul.[99] This sort of relation between νοῦς and αἴσθησις fits Philo's general characterization of Middle-Platonic bipartition: a rational element placed over a non-rational element, one capable of opposing or even *usurping* reason's hegemony. This emphasis on νοῦς over against αἴσθησις allows Philo to press another model of the soul, an otherwise *Stoic* model, into Middle-Platonic service.

Reason over against "Stoic" Non-Rational Soul

For Stoics, the soul has eight parts: the rational mind (ἡγεμονικόν), plus the five senses, the faculty of speech, and the faculty of reproduction.[100] On the surface, this Stoic model resembles Philo's Middle-Platonic dichotomy of νοῦς over against αἴσθησις: not only does the Stoic soul divide into a rational and a non-rational component (ἡγεμονικόν plus collective seven), but the senses account for five of the seven non-rational parts. So a loose description of *both* models as rational mind over non-rational sense-perception fits the data reasonably well. In terms of moral psychology, however, the two models are fundamentally incompatible. The non-rational parts of the Stoic soul operate *only* by order of the ἡγεμονικόν in a *strictly* instrumental capacity.[101] Under no circumstances would—or *could*—αἴσθησις ever oppose, let alone usurp, the ἡγεμονικόν.[102] Yet Philo, who clearly

---

[98] E.g., *Det.* 53: τιμή ... τῆς δὲ αἰσθήσεως τὸ μὴ ἀφεθῆναι ῥύμῃ μιᾷ φέρεσθαι πρὸς τὰ ἐκτὸς αἰσθητά, ἐγχαλινωθῆναι δὲ ὑπὸ νοῦ κυβερνᾶν καὶ ἡνιοχεῖν τὰς ἀλόγους ἐν ἡμῖν δυνάμεις ἐπισταμένου.
[99] E.g., *Leg.* 3.224: ἐπειδὰν μὲν ὁ τῆς ψυχῆς ἡνίοχος ἢ κυβερνήτης ὁ νοῦς ἄρχῃ τοῦ ζῴου ὅλου ... εὐθύνεται ὁ βίος, ὅταν δὲ ἡ ἄλογος αἴσθησις φέρηται τὰ πρωτεῖα, σύγχυσις καταλαμβάνει δεινή, οἷα δούλων δεσπόταις ἐπιτεθειμένων.
[100] See Inwood, *Ethics and Human Action*, 27–41; Long, *Stoic Psychology*, esp. 560–72.
[101] Inwood, *Ethics and Human Action*, 33.
[102] Because αἴσθησις clearly *does* function in this way for Philo, his understanding of αἴσθησις cannot be called Stoic (cf. Pohlenz, *Philon*, 456–57, esp. 456: "[F]ür ihn wächst die Aisthesis weit über die Rolle hinaus, die ihr nach der Stoa zukommen kann. Sie wird zu einem selbständigen seelischen Vermögen, das dem Nus wohl unentbehrlich für die Erkenntnis der Außenwelt ist und ihm damit gute Dienste tut, aber zugleich, da

knows and *cites* the Stoic eight-part model,[103] characterizes its non-rational component as an antagonist of reason, able not only to oppose but even to supplant and enslave its rightful sovereign:

> [S]ix of [the faculties within us] wage ceaseless and continuous war on land and sea, namely the five senses (αἵ τε πέντε αἰσθήσεις) and speech (ὁ προφορικὸς λόγος), the former in their craving for the objects of sense (πόθῳ τῶν αἰσθητῶν), deprivation of which is painful to them, speech because with unbridled mouth (ἀχαλίνῳ στόματι) it perpetually gives utterance where silence is due. But the seventh faculty is that of the dominant mind (ἡ περὶ τὸν ἡγεμόνα νοῦν), which, *after triumphing over the six and returning victorious through its superior strength* (δυνατωτέρᾳ ῥώμῃ κατακρατήσας), welcomes solitude and rejoices in its own society .... (*Abr.* 29–30)[104]

Philo's omission here of the faculty of reproduction, making a soul of *seven* parts instead of the canonical *eight*, illustrates his willingness to adapt the Stoic model for use in a Middle-Platonic context.[105] He has no real commitment to the *Stoic* doctrine, but he insists on the Middle-Platonic bipartition of rational over against non-rational, with the patently non-Stoic assumption of antagonism between the two components.[106] The Stoic formulation simply gives Philo more options when speaking of the soul's non-rational part: reason's non-rational antagonist can be αἴσθησις (as in the Middle-Platonic νοῦς-αἴσθησις dichotomy), or the faculty of reproduction, or the faculty of speech.[107] Philo does *not* endorse a Stoic understanding of the soul—he merely superimposes Middle-Platonic bipartition onto a Stoic formulation, always presuming a moral psychology incompatible with Stoic monism.

---

es auch die sinnlichen Triebe umfaßt, sein ständiger Widerpart wird und an die Stelle tritt, die in der griechischen Philosophie das Alogon einnimmt."

[103] E.g., *Opif.* 117: τῆς ἡμετέρας ψυχῆς τὸ δίχα τοῦ ἡγεμονικοῦ μέρος ἑπταχῇ σχίζεται, εἰς πέντε αἰσθήσεις καὶ τὸ φωνητήριον ὄργανον καὶ ἐπὶ πᾶσι τὸ γόνιμον (cf. *Leg.* 1.11; *Det.* 168; *Her.* 232; *Mut.* 111).

[104] Emphasis added.

[105] Although he omits one here, Philo *knows* all seven of the Stoic non-rational parts (e.g., *Det.* 168: τὸ ἄλογον τῆς ψυχῆς εἰς ἑπτὰ διανέμεται μοίρας, ὅρασιν ἀκοὴν ὄσφρησιν γεῦσιν ἀφὴν λόγον γόνιμον).

[106] For another example of Philo's recasting of the Stoic model as Middle-Platonic bipartition, see *Agr.* 30–34. On Philo's adaptive use of the Stoic model, see Carlos Lévy, "Le concept de doxa des Stoïciens à Philon d'Alexandrie: Essai d'étude diachronique" in *Passions and Perceptions: Studies in Hellenistic Philosophy of Mind* (ed. J. Brunschwig and M. Nussbaum; Cambridge: Cambridge University Press, 1993), 250–84, esp. 275–84.

[107] On the faculties of reproduction and speech as antagonists, see (e.g.) *Det.* 102–03.

Summary

Despite a variety of formulations, Philo ultimately endorses *one* basic model of the soul, setting rational over against non-rational in an often antagonistic bipartition:

Table Two: Variations of Bipartition in Philo's Writings

	"PLATONIC" THREE PARTS	APPETITE	IMPULSE	EMOTION	SENSE-PERCEPTION	"STOIC" EIGHT PARTS
RATIONAL[108]	λόγος	λόγος	λόγος	λόγος	λόγος (νοῦς)	λόγος (ἡγεμονικόν)
NON-RATIONAL	θυμός ἐπιθυμία	ὄρεξις	ὁρμή	πάθος	αἴσθησις	αἴσθησις (5) γόνη φωνή

Philo's Middle-Platonic contemporaries offered him various ways of framing his discourse on ἐπιθυμία. Undoubtedly, Plato's conviction that the soul contains an independent, enduring source of non-rational desire exerts a powerful influence: the term ἐπιθυμία stands often as a reference to either the Platonic *faculty* of desire (i.e., τὸ ἐπιθυμητικόν) or the *operation* of that faculty (i.e., ἐπιθυμίαι)—either, to use Platonic imagery, the beast itself or the beast in action.[109] Philo's Middle-Platonic moral psychology, however, allows for greater technical precision and more sophisticated conceptions of the phenomenon of desire. Philo can, for example, identify ἐπιθυμία as an ἄλογος ὄρεξις. In addition, he understands that ἐπιθυμία bears analysis as an impulse (ὁρμή), which in turn allows him to speak of discrete instances of desire using the technical language associated with ὁρμή. Or Philo can envision ἐπιθυμία as an *emotion* (πάθος), considering it— along with contemporary Middle Platonists—both a natural and amoral

---

[108] Schmidt (*Anthropologie*, 49–50) comments on Philo's various designations for the soul's rational part: "Für dieses oberste Vermögen, wodurch sich der Mensch von den Tieren unterscheidet, verwendet Philon nun außer Seele und Nus noch gleichbedeutend διάνοια, λογισμός, λόγος und die formale Bezeichnung ἡγεμονικόν, zwischen denen er ... nur des Stiles wegen wechselt". For extensive evidence of the interchangeability of terms, see idem, 139–42 (=n. 14).

[109] For Philo's Platonic comparison of τὸ ἐπιθυμητικόν (ἐπιθυμία) to a beast, see (e.g.) *Abr.* 160: τὸ σύμφυτον ἡμῖν θρέμμα ... τὴν ἐπιθυμίαν; *Spec.* 1.148: ἀλόγου θρέμματος, ἐπιθυμίας.

function of the non-rational, "emotional" part of the soul. Philo's dichotomy of νοῦς over against αἴσθησις offers him not only another model of bipartition, but also another way of envisioning desire: non-rational αἴσθησις yearning for the attractions of the sensible world.[110] Using this same notion of non-rational αἴσθησις, but adding the two non-rational faculties of reproduction and speech, Philo uses a reworked Stoic model for his Middle-Platonic moral psychology, facilitating, for example, his discussion of the *desire* to speak and the *desire* to keep silent.[111] All of these various conceptions of the soul and its faculties make it possible for Philo to understand and describe discrete instances of desire in a variety of equivalent ways. But no instance of ἐπιθυμία, however described, *necessarily* represents for Philo an ethical problem or malfunction of the soul. In fact, amoral desire serves a range of useful purposes. When Philo wants to speak of desire as an aberration, he turns to other conceptual models.

Problematic Malfunctions of Desire

Passionate Desire (πλεονάζουσα [ἄμετρος] ἐπιθυμία)

In Philo's view, the term ἐπιθυμία can refer also to "passionate desire," meaning non-rational desire that has overstepped the bounds of reason. For Middle Platonists, and Plato himself, ἐπιθυμία as such was normal and morally unobjectionable—an inevitable, often useful, part of human life. But certainly there were problematic manifestations of ἐπιθυμία, so Plato's heirs needed a precise model (comparable to the Stoic model) for explaining the mechanics of *problematic* desire. For the Stoics, problematic movements of the soul belonged under one rubric, "passion" (πάθος): the passions (πάθη), including ἐπιθυμία, were always and inherently bad. But for Middle Platonists, the term πάθος did not bear such an exclusively negative meaning. So despite the appeal—from the standpoint of systematic moral theory—of having *one* designated class of problematic phenomena, the label πάθος by itself would not work (as it did for the Stoics) because of its moral ambiguity. The technical Stoic *definition* of πάθος, however, was more promising, in particular the designation of πάθος as

---

[110] E.g., *Her.* 109: αἴσθησιν δὲ ἀκόρεστον, ἐμφορουμένην μὲν αἰεὶ τῶν αἰσθητῶν, ὑπὸ δὲ ἀκράτορος τῆς ἐπιθυμίας μηδέποτε ἐμπλησθῆναι δυναμένην; *Abr.* 29: αἴ τε πέντε αἰσθήσεις ... πόθῳ αἰσθητῶν; *Somn.* 2.267: τὸ κτηνῶδες θρέμμα, τὴν αἴσθησιν (cf. *Spec.* 1.148: ἀλόγου θρέμματος, ἐπιθυμίας).
[111] E.g., *Spec.* 4.90: ἐπιθυμοῦσιν ἢ τὰ λεκτέα σιωπᾶν ἢ τὰ ἡσυχαστέα λέγειν (cf. *Det.* 102).

"excessive impulse" (πλεονάζουσα ὁρμή).[112] Stoics and Middle Platonists, despite radically different views of the human soul, could agree on the following points: (1) the soul generates impulses (ὁρμαί); (2) some impulses are unobjectionable, some are problematic; (3) human appetition, generally speaking, bears analysis as either an unobjectionable or a problematic impulse. Middle Platonists, then, could preserve the analytic value of the Stoic *category* of "passion"(despite the ambiguity of the *term* πάθος from a Platonic perspective) by focusing on the term ὁρμή and radically reworking the Stoic notion of πλεονάζουσα ὁρμή.

What did the Stoics mean by "excessive impulse"? In accordance with Stoic psychology, the impulse had to be a rational impulse, a function of the mind, because the Stoics denied the existence of non-rational impulses in adult human beings. But in what sense is the impulse "excessive"?[113] Ultimately, the excess lies in a faulty—but nevertheless *reasoned*—assessment of something's value: an excessive, exorbitant *appraisal*.[114] The notion is strictly qualitative: an excessive impulse differs in quality from a non-excessive impulse in the same way that strict alternatives like "correct" and "incorrect" differ from one another. In this qualitative model, the only way to eliminate an "excessive impulse" is to abandon an incorrect rational assessment and make a different (correct) rational assessment. Nothing in the Stoic sources suggests a *quantitative* notion of excess: the idea that an impulse, whose essential nature never changes, proceeds along an incremental scale of measurement until at some point it goes too far, becoming too powerful, too intense, too big. On the contrary, the term πλεονάζουσα ὁρμή denoted for the Stoics the *quality* of a *rational* impulse.

The earliest extant evidence for a *Middle-Platonic* definition of πάθος using the *Stoic* terms πλεονάζουσα ὁρμή comes from Eudorus of Alexandria.[115] But no explanation survives from Eudorus of what he *meant* by that

---

[112] E.g., DL 7.110 [*SVF* I 50, 22–23]: αὐτὸ τὸ πάθος κατὰ Ζήνωνα ... ὁρμὴ πλεονάζουσα; *ESE* 10 [=*SVF* III 92, 11]: πάθος δ'εἶναί φασιν ὁρμὴν πλεονάζουσαν.

[113] On this question, see Inwood, *Ethics and Human Action*, 165–73.

[114] Cf. Frede, "Stoic Affections," 107: Due to their faulty assessments of objects, moral agents "feel impelled towards them or away from them, with an intensity which stands in no comparison to their real value, and which hence is excessive."

[115] Impulse was a principal topic in Eudorus's system of ethics: Ταῦτ'ἐστὶ τὰ πρῶτα μέρη τοῦ ἠθικοῦ λόγου θεωρητικόν, ὁρμητικόν, πρακτικόν (Mazz. 1.10 [=*Eclog.* 42.23]; cf. Bonazzi, "Eudorus' Psychology"). He took an interest in both the taxonomy of impulse and the relation between impulse and passions, in particular the notion of passion as an "excessive impulse": Τοῦ δὲ περὶ τῆς ὁρμῆς λόγου ὁ μέν ἐστι περὶ τῆς εἰδικῆς ὁρμῆς, ὁ δὲ περὶ παθῶν. Ἤτοι γὰρ πᾶν πάθος ὁρμὴ πλεονάζουσα ... (Mazz. 1.23–24 [=*Eclog.* 44.3–6]). Ps.-Timaeus (TL 73–74) similarly attests a Middle-Platonic use of Stoic terminology (πλεονάζεν ... ὁρμάς) with reference to the passions (τὰ πάθεα), which both Tobin

definition. If he simply meant what the Stoics meant, he would have endorsed the Stoic theory of impulse, which in turn implies an endorsement of Stoic monistic psychology. In that case, his association with Middle *Platonism*, which disagreed so sharply with the Stoics on the fundamentals of moral psychology, becomes difficult to explain. A more likely conjecture would have Eudorus revising the Stoic definition in accordance with the tenets of Middle-Platonic moral psychology.[116] Given Middle Platonism's strong association of impulse with the non-rational part of the soul, the impulse in question would most certainly be a non-rational impulse (ἄλογος ὁρμή).[117] Since non-rational impulses (like emotions) are not problematic as such, but only *become* problematic when they overstep the bounds of reason, "excessive" would then denote a non-rational impulse whose measure *exceeds* proper limits and becomes "immoderate" in a quantitative sense. When the bounds of reason are transgressed—precisely at that moment—an otherwise benign impulse of *emotion* (say, fear or desire) becomes a *passion*, a morally problematic, injurious force within the soul. In other words, *based on what is otherwise known of Middle-Platonic moral psychology*, a Middle Platonist speaking of πάθος as πελονάζουσα ὁρμή would have meant the excessive *quantity* of a *non-rational* impulse, not the aberrant *quality* of a *rational* impulse.[118] Exactly this sort of Middle-Platonic reinvention of Stoic ideas appears in the writings of Philo.

(*Timaios of Locri*, 79, n. 35) and Baltes (*Timaios Lokros*, 206–07) identify as an allusion to the Stoic definition of πάθος as ὁρμὴ πλεονάζουσα. Plutarch uses a similar Middle-Platonic concept of πάθος: τὰ δὲ πάθη σφωδρότητες ὁρμῶν (*An. corp.* 501 D), identified as an allusion to the Stoic definition by Francesco Becchi, "Plutarco tra Platonismo e Aristotelismo: La Filosofia come ΠΑΙΔΕΙΑ," in *Plutarco, Platón y Aristóteles: Actas del V Congreso Internacional de la I.P.S. : Madrid-Cuenca, 4–7 de mayo de 1999* (ed. Aurelio Peréz Jiménez et al.; Madrid: Ediciones Clásicas, 1999), 25–43, 32 (cf. *Virt. mor.* 444 B–C).

[116] Cf. Dillon, *Middle Platonists*, 122: "Eudorus' terminology is as fully Stoic as that of Antiochus [of Ascalon], although, like Antiochus, he would not have admitted that it was distinctively Stoic, but would claim it as the normal current language of philosophic discourse. We, from our perspective, attach too much importance to ferreting out Stoic, and even Epicurean, terms, in Platonic writers. By Eudorus's time, the technical language of philosophy was very largely uniform. *Only the meanings given to certain terms by the various schools might differ*" (emphasis added). For an example of Eudorus's revision of Stoic formulations in the area of *physics*, see Mauro Bonazzi, "Eudoro di Alessandria alle origini del platonismo imperiale," in *L'eridità platonica: Studi sul platonismo da Arcesilao a Proclo* (ed. Mauro Bonazzi and Vincenza Celluprica; Elenchos 45; Naples: Bibliopolis, 2005), 117–60, esp. 127–49.

[117] Cf. Bonazzi, "Eudorus' Psychology."

[118] John Dillon, *Middle Platonists*, 77–78, entertains this idea as a possibility but does not explore it further or mention it in connection with Eudorus. Speaking of Antiochus of Ascalon, he writes: "Antiochus, then, accepted the Stoic ideal of *apatheia* (freedom from passion) as opposed to the Academic-Peripatetic *metriopatheia* (moderation

In his most obvious citation of the Stoic definition, Philo *adds* one qualifying term, as if to clarify precisely what he means:

> [E]very "passion" (πάθος) is reprehensible (ἐπίληπτον), since we are morally responsible (ὑπαίτιος) for every unmeasured "excessive impulse" (ἄμετρος καὶ πλεονάζουσα ὁρμή). (*Spec.* 4.79)[119]

Philo grants, along with the Stoics, that a passion is an "excessive impulse"—but by "excessive" *he* means "immoderate" (ἄμετρος), something quite different from what the Stoics had in mind. The term ἄμετρος denotes quantitative excess: going beyond the proper *measure* (μέτρον) imposed by reason.[120] As a natural function of the human soul, non-rational impulse (ὁρμή) poses no threat while it operates within the bounds of reason. If, however, an impulse *exceeds* those bounds (i.e., if the non-rational force *usurps* reason's control), it becomes morally problematic (a "passion"). For a Middle Platonist like Philo, the term ἄμετρος best captured what was actually going wrong with the impulse; but the Stoic technical term

---

in the passions). It is not impossible, however, that Antiochus took the Stoic term and gave it a meaning consonant with Peripateticism. After all, he could argue, a passion is defined as an 'immoderate impulse' (*hormê pleonazousa*); if an impulse is under the control of moderation, it is not *pleonazousa*, and therefore not a passion 'within the meaning of the Act'. There were, after all, in Stoic theory, so-called 'equable states' (*eupatheiai*) corresponding to all of the *pathê* (except Distress, of which there could be no reasonable form), and it would not have been beyond the wit of Antiochus to equate these with the Peripatetic 'means'. The difference, he might well say, is more verbal than real." Just such a connection between the Peripatetic notion of mean (μέσον) and the *term* πλεονάζειν appears in *Eth. nic.* 1106 a 29–33: λέγω δὲ τοῦ μὲν πράγματος μέσον τὸ ἴσον ἀπέχον ἀφ'ἑκατέρου τῶν ἄκρων, ὅπερ ἐστὶν ἓν καὶ ταὐτὸν πᾶσιν, πρὸς ἡμᾶς δὲ ὃ μήτε πλεονάζει μήτε ἐλλείπει (cited by Francesco Becchi, "Platonismo medio ed etica Plutarchea," *Prometheus* 7 [1981]: 125–45 [part one], 263–84 [part two], 275, in the context of Middle-Platonic theories of virtue).
[119] My translation. Cf. *Virt. mor.* 444 B–C. Inwood, *Ethics and Human Action*, cites *Virt. mor.* 450 E–451 B & 444 C (304, n. 193) understanding Plutarch to mean that "excessiveness of impulse" is "a reference to the exceeding of some ideal and moderate degree of emotion in the soul" (170).
[120] Cf. *Agr.* 70: σὺν πλείονι ὁρμῇ πέραν ἐκφέρηται τοῦ μετρίου; *Spec.* 4.79: μέτρα ταῖς ὁρμαῖς ὁρίζειν; Petit, *QE* N° 24 (*Fragments non identifiés*) (cf. Marcus, PLCL suppl. 2, 261): Τὰ μέτρα πλεονάζοντα τὸν ὅρον ὑπερβαίνει ὡς γίνεσθαι τὴν μὲν ἄμετρον φρόνησιν πανουργίαν). Note also Plutarch, *Virt. mor.* 444 B: τὴν δ'ὁρμὴν τῷ πάθει ποιεῖ τὸ ἦθος, λόγου δεομένην ὁρίζοντος, ὅπως μετρία παρῇ καὶ μήθ'ὑπερβάλλῃ μήτ'ἐγκαταλείπῃ. On the ethics of *measure* in Middle Platonism, see Opsomer, "L'âme du monde," esp. 45–49 (cf. idem, "Plutarch's Platonism Revisited," in *L'eridità platonica: Studi sul platonismo da Arcesilao a Proclo* [ed. Mauro Bonazzi and Vincenza Celluprica; Elenchos 45; Naples: Bibliopolis, 2005], 163–200, esp. 180–83 [="Moral psychology and ethics"]).

πλεονάζειν worked as a synonym, and this equivalence enabled a deliberate pressing of the Stoic definition of "passion" into Middle-Platonic service.[121]

This Middle-Platonic reinvention of Stoic technical terminology allowed Philo to speak with greater precision about *problematic* desire over against amoral desire. Desire itself—understood variously as the Platonic ἐπιθυμητικόν, ἄλογος ὄρεξις, a type of ὁρμή, a useful *emotion* (πάθος), or some other expression of the non-rational soul (e.g., αἴσθησις)—was unobjectionable. But *passionate desire*—understood as an excessive (i.e., immoderate) desiderative impulse, and thus a "passion" by Stoic definition—was unquestionably a moral problem. In *Her.* 245, among the "deadly and irreconcilable enemies of the soul," Philo lists ὅσαι ἄλλαι ἐκ πλεοναζούσης ὁρμῆς εἰώθασι φύεσθαι ἄλογοι ἐπιθυμίαι, stating plainly that ἄλογοι ἐπιθυμίαι stem from "excessive impulse" (ἐκ πλεοναζούσης ὁρμῆς). He is obviously making use of the Stoic definition, but in Stoic theory an "excessive" desiderative impulse would simply be ἐπιθυμία: the term "irrational desire" (ἄλογος ἐπιθυμία), from their perspective, makes no sense, because ἐπιθυμία is *always* irrational—there is no other type. For a Middle Platonist, however, the term ἐπιθυμία by itself denotes the non-rational desire inherent in the soul, whose presence and operation do not necessarily result in irrational behavior, *provided that reason stays in control.* Only when the impulse of non-rational desire oversteps the bounds of reason does desire become "irrational": a non-rational desire usurps reason and becomes a dangerous force, capable of motivating a rational being to act contrary to reason (i.e., irrationally). So for Philo, as *Her.* 245 illustrates, ἄλογος ἐπιθυμία designates "irrational desire"—in other words, *problematic desire,* which appears only when an otherwise natural desiderative impulse oversteps reason and becomes "immoderate" (πλεονάζουσα [ἄμετρος]).[122] In connection with

---

[121] Cf. *Didask.* 32.2 [186.6–7]: πλεονάζει μέντοι ἐν τῷ λυπεῖσθαι καὶ ὀχλεῖσθαι, and the comments of Whittaker, *Alcinoos,* 148, n. 519: "Le terme stoïcien πλεονάζω (cf. SVF I. 205 et III. 479, etc.) a été adopté tant par les Moyen-platoniciens (cf. Eudore d'Alexandrie *ap.* Stobée, *Anth.* II. 44. 5 W.; Philon d'Alexandrie, *De spec. leg.* IV. 79; Plutarque, *De virt. mor.* 441 C; *Timée de Locres* 222. 14 M.) que par les Péripatéticiens (cf. Arius Didyme *ap.* Stobée, *Anth.* II. 38. 18–24 W.)."

[122] Cf. *Somn.* 2.276: ἡδονῆς καὶ ἐπιθυμίας καὶ πάσης πλεοναζούσης ὁρμῆς ... ἄλογον πάθος ἐπιτειχίζοντες ἡγεμόνι λογισμῷ (N.B. ἐπιθυμία = πλεονάζουσα ὁρμή = ἄλογον πάθος). Despite the apparently Stoic identification of ἐπιθυμία with πλεονάζουσα ὁρμή, Philo reveals his Middle-Platonic position by referring to this as an ἄλογον πάθος. For the Stoics *every* πάθος was irrational, so the term ἄλογον πάθος would strike them as redundant. But for a Middle-Platonist, who believes that non-rational ἐπιθυμία need not be "irrational," the term ἄλογον πάθος makes perfect sense: an *excessive* desiderative impulse represents an otherwise useful emotion (πάθος) that has *become* problematic and thus "irrational" (ἄλογον) This is precisely the idea underlying Philo's use of ἄλογος ἐπιθυμία in *Her.* 245. In other words, a non-rational force no longer under the

the revised Stoic definition of passion (ἄμετρος καὶ πλεονάζουσα ὁρμή), Philo cites the task of reason as μέτρα ταῖς ὁρμαῖς ὁρίζειν (see *Spec.* 4.79). Reason must impose boundaries on non-rational desire (ἐπιθυμία), lest it become *passionate desire* (ἄμετρος ἐπιθυμία).[123] This Middle-Platonic revision of Stoic terminology underlies expressions such as μέτρα ταῖς ἐπιθυμίαις περιθεῖναι (*Cherub.* 33) and μέτροις [ἐπιθυμίας] ... περιορίζων (*Spec.* 4.217).[124] Since ἐπιθυμία bears analysis as an impulse, πλεονάζουσα (ἄμετρος) ἐπιθυμία represents a more specific instance of πλεονάζουσα (ἄμετρος) ὁρμή, both of which are morally problematic. With the concept of "immoderation" (ἀμετρία), Philo could clearly distinguish *passionate desire* from amoral desire, using a reinvented Stoic definition of passion.[125]

---

control of reason, operating contrary to reason, is "irrational." Cf. εὔλογον πάθος in *Her* 192, in reference to a non-rational emotion that is not *ir*rational (opposed to reason) but "*eu*rational" (obedient to reason). This is the Middle-Platonic version of Stoic εὐπάθεια (see also Plutarch, *Virt. mor.* 448 F: πάθος ... ἀκολουθοῦν τῷ λόγῳ; 449 A: πάθη προστιθέμενα ... τῷ λογισμῷ; 449 B: γίνεται γὰρ εὐπάθεια τοῦ λογισμοῦ τὸ πάθος οὐκ ἀναιροῦντος ἀλλὰ κοσμοῦντος καὶ τάττοντος ἐν τοῖς σωφρονοῦσιν; cf. Mauro Bonazzi, "Antiochus' Ethics and the Subordination of Stoicism," in *The Origins of the Platonic System: Platonisms of the Early Empire and their Philosophical Contexts* [ed. Mauro Bonazzi and Jan Opsomer; CEC 23; Louvain: Peeters, 2009], 33–54, 49). Philo's Middle-Platonic take on Stoic εὐπάθεια explains his willingness to defy the Stoic doctrine of *no* rational counterpart to grief by naming δηγμός in *QG* 2.57 as the "good emotion" corresponding to λύπη (see John Dillon and Abraham Terian, "Philo and the Stoic Doctrine of ΕΥΠΑΘΕΙΑΙ: A Note on *Quaes Gen* 2.57," *SPh* 4 [1976–77]: 17–24). For Philo, δηγμός would indicate the *emotion* of grief properly measured by reason. Rather than "a significant modification in basic Stoic doctrine" (idem, 18), Philo offers a Middle-Platonic revision of Stoic *terminology* (εὐπάθεια) similar to the reworking of πλεονάζουσα ὁρμή (cf. Wolfson, *Philo*, 2:275–77). On *QG* 2.57, see also Graver, "Stoic ΠΡΟΠΑΘΕΙΑΙ," 213–16.

[123] *Plant.* 105: ἀμέτρων ἐπιθυμιῶν; *Migr.* 21: ἐπιθυμιῶν καὶ πάντων παθῶν ἀμετρίαις; *Prov.* 2.70: τὴν ἀμετρίαν τῶν ἐπιθυμιῶν; *Legat.* 162: τῆς ἀμέτρου ... ἐπιθυμίας; cf. *Leg.* 2.77: ἀμετρία τῶν ἡδονῶν; *Leg.* 3.111: ἡδονῆς ἀμέτρου; *Conf.* 117: ἀμέτροις ἡδοναῖς; TL 72: ἀδοναὶ ἄμετροι.

[124] Cf. *Spec.* 1.343: τὸ δ'ἄμετρον μέτροις ἐπιστομίζουσα.

[125] And since ἐπιθυμία bears analysis as also a useful *emotion* (πάθος), the Middle-Platonic use of ἄμετρος terminology to analyze non-rational impulse applies also to the analysis of non-rational *emotion*, particularly in connection with the idea of "moderate" emotion (μετριοπάθεια). In *Virt.* 195, Philo clearly identifies ἡ ἀμετρία τῶν παθῶν as the antithesis of μετριοπάθεια (cf. *Migr.* 18: τὰς ἄλλας παθῶν ἀμετρίας; *Migr.* 21: παθῶν ἀμετρίαις; *Mut.* 143: παθῶν ἀμετρίας; *Spec.* 3.209: τὰς ἀμετρίας τῶν παθῶν). For Middle Platonists, the need to distinguish between emotion (πάθος) and passion (πάθος) posed an obvious terminological problem. So they often denoted *passion* by using terms that ascribed excess or lack of measure to *emotion*: e.g., ἀμετρία τῶν παθῶν designates a "passionate emotion," an amoral, potentially useful emotion (πάθος) that exceeds rational bounds and becomes morally problematic, or "passionate" (cf. πλεονάζουσα [ἄμετρος] ὁρμή). Plutarch describes this phenomenon in *Virt. mor.* 444 C, associating τὰς ἀμετρίας τῶν παθῶν with an impulse (ὁρμή) that goes too far (ἐκφέρεται ῥυεῖσα

Tyrannical Desire (ἔρως)

Along with passionate desire (πλεονάζουσα [ἄμετρος] ἐπιθυμία), Philo recognizes a second and even worse type of problematic desire, "tyrannical desire" (ἔρως), which does not simply overstep the bounds of reason—it takes control of the entire soul. Philo's characterization of tyrannical desire relies not on reinvented Stoic terminology but on the writings of Plato himself, who believed that ἔρως can operate as a consuming, injurious, relentless desire for a single beloved object. He describes this type of desire in Books VIII–IX of the *Republic* through his portrait of the "tyrannical soul."[126] Just as governments can degenerate stepwise from a best to a worst type, *souls* can degenerate from a best to a worst type, with tyranny representing the worst of both states and souls. The "tyrannical soul" suffers under the hegemony of an overgrown desire (ἐπιθυμία)—a preeminent, tyrannical desire (ἔρως) that dominates not only other competing desires but also the collective operation of the entire soul.[127]

πολλὴ καὶ ἄτακτος ... τὸ σφοδρόν; cf. 444 B: ὑπερβάλλοντες τὸ μέτριον). Evidence of the terminological problem faced by Middle Platonists appears in *Didask.* 30.5–6 [184.20–36], where Alcinous uses the terms ἀμετριοπαθής and ὑπερπαθής to designate excessive (i.e., "passionate") emotion (cf. 30.5 [184.20–21]: ἐν τοῖς πάθεσιν ἀμετρία). On ἀμετρία in Middle Platonism (including *Virt.* 195), see Whittaker, *Alcinoos*, 62, n. 504, who cites *Resp.* 486 D and *Phileb.* 52 C in connection with the term; cf. Dillon, *Alcinous*, 188–89.

[126] See esp. *Resp.* 572 C–576 B (also 545 C: τυραννικὴν ψυχήν; 577 E: ἡ τυραννουμένη ... ψυχή). On ἔρως as a tyrant, see 573 B: τύραννος ὁ ἔρως λέγεται; 573 D: ἔρως τύραννος ἔνδον οἰκῶν; 574 E: τυραννευθεὶς δὲ ὑπὸ ἔρωτος; 575 A: τυραννικῶς ἐν αὐτῷ ὁ ἔρως. This clearly *negative* image of ἔρως from the *Republic* resonates with the image in *Phaedr.* 237 D–238 C, where Socrates defines ἔρως as an ἐπιθυμία that usurps reason and becomes a tyrant (238 B: τυραννεύσασα; cf. 238 A: ἐπιθυμίας ... ἀρξάσης ἐν ἡμῖν; 238 C: κρατήσασα ἐπιθυμία ... νικήσασα ... ἔρως ἐκλήθη). Plato's *positive* image of ἔρως, by contrast, sees it as a means by which the soul of the philosopher ascends to the realm of true beauty and goodness (see *Symp.* 210 A–212 C; *Phaedr.* 245 B–257 B). Philo employs also this *positive* understanding of ἔρως in his writings (e.g., *Praem.* 84: ὑπ'ἔρωτος οὐρανίου; also *Gig.* 44; *Contempl.* 11–12; cf. *Didask.* 1.2 [152.11–12]: πρὸς τὴν ἀλήθειαν ἔχειν ἐρωτικῶς), on which see esp. Dieter Zeller, *Charis bei Philon und Paulus* (SBS 142; Stuttgart: Verlag Katholisches Bibelwerk, 1990), 75–79 [="Der himmlische Eros"] (cf. Peder Borgen, "Heavenly Ascent in Philo: An Examination of Selected Passages," in *The Pseudepigrapha and Early Biblical Interpretation* [ed. James Charlesworth and Craig Evans; JSPSup 14; SSEJC 2; Sheffield: JSOT Press, 1993], 246–68, esp. 253–56; Holger Thesleff, "Notes on Eros in Middle Platonism," *Arctos* 28 [1994]: 115–28, esp. 119–20). Both views ascribe to ἔρως a consuming motivational power capable of directing the course of one's life (cf. *Post.* 157). On Platonic ἔρως, see Halperin, "Platonic *Erôs*"; idem, "Plato and the Metaphysics of Desire," *PBACAP* 5 (1989): 27–52; Dominic Scott, "*Erôs*, Philosophy, and Tyranny," in *Maieusis: Essays on Ancient Philosophy in Honour of Myles Burnyeat* (ed. Dominic Scott; Oxford: Oxford University Press, 2007), 136–53.

[127] See *Resp.* 572 E: ἔρωτά τινα ... προστάτην τῶν ... ἐπιθυμιῶν; 573 B: [ἔρως] ὁ προστάτης τῆς ψυχῆς; 573 D: ἔρως τύραννος ἔνδον οἰκῶν διακυβερνᾷ τὰ τῆς ψυχῆς ἅπαντα; 573 E: τοῦ

Without explicitly citing Plato's text, Philo nevertheless demonstrates familiarity with Plato's description of soul tyranny in the *Republic*.[128] In particular, he incorporates Plato's notion of tyrannical desire (ἔρως) into his moral psychology to describe the ultimate victory of non-rational desire (ἐπιθυμία) over reason (λόγος).[129]

Ἔρως *as Advanced Grade of Desire*

Unlike *amoral desire*, which proves useful under reason's command, *passionate desire* and *tyrannical desire* both counteract reason, but to different extents and in different ways. Generally speaking, passionate desire and tyrannical desire correspond to the ethical categories of "lack of self-control" (ἀκρασία) and "intemperance" (ἀκολασία), which in turn represent two distinct types of relation between non-rational desire (ἐπιθυμία) and reason (λόγος) within the soul.[130] In the case of passionate desire,

---

ἔρωτος, πάσαις ταῖς ἄλλαις [ἐπιθυμίαις] ὥσπερ δορυφόροις ἡγουμένου; 575 A: τυραννικῶς ἐν αὐτῷ ὁ ἔρως ... αὐτὸς ὢν μόναρχος. Ἔρως is a type of desire (*Phaedr.* 237 D: ἐπιθυμία τις ὁ ἔρως), originating in the Platonic ἐπιθυμητικόν. Philo clearly associates ἔρως with ἡ ἐπιθυμία (i.e. the ἐπιθυμητικόν) in *Conf.* 21. A scholium on *Didask.* 34.3 [188.30–35] from the ninth-century codex Parisinus Graecus 1962 (see Whittaker, *Alcinoos*, 167) correlates the various constitutions of *Resp.* IX with the corresponding parts of the Platonic soul: κατὰ τὸ λογικόν: ἡ ἀριστοκρατική; κατὰ τὸ θυμικόν: ἡ τιμοκρατική; κατὰ τὸ ἐπιθυμητικόν: ἡ δημοκρατική, ἡ ὀλιγαρχική, ἡ τυραννίς.

[128] Esp. *Agr.* 45–46, where Philo speaks of "bad governments" (κακοπολιτειῶν), noting the danger of "mob-rule" (ὀχλοκρατία) and the *additional* danger of an arising tyrant (τύραννος), which *in cities* involves a man (πόλεων μὲν ἄνθρωπος), but *in body and soul* involves a savage mind (σώματος δὲ καὶ ψυχῆς ... θηριωδέστατος νοῦς). See also *Leg.* 2.91: τυράννου τρόπον; *Leg.* 3.80: ὁ ... τύραννος νοῦς; *Conf.* 164: τὰς τῶν τυράννων τύχας (see Colson, PLCL 4, 558); *Abr.* 242: ἀντὶ τυραννίδων καὶ δυναστειῶν ἐν τῇ ψυχῇ; *Prob.* 45: ὥσπερ τῶν πόλεων αἱ μὲν ὀλιγαρχούμεναι καὶ τυραννούμεναι δουλείαν ὑπομένουσι ... οὕτως καὶ τῶν ἀνθρώπων.

[129] Cf. Emma Wasserman, *The Death of the Soul in Romans 7: Sin, Death, and the Law in Light of Hellenistic Moral Psychology* (WUNT 256; Tübingen: Mohr Siebeck, 2008), 60–76 [="The Death of the Soul in Philo of Alexandria"]. Wasserman similarly notes the influence of *Resp.* VIII and IX on Philo's Platonic notion of an inferior part of the soul utterly defeating reason, but she does not explore this connection in terms of ἔρως (tyrannical desire). Instead, she suggests a link between Philo's motif of "soul death" (e.g., *Leg.* 1.105–107) and the "extreme immorality" (broadly conceived) represented by Plato's image of tyranny in the *Republic* (see 67–76 [="Extreme Immorality in Platonic Discourse"], esp. 67–70).

[130] In descending order of moral value, the four relations are "self-mastery" (σωφροσύνη), in which reason enjoys uncontested dominion over compliant desire; "self-control" (ἐγκράτεια), in which reason asserts contested control over opposing desire; "lack of self-control" (ἀκρασία), in which desire asserts contested control over opposing reason; and "intemperance" (ἀκολασία), in which desire enjoys uncontested dominion over compliant reason. The ethical theory underlying this scale of morality comes from Book VII of Aristotle's *Nicomachean Ethics* (see Helen North, *Sophrosyne: Self-*

ἐπιθυμία impulsively counteracts the dictates of reason—overstepping the bounds of reason (becoming ἄ-μετρος)—despite reason's attempt to enforce those dictates. In other words, desire forcibly asserts its inclination over against the inclination of reason *in a contest of power*. The moral agent simply does not have the requisite power (κράτος) to control desire (i.e., ἀ-κρασία), and thus acts under compulsion "against his or her will." In the case of tyrannical desire, however, the moral agent no longer experiences internal conflict, because desire has defeated reason entirely. Desire has become the undisputed ruler of the soul, a tyrant whose agenda determines the overall orientation and course of life.[131] The moral agent, whose reason offers no opposition—no correction (κόλασις) of desire's errant ways (i.e., ἀ-κολασία)—acts as the compliant *slave* of desire.[132] In terms of moral psychology, what this means is that the invariable, sole aim of ἐπιθυμία, which the Platonic tradition identifies as pleasure (ἡδονή), has become the invariable, sole aim of the moral agent, who thus becomes a "Lover of Pleasure" (φιλήδονος).[133]

Just as ἐπιθυμία can invariably seek pleasure through a variety of means (food, money, fame), tyrannical desire (ἔρως) can invariably amount to "love of pleasure" (φιληδονία) despite a variety of distinct *means* to pleasure. Philo speaks of the trouble caused by:

Knowledge and Self-Restraint in Greek Literature [CSCP 35; Ithaca: Cornell University Press, 1966], 203). For the scale from a Middle-Platonic perspective similar to Philo's, see esp. Plutarch *Virt. mor.* 445 B–446 C (cf. *PHP* IV 2.39–42).

[131] Cf. Annas, "Humans and Beasts," on *Resp.* VIII–IX: "[T]he 'tyrannical' man is the only one to have lost all overall control, once a master desire has been implanted within him" (129).

[132] Cf. *Ios.* 40: ἐξ ἔρωτος ἀκολάστου. On the *slavery* associated with (tyrannical) desire, see *Her.* 269: ἡ δουλεία ... ὅταν δὲ ἐπιθυμία κρατήσῃ, ἔρως ἐγγίνεται. In *Leg.* 2.90–91, Philo associates the absence of *discipline* (παιδεία [cf. ἀ-κολασία]) with the eventual rise of tyranny in the soul.

[133] Philo sees ὁ φιλήδονος as a particular type (τρόπος) of soul (*Leg.* 3.212: φιλήδονος τρόπος; *Sobr.* 24: φιλήδονον ... ἐν ψυχῇ τρόπον) equivalent to the tyrannical soul—in other words, a soul dominated by desire and possessed of ἀκολασία: e.g., *Leg.* 2.90: ἐὰν γὰρ ἡ ψυχὴ ἀπορρίψῃ τὴν παιδείαν (cf. ἀκολασία), γέγονε φιλήδονος; *Leg.* 3.37–38: τόν ... τέλος ἡγούμενον τὰς ἡδονάς ... τὸν φιλήδονον; *Spec.* 3.23: ἀκολασία καὶ φιληδονία;. Cf. Ranocchia, "Anti-Epicurean Polemic," 93: "Philo never tires of attacking in his writings the 'pleasure-seeker' (ἡδονικός) or 'pleasure lover' (φιλήδονος) *who has chosen pleasure as the only yardstick of judgment and has made it his supreme rule of life*" (emphasis added). Philo's disdain for the φιλήδονος may indeed reflect a polemic against Epicurean philosophy, but he understands the moral psychology of hedonism along fundamentally Platonic lines. (On the Epicurean notion of pleasure as "the good," see LS 21A–X, esp. 21B, lines 12–14 [from Epicurus, *Letter to Menoeceus*]: τὴν ἡδονὴν ἀρχὴν καὶ τέλος λέγομεν εἶναι τοῦ μακαρίως ζῆν· ταύτην γὰρ ἀγαθὸν πρῶτον καὶ συγγενικὸν ἔγνωμεν; cf. John Cooper, "Pleasure and Desire in Epicurus," in *Reason and Emotion*, 485–514.)

[A] tyrannical desire for money (χρημάτων ἔρως) or a woman (γυναικός) or fame (δόξης) or *any other source of pleasure* (τινος ἄλλου τῶν ἡδονὴν ἀπεργαζομένων) .... (*Decal.* 151)[134]

Plato's general theory of ἔρως makes a distinction between the *object* and the *aim* of ἔρως, which accounts—in the case of tyrannical desire (ἔρως)— for the relation between various *means* to the one ultimate *end* of pleasure (ἡδονή).[135] For Plato, ἔρως engages the rational mind, whose scope includes the convictions and aspirations of the moral agent, not just the impulsive activity of a non-rational element within the soul.[136] Ἔρως fundamentally involves a passionate pursuit of the Beautiful (τὸ καλόν), the *object* of ἔρως, in an effort to secure the Good (τὸ ἀγαθόν), the ultimate *aim* of ἔρως.[137] By properly evaluating *reflections* of the Beautiful manifested in a variety of sources in the sensible realm, the student of philosophy can ultimately ascend to the one *source* of those reflections in the intelligible realm, the Beautiful *itself*, in order to secure the Good *itself*, which results in happiness (εὐδαιμονία). But this philosophical use of ἔρως presumes that the moral agent values *as* good what truly *is* good. In the case of tyrannical desire, the moral agent operates under the erroneous conviction that *pleasure* (ἡδονή) is good and thus worthy of pursuit.[138] Enamored of a false good, the moral

---

[134] My translation (emphasis added). Cf. *Leg* 2.107: ὁ βίος ὁ τῶν φαύλων δεσπόζεται ὑφ'ἡδονῆς· τὰ γοῦν ποιητικὰ αὐτῆς εὑρίσκεται διὰ πανουργίας πάσης, χρυσὸς ἄργυρος δόξα τιμαὶ ἀρχαί, αἱ ὗλαι τῶν αἰσθητῶν, καὶ τέχναι αἱ βάναυσοι καὶ ὅσαι ἄλλαι κατασκευαστικαὶ ἡδονῆς πάνυ ποικίλαι; *Ios.* 70: τιμῶν ἔρως. Plutarch speaks of Epicurus's ἔρως for δόξα in *Suav. viv.* 1100 A-D; cf. the discussion of Caeser's καινῆς ἔρωτα δόξης and ὁ τῆς βασιλείας ἔρως in Duff, *Plutarch's Lives*, 86–87.
[135] On this distinction, see Halperin, "Platonic *Erôs*," esp. 176–82.
[136] Cf. J. M. E. Moravcsik, "Reason and Eros in the 'Ascent'-Passage of the *Symposium*," in *Essays in Ancient Greek Philosophy* (ed. J. P. Anton and G. L. Kustas; Albany: State University of New York Press, 1971), 283–302, 290: "Plato is using 'eros' in a wide sense, including any over-all desire or wish for what is taken to be good. The qualification 'over-all' is needed, for Plato is not talking about momentary impulses but about wishes, desires, aspirations that determine the ultimate goals of one's life. Thus eros is not blind passion; it is the wish or desire ... for things deemed on account of their nature to be worthy of having their attainment become a man's ultimate goal."
[137] N.B. *Symp.* 205 D: οὕτω τοίνυν καὶ περὶ τὸν ἔρωτα· τὸ μὲν κεφάλαιόν ἐστι πᾶσα ἡ τῶν ἀγαθῶν ἐπιθυμία καὶ τοῦ εὐδαιμονεῖν; 206 A: οὐδέν γε ἄλλο ἐστὶν οὗ ἐρῶσιν ἄνθρωποι ἢ τοῦ ἀγαθοῦ ... οἱ ἄνθρωποι τοῦ ἀγαθοῦ ἐρῶσιν ... ὁ ἔρως τοῦ τὸ ἀγαθὸν αὐτῷ εἶναι ἀεί. Cf. Gerasimos Santas, "Plato's Theory of Eros in the *Symposium*," in *Plato and Freud: Two Theories of Love* (Oxford: Basil Blackwell, 1988), 14–57, esp. 32–34 [="Generic Desire: Desire for the Good to be One's Own Forever"].
[138] Cf. Philo's allegorical interpretation (*Leg.* 3.59–64) of Gen 3:13: ὁ ὄφις [ἡδονή] ἠπάτησέν με, καὶ ἔφαγον. Pleasure *appears* to be good and its deceptive charm leads people to embrace it *as* good (see Jessica Moss, "Pleasure and Illusion in Plato," *Ph&PhenR* 72 [2006]: 503–35).

agent vehemently pursues objects that secure the "good"—pursues, in other words, objects capable of producing pleasure. The moral agent focuses only on what is "good" for non-rational desire, which has commandeered all faculties of the soul—including the rational faculty—to serve its pursuit of pleasure.[139] Tyrannical desire (ἔρως) thus represents the terminal stage of a disastrous process that begins with reason *outmatched* by ἐπιθυμία and ends with reason *enslaved* by ἐπιθυμία.[140]

Philo emphasizes the distinct nature of ἔρως as an advanced grade of desire by representing passionate desire (and thus ἀκρασία) as a preliminary condition that *engenders* tyrannical desire (and thus ἀκολασία):

> When desire prevails within the soul (ὅταν δὲ ἐπιθυμία κρατήσῃ), a tyrannical desire arises for things one does not have (ἔρως ἐγγίνεται τῶν ἀπόντων)—a tyrannical desire that hangs the soul on unmet expectation as on a noose (τὴν ψυχὴν ὥσπερ ἀπ'ἀγχόνης ἐλπίδος ἀτελοῦς ἐκρέμασε). Always thirsty, yet never able to drink, such a soul suffers the awful fate of Tantalus (διψῇ μὲν γὰρ ἀεί, πιεῖν δὲ ἀδυνατεῖ ταντάλειον τιμωρίαν ὑπομένουσα). (*Her.* 269)[141]

In order for tyrannical desire to come into existence, ἐπιθυμία must first overpower reason (κρατεῖν), subjecting the soul to passionate desire—in other words, tyrannical desire is born *only* in souls predisposed to its genesis by passionate desire and the accompanying state of ἀκρασία. Advancement to this terminal grade of desire invariably brings disaster.

Negative Impact of Ἔρως

Once established, tyrannical desire's hegemony ravages the soul by imposing the "fate of Tantalus" (*Her.* 269). For Tantalus, this meant the torturous circumstance of being *always* thirsty yet *never* able to take a drink.[142] Framed as a more general predicament, this means suffering under an

---

[139] I.e., tyrannical desire has made pleasure "the good" (cf. *Symp.* 205 D; 206 A).

[140] Cf. Kahn, "Plato's Theory of Desire," 88: "If reason is able to rule in the soul, it will specify the life of virtue (the life of philosophy) as the good to be aimed at. If it does not succeed in doing so, that is because it has been so 'overpowered' by spirit or appetite that it mis-identifies the good. Since it is only the rational part that can form any conception of the good, even an erroneous conception, the domination of the other parts has the consequence of *causing reason to make a mistake* in its recognition of the ends to be pursued. That is what it means for reason to be enslaved" (original emphasis) (see also Cooper, "Human Motivation," 132, n. 18; Lorenz, *Brute Within*, 46: "the rule of the appetitive part consists in the fact that its central object of desire has become the person's central object of desire ... ").

[141] My translation. For passionate desire as a preliminary condition engendering ἔρως, see also *Spec.* 4.80–81.

[142] See *Od.* 11.582–92.

insatiable desire: *always* wanting something yet *never* able to get it.[143] This experience of *chronic* insatiability (ἀπληστία) distinguishes tyrannical desire (ἔρως) from all other types.[144] In fact, *only* the abject defeat of reason (ἀκολασία) presupposed by tyrannical desire can explain the phenomenon of chronic insatiability. Unlike a physical receptacle such as the stomach, whose physical limits can be reached to induce satiety, desire itself (ἐπιθυμία)—as a function of the *soul*—has no inherent limit. Philo explains:

> [T]he craving of the soul that is out of control (ἡ τῆς ἀκράτορος[145] ψυχῆς ἐπιθυμία) is not restricted as the bodily organs are by their size. These are vessels of a fixed capacity admitting nothing that exceeds it (ἄμετρον), but ejecting all that is superfluous. Desire is never filled up (ἡ δὲ ἐπιθυμία πληροῦται μὲν οὐδέποτε), but continues always thirsty and in want of more (μένει δὲ ἐνδεὴς καὶ διψαλέα ἀεί). (*Leg.* 3.149)[146]

Once activated in the soul, desire impulsively extends toward its object, with nothing to limit it *other than reason*. In the virtuous soul, reason imposes limits, allowing desire to pursue its object only so far as that pursuit serves a rational end: to secure, for example, something necessary or useful. But in the soul under tyrannical desire (ἔρως), reason *never* exercises its limiting capacity, so nothing counteracts this appetitive extension. The moral agent consumed with tyrannical desire continually holds the object of desire in mind, causing non-rational desire to pursue reflexively the pleasure afforded by that object, which in turn leads to the unending frustration of insatiable desire in a soul racked with longing. Although Philo alludes to this phenomenon in a variety of passages, he finds it signified explicitly under the allegorical figure of Tubal (Θοβέλ), a descendant of Cain mentioned in Gen 4:22.[147] Tubal represents for Philo the torturous

---

[143] Cf. *Resp.* 578 A: ψυχὴν ἄρα τυραννικὴν πενιχρὰν καὶ ἄπληστον ἀνάγκη ἀεὶ εἶναι. See Halperin, "Metaphysics of Desire," 36–43 [="Eros: Suffering Without Satisfaction"].

[144] Insatiability characterizes also the ἔρως of the philosopher: *Leg.* 3.39: ἄπληστοι τῶν ἀρετῆς ὄντες ἐρώτων; *Gig.* 31: ἄπληστος ... ἔρως.

[145] What applies here to the ἄκρατος soul applies also to the ἀκόλαστος soul. Desire itself is insatiable, whether the absence of restraining reason is *temporary* (ἀκρασία) or *chronic* (ἀκολασία).

[146] Cf. *Ebr.* 6: ἀπληστίας δὲ [αἴτιον] ἡ ἀργαλεωτάτη παθῶν ψυχῆς ἐπιθυμία; *Ebr.* 206: τὰς τοῦ σώματος δεξαμενὰς ἀποπληρωθῶσι πάσας, ἔτι κενοὺς τὰς ἐπιθυμίας ὄντας; *Contempl.* 55: τὰς μὲν γαστέρας ἄχρι φαρύγγων πεπληρωμένοι, κενοὶ δὲ πρὸς τὰς ἐπιθυμίας.

[147] On Philo's etymological interpretation, see Lester L. Grabbe, *Etymology in Early Jewish Interpretation: The Hebrew Names in Philo* (BJS 115; Atlanta: Scholars Press, 1988). On "Θοβέλ," see idem, 165–66 (cf. 29–33). Grabbe correctly notes that Philo in general does not so much *draw* meaning as *inject* meaning: "Philo has a definite philosophical and theological system in mind. While certain modifications have been made to accommodate it to Judaism, this system is still evidently a representative of Middle

extension of a soul consumed by tyrannical desire (ἔρως)[148] for the *pleasure* (ἡδονή) derived from false "goods" (ἀγαθά):

> [T]he soul of someone vexed by the pleasures derived from either bodily or external "goods" (τοῦ γὰρ σεσοβημένου περὶ τὰς ἢ σωματικὰς ἡδονὰς ἢ τὰς ἡδονὰς [ἢ] τὰς ἐκτὸς ὕλας ἡ ψυχή)[149] gets hammered thin as if on an anvil (καθάπερ ἐπ'ἄκμονος σφυρηλατεῖται), driven by the long and cavernous extensions of its desires (κατὰ τὰς τῶν ἐπιθυμιῶν μακρὰς καὶ διωλυγίους ἐκτάσεις ἐλαυνομένη). (*Post.* 116)[150]

Philo notes that such people have literally boundless appetites (ταῖς ἀορίστοις αὐτῶν ὀρέξεσιν [*Post.* 116]), meaning that their desire is insatiable.[151]

Tyrannical desire harms not only the individual, but also the community at large *through* the individual, whose obsessive pursuit of pleasure via false

---

Platonism. Philo is not in reality exegeting the biblical text, any more than the Stoic allegorists exegeted the text of Homer. He is only building an extensive bridgework between the Jewish sacred text and his philosophico-theological system. Although Philo probably would not have thought consciously in such terms, his question is, ultimately, not what the text means but how can he funnel his philosophical system into it" (116). See also David Runia, "Etymology as an Allegorical Technique in Philo of Alexandria," *SPhA* 16 (2004): 101–21.

[148] Although the *term* ἔρως does not appear in *Post.* 116, Philo clearly has ἔρως in mind. First, the broader context of the passage (*Post.* 113: esp. ὡς δι'ἀναβαθμῶν) alludes to Plato's teaching on ἔρως in the *Symposium* (211 C: esp. ὥσπερ ἐπαναβαθμοῖς; cf. Arnaldez, PAPM 6, 110, n.3). Second, Philo links the term σεσοβημένου (*Post.* 116), which Colson translates as "vehemently concerned," with ἔρως elsewhere (*Her.* 70: ἔρωτι οὐρανίῳ σεσοβημένης). Third, the terms οἶστρον and ἵμερον, which appear in *Post.* 116, signal the involvement of ἔρως (cf. οἰστράω and ἵμερος in *Phaedr.* 251 C–E). Philo describes a person whose *state of mind* is characterized by ἔρως, although discrete *instances* of desire still bear description with terms like ἐπιθυμία and ὄρεξις, both found in *Post.* 116.

[149] Cohn's emendation, τοῦ γὰρ σεσοβημένου περὶ τὰς ἢ σωματικὰς ἡδονὰς [ἢ τὰς ἡδονὰς] ἢ τὰς ἐκτὸς ὕλας ἡ ψυχή, suggests that Philo means *either* (1) bodily pleasures *or* (2) the materials of external things. But the phrase τὰς ἢ σωματικὰς ἡδονάς (*not* ἢ τὰς σωματικὰς ἡδονάς) suggests that Philo has in mind one type of pleasure over against another: τὰς ἢ (1) σωματικὰς ἡδονὰς ἢ (2) τὰς ἡδονὰς τὰς ἐκτὸς ὕλας. The context of Philo's statement (*Post.* 112–15) clearly shows that he has in mind two classes of false "goods," those related to the body (e.g., health) and those related to the external world (e.g., wealth): "Sella" is a symbol (σύμβολον) of the "goods" of the body and external "goods" (esp. §112: τῶν περὶ σῶμα καὶ ἐκτὸς ἀγαθῶν) and "Tubal" is the "son" of "Sella." In this context, τὰς σωματικὰς ἡδονάς must refer to pleasures derived from (associated with) "goods" of the body, and τὰς ἡδονὰς τὰς ἐκτὸς ὕλας, although an awkward expression, must refer to pleasures derived from (associated with) external "goods," with τὰς ἐκτὸς ὕλας serving as an adjective modifying ἡδονάς, just as σωματικάς modifies ἡδονάς. This emphasis on *pleasure* complements Philo's subsequent emphasis on *desire* (τὰς τῶν ἐπιθυμιῶν μακρὰς καὶ διωλυγίους ἐκτάσεις ἐλαυνομένη), since he knows that ἐπιθυμία fundamentally involves a desire for pleasure.

[150] My translation.

[151] Cf. *Conf.* 117: σὺν ἀμέτροις ἡδοναῖς ἀόριστος ἐπιθυμία.

"goods" leads to lawless behavior and violent conflict. Plato associates tyrannical desire with lawlessness in the *Republic*, in his portrait of the tyrannical man:

> Consumed by tyrannical desire (τυραννευθεὶς δὲ ὑπὸ ἔρωτος), he is continuously and in waking hours what he rarely became in sleep, and he will refrain from no atrocity of murder nor from any food or deed, but the tyrannical desire inside of him (τυραννικῶς ἐν αὐτῷ ὁ ἔρως) will live in utmost anarchy and lawlessness (ἐν πάσῃ ἀναρχίᾳ καὶ ἀνομίᾳ), and, since it is itself sole autocrat (αὐτὸς ὢν μόναρχος), will urge (ἄξει) the polity (πόλιν), so to speak, of him in whom it dwells to dare anything (ἐπὶ πᾶσαν τόλμαν) .... (*Resp.* 574 E–575 A)[152]

Philo too links inner tyranny with lawless behavior, in an allusion to Plato's *Republic*:

> Anarchy (ἀναρχία) ... is not our only danger. We have to dread also the uprising of some aspirant to sovereign power, forcibly setting law at naught (ἡ καὶ παρανόμου καὶ βιαίου τινὸς ἐφ'ἡγεμονίαν ἐπανάστασις). For a tyrant is a natural enemy (τύραννος γὰρ ἐκ φύσεως ἐχθρός). In cities this enemy is man (πόλεων μὲν ἄνθρωπος); to body and soul and all the interests of each of these (σώματος δε καὶ ψυχῆς καὶ τῶν καθ'ἑκάτερον πραγμάτων), it is an utterly savage mind, that has turned our inner citadel into a fortress from which to assail us (ὁ τὴν ἀκρόπολιν ἐπιτετειχικὼς ἑκάστῳ θηριωδέστατος νοῦς). (*Agr.* 46)[153]

People consumed by tyrannical desire will do *anything* to get what they want: nothing deters them, not even the law. For instance, Philo in *Spec.* 4.7 speaks of someone "crazed with a tyrannical desire for what belongs to others" (ἔρωτι τῶν ἀλλοτρίων ἐπιμανείς), who as a result "attempts to steal" (κλέπτειν ἐπιχειρῇ). As in *Agr.* 46, the tyrannical desire for possessions has "set law at naught." Tyrannical desire leads not only to individual acts of lawlessness, but also to violent conflict among entire groups of people. Philo states this most clearly in his exposition of the Tenth Commandment:

---

[152] Trans. Paul Shorey. Substituting "consumed by tyrannical desire" for "under the tyranny of his ruling passion"; "the tyrannical desire inside of him" for "the passion that dwells in him as a tyrant."

[153] On ὁ τὴν ἀκρόπολιν ἐπιτετειχικὼς ἑκάστῳ θηριωδέστατος νοῦς, see André Pelletier, "Les passions à l'assaut de l'âme d'après Philon," *REG* 78 (1965): 52–60, 56. Cf. *Leg.* 3.79–80: "[A] 'king' (βασιλεύς) is a thing at enmity with a despot (τυράννῳ), the one being the author of laws, the other of lawlessness (ἀνομίας ... εἰσηγητής). So mind, the despot (ὁ ... τύραννος νοῦς), decrees for both soul and body harsh and hurtful decrees (ἐπιτάγματα ... βίαια καὶ βλαβερά) working grievous woes (σφοδρὰς λύπας), conduct, I mean, such as wickedness prompts (τὰς κατὰ κακίαν λέγω πράξεις), and free indulgence of the passions (τὰς τῶν παθῶν ἀπολαύσεις)" (see also *Abr.* 242).

> [A]mong the passions, only passionate desire deserves the name "Master Vice," whose one little offspring (ἔγγονον) tyrannical desire (ἔρως) has repeatedly filled the world with unspeakable disasters—which, too numerous for land, have spilled out into the sea. Everywhere the vast watery expanse has been filled with ships of war and all the terrible inventions of war. Charging out to sea, their violence runs its course then crashes back like a tide upon the shores of home. (*Spec.* 4.85)[154]

This same idea appears in Philo's allegorical reading of Tubal, who represents the soul consumed by tyrannical desire (ἔρως)[155] and thus all "war makers" (δημιουργοί ... πολέμου):

> [A]nd that is why they are said to be workers in iron and bronze,[156] and these are the instruments with which wars are waged (δι'ὧν οἱ πόλεμοι συνίστανται). For any who are looking into the matter would find, that the greatest quarrels both of men individually and of states corporately, have arisen in the past, and are going on now, and will take place in the future, either for a woman's beauty (εὐμορφίας γυναικὸς εἵνεκα), or for money (χρημάτων), or glory (δόξης) or honor (τιμῆς) or dominion (ἀρχῆς), or to acquire something (κτήσεως), or, in a word, to gain advantages pertaining to the body and outward things (συνόλως ὅσα σώματος καὶ τῶν ἐκτός ἐστι πλεονεκτήματα). (*Post.* 117)[157]

Tyrannical desire (ἔρως) thus poses a unique threat to both the individual and society, since it brings the maximum ill effect of unrestrained ἐπιθυμία.

Conclusion

Philo holds a coherent, consistently Middle-Platonic theory of ἐπιθυμία involving a variety of terms and concepts. Philo consistently locates ἐπιθυμία in the non-rational part of the soul, although he uses different terms to *describe* that part. In other words, he considers ἐπιθυμία a fundamentally non-rational phenomenon, which operates according to a non-rational mechanism of stimulus (pleasurable object) and response (pursuit). Discrete *instances* of ἐπιθυμία may receive different labels (ἐπιθυμία, ὄρεξις, ὁρμή, πάθος), but each describes the *same* phenomenon, only from a different conceptual perspective. Desire serves a variety of useful purposes for human beings—most notably the *necessary* desire for food and drink—and so forms an integral part of life. If not properly managed by reason, however, desire can become an injurious force. Passionate desire signals

---

[154] My translation. Cf. *Decal.* 151–53.
[155] On ἔρως in *Post.* 116–17, see above, n. 148.
[156] See Gen 4:22: σφυροκόπος χαλκεὺς χαλκοῦ καὶ σιδήρου.
[157] Cf. *Conf.* 45–50.

the partial victory of non-rational desire over reason, in which desire forcibly oversteps the bounds of reason, despite the moral agent's knowledge of what reason requires. Tyrannical desire (ἔρως) signals the complete defeat of reason by non-rational desire, in which desire *enslaves* reason, compelling the entire soul to pursue desire's single aim of pleasure. So the non-rational desire (ἐπιθυμία) found in every human soul poses a latent threat, and tyrannical desire (ἔρως) represents the absolute realization of that threat. Instead of a useful source of non-rational motivation, desire becomes an awful tyrant, whose despotic rule harms both the individual and the society at large.

Clearly, effective management of the threat posed by non-rational desire requires preemptive intervention, an effort to *contain* the threat before it ever matures. Since the terminal state of intemperance (ἀκολασία) accompanying tyrannical desire always develops from a prior lack of self-control (ἀκρασία), preemptive therapeutic intervention must target the preliminary state and the *passionate desire* associated with it. If non-rational desire always remains within rational bounds, then passionate desire can never emerge, which in turn removes the precondition for tyrannical desire and precludes its development. The moral quality necessary for keeping non-rational desire in check is self-control (ἐγκράτεια)—literally the *power* (κράτος) to restrain desire when it tries to usurp the dictates of reason. So a complete system of practical ethics must include provisions for the development and exercise of self-control (ἐγκράτεια).

CHAPTER THREE

PHILO ON SELF-CONTROL (ΕΓΚΡΑΤΕΙΑ) AND PRACTICE (ΑΣΚΗΣΙΣ)

Introduction

Philo considers non-rational desire (ἐπιθυμία) a necessary, even useful component of human life, but its innate and invariable tendency to pursue pleasure (ἡδονή) apart from rational calculation (λογισμός) threatens human well being. The initial danger lies in the ability of ἐπιθυμία to oppose and overpower the dictates of reason, to compel moral agents to pursue pleasure against their better judgment in an instance of ἀκρασία ("lack of self-control"). When an otherwise benign *emotion* overpowers reason in this way, it becomes a malignant *passion*, and Middle Platonists conceptualized this transformation as an impulse (ὁρμή) becoming "immoderate" (ἄμετρος) as it transgresses the limit or "measure" (μέτρον) set by reason. Passionate desire unquestionably harms the soul, but the ultimate danger of ἐπιθυμία lies not so much in its ability to get the occasional upper hand as in its ability to usurp reason entirely, to rule the moral agent without opposition in a state of ἀκολασία ("intemperance"). At this terminal stage, ἐπιθυμία becomes an all-consuming tyrannical desire (ἔρως) and the moral agent becomes thoroughly corrupt.

Self-control (ἐγκράτεια) involves the moral agent's ability to assert the dictates of reason over against the demands of desire whenever the two conflict, and by preventing desire from *ever* getting the upper hand, ἐγκράτεια eliminates the risk of tyrannical desire entirely. Recognizing its critical importance for the overall health of the soul, Philo speaks highly of ἐγκράτεια and gives it a prominent role in his ethical theory.[1] This chapter explains Philo's concept of ἐγκράτεια in light of Middle-Platonic moral

---

[1] E.g., *Spec.* 1.173: τὴν ὠφελιμωτάτην τῶν ἀρετῶν ἐγκράτειαν (cf. *Spec.* 1.175); *Contempl.* 34: ἐγκράτειαν δὲ ὥσπερ τινὰ θεμέλιον προκαταβαλλόμενοι τῆς ψυχῆς τὰς ἄλλας ἐποικοδομοῦσιν ἀρετάς. A similar emphasis on ἐγκράτεια appears in Xenophon's portrait of Socrates in the *Memorabilia* (see Louis-André Dorion, "*Akrasia* et *enkrateia* dans les *Mémorables* de Xénophon," *Dialogue* 42 (2003): 645–72, esp. 646–50 [="La prééminence de l'*enkrateia*"]. On the valorization of ἐγκράτεια among Philo's contemporaries as a context for his own emphasis on ἐγκράτεια, see Stowers, *Romans*, 46–56; also Niehoff, *Philo on Jewish Identity*, 75–110 [= "Jewish Values: Religion and Self-Restraint"]; cf. A. A. Long, "Hellenistic Ethics and Philosophical Power," in *Hellenistic History and Culture* (ed. Peter Green; HCS 9; Berkeley: University of California Press, 1993), 138–56.

psychology, addressing in turn the fundamental questions of *what* ἐγκράτεια is and *how* to acquire it.

The Nature of Ἐγκράτεια

Philo has a coherent but multi-faceted concept of ἐγκράτεια, whose character emerges best by considering three of its aspects. First, ἐγκράτεια involves a basic *power dynamic*, in which reason engages and overpowers a separate, unruly element of the soul. Second, ἐγκράτεια involves the *curtailing of excessive impulse*, and so it figures prominently in a Middle-Platonic theory of passion, especially through the Platonic image of reason as charioteer. Finally, ἐγκράτεια involves a *predominance of rational motivation*, in which the urge to secure a rationally determined, *ultimate* benefit for the entire soul outweighs the urge to experience an immediate pleasure.

Ἐγκράτεια – Victory of Rational over Non-Rational

The Platonic tradition associates ἐγκράτεια with the victory of reason, but it characterizes reason's opponent in different ways. One *broad* formulation simply pits reason against the rest of the soul, understood more or less as a single inferior "part" whose inferiority stems from a lack of reasoning capacity. One *narrow* formulation pits reason against *only* desire (ἐπιθυμία), based on a theoretical correlation of specific virtues with specific elements of the tripartite Platonic soul. Philo uses both of these formulations in his ethical discourse.

The broad formulation appears in Plato's *Republic* as a reflection on the division within the soul presumed by the very *term* ἐγκράτεια, which commonly denotes power (κράτος) *over oneself*.[2] Socrates notes the association of ἐγκράτεια with the expression κρείττω αὑτοῦ, whose literal sense—"stronger than himself"—creates confusion:

---

[2] See *Resp.* 430 D–432 A. Κράτος takes the genitive to indicate the domain of power: power *over* someone or something (see LSJ, s.v.). Walter Grundmann suggests that ἐγκράτεια derives from "ἐν κράτει ὤν," which implies a "status of power" ("ἐγκράτεια," *TDNT* 2:339–42, 340)—i.e., a state of *being in power*, namely *over oneself*. As with κράτος, the term ἐγκράτεια can also take the genitive, at least in earlier usage (e.g., *Resp.* 390 B: ἐγκράτειαν ἑαυτοῦ). But the reflexive pronoun eventually became unnecessary (see Long, "Ethics and Power," esp. 144). Philo never uses ἐγκράτεια with the reflexive pronoun, despite his use of equivalent expressions elsewhere: *Post.* 42: ὃς μηδ'αὑτοῦ κρατεῖν ἱκανὸς ὤν; *Agr.* 37: οὐκέτι κρατεῖν ἑαυτῶν δύνανται; *Ebr.* 221: οὐκέτι κρατεῖν ἑαυτῶν δυνάμενοι.

Now the expression "stronger than himself" (κρείττω αὑτοῦ) is ridiculous, is it not? For anyone stronger than himself (ὁ γὰρ ἑαυτοῦ κρείττων) would also be weaker than himself (ἥττων ... αὑτοῦ), and anyone weaker (ὁ ἥττων) would also be stronger (κρείττων). For the same person (ὁ αὐτός) is spoken of in all of these expressions. (*Resp.* 430 E–431 A)[3]

Socrates, however, further explains what people really *mean* by such expressions, despite the obscurity:

> [T]he soul of a man within him has a better part (τὸ μὲν βέλτιον) and a worse part (τὸ δὲ χεῖρον), and the expression "being stronger than himself" (τὸ κρείττω αὑτοῦ) means the control of the worse by the naturally better part (τὸ βέλτιον φύσει τοῦ χείρονος ἐγκρατές). (*Resp.* 431 A)[4]

Here the "naturally better part" (τὸ βέλτιον φύσει) stands for reason, which ought to be in control (ἐγκρατές). But Plato never clearly identifies the "worse part" (τὸ χεῖρον), here or elsewhere, because he never clearly formulates a bipartite model of the soul.[5] Middle Platonists, however, ultimately *preferred* a bipartite model of the soul, envisioning a "rational part" over a "non-rational part," and they developed a concept of ἐγκράτεια along these lines:

> When the rational part of the soul overpowers the non-rational part (τὸ λογιστικὸν μέρος τᾶς ψυχᾶς ἐπικρατῇ τῷ ἀλόγῳ), self-control comes into being (γίνεται ... ἐγκράτεια). When the non-rational part of the soul overpowers the rational part (τὸ ἄλογον μέρος τᾶς ψυχᾶς τῷ λογιστικῷ), lack of self-control comes into being ([γίνεται] ἀκρατία ...). (Ps.-Metop.117.16–18)[6]

Although Philo never *defines* ἐγκράτεια in this way, he presumes this sort of definition when, for example, he interprets biblical references to "shepherding" (ποιμενικὴ τέχνη) allegorically as an ethical discourse about reason's management of the "herd" (ἀγέλη) of non-rational powers within

---

[3] My translation. On this passage, see Plutarch, *Virt. mor.* 450 D–E. Cf. *Leg.* 626 E: "[T]he victory over self (τὸ νικᾶν αὐτὸν αὑτόν) is of all victories the first and best while self–defeat (τὸ δὲ ἡττᾶσθαι αὐτὸν ὑφ'ἑαυτοῦ) is of all defeats at once the worst and the most shameful. For these phrases signify that a war exists within each one of us (πολέμου ἐν ἑκάστοις ἡμῶν ὄντος πρὸς ἡμᾶς αὐτούς)."

[4] Trans. Paul Shorey; substituting "being stronger than himself" for "self-mastery."

[5] Despite evidence for a *concept* of bipartition (see Rees, "Bipartition").

[6] My translation. Cf. Plutarch, *Virt. mor.* 442 A: "[The soul of man] has as one part the intelligent and rational (ἕτερον μὲν ἔχει τὸ νοερὸν καὶ λογιστικόν), whose natural duty is to govern and rule the individual (ᾧ κρατεῖν τοῦ ἀνθρώπου κατὰ φύσιν καὶ ἄρχειν προσῆκόν ἐστιν), and as another part the passionate and irrational (ἕτερον δὲ τὸ παθητικὸν καὶ ἄλογον) ..., which has need of a director (ἐξεταστοῦ δεόμενον)" (trans. W.C. Helmbold; unless otherwise noted, all translations of Plutarch's writings are from LCL); *Eclog.* 38.5–6: Ἄλογον μέρος τῆς ψυχῆς εἰθισμένον ὑπακούειν τῷ λόγῳ.

the soul (*Agr.* 26–66).[7] Consistent with Philo's Middle-Platonic moral psychology, this line of interpretation envisions a basic power dynamic in the soul between a *rational* component fit to govern and a separate, *non-rational* component in need of governance.[8] As long as the non-rational component tractably *accepts* governance, all is well. But when the two components conflict, moral well being depends on the presence or absence of ἐγκράτεια. Its *presence* consists in the ability of the rational to overpower the non-rational, and Philo attributes precisely this ability to "shepherds," who use their rational powers to rule (κρατεῖν) over the non-rational forces within.[9] The *absence* of ἐγκράτεια (ἀκρασία) similarly involves a question of power, but in this case *non-rational* forces overpower the rational. Philo uses the shepherding allegory to depict this disastrous situation:

> [T]he stream of these evils becomes most grievous when the non-rational forces of the soul (αἱ ἄλογοι δυνάμεις τῆς ψυχῆς) attack and overpower the forces of reason (ἐπιθέμεναι ταῖς τοῦ λογισμοῦ κρατήσωσιν). While the herd obeys its herdsman (βουκόλια βουκόλοις ... πειθαρχεῖ), or the flocks of sheep or goats obey the shepherd or goatherd (ποιμέσι ποίμνια ἢ αἰπόλοις αἰπόλια), all goes well with them; but, when the controlling herdsmen

---

[7] Moses uses the figures of "shepherd" (ποιμήν) and "feeder of livestock" (κτηνοτρόφος) respectively to speak of the rational faculty engaged in either *good* or *bad* management of its non-rational "herd" (ἀγέλη) (esp. *Agr.* 29: φαῦλος μὲν γὰρ ὢν ὁ ἀγελάρχης οὗτος [λογισμός] καλεῖται κτηνοτρόφος, ἀγαθὸς δὲ καὶ σπουδαῖος ὀνομάζεται ποιμήν) (cf. *Sacr.* 104–06). Figurative representations of the soul as a combination of "Man" (rational) and "Beast" (non-rational) suit Platonic moral psychology well; see Annas, *Platonic Ethics*, 117–36 [="Humans and Beasts: Moral Theory and Moral Psychology"], esp. 134–36; cf. Theo Heckel, *Der innere Mensch: Die paulinische Verarbeitung eines platonischen Motivs* (WUNT 53; Tübingen: J.C.B. Mohr, 1993). Heckel considers the Platonic image of the tripartite soul as "man" (τὸ λογιστικόν, the "inner man"), lion (τὸ θυμοειδές), and many-headed beast (τὸ ἐπιθυμητικόν) (*Resp.* 588 B–D), especially its use among authors postdating Plato (see ch. 3, "Der Aufstieg der Metapher vom 'Inneren Menschen' und die neue Platonhermeneutik ab dem ersten Jh. v. Chr.," 31–88, esp. 42–76 [="Der 'Innere Mensch' bei Philon"]).

[8] Philo's subdivision of the non-rational component into five senses, the organs of speech, and the organs of reproduction (*Agr.* 30) in no way undermines the fundamentally *bipartite* conception of the soul presumed in his shepherding allegory (see above, pp. 60–65). In this case, the manifold nature of the non-rational part fits the characterization of reason as manager of a non-rational "herd." On Philo's conviction that the "better" (rational) part ought to govern the "worse" (non-rational) part, note for example *Leg.* 1.72: δίκαιον γὰρ τὸ μὲν κρεῖττον ἄρχειν ἀεὶ καὶ πανταχοῦ, τὸ δὲ χεῖρον ἄρχεσθαι· κρεῖττον μὲν δὴ τὸ λογικόν, χεῖρον δὲ τὸ ἐπιθυμητικὸν καὶ τὸ θυμικόν (cf. *Leg.* 3.222; *Fug.* 24; *Praem.* 59; *QG* 4.218). In *Opif.* 83–86, Philo expresses a similar conviction: human beings (rational) ought to govern animals (non-rational).

[9] E.g., *Agr.* 63: δύνανται κρατεῖν τῶν ἀλόγων [δυνάμεων] ... χρώμενοι ταῖς λογικαῖς [δυνάμεσι].

(ἀγελάρχαι) prove weaker than their charges (ἀσθενέστεροι τῶν θρεμμάτων), everything goes awry. (*Somn.* 2.151–52)[10]

Although Philo sees reason engaged in a struggle against certain "powers of the soul" (δυνάμεις τῆς ψυχῆς), he disregards the specific *identity* of those powers and notes only a common *property*, their lack of reason (ἄλογοι). Here he construes ἐγκράτεια in the broadest possible terms: a variety of distinct opponents (desire, anger, fear, etc.) may contend with reason, but they necessarily offer only one *type* of opposition, non-rational opposition. The value of such a broad formulation lies in its ability to construe the forcible control of *any* non-rational movement as an instance of ἐγκράτεια.

A *narrower* formulation of ἐγκράτεια results from a development within Platonic tradition regarding the nature of σωφροσύνη, "self-mastery." Plato himself had conceived of σωφροσύνη in terms of "order" (κόσμος) or "concord" (ξυμφωνία) among all parts of the soul as to which part should rule (ὁπότερον δεῖ ἄρχειν).[11] But Middle Platonists, dogmatically assigning a single cardinal virtue to each of the soul's parts, narrowed the scope of σωφροσύνη from an agreement involving the entire soul to governance of τὸ ἐπιθυμητικόν, the seat of ἐπιθυμία.[12] Philo reflects this trend:

> We must understand, then, that our soul has three parts (ἐστὶν ἡμῶν τριμερὴς ἡ ψυχή): the rational (τὸ μὲν λογικόν), the assertive (τὸ δὲ θυμικόν), and the desirous (τὸ δὲ ἐπιθυμητικόν).... [T]o each of the parts an appropriate virtue has been attached (ἀρετὴν δὲ ἑκάστῳ τῶν μερῶν οἰκείαν προσηρμόσθαι): prudence to the rational part (τῷ μὲν λογικῷ φρόνησιν) .... courage to the assertive part (τῷ δὲ θυμικῷ ἀνδρείαν), and self-mastery to the desirous part (τῷ δὲ ἐπιθυμητικῷ σωφροσύνην). For it is by self-mastery that we heal

---

[10] Substituting "non-rational" for Colson's "unreasoning."
[11] *Resp.* 430 E and 432 A. On σωφροσύνη in Plato's writings, see North, *Sophrosyne*, 150–96.
[12] Cf. North, *Sophrosyne*, 173: "[S]ophrosyne must be practiced by all three parts of the soul; it is never, for Plato, as for many later Platonists, solely the virtue of the appetitive part" (cf. Lilla, *Clement of Alexandria*, 78, n. 2). On the doctrine of particular virtues for each part of the soul in Middle Platonism, see Lilla, *Clement of Alexandria*, 72–84, esp. 80–83. In addition to the passages Lilla cites, note also Ps.-Metop.118.9–13: τῷ μὲν γὰρ λογιστικῷ μέρεος τᾶς ψυχᾶς ἀρετὰ ἁ φρόνασις ... τῷ δὲ θυμοειδέος ἀνδρεία ... τῷ δ'ἐπιθυματικῷ ἁ σωφροσύνα ... ὅλας δὲ τᾶς ψυχᾶς ἁ δικαιοσύνα; cf. *Didask.* 29.1 [182.22]: περὶ δὲ τὸ ἐπιθυμητικὸν τῆς σωφροσύνης. On Philo's understanding of the cardinal virtues, see Carl Joachim Classen, "Der platonisch-stoische Kanon der Kardinaltugenden bei Philo, Clemens Alexandrinus und Origenes," in *Kerygma und Logos: Beiträge zu den geistesgeschichtlichen Beziehungen zwischen Antike und Christentum: Festschrift für Carl Andresen zum 70. Geburtstag* (ed. Adolf Ritter; Göttingen: Vandenhoeck & Ruprecht, 1979), 68–88, esp. 70–75; Wofson, *Philo*, 2:218–35; and, in general, Pierre Daubercies, "La vertu chez Philon d'Alexandrie," *RTL* 26 (1995): 185–210.

and cure our desires (σωφροσύνη γὰρ τὰς ἐπιθυμίας ἀκούμεθα καὶ ἰώμεθα). (*Leg.* 1.70)[13]

As the "appropriate virtue" for the ἐπιθυμητικόν, σωφροσύνη accordingly manages the non-rational desires (τὰς ἐπιθυμίας) generated in that part of the soul—and it manages them well. Philo associates σωφροσύνη with the "healing" and "curing" of desire, suggesting a state of moral wellness in which desire operates only as it should. In other words, σωφροσύνη represents the *ideal* sort of management, in which ἐπιθυμία operates as the obedient servant of reason, acting only with reason's authorization and never opposing its dictates. Plutarch characterizes the man of self-mastery along similar lines:

> And you would say, as you looked at the man, "Then, indeed ceased the gale; a windless calm arose; some god had laid the waves to rest" [*Od.* 12.168], since by reason the violent, raging, and furious movements of the desires (κινήματα τῶν ἐπιθυμιῶν) had been quenched and those movements which Nature absolutely requires (ὧν δ'ἡ φύσις ἀναγκαίως δεῖται) had been made sympathetic (ὁμοπαθῆ), submissive (ὑπήκοα), friendly (φίλα), and, when the man chose a course of action, willing to co-operate (συνεργά), so that they did not outstrip the dictates of reason (μὴ προεκθεῖν τοῦ λογισμοῦ), nor fall short of them (ὑπενδιδόναι), nor misbehave (ἀτακτεῖν), nor disobey (ἀπειθεῖν), but so that every impulse was easily led (πᾶσαν ὁρμὴν εὐάγωγον οὖσαν) .... (*Virt. mor.* 446 D–E)[14]

Plutarch situates this concept of self-mastery at the top of a four-point scale depicting four possible relations between reason and desire: reason rules desire *without* conflict (σωφροσύνη), reason rules desire *with* conflict (ἐγκράτεια), desire rules reason *with* conflict (ἀκρασία), and desire rules reason *without* conflict (ἀκολασία).[15] Despite occasional lapses in technical precision, Philo demonstrates a fundamental acceptance of this same scale in his ethical theory. For example, he identifies moral "opposites" according to the terms of the scale, correlating the terms denoting *absence* of conflict (σωφροσύνη and ἀκολασία) and the terms denoting its *presence* (ἐγκράτεια and ἀκρασία).[16] Furthermore, Philo's ethical theory presumes and depicts, in a variety of ways, the four types of relation between reason and desire outlined by the scale, so he affirms its distinctions by implication

---

[13] My translation.
[14] Cf. TL 82: ὅρος σωφροσύνας εὐπείθια.
[15] *Virt. mor.* 445 B–446 E. See above, p. 72, n. 130.
[16] For σωφροσύνη opposed to ἀκολασία, see for example *Opif.* 73: τἀναντία ... σωφροσύνην καὶ ἀκολασίαν; *Her.* 209: ἐναντία ... σωφροσύνη, ἀκολασία. For ἐγκράτεια opposed to ἀκρασία, see for example *Abr.* 103: πρὸς ἐγκράτειαν ὁ ἀκρατής; *Mos.* 1.161: ἀκράτορες μεταβάλλουσι πρὸς ἐγκράτειαν; *Virt.* 180: ἐξ ἀκρατείας εἰς ἐγκράτειαν.

if not always by name.[17] Philo's general acceptance of such a well-developed scheme, especially its distinction between self-mastery and self-control, helps to clarify his concept of ἐγκράτεια.

Like σωφροσύνη, which in Middle-Platonic theory deals specifically with the ἐπιθυμητικόν, ἐγκράτεια deals specifically with ἐπιθυμία, but in a different way. In *Spec.* 1.149, Philo calls ἐγκράτεια the "antagonist" of desire (ἀντίπαλον ... ἐπιθυμίας), and this image captures the essential difference between ἐγκράτεια and σωφροσύνη. In the case of "self-mastery," reason placidly manages an ever docile desiderative faculty. But in the case of "self-control," reason struggles against desire in an active contest of power: reason *does* manage to assert its directives, but only against—and *over*—desire's positive opposition to those directives. Plutarch characterizes the man of self-control along these lines:

> [T]he self-controlled man (ὁ δ'ἐγκρατής), while he does indeed direct his desire by the strength and mastery of reason (ἄγει μὲν ἐρρωμένῳ τῷ λογισμῷ καὶ κρατοῦντι τὴν ἐπιθυμίαν), yet does so not without pain (οὐκ ἀλύπως), nor by persuasion (οὐδὲ πειθομένην), but as it plunges sideways and resists (πλαγίαν καὶ ἀντιτείνουσαν), as though with blow and curb (ὑπὸ πληγῆς καὶ χαλινοῦ), he forcibly subdues it and holds it in (καταβιαζόμενος καὶ ἀνακρούων), being the while himself full of internal struggle and turmoil (ἀγῶνος ὢν ἐν ἑαυτῷ καὶ θορύβου μεστός). (*Virt. mor.* 445 B–C)

Because self-control involves an active conflict between reason and desire, Plutarch uses terms of strength, force, and violent opposition to characterize it.[18] Philo demonstrates a similar view of self-control and uses similar language in his own characterizations, although he never states his theoretical positions as clearly as Plutarch.[19] He does, however, encapsulate his understanding of ἐγκράτεια in an interpretive reflection on the creature known as the "snake-fighter" (ὀφιομάχης):

> For the snake-fighter is, I think, nothing but a symbolic representation of self-control (συμβολικῶς ἐγκράτεια εἶναί μοι δοκεῖ), waging a fight that never ends (μάχην ἀκαθαίρετον) and a truceless war (πόλεμον ἄσπονδον) against intemperance and pleasure (ἀκρασίαν καὶ ἡδονήν). (*Opif.* 164)

The notions of "never ending fight" (μάχην ἀκαθαίρετον) and "truceless war" (πόλεμον ἄσπονδον) obviously convey the element of conflict characteristic of ἐγκράτεια. And despite Philo's naming here of ἀκρασία and

---

[17] See above, pp. 71–75.
[18] For a consideration of Plutarch's concept of self-control, including its place within the four-point spectrum (σωφροσύνη, ἐγκράτεια, ἀκρασία, ἀκολασία), see Margaret DeMaria Smith, "*Enkrateia*: Plutarch on Self-Control and the Politics of Excess" *Ploutarchos*, n.s., 1 (2003/2004): 79–88.
[19] E.g., *Leg.* 1.86: οἱ ἐγκρατέστατοι ... ἀντιβῆναι καὶ μαχέσασθαι τῷ γένει τῆς ἐπιθυμίας.

ἡδονή as the opponents of ἐγκράτεια, he in no way contradicts the notion of a fundamental opposition between ἐγκράτεια and *desire* (ἐπιθυμία). By pitting ἐγκράτεια against ἀκρασία, Philo notes that self-control subverts the victory of desire over reason (ἀκρασία) by enforcing instead the victory of reason over desire (ἐγκράτεια). By pitting ἐγκράτεια against ἡδονή, Philo recognizes pleasure as the constant and necessary counterpart of desire. Since Platonic ἐπιθυμία invariably seeks ἡδονή as its object, pleasure and desire ultimately represent twin aspects of the same phenomenon, and for that reason ἐγκράτεια can interchangeably represent the antagonist of either one—but in either case ἐγκράτεια involves active management of the ἐπιθυμητικόν.[20]

Whether formulated *broadly* as the dominance of rational over non-rational forces or *narrowly* as the dominance of reason over desire, ἐγκράτεια always involves a decisive contest of power. Since only *reason* can successfully direct the soul on a virtuous course of life, moral well being demands an ability to overcome *any* opposition to reason, no matter the source. Conceiving ἐγκράτεια along these lines, as basically a power dynamic, rightly identifies self-control with the victory of reason, but it does not *define* that victory. A more precise concept of ἐγκράτεια emerges through Philo's use of what he and other Middle Platonists took as a model of self-control in action: the two-horse chariot.

Ἐγκράτεια – *Curtailing Excessive Impulse*

While he owes the analogy between soul and chariot to Plato's *Phaedrus* (esp. 246 A–B; 253 D–256 D), Philo's particular use of the chariot figure to depict ἐγκράτεια reflects a decidedly *Middle*-Platonic moral psychology and a set of didactic aims different from Plato's.[21] In the *Phaedrus*, the chariot

---

[20] In Philo's discussion of σωφροσύνη in *Leg.* 1, he links self-mastery with *only* the ἐπιθυμητικόν (§§70–71), yet—in line with the Platonic view of ἐπιθυμία—he presumes its dealing with *both* desire *and* pleasure (§86: ἡ δὲ σωφροσύνη ἀδυνατεῖ κυκλώσασθαι τὴν ἐπιθυμίαν καὶ ἡδονήν· χαλεπαὶ γὰρ ἀντίπαλοι). Since ἐγκράτεια deals with the same part of the soul, it too deals with both desire and pleasure: either the forcible *subjugation* of ἐπιθυμία or the forcible *abstention* from ἡδονή (cf. Ps.-Metop. 117.21-22: ἃ δὲ ἐγκράτεια ἐν τῷ ἀντέχεν ἀδονᾷ).

[21] On Philo's use of the *Phaedrus* image, see esp. Méasson, *Char ailé*, 141–76; also Billings, *Platonism of Philo*, 88–92. On the use of the *Phaedrus* image in Middle Platonism broadly, see Vander Waerdt, "Moral Psychology," 390 (cf. Lilla, *Clement of Alexandria*, 92–103, esp. 97). Within Middle Platonism, Philo's use is significantly early, as Méasson notes: "l'œuvre de Philon est sans doute le plus ancien témoignage subsistant de l'utilisation de cette image destiné à devenir un des themes familiers du moyen platonisme" (176). Philo, however, reflects an earlier trend launched perhaps by the Stoic Posidonius, who may have been the one to popularize Plato's chariot figure as an

figure helps to narrate a myth of the soul's journey to transcendent reality, *not* to expound moral theory.[22] The struggle between charioteer and horse obviously symbolizes conflict within the soul, but Plato examines this conflict strictly in terms of the myth, not as a separate ethical concern.[23] In Philo's writings, by contrast, the chariot figure serves mainly as a working model for moral psychology, stripped of any explicit connection with the *Phaedrus* myth and framed according to Middle-Platonic conceptions of the soul.[24] And just as Middle-Platonic bipartition recast θυμός as more of an *opponent* of reason than an ally, Philo pits *both* horses against the driver, replacing the *Phaedrus* notion of a "bad" horse (ἐπιθυμία) yoked to an obedient "good" horse (θυμός).[25] In further agreement with Middle-Platonic moral psychology, which offered variant conceptions of the soul's non-rational part (ἄλογον μέρος) over against its rational part (λογικὸν μέρος), Philo offers variant conceptions of what exactly the soul's driver, reason, must manage. Reflecting Middle Platonism's configuration of tripartition as bipartition, Philo can speak of either *two* horses, θυμός and ἐπιθυμία, or a *single* horse, representing simply the non-rational part of the soul.[26]

---

effective model for moral psychology (see Vander Waerdt, "Moral Psychology," 86, 90; cf. Méasson, *Char ailé*, 64–65). In any case, Philo does *not* accept Posidonius's Stoic theory of emotion (see above, p. 46, n. 49), even if he *does* follow Posidonius—or some other Middle-Platonic philosopher who followed Posidonius—in using the chariot figure to articulate a theory of emotion. On the chariot as a model of ἐγκράτεια, see esp. Plutarch's explicit statement to that effect in *Virt. mor.* 445 B–D. On the *Phaedrus* image in Plutarch's writings, see François Fuhrmann, *Les images de Plutarque* (Paris: Klincksieck, 1964), 141, n. 2; also Rhiannon Ash, "Severed Heads: Individual Portraits and Irrational Forces in Plutarch's *Galba* and *Otho*," in *Plutarch and His Intellectual World: Essays on Plutarch* (ed. Judith Mossman; London: Duckworth, 1997), 189–214, 192–96; Opsomer, "L'âme du monde," 46–47; Méasson, *Char ailé*, 165–66.

[22] See Anne Lebeck, "The Central Myth of Plato's *Phaedrus*," *GRBS* 13 (1972): 267–90.

[23] See Jacqueline de Romilly, "Les conflits de l'âme dans le *Phèdre* de Platon" *WS* 16 (1982): 100–13, esp. 112, where she concludes regarding the conflict depicted through the chariot figure: "Il s'agit, en commandant mieux à l'attelage de notre âme, de pouvoir monter jusqu'au lieu supracéleste, et, pour finir, d'échapper au cycle des incarnations. Ou bien il s'agit, dans le cas contraire, de s'empêtrer dans la matière et les souffrances infinies qu'entraîne cette déchéance."

[24] For example, Philo's use of the chariot model in the context of moral psychology includes no talk of *wings*, which figure prominently in the mythical narrative (e.g., *Phaedr.* 246 A: ἐοικέτω δὴ ξυμφύτῳ δυνάμει ὑποπτέρου ζεύγους τε καὶ ἡνιόχου); cf. Méasson, *Char ailé*, 164.

[25] See Méasson, *Char ailé*, 148–49 [="De l'attelage de Platon à celui de Philon"]; 158–60 [="Le «thumos» chez Platon et chez Philon"].

[26] Two horses, θυμός and ἐπιθυμία: e.g., *Agr.* 72–73; *Migr.* 67; cf. *Leg.* 1.72; single horse: e.g., *Leg.* 2.99, cited in Inwood, *Ethics and Human Action*, 142, n. 63. On the single horse variation (142), Inwood writes: "In Plato the two horses represent the two distinct irrational elements in the soul. When a dualistic contrast of reason and the irrational

Elsewhere, he identifies the team of horses more broadly as emotion(s).[27] He can also envision the team as sense-perception (αἴσθησις).[28] But no matter what sort of team Philo envisions, he always casts the soul's rational element as the charioteer charged with *controlling* the team.[29] In this way, his chariot figure *always* serves as a model of ἐγκράτεια in action—as a model of reason managing or "driving" the non-rational elements of the soul—and in this respect it perfectly suits the Platonic tradition's *broad* formulation of ἐγκράτεια as a power dynamic of rational over against non-rational. But since it can *also* depict reason managing the discrete *movement* of those elements—managing, in other words, discrete instances of non-rational *impulse* (ὁρμή)—the figure accommodates a more precise concept of ἐγκράτεια tailored to a Middle-Platonic view of "passion."

Philo's use of the concept of impulse (ὁρμή) to develop his chariot figure into a more elaborate model of ἐγκράτεια presumes a suitable basis in the *actual* dynamic between horses and drivers:[30]

> Drivers (ἡνίοχοι) ... lead [their team] just as they please by keeping hold of the reins (τῶν ἡνιῶν). Sometimes they give rein for a brisk trot (ἐφιέντες πρὸς ὀξὺν δρόμον), other times they pull back violently (ἀναχαιτίζοντες), if an excessive surge (φορᾷ τοῦ δέοντος πλείονι) gets the team running. (*Opif.* 88)[31]

---

part of the soul in its undifferentiated formulation was preferred, an analogy with only one horse was substituted."

[27] E.g., *Leg.* 3.193: ὑποζεύξας σεαυτὸν ὀχήματι παθῶν, ἡνιοχούσης ἀφροσύνης.

[28] E.g., *Leg.* 3.222–24 (esp. §224: ἐπειδὰν μὲν ὁ τῆς ψυχῆς ἡνίοχος ... ὁ νοῦς ἄρχῃ τοῦ ζῴου ὅλου καθάπερ ἡγεμὼν πόλεως, ὅταν δὲ ἡ ἄλογος αἴσθησις φέρηται τὰ πρωτεῖα, σύγχυσις καταλαμβάνει δεινή, οἷα δούλων δεσπόταις ἐπιτεθειμένων). See Méasson, *Char ailé*, 160–63.

[29] In *Agr.* 93, Philo characterizes the "art of driving" (τέχνην τὴν ἡνιοχικήν) as ἱκανὸς εἶναι δύνασθαι <u>κρατεῖν ἵππων</u> (cf. *Virt.* 13: ὑγεία δὲ ψυχῆς εὐκρασία δυνάμεών ἐστι τῆς τε κατὰ τὸν θυμὸν καὶ τὴν ἐπιθυμίαν καὶ τὸν λόγον, <u>ἐπικρατούσης τῆς λογικῆς</u> καὶ ὥσπερ ἀφηνιαστὰς ἵππους ἡνιοχούσης ἑκατέρας). Conversely, Philo assumes the capacity of the *team* to overpower the *driver* (i.e., ἀκρασία) and bring everything to ruin (e.g., *Leg.* 3.223: ὥσπερ οὖν ἄρχοντος μὲν ἡνιόχου καὶ ταῖς ἡνίαις τὰ ζῷα ἄγοντος ᾗ βούλεται ἄγεται τὸ ἅρμα, ἀφηνιασάντων δὲ ἐκείνων καὶ <u>κρατησάντων</u> ὅτε ἡνίοχος κατεσύρη πολλάκις τά τε ζῷα ἔστιν ὅτε τῇ ῥύμῃ τῆς φορᾶς εἰς βόθρον κατηνέχθη πλημμελῶς τε πάντα φέρεται).

[30] Philo himself had seen chariots in action: "Thus in chariot races (ἐν ἱπποδρομίαις) too *I have seen people* (εἶδόν τινας) giving way to thoughtlessness who, instead of sitting in their places as they should as orderly spectators, stood in the middle of the course and pushed over by the rush of the chariots were crushed under the feet and wheels, a proper reward for their folly" (*Prov.* 2.58; emphasis added). Philo's knowledge of chariots included familiarity with obscure technical terminology, on which see H. A. Harris, "The Foot-Rests in Hippolytus's Chariot," *CR* 18 (1968): 259–60. On Philo's extensive familiarity with a variety of competitive sports, see esp. H. A. Harris, *Greek Athletics and the Jews* (TSP 3; Cardiff: University of Wales Press, 1976), 51–95.

[31] My translation.

Here Philo reviews the fundamentals of managing an unruly team. Of course, the problem lies not in the team's movement per se, but in its movement *beyond* what the driver sanctions, in its "excessive surge." Philo uses the term φορά—a synonym of ὁρμή—to describe this surge and qualifies it with the expression πλείων τοῦ δέοντος, "greater than the need," meaning greater than the movement needed to accomplish the driver's purpose. Philo elsewhere denotes this type of unruly, excessive movement using a number of specialized terms, most commonly ἀφηνιάζειν, "to throw off the reins."[32] To counter this unruliness, drivers must reassert their control, whether by "pulling back violently" (ἀναχαιτίζειν), as Philo indicates here, or by some other technique, such as "curbing" (ἐπιστομίζειν), as Philo indicates elsewhere.[33] In any case, Philo envisions controlling a team of horses as a matter of curtailing their *excessive* movements, which bear description in terms of impulse. Philo's characterization of chariot driving applies also to the mounted horseman:

> When the horse goes forward in obedience to the reins (εὐηνίως), the horseman gives a few pats as if to praise the horse, but when the horse gets carried away beyond proper measure by excessive impulse (σὺν πλείονι ὁρμῇ πέραν ἐκφέρηται τοῦ μετρίου), the horseman pulls back violently with force (μετὰ βίας ... ἀναχαιτίζει) to slow the horse down. (*Agr.* 70)[34]

Here again Philo equates *control* with the curtailing of excessive impulse (πλείονι ὁρμῇ), which involves movement beyond the limit or measure (πέραν ... τοῦ μετρίου) set by the horseman's purpose. He also highlights a key element of managing *any* unruly non-rational power, horse or not: the use of brute force (μετὰ βίας). By the application of force, a horseman bends the steed to his will, not to *eliminate* its movement, but simply to *control* it. While neither of these passages explicitly describes the workings of the *soul*, they clearly allude to the Middle-Platonic definition of "passion" that Philo formulates in *Spec.* 4.79:

- ἄμετρος καὶ πλεονάζουσα ὁρμή (*Spec.* 4.79)
- φορᾷ τοῦ δέοντος πλείονι (*Opif.* 88)
- πλείονι ὁρμῇ πέραν ... τοῦ μετρίου (*Agr.* 70)

---

[32] ἀφηνιάζειν and its variants appear over fifty times in Philo's writings. Méasson (*Char ailé*, 146) considers it part of a larger vocabulary "inspiré du *Phèdre*."
[33] ἀναχαιτίζειν: lit. *to throw back the mane* (χαίτη), i.e., *to cause to rear up*; e.g., *Mos.* 1.25: ὥσπερ τισὶν ἡνίαις ... τὴν εἰς τὸ πρόσω φορὰν ἀνεχαίτιζε βίᾳ. In other words, the driver pulls back with such violence that the team rears up. ἐπιστομίζειν: *to curb with the bit* (cf. στόμα); e.g., *Leg.* 2.104: ἱππέως ... ἔργον δαμάζειν τὸν ἵππον καὶ ἀφηνιάζοντα ἐπιστομίζειν.
[34] My translation.

In other words, Philo sees in the management of horses an effective means of representing the management of non-rational impulse, specifically the "excessive" impulse Middle Platonists counted as "passion." Capitalizing on this analogy, Philo applies the language of horsemanship *directly* to the realm of moral psychology to characterize ἐγκράτεια as the curtailing of excessive impulse.

Since Middle Platonists defined passion in terms of non-rational impulse, Philo can depict the *management* of passion strictly in terms of non-rational impulse, without naming a specific *type* of passion (desire, fear, grief, etc.):[35]

> For ["horsemen"] are able (δύνανται), by applying a bridle to the soul's non-rational faculties (χαλινὸν ταῖς ἀλόγοις δυνάμεσιν ἐμβαλόντες), to curb the surge of their excessive impulse (ἐπιστομίζειν τῆς πλεοναζούσης τὴν φορὰν ὁρμῆς). (*Agr.* 94)[36]

As Philo suggests here, the soul has a variety of non-rational faculties (ἄλογοι δυνάμεις), whose existence per se poses no problem. But since these faculties can usurp reason's authority and become "passionate," the moral agent must be able to exercise ἐγκράτεια, which Philo depicts here as "applying a bridle" (χαλινόν ... ἐμβαλόντες). In particular, the moral agent must be able to curb the surge of *excessive* non-rational impulses, whatever their source. Desire (ἐπιθυμία), for example, represents a perfectly natural faculty of the soul. But when the impulses of desire become *excessive*, ἐπιθυμία the benign emotion becomes ἐπιθυμία the malignant passion. Controlling ἐπιθυμία (exercising ἐγκράτεια) specifically involves the curtailment of this excess:

> But there are others, boastful persons, of the sort that is puffed up by arrogance, who in their craving for high position determine to have nothing to do in any way with the frugal, the truly profitable mode of living. Indeed, if any rebuke them in order to rein in the unruliness of their desires (ἕνεκα τοῦ τὸν ἀφηνιασμὸν τῶν ἐπιθυμιῶν ἀναχαιτίσαι), they regard the admonition as an insult .... (*Spec.* 2.18)[37]

The rebuke here stands against *passionate* desire, since it involves "pulling back violently" (ἀναχαιτίσαι) not on desire per se but on the "unruliness" of desire (τὸν ἀφηνιασμόν), which represents the movement *in excess of* the

---

[35] Cf. *Leg.* 3.118: ἡ ... ὁρμὴ πάθους.
[36] My translation. Cf. *Agr.* 58: τὰ περιττὰ τῆς εἰς ἀπληστίαν ὁρμῆς αὐτῶν ἐπιστομίζοντες; *Spec.* 1.193: ἐπιστομίζοντας τὰς ἐφ'ἡδονὴν ὁρμάς.
[37] Cf. *Spec.* 2.135: χαλινόν ... ἐμβαλεῖν ταῖς ἐπιθυμίαις ὑπὲρ τοῦ μὴ ἀνασκιρτᾶν ἐπὶ πλέον; *Virt.* 113: οὐκ εἴασεν ἀχάλινον φέρεσθαι τὴν ἐπιθυμίαν ἀπαυχενίζουσαν, ἀλλ'ἐστείλατο τὸ σφοδρόν αὐτῆς.

"frugal mode of living" reason would otherwise allow. And the dynamic envisioned here in regard to ἐπιθυμία applies in theory to *any* emotion. In *Leg.* 3.118–37, for example, Philo uses the chariot figure to represent the work of Aaron, who stands as the allegorical exemplar of the *moderation of emotion* (μετριοπάθεια).[38] While cues in the biblical text prompt Philo to highlight θυμός in his allegorical consideration of μετριοπάθεια, he clearly has *all* emotions in view.[39] In general, he portrays the moderating effect of ἐγκράτεια as bringing *reason* (λόγος) to bear on the *emotions* (πάθη), "so that [reason] like a charioteer (ἡνιόχου τρόπον) may curb their surge to excess (ἐπιστομίζῃ τὴν ἐπὶ πλέον αὐτῶν φοράν)" (*Leg.* 3.134).[40] In other words, reason seeks not to eliminate emotions but only to curb their *excessive impulse*. With reason in command, emotion never oversteps the limits of moderate expression—it never becomes, in other words, a "passion," a disruptive force leading the soul to destruction, like a runaway horse pulling a hapless chariot to ruin. Here again Philo conceives ἐγκράτεια as the curtailing of *excessive* non-rational impulse, and he formulates this concept in light of a Middle-Platonic definition of "passion." While this notion of *curtailing excess* lends precision to Philo's concept of ἐγκράτεια, a more practical concept of what it means for a rational part to rule over non-rational parts within the soul—especially for reason to rule over *desire* (ἐπιθυμία)—involves the different and often conflicting sources of human motivation.

---

[38] *Leg.* 3.131: Ἀαρὼν μετριοπάθειαν ... ἀσκεῖ, ἐκτεμεῖν γὰρ ἔτι τὸ στῆθος καὶ τὸν θυμὸν ἀδυνατεῖ· φέρει δ'ἐπ'αὐτὸν τὸν ἡνίοχον ... λόγον. Philo contrasts the μετριοπάθεια of Aaron, a lower ethical stage, with the ἀπάθεια of Moses, a higher ethical stage (*Leg.* 3.128–29). For this distinction between μετριοπάθεια and ἀπάθεια in Middle Platonism, see Lilla, *Clement of Alexandria*, 92–106 (cf. John Dillon, "Plotinus, Philo and Origen on the Grades of Virtue," in *Platonismus und Christentum: Festschrift für Heinrich Dörrie* [ed. Horst-Dieter Blume and Friedhelm Mann; JACE 10; Münster: Aschendorff, 1983], 92–105, esp. 102–03).

[39] On reason as the "charioteer" of θυμός, see, for example, *Leg.* 3.123: ἐπὶ τοῦ θυμοῦ, ἵν'οὗτος ἡνιοχῆται λόγῳ; *Leg.* 3.127: ἡνιοχθήσεται ὁ θυμὸς ὑπό τε λόγου. Philo, however, sets this long discourse on "Aaronic" moderation in the broader context of a Middle-Platonic bipartite opposition between *reason* (λόγος) and *emotion* (πάθος). At the outset (*Leg.* 3.115), he seems to endorse Platonic *tripartition*, but he immediately reveals his Middle-Platonic affinities in *Leg.* 3.116 by making bipartition the overarching frame of reference: the soul consists of reason opposed to *emotion* (μάχεται ὁ λόγος τῷ πάθει), for instance *pleasure* (κρατοῦντος ... λόγου φροῦδος ἡ ἡδονή, νικώσης δὲ ἡδονῆς φυγὰς ὁ λόγος), or of reason opposed to θυμός and ἐπιθυμία, elements of the *non-rational part* (ὁ θυμὸς καὶ ἡ ἐπιθυμία, μέρη τοῦ ἀλόγου), abode of *the emotions* (τὰ πάθη). In Philo's Middle-Platonic tripartition as bipartition, θυμός and ἐπιθυμία represent emotions (πάθη) stemming from the soul's non-rational part, but they are only two of many (cf. *Agr.* 78: θυμοῦ γὰρ καὶ ἐπιθυμίας καὶ συνόλως ἁπάντων παθῶν).

[40] My translation.

Ἐγκράτεια – Predominance of Rational Motivation

Reason and desire represent two distinct sources of motivation in the human soul, each with its own characteristic aim.[41] Desire (ἐπιθυμία) represents a source of motivation whose invariable aim is pleasure (ἡδονή). Given a sensory impression of something pleasurable, desire *always* responds by motivating the moral agent to pursue pleasure. Reason (λόγος), by contrast, represents a source of motivation whose invariable aim is the good (ἀγαθός). Given a set of circumstances, reason—unless captive to another component of the soul—*always* responds by motivating the moral agent to do what rational calculation (λογισμός) deems best in those circumstances. These two sources of motivation do not necessarily oppose one another, but they obviously *can*. Desire overcomes reason (ἀκρασία) whenever the moral agent acts *for the sake of* pleasure despite reason's contrary motivation to act *for the sake of* rational benefit.[42] Conversely, reason overcomes desire (ἐγκράτεια) whenever the moral agent acts *for the sake of* rational benefit despite desire's contrary motivation to act *for the sake of* pleasure.[43] In other words, ἐγκράτεια restricts desire with the "measure" of rational benefit: desire may pursue its aim of pleasure, *as long as* that pursuit serves a rational end and bears rational justification.[44] The pursuit of pleasure *beyond* reasonable measure—the pursuit of pleasure for pleasure's sake—represents the triumph of desire (as a source of motivation) over reason (as a source of motivation), and desire at that moment, as *its* characteristic motivation predominates, becomes "excessive" and so "passionate." While this dynamic applies in theory to *any* desire, the desire for food illustrates it well.[45]

---

[41] For analysis of the Platonic theory in terms of *motivation*, see for example Lorenz, *Brute Within*, 35: "the embodied human soul is a composite object, composed of a number of parts which (strictly and accurately speaking) are the *subjects or bearers of different kinds of motivating conditions*" (emphasis added; cf. passages in the General Index under "Motivating condition" [218]); see also Cooper, "Human Motivation."

[42] E.g., *Det.* 95: τὴν ἡδονὴν ἀποδεχόμεθα ἐγκράτειαν πέραν ὅρων ἐλαύνοντες.

[43] E.g., *Agr.* 48: χρή ... τὸν ἡμέτερον ἄρχειν νοῦν τὸ συμφέρον πρὸ τοῦ ἡδέος ... αἱρούμενον.

[44] E.g., *QG* 2.68 (Petit): δι'ἐγκράτειαν δι'ἣν ἐμέτρει τὴν χρῆσιν.

[45] For an illustration of this basic dynamic relative to *sexual* desire, see Kathy L. Gaca, "Philo's Principles of Sexual Conduct and Their Influence on Christian Platonist Sexual Principles," *SPhA* 8 (1996): 21-39, esp. 22–27, where Gaca outlines Philo's (Pythagorean) "procreationist principle." Although Gaca does not analyze it in terms of moral psychology, the procreationist principle resonates with the concept of ἐγκράτεια as predominance of rational motivation by endorsing sex for the sake of reproduction (*reason* as source of motivation) and rejecting sex for the sake of pleasure (*desire* as source of motivation). Niehoff (*Philo on Jewish Identity*, 99–102) examines the same

With regard to food, desire invariably seeks *only* the pleasure of eating, while reason seeks the moral agent's overall well being.[46] Desire always urges indulgence, due to its reflexive, non-rational mode of operation—in other words, given an opportunity to eat pleasurably, desire will always say "yes." Reason, by contrast, taking all factors into account, can accordingly urge either *for* or *against* indulgence on an ad hoc basis. While reason could not in principle *categorically* endorse a certain type of indulgence, human beings must eat to live, so—barring exceptional circumstances—reason always approves eating for nourishment as the proper indulgence of a "necessary" desire, an indulgence perfectly consistent with the demands of ἐγκράτεια:

> Mark you not that even the most self-controlled of men (οἱ ἐγκρατέστατοι) under compulsion of the mortal element in them (ἀνάγκῃ τοῦ θνητοῦ) resort to food and drink (παραγίνονται ἐπὶ σιτία καὶ ποτά), out of which the pleasures of the appetite develop (αἱ γαστρὸς ἡδοναὶ συνεστᾶσιν)? (*Leg.* 1.86)[47]

So a moral agent who genuinely *needs* to eat can satisfy both reason and desire with a good meal: rational calculation (λογισμός) motivates the eating as a logical means of sustaining life and health, while desire (ἐπιθυμία) motivates the eating as a pleasurable experience. Of course, rational calculation (λογισμός) may compel the same hungry moral agent to *reject* a meal despite desire's pressing motivation to eat for the sake of pleasure—if, for instance, the meal is poisoned or belongs to someone else. But the conflict

---

principle of limiting sex to reproduction but downplays the Pythagorean associations, instead framing the issue in terms of Philo's ideal of Jewish ἐγκράτεια.

[46] Much of Philo's discourse on ethical eating reflects elements of the diatribe tradition, especially the works of Musonius Rufus (see Paul Wendland, "Philo und die kynisch-stoische Diatribe," in *Beiträge zur Geschichte der griechischen Philosophie und Religion* [Berlin: Georg Reimer, 1895], 1–75, esp. 8–15; cf. Bréhier, *Idées philosophiques et religieuses*, 261–62; Niehoff, *Philo on Jewish Identity*, 105). Musonius, for example, endorses the standard of *need* over *pleasure*. e.g., *Troph.*[B] 116.9–11: γαστριμαργία τί ἂν εἴη ἄλλο ἢ ἀκρασία περὶ τροφήν, δι'ἣν ἄνθρωποι τὸ ἡδὺ τὸ ἐν σίτῳ τοῦ ὠφελίμου προτιμῶσιν; 118.6–7: ἀσκῶν καὶ ἐθίζων αὐτὸν αἱρεῖσθαι σῖτον οὐχ ἵνα ἥδηται ἀλλ'ἵνα τρέφηται. Such similarities, however, do not indicate the acceptance of Cynic-Stoic *philosophical* commitments on Philo's part but only his use of a widespread ethical topos (cf. A.C. van Geytenbeek, *Musonius Rufus and Greek Diatribe* [trans. B. L. Hijmans; rev. ed.; WTS 8; Assen: Van Gorcum, 1963], 106: "Like nearly all moralists who treat the problem of food, Musonius rejects pleasure as the aim"). Although he frames ethical discourse in ways comparable to Musonius, Philo presupposes a moral psychology quite different from that of Musonius or any other Stoic.

[47] Cf. *Leg.* 3.147: τοῖς γὰρ ἀναγκαίοις σιτίοις καὶ ποτοῖς ἡ φύσις βιάζεται χρῆσθαι; *Ebr.* 131: σιτίων καὶ ποτῶν καὶ ὕπνου καὶ πάντων ὅσα ἀναγκαῖα τῇ φύσει. For Plato's understanding of "necessary desires," see *Resp.* 558 C–559 D.

between reason and desire in matters of food more commonly involves the question of eating *in excess of* rational necessity. Having eaten enough to survive in good health, and so having no real *need* to eat, how does the moral agent handle further *opportunities* to eat? At this point, Philo's moral theory can explain indulgence and abstinence in term of ἀκρασία and ἐγκράτεια, understanding each as the victory of a certain type of motivation. *To eat* represents a victory of desire over reason (ἀκρασία), since the moral agent eats strictly for the sake of pleasure: the motivation for pleasure has in effect *overpowered* the motivation for rational benefit, which urges abstinence as the reasonable course. Philo understands ἀκρασία along these lines in *Mos.* 1.160–61, where he attributes a lack of ἐγκράτεια to those who incite desires, including desires of the stomach (τὰς γαστρός ... ἐπιθυμίας), *beyond necessities* (ἔξω τῶν ἀναγκαίων)—by eating more than they need, they eat for pleasure and reflect the predominance of ἐπιθυμία as a motivating disposition.[48] Conversely, *not to eat* represents a victory of reason over desire (ἐγκράτεια), since the moral agent *controls* the desire for food by keeping it within the bounds of rational necessity. Philo equates ἐγκράτεια with eating (and drinking) according to need, since it involves reason motivating the moral agent to indulge desire only *to the point of need* and no further. Commenting on Exodus 23:25b[49] Philo writes:

> He symbolically indicates nourishment and health (τροφὴν καὶ ὑγίειαν αἰνίττεται): nourishment through the mention of food and water (δι'ἄρτου καὶ ὕδατος), and health through the expression "turn away weakness" (διὰ τοῦ μαλακίαν ἀποστρέφειν). Second, he represents self-control (ἐγκράτειαν εἰσηγεῖται) by talking about the consumption of necessities only (τὴν τῶν ἀναγκαίων μετουσίαν μονὸν ἐνειπῶν). (*QE* 2.18)[50]

---

[48] In this passage, Philo contrasts ἀκρασία and ἐγκράτεια (N.B. *Mos.* 1.161: οἱ ... ἀκράτορες μεταβάλλουσι πρὸς ἐγκράτειαν), associating the former not only with desire ἔξω τῶν ἀναγκαίων but also with the enjoyment of pleasure (§160: καθηδυπαθεῖν [cf. ἡδύς]); cf. *Opif.* 158: ὁ φιλήδονος ... ἐκτραχηλιζούσης καὶ ὑποσκελιζούσης τῆς ἀκρασίας; *Det.* 95: τὴν ἡδονὴν ἀποδεχόμεθα ἐγκράτειαν πέραν ὅρων ἐλαύνοντες; *Somn.* 2.48: πρὸς ἀπόλαυσιν ἡδονῆς μᾶλλον ἢ πρὸς μετουσίαν τροφῆς. In *Det.* 113, Philo associates ἀκρασία with those whose desires continue despite a full stomach. With no rational motivation for eating, only a desire for pleasure can explain their behavior (cf. *Leg.* 2.16: ἕνεκα τοῦ ἀναγκαίου μόνον ... ἢ καὶ ἕνεκα τοῦ ἀμέτρου καὶ περιττοῦ).

[49] Exodus 23:25b: εὐλογήσω τὸν ἄρτον σου καὶ τὸν οἶνόν σου καὶ τὸ ὕδωρ σου καὶ ἀποστρέψω μαλακίαν ἀφ'ὑμῶν. As Marcus notes (PLCL suppl. 2, 56, n. c), "Philo agrees with Heb. against LXX in omitting 'and wine' after 'bread'" (cf. Petit, 254, n. b).

[50] My translation of Petit's text of the Greek fragment (Petit, 254). The passage continues from the Armenian, "for bread is a plain food without anything extra, and flowing water is (a similarly plain) drink, and upon these (depends) health" (trans. Marcus; PLCL suppl. 2, 56). In *Leg.* 3.154, Philo likewise associates the restraint of desire (συνεστάλθαι τὰς ἐπιθυμίας) with only necessary indulgence(s) (μόνοις χρησόμεθα

Philo's identification here of ἐγκράτεια with the indulgence of *necessary* desire clarifies the notion of curtailing excess from the chariot figure by further characterizing "excessive" as "unnecessary." Conceived in these terms, ἐγκράτεια works to counteract *passionate* desire (πλεονάζουσα [ἄμετρος] ἐπιθυμία) by consistently enforcing the "measure" urged by reason (necessity) over against desire's persistent urge toward pleasure. In other words, ἐγκράτεια eliminates excessive, *unnecessary* desire and the *unnecessary* pleasure it entails. Philo symbolically interprets the rite of circumcision along these lines:

> They say that circumcision of the skin is a symbol, as if (to show that) it is proper to cut off superfluous and excessive desires (τὰς περιττὰς καὶ πλεοναζούσας ἐπιθυμίας) by exercising self-control (ἐγκράτειαν) .... For just as the skin of the foreskin is superfluous in procreation ... so the excess of desire is superfluous .... It is superfluous because it is not necessary .... (*QG* 3.48)[51]

So the moral agent possessed of ἐγκράτεια moderates ἐπιθυμία and avoids passion by indulging according to *need*, curtailing the excess of unnecessary indulgence by ensuring the predominance of a motivation to secure rational benefit (necessity) over a motivation to secure pleasure.

Summary

Although Philo never formally defines ἐγκράτεια, he nevertheless reveals through incidental remarks a substantive *concept* of ἐγκράτεια framed along three distinct but complementary lines. First, ἐγκράτεια involves a power dynamic of rational over non-rational forces, understood either broadly as λόγος defeating *any* challenge from elsewhere in the soul, or narrowly as λόγος defeating ἐπιθυμία. Second, ἐγκράτεια involves the curtailing of excessive impulse. Finally, ἐγκράτεια involves the predominance of rational motivation over against a non-rational urge toward pleasure. But how, in Philo's view, does the moral agent acquire ἐγκράτεια?

τοῖς ἀναγκαίοις, τῶν δὲ περιττῶν ἀφεξόμεθα); cf. *Mos.* 1.28: γαστρί τε γὰρ ἔξω τῶν ἀναγκαίων δασμῶν, οὓς ἡ φύσις ἔταξεν, οὐδὲν πλέον ἐχορήγει.
[51] Trans. Ralph Marcus; substituting "self-control" for "continence"; Greek text reconstructed by Marcus from the Armenian (see PLCL suppl. 1, 245, n. h and i).

The Acquisition of Ἐγκράτεια

Because ἐγκράτεια involves the control of *non-rational* forces, the means of acquiring it have a correspondingly non-rational character, insofar as they do not involve the formulation or deployment of rational argument. Without a *capacity* for reason, ἐπιθυμία cannot accept or reject a moral agent's reasoned guidance. Instead, the moral agent must manage ἐπιθυμία through the application of *force*—just as the charioteer does not *reason* with an unruly team (he cannot), but simply *acts* to bring it into submission. In other words, ἐγκράτεια comes from *doing*, not *thinking*: the moral agent becomes good at controlling ἐπιθυμία only by *exerting* or *practicing* control, not by theoretical reflection.[52] Philo's philosophical contemporaries considered the importance of *practice* in moral development under the conceptual rubric of ἄσκησις.[53] Although the term appears nowhere in the Pentateuch, Philo has much to say about ἄσκησις, because he believes that Moses considered the topic *allegorically* under the figure of Jacob.

Ἐγκράτεια through Ἄσκησις

Philo's view of Jacob fits into a broader interpretive scheme involving the *three* patriarchs Abraham, Isaac, and Jacob, who each represent a different way of acquiring virtue: through instruction (μάθησις), nature (φύσις), and practice (ἄσκησις) respectively:[54]

> For the holy word seems to be searching into the types of souls (τρόπους ... ψυχῆς), all of them of high worth, one which pursues the good through teaching (ἐκ διδασκαλίας), one through nature (ἐκ φύσεως) and one through practice (ἐξ ἀσκήσεως). The first called Abraham, the second Isaac

---

[52] Philo clearly distinguishes between theoretical and *practical* virtue: e.g., *Leg.* 1.57: ἡ δὲ ἀρετὴ καὶ θεωρητική ἐστι καὶ πρακτική; cf. *Congr.* 46: ἡ γὰρ ἄνευ πράξεως θεωρία ψιλὴ πρὸς οὐδὲν ὄφελος τοῖς ἐπιστήμοσιν.

[53] As noted earlier (p. 15, n. 45), the term ἄσκησις in Philo's usage has little to do with modern terms such as "ascetic" or "asceticism," whose connotations derive mostly from Christian monasticism. The Greek term has no intrinsic association with religious practice (see Dressler, *Usage of Ἀσκέω*). For use of the term in Middle Platonism, see, for example, *Didask.* 24.4 [177.14–15]: τοῦ μὲν [λογιστικοῦ] διὰ διδασκαλίας, τοῦ δὲ [παθητικοῦ] διὰ τῆς τοῦ ἔθους ἀσκήσεως; (cf. 30.3 [184.1–2]: ἐξ ἔθους ἐγγινόμεναι καὶ ἀσκήσεως); Plutarch, *Garr.* 510 C: τῶν γὰρ παθῶν κρίσει καὶ ἀσκήσει περιγινόμεθα; *Eclog.* 37.18–38.1: Ἠθική ἐστι δύναμις ψυχῆς, δι᾽ἧς ἀσκηθείσης καλῶς ἡ πρακτικὴ κατασκευάζεται ἀρετή. For the concept in contemporary Stoicism, see Geytenbeek, *Musonius Rufus*, 28–29; Richard Valantasis, "Musonius Rufus and Roman Ascetical Theory," *GRBS* 40 [1999]: 207–31; cf. B. L. Hijmans, *ΑΣΚΗΣΙΣ: Notes on Epictetus' Educational System* [WTS 2; Assen: Von Gorcum, 1959]). For the concept in Cynic philosophy, see Marie-Odile Goulet-Cazé, *L'ascèse cynique: Un commentaire de Diogène Laërce VI 70–71* (2d ed.; Paris: J. Vrin, 2001).

[54] See Birnbaum, "Exegetical Building Blocks."

and the third Jacob, are symbols of virtue (σύμβολον [sic] ... ἀρετῆς) acquired respectively by teaching (διδασκαλικῆς), nature (φυσικῆς) and practice (ἀσκητικῆς). (*Abr.* 52)[55]

Although Philo ostensibly discovers this threefold scheme through allegorical exegesis of the Pentateuch, the notion of virtue accruing by nature, instruction, and practice comes from Greek philosophy, appearing in systematic formulation at least as early as Aristotle and gaining later acceptance among Philo's philosophical contemporaries, including his fellow Middle Platonists.[56] Philo's reason for choosing *Jacob* as the model of practice (ἄσκησις) derives mainly from the patriarch's wrestling match at the ford of the Jabbok (Gen 32:22–32).[57] Since wrestling plays a definitive role in the life of Jacob, Philo makes it an essential attribute of the type of *soul* Moses represents through the *story* of Jacob. Wrestlers are athletes, and, in the athletic discourse of antiquity, the term ἄσκησις refers to the *practice* (i.e., *exercise, training*) that every athlete—wrestler or not—must undergo to achieve excellence. And the discourse of ἄσκησις belongs to an even larger stock of athletic imagery and terminology deployed in connection with the Jacob soul: an "agon motif" that suits Philo's allegorical method well because it operates on two levels.[58] Literally, the agon motif speaks of an

---

[55] Cf. *Mut.* 12; *Ios.* 1; *Mos.* 1.76.
[56] Diogenes Laertius (DL 5.18), attributes the formulation to Aristotle: "Three things he declared to be indispensable for education: natural endowment (φύσεως), study (μαθήσεως), and constant practice (ἀσκήσεως)" (trans. R. D. Hicks). Noting the threefold scheme in *Didask.* 28.4 [182.3–6], Dillon writes (citing *Abr.* 52–54) that "it is thus likely to be the basic Middle-Platonic doctrine" (*Alcinous*, xxiii) (cf. Lilla, *Clement of Alexandria*, 66–68).
[57] Cf. Birnbaum, "Exegetical Building Blocks," 86–88. Gen 32:25: ἐπάλαιεν ἄνθρωπος μετ'αὐτοῦ ἕως πρωΐ; Gen 32:26 : ἐν τῷ παλαίειν αὐτὸν μετ'αὐτοῦ. For Philo, the etymological tale of Jacob's "heel grabbing" (Gen 25:26 : ἡ χεὶρ αὐτοῦ ἐπειλημμένη τῆς πτέρνης Ἠσαυ) illustrates his skill as a wrestler, who grabs the heel to trip up and overthrow an opponent (e.g., *Leg.* 3.93: ὁ πτερνιστής ... Ἰακώβ; *Leg.* 3.190: πτερνισθήσεται πρὸς τοῦ πάλην ἠσκηκότος Ἰακώβ). On Philo's portrait of Jacob in terms of ancient wrestling, see Harris, *Greek Athletics*, 68–71. On Philo's understanding of Jacob more broadly, see Petra von Gemünden, "La figure de Jacob à l'époque hellénistico-romaine: L'example de Philon d'Alexandrie," in *Jacob: Commentaire à plusieurs voix de Gen 25–36 : Mélanges offerts à Albert de Pury* (ed. Jean-Daniel Macchi and Thomas Römer; MdB 44; Genève: Labor et Fides, 2001), 358–70; C. T. R. Hayward, "Philo, the Septuagint of Genesis 32:24–32 and the Name 'Israel': Fighting the Passions, Inspiration and the Vision of God," *JJS* 51 (2000): 209–226; Michael Poliakoff, "Jacob, Job, and Other Wrestlers: Reception of Greek Athletics by Jews and Christians in Antiquity," *JSH* 11 (1984): 48–65, esp. 63–65; Mark Sheridan, "Jacob and Israel: A Contribution to the History of an Interpretation," in *Mysterium Christi: Symbolgegenwart und theologische Bedeutung* (ed. M. Löhrer and Elmar Salmann; SA 116; Rome: Pontificio Ateneo S. Anselmo, 1995), 219–42.
[58] On the agon motif in Philo, see esp. Martin Brändl, *Der Agon bei Paulus: Herkunft und Profil paulinischer Agonmetaphorik* (WUNT 222; Tübingen: Mohr Siebeck, 2006), 85–115

athlete's struggle to train in pursuit of tangible prizes. Figuratively, the motif speaks of the *soul's* struggle to train in pursuit of intangible—yet more valuable—prizes, especially virtue. While ἄσκησις can in theory yield a number of virtues, Philo sees it primarily as a means of acquiring ἐγκράτεια.[59] He thematically highlights ἐγκράτεια as a prominent goal of the Jacob soul by characterizing its struggle as a contest with non-rational forces—a wrestling match against *emotion* (πάθος).[60]

[="Die Agon-Metaphorik bei Philo von Alexandrien"]. On Philo's knowledge of agon terminology, Brändl notes: "Dabei handelt es sich nicht nur um das gängige agonistische Wortfeld, sondern auch um detaillierte Einzelheiten und zahlreiche *termini technici*" (87). As examples of "das gängige agonistische Wortfeld," Brändl lists: "ἀγωνίζεσθαι, ἀθλεῖν, ἀλείφειν, ἀσκεῖν, βραβεύειν, γυμνάζειν, κηρύσσειν, κονιοῦσθαι, παγκρατιάζεσθαι, παλαίειν, πενταετηρίς, πόνος, πυκτεύειν, σταδιεύειν, στεφανοῦν, τρέχειν mit ihren Derivaten und Komposita" (87, n. 39). See also Uta Poplutz, *Athlet des Evangeliums: Eine motivgeschichtliche Studie zur Wettkampfmetaphorik bei Paulus* (HBS 43; Freiburg im Breisgau: Herder, 2004), 174–201 [="Die Agonmetaphorik im hellenistischen Judentum: Philo von Alexandrien"]; Victor C. Pfitzner, *Paul and the Agon Motif: Traditional Athletic Imagery in the Pauline Literature* (NovTSup 16; Leiden: Brill, 1967), 38–48 [="Hellenistic Judaism and the Agon Tradition: Philo"].

[59] When Philo lists the elements of ἄσκησις, he mentions only one virtue, ἐγκράτεια: *Leg.* 3.18: μέρη τῆς ἀσκήσεως [=] ἀναγνώσεις, μελέται, θεραπεῖαι, τῶν καλῶν μνῆμαι, ἐγκράτεια, τῶν καθηκόντων ἐνέργειαι; *Her.* 253: πάντα ... τὰ τῆς ἀσκήσεως [=] ἡ ζήτησις, ἡ σκέψις, ἡ ἀνάγνωσις, ἡ ἀκρόασις, ἡ προσοχή, ἡ ἐγκράτεια, ἡ ἐξαδιαφόρησις τῶν ἀδιαφόρων.

[60] Cf. Völker, *Fortschritt und Vollendung,* 126–37 [="Der kampf gegen die πάθη"], esp. 129–30: "Daneben fordert Philo eine willensmäßige Anspannung, um die πάθη zu überwinden, ein systematsiches Sich-Üben in der ἐγκράτεια." Although a *prominent* goal, ἐγκράτεια does not represent for Philo the *ultimate* goal of the Jacob soul. Philo translates "Israel" as "seeing God" (*Congr.* 51: Ἰσραὴλ γὰρ ὁρῶν θεὸν ἑρμηνεύεται; cf. *Ebr.* 82: Ἰσραὴλ δὲ τελειότητος· ὅρασιν γὰρ θεοῦ μηνύει τοὔνομα; on the etymology see Grabbe, *Etymology,* 172–73), so the Jacob soul must become "Israel" and obtain a vision of God to achieve its *final* end. This ultimate emphasis on *seeing* God—representing detachment from the sensible world in favor of the intelligible—gives Philo's understanding of Jacob, and thus his concept of ἄσκησις, an overarching *Platonic* framework (see esp. *Praem.* 36–40; cf. *Migr.* 214; *Somn.* 1.46). On the Platonic nature of such a vision, see David Bradshaw, "The Vision of God in Philo of Alexandria," *ACPQ* 72 (1998): 483–500; Frederick E. Brenk, "Darkly Beyond the Glass: Middle Platonism and the Vision of the Soul," in *Platonism in Late Antiquity* (ed. Stephen Gersh and Charles Kannengiesser; CJA 8; Notre Dame, Ind.: University of Notre Dame Press, 1992), 39–60; cf. Irl Goldwin Whitchurch, *The Philosophical Bases of Asceticism in the Platonic Writings and in Pre-Platonic Tradition* (CSP 14; New York: Longmans, Green & Co., 1923); Sarah J. K. Pearce, *The Land of the Body: Studies in Philo's Representation of Egypt* (WUNT 208; Tübingen: Mohr Siebeck, 2007), 30–33 [="Migration and Allegory"]. Despite his identification of Cynic *elements* in Philo's concept of ἄσκησις, Émile Bréhier's suggestion that it derives *entirely* from Cynicism must be rejected (*Idées philosophiques et religieuses,* 261: "L'on ne saurait réduire toute la morale philonienne au cynisme ... nous allons essayer de montrer que *tout son ascétisme en provient*" [emphasis added]; see idem, 261–71 [="Le cynisme et l'ascétisme"]).

While the *patriarch* Jacob played the athlete by literally wrestling with a physical opponent, the Jacob *soul*—the soul possessed of Jacob's athletic qualities—takes its practice (ἄσκησις) by figuratively wrestling with an intangible yet dangerously *real* opponent, the emotions (πάθη).[61] Philo's vision of the moral agent grappling with, and so struggling *against*, the emotions reflects the division of soul presumed in Middle-Platonic moral psychology: πάθος has an independent existence over against the rational faculty. The Jacob soul, in other words, contends with distinct, non-rational πάθη—but *how* and *to what end*? Philo depicts the Jacob soul engaged in a contest of power whose outcome rests solely on the relative strength of opponents: the reason (λόγος) of the moral agent either *is* or *is not* stronger than emotion, and so either *will* or *will not* succeed in forcibly controlling emotion.[62] And the Jacob soul clearly does, in Philo's view, wrestle for *control* of the emotions, not their elimination or absolute suppression. Specifically, the Jacob soul seeks to *moderate* emotion and keep it from overstepping the limits or bounds set by reason.[63] In Philo's view, the *historical* patriarch Abraham exhibits this type of soul, as he "wrestles" with the emotion of grief at the loss of Sarah and rightly aims for μετριοπάθεια:[64]

> [W]hen grief was making itself ready to wrestle with his soul (τῆς λύπης ἐπαποδυομένης ἤδη καὶ κατὰ τῆς ψυχῆς κονιομένης), he grappled with it, as in the arena, and prevailed (ὥσπερ ἀθλητὴς ἐπεκράτησε). He gave strength and high courage to the natural antagonist of emotion, reason (τὸν ἀντίπαλον φύσει τῶν παθῶν λογισμόν), which he had taken as his counselor throughout his life and now particularly was determined to obey .... (*Abr.* 256)[65]

---

[61] E.g., *Leg.* 3.93: ὁ πτερνιστὴς τῶν παθῶν καὶ ἀσκητὴς ἀρετῆς Ἰακώβ; *Sobr.* 65: ἀθλητής ἐστιν ὁ πρὸς πάθη πάλην γεγυμνασμένος Ἰακώβ (cf. *Leg.* 3.190; *Sacr.* 17; *QG* 4.163).

[62] E.g., *Leg.* 3.18: ὁ ἀσκητὴς οὖν Ἰακὼβ νοῦς, ὅτε μὲν ὁρᾷ ταπεινὸν τὸ πάθος, περιμένει λογιζόμενος αὐτὸ νικήσειν κατὰ κράτος; *Mut.* 85: ὁ δ'ἀσκητὴς καὶ τὸ ἑκούσιον ἔχων αὐτὸ μόνον καὶ τοῦτο γυμνάζων καὶ συγκροτῶν, ἵνα τὸ οἰκεῖον πάθος τῷ γενητῷ καταβάλῃ.

[63] In general, Philo suggests a necessary correlation between μετριοπάθεια and ἄσκησις as common characteristics of a moral agent occupying a lower stage of ethical development and making *progress* (προκόπτων) toward perfection: e.g., *Leg.* 3.132: ὅ γε προκόπτων δεύτερος ὢν Ἀαρὼν μετριοπάθειαν ... ἀσκεῖ; *Det.* 65: ἡ μὲν οὖν ἄσκησις μέσον, οὐ τέλειον; *Post.* 78: τοῖς μὲν γὰρ ἀσκηταῖς προκόπτουσι καὶ βελτιουμένοις; for an overview of the topic of moral progress, see John T. Fitzgerald, "The Passions and Moral Progress: An Introduction," in *Passions and Moral Progress*, 1–25, esp. 15–16. Ἐγκράτεια fits with μετριοπάθεια and ἄσκησις, insofar as it always involves *conflict* and thus always denotes a measure of imperfection on the part of the moral agent, who has failed at some level to settle the issue of who—or what—shall rule the soul (see above, pp. 82–88).

[64] In *Abr.* 257, Philo explicitly identifies the goal of Abraham's struggle as "μετριοπαθεῖν."

[65] Substituting "grief" for Colson's "sorrow"; "emotion" for "passion."

Philo's conception of what the ascetic soul achieves in grappling with the emotions mirrors the Middle-Platonic theory of "passion" sketched elsewhere in his writings. Benign emotions become malignant "passions" by becoming "immoderate" (ἄμετρος), so the Jacob soul targets any expression of emotion *in excess of* the measure (μέτρον) set by reason, "wrestling" it down into a more appropriate form.[66] Allegorically interpreting the "numbing of the broad part" (πλάτους νάρκη)[67] as a "prize" (βραβεῖον) awarded to Jacob the "practiser" (ὁ ἀσκητής) after his wrestling match (*Praem.* 47), Philo writes:

> [N]othing is so profitable as that the laxity and free play of the impulses (τὸ κεχαλασμένον καὶ ἀνειμένον τῶν ὁρμῶν) should be hampered and numbed (ἀνακοπῆναί τε καὶ ναρκῆσαι) with their vitalizing forces paralyzed so that the inordinate strength of the emotions may be exhausted (ἵν'ἡ τῶν παθῶν ἄμετρος ἰσχὺς ἐξασθενήσασα) and thus provide a breadth in which the better part of the soul may expand (πλάτος ἐμπαράσχῃ ψυχῆς τῷ βελτίονι μέρει). (*Praem.* 48)[68]

Since *curtailing excess* stands in Philo's mind as one aspect of ἐγκράτεια, he characterizes here the laborious wrestling of the Jacob soul as the *practice* (ἄσκησις) of ἐγκράτεια.[69] Speaking allegorically of "Jacob," Philo elsewhere notes:

> The Man of Practice (ὁ ἀσκητής) ... wrestles with the emotions (πρὸς τὰ πάθη παλαίων) and ... goes into training to gain self-control (πρὸς ἐγκράτειαν ἀλειφόμενος) .... (*Congr.* 31)[70]

Insofar as he identifies the emotions *generically* as the wrestling opponent of the Jacob soul, Philo brings a broad formulation of ἐγκράτεια ("rational" over "non-rational") to his consideration of ἄσκησις. But the emotions *specifically* include ἐπιθυμία, which the narrow formulation of ἐγκράτεια singles out as the principal antagonist of reason. When Philo considers the specific types of practice needed to acquire ἐγκράτεια, he tends to have this narrow formulation—with its emphasis on ἐπιθυμία—in mind.

---

[66] N.B. Philo's characterization of μετριοπαθεῖν in *Abr.* 257: μήτε πλέον τοῦ μετρίου σφαδάζειν.
[67] Gen 32:26: ἐνάρκησεν τὸ πλάτος τοῦ μηροῦ Ιακωβ ἐν τῷ παλαίειν αὐτὸν μετ'αὐτοῦ.
[68] Substituting "impulses" for Colson's "appetites"; "emotions" for "passions." On κεχαλασμένον, see Philo's interpretation of "girding the loins" (ὀσφῦς περιεζῶσθαι [Exod 12:11]) which likewise speaks of moderating emotion (e.g., *Leg.* 3.153–54: ἀνεζῶσθαι γὰρ βούλεται ἡμᾶς τὰ πάθη, ἀλλὰ μὴ ἀνειμένα καὶ κεχαλασμένα φορεῖν; cf. *Leg.* 2:28: ἐπὶ τοῦ πάθους, ὃ ἀνεζῶσθαι χρὴ καὶ μὴ ἐᾶν κεχαλάσθαι καὶ ἀνεῖσθαι).
[69] Cf. *Praem.* 100: ἐγκράτειαν ἀσκήσαντες; *Hypoth.* 7.11: πρὸς ἀσκήσεως ... ἐγκρατείας.
[70] Substituting "emotions" for Colson's "passions."

Ἐγκράτεια through Ascetic Precepts

In light of his understanding of what Jacob represents, Philo sees the acquisition of ἐγκράτεια as a matter of *practice* (ἄσκησις): strenuous, active engagement with an opponent (in this case, ἐπιθυμία), in a contest of power that builds strength and skill. But exactly what *sort* of practice endows the moral agent with ἐγκράτεια? What *sorts* of exercises make for good training? In general, Philo believes that the Law of Moses promotes virtue among its adherents.[71] But he also believes that Moses designed *specific* laws to promote *specific* virtues, including ἐγκράτεια. In other words, Moses had a clear grasp of the activities of soul capable of effecting ἐγκράτεια, and—like a good trainer—he *prescribed* those activities through specific laws.[72] Apart from any *religious* significance, such precepts have great *philosophical* significance, because their formulation reflects principles of moral psychology and ἄσκησις derived from Philo's philosophical milieu.[73] To coin a term, they are "ascetic precepts," and they signal Philo's attempt to understand Mosaic legislation in light of contemporary Middle-

---

[71] E.g., *Spec.* 4.179: νόμοις ἐξαιρέτοις χρωμένῳ· σεμνοὶ δ'εἰσὶν ἐξ ἀνάγκης, ἄτε πρὸς τὴν ἄκραν ἀρετὴν ἀλείφοντες; cf. *Mos.* 2.10: Μωυσῆς ... τρανώσας εὖ μάλα τὰς εἰρημένας ἀρετὰς ἐν οἷς διετάξατο. See Wolfson, *Philo*, 2:200–225 [="Commandments and Virtues"] (cf. John W. Martens, *One God, One Law: Philo of Alexandria on the Mosaic and Greco-Roman Law* [AMMTC; SPhAMA 2; Boston: Brill Academic Publishers, 2003], 95–99 [="The Law of Moses"]; André Myre, "La loi de la nature et la loi mosaïque selon Philon d'Alexandrie," *ScEs* 28 [1976]: 163–81, esp. 167–71 [="La loi mosaïque et la loi morale"]; Michael Satlow, "Philo on Human Perfection," *JTS* 59 [2008]: 500–519, 517–18).

[72] In Philo's view, Moses could formulate helpful exercises in ἐγκράτεια because he himself had mastered desire: "When [Moses] was now passing beyond the term of boyhood, his good sense became more active. He did not, as some, allow the desires of adolescence to go unbridled (οὐχ ὡς ἔνιοι τὰς μειρακιώδεις ἐπιθυμίας ἀχαλινώτους ἐῶν), though the abundant resources which palaces provide supply numberless incentives to foster their flame. But he kept a tight hold on them with the reins, as it were, of self-mastery and endurance (σωφροσύνῃ καὶ καρτερίᾳ ὥσπερ τισὶν ἡνίαις ἐνδησάμενος αὐτάς), and forcibly pulled them back from their forward course (τὴν εἰς τὸ πρόσω φορὰν ἀνεχαίτιζε βίᾳ)" (*Mos.* 1.25–26; substituting "desires" for Colson's "lusts"; "self-mastery and endurance" for "temperance and self-control"). On Philo's view of Moses, see Hywel Clifford, "Moses as Philosopher-Sage in Philo," in *Moses in Biblical and Extra-Biblical Traditions* (ed. Axel Graupner and Michael Wolter; BZAW 372; Berlin: de Gruyter, 2007), 151–67.

[73] These *Mosaic* philosophical exercises fit the definition of "sittliches Exerzitium" (also "sittliche Übung"), the term Paul Rabbow offers to describe a type of methodical practice popular among philosophers of the early Roman Era: "a particular exertion, a calculated act of self-influence, carried out with the express purpose of achieving a specific ethical effect; it always transcends itself, insofar is it is either repeated or forms part of a larger network of acts designed for the same purpose" (my translation of Paul Rabbow, *Seelenführung: Methodik der Exerzitien in der Antike* [München: Kösel, 1954], 18).

Platonic ethical concerns.[74] Although Philo casts a number of laws as ascetic precepts to engender ἐγκράτεια, he never couples an individual law with a complete explanation of how it works. But considering his remarks on *several* such laws provides enough material to create a working concept of the ascetic precept.

In the law regarding a year of Sabbath rest for the land (Exod 23:10–11; Lev 25:2–7), the law regarding fasting on the Day of Atonement (Lev 16:29–31; Num 29:7–11), and the law regarding marrying female prisoners of war (Deut 21:10–14), Philo recognizes deliberate efforts on Moses' part to promote ἐγκράτεια through ἄσκησις.[75] First of all, Moses understood that

---

[74] In general, research into Philo's theory of ἄσκησις has overlooked the place of Mosaic legislation within that theory. Studies of Philo that deal directly with ἄσκησις but do not consider the ascetic function of precepts include Bréhier, *Idées philosophiques et religieuses*, 261–71 [="Le cynisme et l'ascétisme"]; Völker, *Fortschritt und Vollendung*, 198–239 [="Die ἄσκησις als Weg zur Vollkommenheit"]; and Winston, "Philo's Ethical Theory," esp. 405–14 [="Asceticism"]. Similarly, David Charles Aune, "Mastery of the Passions," while he intends in part to "illustrate Philo's ... ascetic program" (128), does not consider the role of precepts. Siegfried, *Philo*, does speak of "das mosaische Gesetz als das zweckmässigste Anleitungsmittel für ... sittlichen Uebungen" (257) in the context of Philo's theory of ἄσκησις (Uebung), but he does not explore the connection between precepts and ἄσκησις in depth (cf. idem, 21 [on 4 Macc]: "durch die Uebung des Gesetzes ... diese vier Tugenden Entstehen"). In their study of Jacob as Philo's allegorical paradigm of ἄσκησις, Hayward ("Philo and the Name 'Israel'") and Sheridan ("Jacob and Israel") do not consider the role of precepts within that paradigm. Steven Fraade does note the role of precepts in his "Ascetical Aspects of Ancient Judaism," in *Jewish Spirituality: From the Bible through the Middles Ages* (ed. Arthur Green; WS 13; New York: Crossroad, 1986), 253–88, 265: "Such strength is only *gradually* achieved with the help of the commandments of the Torah, which are often interpreted by Philo as exercises intended to strengthen the soul by repeatedly accustoming it to abstinence from and moderation of desires for food, drink, sex, etc." But Fraade does not explore the connection between precepts and ἄσκησις in depth, or from the standpoint of moral psychology. Studies of ἄσκησις per se that consider Philo tend *not* to consider the role of precepts (e.g., Bernhard Lohse, *Askese und Mönchtum in der Antike und in der alten Kirche* [RKAM 1; Munich and Vienna: R. Oldenbourg, 1969], 102–10 [="Philo"]). Pierre Hadot, "Spiritual Exercises," provides an excellent survey of therapeutic exercises in Greco-Roman philosophy, including Philo. He cites Philo's general lists of what constitutes ἄσκησις (*Leg.* 3.18, *Her.* 253) (84) but does not mention Mosaic precepts, which are for Philo just the sort of therapeutic exercises Hadot seems to have in mind.

[75] On the law of Sabbath rest, see esp. *Spec.* 2.86–109, *Spec.* 4.212–18, and *Praem.* 153–56 (cf. *Hypoth.* 7.15–19). On fasting, see esp. *Spec.* 1.186–88 (cf. *Mos.* 2.23–24; *Spec.* 1.192–93) and *Spec.* 2.193–203 (esp. §195). On female prisoners of war, see *Virt.* 110–15. In *Virt.* 110–15, Philo himself seems to acknowledge the barbaric setting of a law treating women as spoils of war subject to nonconsensual marriage. He takes an apologetic tack, including this law in his discussion of Mosaic *humanity* (φιλανθρωπία) and highlighting the kindness it enjoins (N.B. *Virt.* 110: μὴ ὡς αἰχμαλώτῳ, φησίν, ἐναπερύγῃς τὸ πάθος, ἀλλ'ἡμερώτερον οἰκτισάμενος τῆς μεταβολῆς ἐπικούφισον τὴν συμφοράν,

the dominance of λόγος over ἐπιθυμία can involve either the complete suppression of desire (*no* indulgence) or simply the constraint of desire within certain limits (*moderate* indulgence). In either case, the moral agent controls desire and effectively *exercises* a capacity for ἐγκράτεια. The law of Sabbath rest, for example, calls for a *moderate* indulgence of ἐπιθυμία, because it prohibits farmers from working their land every seventh year: by enjoining the *deliberate* forgoing of potential gain from a seventh year, this law trains its adherents to keep their desires within moderate bounds.[76] In Philo's view, the command targets πλεονεξία, a form of *excessive* desire.[77] Speaking of those who do *not* observe the law of Sabbath rest, Philo writes:

> They have burdened the fields by continually pursuing unjust gains based on greedy cravings (ἀεὶ κέρδη μεταδιώκοντες ἐκ πλεονεξιῶν ἄδικα), having added to otherwise reasonable desires (ταῖς ἐπιθυμίαις ἐπιστάντες) unbridled and unjust impulses incapable of fulfillment (ἀχαλίνους καὶ ἀδίκους ὁρμὰς εἰς τὸ ἀκόρεστον). (*Praem.* 154)[78]

Philo clarifies here precisely how πλεονεξίαι count as *excessive desires* in terms of Middle-Platonic theory. The ἐπιθυμίαι he names represent the unobjectionable *emotion* desire, whose otherwise benign impulse becomes malignant *with the addition* (ἐπιστάντες) of excessive impulse. In other

---

μεθαρμοσάμενος πάντα πρὸς τὸ βέλτιον; *Virt.* 114: ἐλεεῖ τὴν αἰχμάλωτον). Unlike the laws of Sabbath rest and fasting, which conceivably had practical application for Alexandrian Jews, the law regarding marrying female prisoners surely had more theoretical interest for Philo.
[76] It *also*, in Philo's view, trains its adherents to bear unexpected hardship, as he explains in *Spec.* 2.87–88: ἑκὼν ζημίαν ὑπόμεινον, ἵνα καὶ τὴν ἀκούσιον βλάβην, εἴ ποτε γένοιτο, ῥᾳδίως ἐνέγκῃς (§87); ἐθίζονται τὰς ἐνδείας εὐμαρῶς ὑπομένειν (§88). (Philo makes the ascetic function of this precept explicit in *Spec.* 2.88: καλοῖς ἐνασκούμενοι νομίμοις.) Philo explains how the law of Sabbath rest works *to moderate desire* in (esp.) *Spec.* 4.215–18, as part of a larger explanation in *Spec.* 4.208–18 of the law against sowing two kinds of seed (Lev 19:19; Deut 22:9), to which he attributes the *same* ascetic function of moderating desire (*Spec.* 4.212–18). Both laws command the farmer to forgo a potentially *greater* yield from a plot of land (either a seventh year of one crop or two crops in one year), so both limit desire in the same way. And both, conversely, aim to produce the same sort of self-controlled farmer: "For he who can bring himself to let his own farms go free in the seventh year and draw no income from them in order to give the land fresh life after its labors is not the man to overload and oppress them with a double burden" (*Spec.* 4.216).
[77] Cf. πλεονέκτης (ὁ πλέον ἔχων) (see LSJ, s.v.). On πλεονεξία and excessive desire, see *Spec.* 4.5: τοῖς οὖσιν οὐκ ἀρκούμενος περιττοτέρων ὀρέγεται, πλεονεξίαν, ἐπίβουλον καὶ δυσίατον πάθος, ἐπιτειχίζων; also *Spec.* 4.129: αἱ γὰρ ἄγαν πλεονεξίαι μέτρον οὐκ ἔχουσι (cf. *Virt.* 100).
[78] My translation. The phrase "ταῖς ἐπιθυμίαις ἐπιστάντες ἀχαλίνους καὶ ἀδίκους ὁρμὰς εἰς τὸ ἀκόρεστον" has caused some difficulty (e.g., PLCL 8, 411, n. d), but it makes sense in light of a Middle-Platonic concept of passion, *without* Cohn's emendation of present (ἐφιστάντες) for the manuscript aorist (ἐπιστάντες).

words, the ἀχαλίνους καὶ ἀδίκους ὁρμάς correspond to the πλεονάζουσα (ἄμετρος) ὁρμή of Middle-Platonic theory, the *quantitative* excess constituting passion. To observe the law, farmers need not *deny* their reasonable desire for produce; they exercise ἐγκράτεια and *curtail* their desire within limits prescribed by Moses.[79] *Outright* denial—at least for a time—figures in the laws of fasting on the Day of Atonement and marrying female prisoners of war. Here reason cedes *nothing* to ἐπιθυμία, compelling it to wait for a fixed interval of time deprived of the pleasure it seeks. The fast, for example, involves *one day* of "bridling impulses for pleasure" (*Spec.* 1.193: ἐπιστομίζοντας τὰς ἐφ'ἡδονὴν ὁρμάς).[80] The marriage law involves thirty days of postponing consummation, reflecting Moses' unwillingness to "let desire get swept away in unbridled disobedience" (*Virt.* 113: οὐκ εἴασεν ἀχάλινον φέρεσθαι τὴν ἐπιθυμίαν ἀπαυχενίζουσαν).[81] In either case, Moses has designed an effective exercise in ἐγκράτεια, since obedience requires a stark denial of desire on reason's part. Like the moderation enjoined by the law of Sabbath rest, the abstinence enjoined by these laws of fasting and marriage strengthen the capacity of λόγος to subjugate ἐπιθυμία, which in turn promotes self-control in contexts beyond those contrived by Moses.

In fact, the ascetic value of these laws hinges on their *not* being ends in themselves, since training exercises necessarily serve as a *means* for cultivating broader proficiencies. In other words, Philo admires Moses' ascetic precepts not so much for the successful *instances* of ἐγκράτεια they enjoin as for the successful *life* of ἐγκράτεια they collectively promote. The moral capacities derived from observing particular commands transfer broadly to analogous situations Moses never addressed, so those trained by Mosaic legislation can operate *apart from law* as free moral agents possessed of ἐγκράτεια. Philo illustrates this principle of transference in *Spec.* 4.218, where he praises both the injunction to give the land a year of rest after seven years of labor and the law against planting two types of seeds in a vineyard (Deut 22:9; cf. Lev 19:19):

---

[79] In *Spec.* 4.217, Philo characterizes the one who would violate the law of Sabbath rest as: προσαναρρηγνὺς τὰς ἀδίκους ἐπιθυμίας αὑτοῦ, μέτροις αὐτὰς μὴ περιορίζων (cf. *Cher.* 33: μέτρα ταῖς ἐπιθυμίαις περιθεῖναι).
[80] My translation. τὰς ἐφ'ἡδονὴν ὁρμάς = ἐπιθυμίας, in accordance with Platonic theory. Philo contrasts this restraint with the *incitements* to desire characteristic of pagan holidays (e.g., *Spec.* 1.192: τὰς γαστρὸς ἀκορέστους ἐπιθυμίας ἐγείρουσαι; *Spec.* 2.193: δι'ὤτων ἐγείρει τὰς ἀκαθέκτους ἐπιθυμίας).
[81] My translation. Cf. *Virt.* 113: λογισμὸς γὰρ πεδήσει τὴν ἐπιθυμίαν οὐδὲν ὑβριστικὸν ἐάσας αὐτὴν ἐξεργάσασθαι, ἀλλὰ τὴν μηνιαίαν προθεσμίαν ἐπισχεῖν.

Should not our passionate affection go out to such enactments as these which by extension restrain and beat back (μακρόθεν ... ἀνείργουσι καὶ ἀνακόπτουσιν)[82] the madness of greedy cravings aimed at *people* (τῶν ἐπ'ἀνθρώποις πλεονεξιῶν τὴν λύσσαν)? For he who as a commoner has learned to shun unjust gains (κέρδος ἄδικον) in the treatment of his plants will, if he becomes a king with greater matters in his charge (λαβόμενος μειζόνων πραγμάτων), follow his acquired habit (τῷ ἔθει) when he comes to deal with men and also women. He will not exact a double tribute nor wring the life out of his subjects with his imposts (δασμοῖς). For long familiar habit (τὸ σύντροφον ἔθος) has the power to soften harsh temperaments and in a sense to tutor and mold them to better forms (πρὸς βελτιόνας τύπους). (*Spec.* 4.218)

Through the repeated *practice* (ἄσκησις) of Moses' agricultural laws, the moral agent develops a "habit" (ἔθος) of successfully managing desire.[83] Since ἐγκράτεια per se stands as the ultimate goal, the original context of the precept has little significance, except that it stages a contest of power between λόγος and ἐπιθυμία whose result is the moral *habit* of moderating desire. Once acquired through Moses' ascetic precepts, this habit of moderation transfers to "greater matters" (μειζόνων πραγμάτων), such as the duties of a king. Instead of indulging an *inordinate* desire for revenue, a ruler trained by Moses' regimen will exercise moderation and not exhaust the wealth of his subjects. The same principle of transference appears in Philo's analysis of the fasting prescribed for the Day of Atonement, which he calls a day "devoted to ἐγκράτεια" (*Spec.* 2.195: ἐξαίρετον ἡμέραν ἀναθεὶς αὐτῇ [ἐγκρατείᾳ]):

---

[82] Substituting "by extension" for Colson's "by implication"; "beat back" for "shackle"; "madness of greedy cravings aimed at *people*" for "mad covetous desires which beset mankind" (see PLCL 8, 144, n. a). For this use of μακρόθεν, see also *Spec.* 4.104: μακρόθεν ἀνεῖρξαι βουλόμενος τὴν ἐπὶ τὰ λεχθέντα ὁρμήν. For the language of restraint used here (ἀνείργουσι καὶ ἀνακόπτουσιν) to describe the *function* of these laws, see also *Decal.* 173: πέμπτον δὲ [κεφάλαιον] τὸ ἀνείργον τὴν τῶν ἀδικημάτων πηγήν, ἐπιθυμίαν; *Spec.* 2.163: ὑφηγήσεσι νόμων θείων, οἳ τάς τε γαστρὸς ἡδονὰς καὶ ὑπογαστρίους ἔστειλαν ... ἔτι δὲ καὶ τὰς τῆς ψυχῆς ἀκρίτους καὶ πλεοναζούσας ὁρμὰς ἀνέκοψαν καὶ ἀνεχαίτισαν.

[83] Aristotle articulated a substantial theory of the role played by ἔθος in the acquisition of moral virtue (e.g., *Eth. nic.* 1103 a 17–18: ἡ δ'ἠθικὴ ἐξ ἔθους περιγίνεται; cf. Nancy Sherman, "The Habituation of Character," in *Aristotle's Ethics: Critical Essays* [ed. Nancy Sherman; Lanham, Md.: Rowman & Littlefield, 1999], 231–60). In Middle-Platonic moral theory, the concepts of ἄσκησις and ἔθος bear close relation, since both involve a process of training non-rational elements of the soul to obey reason. E.g., *Didask.* 24.4 [177.15]: διὰ τῆς τοῦ ἔθους ἀσκήσεως; *Didask.* 30.3 [184.1–2]: ἐξ ἔθους ἐγγινόμεναι καὶ ἀσκήσεως; *Didask.* 28.4 [182.4–5] cites the threefold means to acquiring virtue familiar to Philo (e.g., *Abr.* 52), expanding ἄσκησις to include ἔθεσί τε καὶ ἀγωγῇ καὶ ἀσκήσει τῇ κατὰ νόμον; Plutarch, *Garr.* 510 C–D: ἀσκήσει ... ἐθίζεται. The association appears in Plato as well: e.g., *Resp.* 518 E: τῷ ὄντι γὰρ οὐκ ἐνοῦσαι [ἀρεταὶ] πρότερον ὕστερον ἐμποιεῖσθαι ἔθεσί τε καὶ ἀσκήσεσιν.

> To one who has learnt to disregard food and drink which are absolutely necessary (σιτίων γὰρ τις καὶ ποτῶν μαθὼν ἀλογεῖν τῶν οὕτως ἀναγκαίων), are there any among the superfluities of life (τῶν περιττῶν) which he can fail to despise, things which exist to promote not so much preservation and permanence of life (ἃ γέγονεν οὐ διαμονῆς καὶ σωτηρίας ἕνεκα) as pleasure with all its powers of mischief (μᾶλλον ἢ βλαβερωτάτης ἡδονῆς)? (*Spec.* 2.195)

Philo admires the *lifestyle* of ἐγκράτεια this law promotes, not simply the temporary *exercise* of ἐγκράτεια it requires. By practicing on a limited basis the more challenging denial of *necessary* desires, the moral agent masters the comparatively easy denial of *superfluous* desires. And this broader capacity for consistent denial of superfluous desires amounts to ἐγκράτεια, because it involves the *enforcement* of reason's measure (necessity) over against desire's tendency to pursue pleasure in excess of that measure.

Conclusion

Philo has a multi-faceted but theoretically consistent understanding of ἐγκράτεια. In essence, ἐγκράτεια involves the rule of reason over antagonistic non-rational forces within the soul, especially ἐπιθυμία. In particular, ἐγκράτεια involves the curtailing of excessive non-rational impulses through the enforcement of limits set by reason. Framed in terms of human motivation, this involves reason's consistent enforcement of *its* goal, the greatest overall good for the soul, over against *desire's* goal of pleasure. In any case, ἐγκράτεια stands as the indispensable guard against passion, because it keeps the *emotion* ἐπιθυμία from ever usurping reason's authority and overtaking the soul. For this reason, Philo commends the acquisition of ἐγκράτεια, identifying ἄσκησις as the principle means to that end. By repeatedly *practicing* reason's dominance over desire, the moral agent develops an increased capacity for ἐγκράτεια. Moses understood this principle and so designed a number of ascetic precepts, which enjoin the subjugation of desire in a limited, artificial setting in order to cultivate a broader lifestyle of ἐγκράτεια among those trained by his precepts.

CHAPTER FOUR

PHILO'S EXPOSITION OF THE TENTH COMMANDMENT: TRANSLATION AND COMMENTARY

Philo's Expository Agenda

In his exposition of the Tenth Commandment, Philo uses the conceptual nexus of ἐπιθυμία, ἐγκράτεια, and ἄσκησις as an overarching framework for his work. Within this framework, his concept of *desire* figures most prominently, since a substantial attempt to explain the prohibition οὐκ ἐπιθυμήσεις requires also a substantial concept of ἐπιθυμία—substantial enough to enable a precise statement of what *exactly* the Tenth Commandment prohibits. For Middle Platonists, the operation of ἐπιθυμία can represent either a perfectly natural, amoral *emotion* (πάθος) or an immoral *passion* (πάθος), depending on whether or not reason stays in control. Reading οὐκ ἐπιθυμήσεις as a categorical prohibition of the *emotion* desire—ἐπιθυμία *itself*—makes no sense from a Middle-Platonic standpoint for two reasons: (1) the emotion itself involves nothing morally objectionable and (2) human existence requires, at minimum, the indulgence of necessary desires for food and drink. So on theoretical grounds alone, Philo must take οὐκ ἐπιθυμήσεις as a prohibition of *passionate* desire, which in fact he *does* in the course of his exposition, explaining the prohibition in light of dangers posed both by passionate desire itself *and* by the propensity of passionate desire to burgeon into tyrannical desire (ἔρως). But how does someone actually observe a prohibition of passionate desire? Here the concept of ἐγκράτεια figures into Philo's conceptual framework as the *solution* to the problem addressed by the Tenth Commandment. Because Middle Platonists conceived passionate desire as "immoderate" desire (πλεονάζουσα [ἄμετρος] ἐπιθυμία), abstaining from the *passion* (and thereby observing the prohibition) means keeping the *emotion* within the bounds of moderation, which requires ἐγκράτεια. For this reason, Philo's exposition programmatically commends ἐγκράτεια as the means to observing the Tenth Commandment. In addition, Philo outlines the Mosaic program for *acquiring* ἐγκράτεια, and this explains the presence of ἄσκησις in his conceptual framework. In particular, he casts the Mosaic dietary laws as a set of ascetic precepts designed to inculcate ἐγκράτεια *through* ἄσκησις. So Philo's entire exposition can be summarized in terms of these three concepts: (1) the Tenth Commandment prohibits passionate ἐπιθυμία, (2) obeying the prohibition amounts to the exercise of ἐγκράτεια, and (3) the Mosaic dietary laws inculcate ἐγκράτεια *through* ἄσκησις.

Recognizing ἐπιθυμία, ἐγκράτεια, and ἄσκησις as Philo's overarching conceptual framework helps to explain the various interpretive moves he makes in connection with both the prohibition οὐκ ἐπιθυμήσεις and the dietary laws presumed to support observance of the prohibition. Before composing an exposition of the Tenth Commandment, Philo undoubtedly understood these three concepts to stand in a distinct theoretical relationship, conceived along Middle-Platonic (rather than biblical) lines. So when he encounters a biblical prohibition of ἐπιθυμία, he tries to make sense of it in light of the Middle-Platonic theory at his disposal, framing a *philosophical* notion of (1) the type of desire proscribed, (2) the reason for its proscription, and (3) how to observe the proscription. Similarly, once Philo identifies the dietary laws as the legal species of the genus οὐκ ἐπιθυμήσεις, his interest involves not so much the laws themselves as the Mosaic program of ἄσκησις they represent. In other words, Philo operates according to a clear *expository agenda*: a deliberate effort to correlate the Tenth Commandment and its dietary laws with the best of contemporary philosophy by carefully highlighting the principles of ἐπιθυμία, ἐγκράτεια, and ἄσκησις at work in the formulation of this legislation. Philo implements this agenda in a variety of ways throughout his exposition, but two *particular* ways presume his knowledge of (1) traditional interpretations of the dietary laws, particularly laws concerning clean and unclean animals, and (2) contemporary genres of philosophical literature. Giving preliminary consideration to these topics clarifies their relevance to Philo's agenda.

Traditional Interpretations of Clean and Unclean Animals

In his extended interpretation of the Mosaic regulations concerning clean and unclean animals (*Spec.* 4.100–118), Philo demonstrates familiarity with a line of interpretation developed by an earlier generation of Hellenistic Jews in Alexandria—namely, the symbolic interpretation of clean and unclean animals attributed to the High Priest Eleazar in the *Letter of Aristeas*.[1]

---

[1] See *Let. Arist.* 144–69. Eleazar's interpretation includes consideration of the Mosaic prohibition of unclean birds (Lev 11:13–19; see *Let. Arist.* 145–49), the criteria regarding cloven hooves and rumination (Lev 11:1–8; see *Let. Arist.* 150–60), and the prohibition of mice and weasels (Lev 11:29; see *Let. Arist.* 163–67). On the *Letter of Aristeas*, see Moses Hadas, ed., trans., *Aristeas to Philocrates: Letter of Aristeas* (New York: Harper, 1951; repr., Eugene, Oreg.: Wipf & Stock, 2007). On Eleazar's interpretation of the dietary laws, see esp. Berthelot, "Interprétation symbolique"; also Fausto Parente, "La *Lettera di Aristea* come fonte per la storia del giudaismo alessandrino durante la

Essentially, Eleazar argues that Moses formulated his legislation on clean and unclean animals to promote *justice* (δικαιοσύνη) among his followers.[2] The designations "clean" and "unclean" have little to do with the properties of animal flesh *for eating*—instead they derive from physical and behavioral traits that symbolize analogous *ethical* traits among human beings.[3] Eleazar's most extensive interpretation along these lines involves various species of birds (*Let. Arist.* 145–49). Unclean birds, for example, "are wild and carnivorous and with their strength oppress the rest and procure their food with injustice ..." (*Let. Arist.* 146).[4] As Eleazar explains further:

> Through these creatures then, by calling them "unclean" (ἀκάθαρτα), [Moses] set up a symbol (παράσημον) that those for whom the legislation was drawn up must practice justice (δικαιοσύνη) in spirit and oppress no one, trusting in their own strength, nor rob anyone of anything, but must guide their lives in accordance with justice (ἐκ δικαίου) .... (*Let. Arist.* 147)

In other words, Mosaic legislation functions as a symbolic discourse in which the command to abstain from eating a certain type of bird translates directly into a moral exhortation to abstain from violent oppression. This

---

prima metà del I secolo a.C.," *ASNSP* 3.2.1–2 (1972): 177–237 (part one), 517–67 (part two), esp. 222–31; Vian, "Purità e culto," 71–74. For general comparisons of Philo and Eleazar's respective treatments of laws regarding clean and unclean animals, see Rhodes, "Diet and Desire"; also James G. Février, *La date, la composition et les sources de la Lettre d'Aristée à Philocrate*, BEHE 242 (Paris: Édouard Champion, 1925), 59–63; Hecht, "Patterns of Exegesis," 112–14; Raffaele Tramontano, *La Lettera di Aristea a Filocrate: Introduzione, testo, versione e commento* (Naples: Ufficio succursale della civiltà cattolica, 1931), 180–84. For detailed consideration of Philo and Eleazar's respective treatments of unclean *birds* in particular, see Hans Svebakken, "Exegetical Traditions in Alexandria: Philo's Reworking of the *Letter of Aristeas* 145–149 as a Case Study," in *From Judaism to Christianity*, 93–112. Philo's work contains subtle but telling indications of his knowing the actual *text* of the *Letter of Aristeas* (see Svebakken, "Exegetical Traditions," 95–101; cf. Hadas, *Aristeas to Philocrates*, 25–26: "The balance of probability seems to be rather on the side of Philo's having read our Aristeas"; also Tramontano, *Lettera di Aristea*, 180–84, esp. 184). Philo's knowledge of the *Letter of Aristeas* suggests more broadly the existence, development, and continued use of *traditions of interpretation* among Alexandrian Jews, on which see, for example, Burton L. Mack, "Philo Judaeus and Exegetical Traditions in Alexandria," *ANRW* 21.1:227–271; Gregory E. Sterling, "'The School of Sacred Laws': The Social Setting of Philo's Treatises," *VC* 53 (1999): 148–64, esp. 151–54; Tobin, *Creation of Man* (cf. Svebakken, "Exegetical Traditions," 107–11).

[2] Esp. *Let. Arist.* 169: περὶ βρωτῶν οὖν καὶ τῶν ἀκαθάρτων ἑρπετῶν καὶ κνωδάλων καὶ πᾶς λόγος ἀνατείνει πρὸς δικαιοσύνην καὶ τῶν ἀνθρώπων συναναστροφὴν δικαίαν; cf. *Let. Arist.* 144: δικαιοσύνης ἕνεκεν ... πάντα ἀνατέτακται; *Let. Arist.* 148: διὰ τῶν τοιούτων ... ὁ νομοθέτης σημειοῦσθαι τοῖς συνετοῖς εἶναι δικαίους.

[3] On this sort of ethical interpretation, see Berthelot, "Interprétation symbolique."

[4] Trans. Hadas (unless otherwise noted, all translations of the *Letter of Aristeas* are from Hadas, *Aristeas to Philocrates*).

line of interpretation makes *actual* abstinence practically irrelevant, since eating an unclean bird would not in fact undermine Moses' purpose, as long as the moral agent abstains from the type of *behavior* the bird represents.[5] Similarly, the clean birds are all "gentle" (ἥμερα) herbivores, which never violently oppress another creature (*Let. Arist.* 147). By calling them "clean," Moses commends the disposition they represent, again with no real concern for the consumption (or not) of their flesh:

> By such examples, then, the lawgiver has commended to men of understanding a symbol (σημειοῦσθαι) that they must be just (δικαίους) and achieve nothing by violence (βίᾳ), nor confiding in their own strength (ἰσχύι), must they oppress others (ἑτέρους καταδυναστεύειν). (*Let. Arist.* 148)

In sum, the exegetical method of Eleazar involves recognizing in the designations "clean" and "unclean" an animal *behavioral* trait analogous to a human *ethical* trait—and further recognizing Moses' *primary* intention as the commendation or condemnation of ethical traits, not types of meat. As a result of this method—especially regarding the traits "savage" and "carnivorous," "tame" and "herbivorous"—Eleazar identifies justice (δικαιοσύνη) as Moses' real ethical concern.

---

[5] Eleazar downplays the literal significance of the dietary laws at the beginning of his interpretation (*Let. Arist.* 144): "Do not accept the debased idea that it was out of regard for 'mice' and the 'weasel' and other such creatures that Moses ordained these laws with such scrupulous care" (substituting "debased" [καταπεπτωκότα] for Hadas' "exploded"). According to Eleazar's analysis, abstinence *in itself* has no practical bearing on the achievement (or not) of Moses' purpose in prohibiting certain birds. Parente (*Lettera di Aristea*, 222–31) takes this relative disregard for literal observance as evidence for the *Letter of Aristeas* approving (if not promoting) the *discontinuance* of literal observance, even suggesting the influence of the *Letter of Aristeas* on exegetes chided by Philo in *Migr.* 89–93 for neglecting the literal sense of the laws (idem, 230–31). But the *Letter of Aristeas* nowhere speaks *against* observing the law—in fact, it seems to credit literal observance with keeping the Jewish community intact: "[our lawgiver] fenced us about (περιέφραξεν ἡμᾶς) with impregnable palisades and with walls of iron, to the end that we should mingle in no way with any of the other nations, remaining pure in body and in spirit ..." (*Let. Arist.* 139; cf. 142). The ambivalence reflects a desire both to maintain group identity and embrace the broader culture (cf. Ellen Birnbaum, "Allegorical Interpretation and Jewish Identity among Alexandrian Jewish Writers," in *Neotestamentica et Philonica: Studies in Honor of Peder Borgen* [ed. David E. Aune, Torrey Seland, and Jarl Henning Ulrichsen; NovTSup 106; Leiden: Brill, 2003], 307–329, 311–14; Reinhard Feldmeier, "Weise hinter 'eisernen Mauern': Tora und jüdisches Selbstverständnis zwischen Akkulturation und Absonderung im Aristeasbrief," in *Die Septuaginta zwischen Judentum und Christentum* [ed. Martin Hengel and Anna Maria Schwemer; WUNT 72; Tübingen: Mohr, 1994], 20–37; also Victor Tcherikover, "The Ideology of the *Letter of Aristeas*," *HTR* 51 [1958]: 59–85). Parente, however, correctly notes the *compatibility* of Eleazar's mode of interpretation with abandonment of literal observance.

Although he uses elements of this traditional interpretation, Philo fundamentally reworks these elements to suit his expository agenda, adapting Eleazar's method *and* its results to his own particular frame of reference: ἐπιθυμία, ἐγκράτεια, and ἄσκησις.[6] Above all, Philo tries to show that Moses had in mind the promotion of ἐγκράτεια—*not* δικαιοσύνη—when he formulated laws concerning clean and unclean animals. As a result, Philo tends to emphasize the *literal* significance of Moses' regulations in two important respects: (1) in drawing a connection between the *actual* eating (or not) of certain meats and the operation of ἐπιθυμία in the human soul, and (2) in casting the commands to eat or abstain as the *substance* of a practical regimen of ἄσκησις, not the dispensable symbolic *form* of Moses' ethical exhortations. And when Philo *does* use a symbolic mode of interpretation comparable to Eleazar's, he uses it to demonstrate Moses' ultimate concern for issues of ἐπιθυμία, ἐγκράτεια, and ἄσκησις.

Contemporary Genres of Philosophical Literature

Philo models his exposition of the Tenth Commandment on a type of philosophical literature whose attention to issues of πάθος, ἐγκράτεια, and ἄσκησις resonates with Philo's exegetical agenda. Five examples of the genre appear among the *Moralia* of Plutarch, and Heinz Gerd Ingenkamp calls these essays "praktische Seelenheilungsschriften."[7] Essentially, the *Seelenheilungsschrift* names one particular passion (πάθος) as its topic and consists of two parts: a "diagnosis" (κρίσις) of that passion and a prescription for "treatment" (ἄσκησις).[8] Plutarch explains the relation between the two parts:

> [W]e get well by the diagnosis and treatment of our passions (τῶν γὰρ παθῶν κρίσει καὶ ἀσκήσει), but the diagnosis must come first (προτέρα δ'ἡ κρίσις); since no one can become habituated to shun or to eradicate from his soul what does not distress him (οὐδεὶς γὰρ ἐθίζεται φεύγειν καὶ ἀποτρίβεσθαι τῆς ψυχῆς ὃ μὴ δυσχεραίνει), and we only grow distressed with the passions (τὰ πάθη) when we have perceived, by the exercise of reason, the injuries and shame which result from them (τὰς βλάβας καὶ τὰς αἰσχύνας τὰς ἀπ'αὐτῶν). (*Garr.* 510 C–D)[9]

---

[6] See Svebakken, "Exegetical Traditions."
[7] See Ingenkamp, *Schriften*, 7, where he introduces the term and lists the five treatises: *De curiositate, De cohibenda ira, De garrulitate, De vitioso pudore,* and *De laude ipsius.*
[8] See Ingenkamp, *Schriften*, 74–124. Cf. Rabbow, *Seelenfürung*, 340: "Plutarchs System der Seelenheilung scheidet κρίσις und ἄσκησις; die κρίσις gibt die Erkenntnis des Übels in seinem Wesen, seiner Schädlichkeit; die ἄσκησις die praktische Übung gegen das Übel."
[9] Substituting "the passions" for Helmbold's "our ailments."

In other words, a *Seelenheilungsschrift* tries to convince the reader of the horrible nature of a particular passion, in hopes of motivating the reader to embrace the practical exercises offered as a therapeutic treatment for that passion. Philo's knowledge of the *Seelenheilungsschrift* genre could not have come from Plutarch himself (b. ca. 45 C.E.), but it *could* have come through acquaintance with the philosophical milieu of Plutarch's teacher, Ammonius, a contemporary of Philo and native of Alexandria.[10] Philo, then, provides early attestation for the *Seelenheilungsschrift* tradition preserved *later* in the writings of Plutarch, especially in his essay *On Talkativeness* (*De garrulitate*).[11]

Although Plutarch makes *talkativeness* (ἀδολεσχία) the explicit subject of his earliest *Seelenheilungsschrift*, he ultimately considers the issue of *desire* (ἐπιθυμία)—in particular, a desire for listeners:

> [B]ut even in that which they desire (περὶ αὐτὴν τὴν ἐπιθυμίαν) especially they fail miserably. For in other diseases of the soul (νοσήμασι τῆς ψυχῆς), such as love of money (φιλαργυρίᾳ), love of glory (φιλοδοξίᾳ), love of pleasure (φιληδονίᾳ), there is at least the possibility of attaining their desires (τυγχάνειν ὧν ἐφίενται), but for babblers (τοῖς δ'ἀδολέσχοις) this is very difficult: they desire listeners (ἐπιθυμοῦντες ... ἀκροατῶν) and cannot get them, since every one runs away headlong. (*Garr.* 502 E)

Here Plutarch suggests that ἐπιθυμία *as it relates to speech* can manifest itself in a "diseased" way as talkativeness (ἀδολεσχία), even though the desire itself involves nothing objectionable.[12] Thinking along Middle-Platonic lines, Plutarch understands the critical importance of *reason's* position over against this type of desire, consistently framing his discussion of talkative-

---

[10] See above, p. 36, n. 12.

[11] Ingenkamp identifies *De garrulitate* as the earliest of the five *Seelenheilungsschriften*, written sometime after 68 C.E. (*Schriften*, 115–18), which makes it closest in time to the milieu of Philo's Alexandria. In addition, of the five *De garrulitate* bears the least evidence of Plutarch's personal development of the genre (*Schriften*, 118, 145). While this particular Middle-Platonic *Seelenheilungsschrift* postdates Philo, the unmistakable conformity of Philo's exposition with the basic structure and function of *De garrulitate* indicates Plutarch's use of a preexisting genre known also to Philo. On *De garrulitate*, see William A. Beardslee, "De Garrulitate (Moralia 502B–515A)," in *Plutarch's Ethical Writings and Early Christian Literature* (ed. Hans Dieter Betz; SCHNT 4; Leiden: Brill, 1978), 264–88; also Lieve Van Hoof, *Plutarch's Practical Ethics: The Social Dynamics of Philosophy* (Oxford: Oxford University Press, 2010), 151–75 [="*On Talkativeness*"].

[12] *Garr.* 504 E: "[S]peech, which is the most pleasant and human of social ties, is made inhuman and unsocial by those who use it badly and wantonly ...." Although Philo never *explicitly* links ἐπιθυμία with ἀδολεσχία, he does so implicitly by characterizing the "lover of pleasure" (φιλήδονος) as "talkative" (ἀδολέσχης) (*Sacr.* 32). He also speaks of desire "overtaking the tongue" (ἐπὶ γλῶτταν φθάσασα), recognizing that some people ἐπιθυμοῦσιν ... τὰ ἡσυχαστέα λέγειν (*Spec.* 4.90).

ness as a matter of self-control (ἐγκράτεια) or its absence (ἀκρασία).[13] With reason in control, the moral agent speaks in an appropriate manner. But if the moral agent's desire for listeners becomes excessive and overcomes reason, a "passion" (πάθος) results, and since the excessive desire here involves *speech*, the resulting passion accordingly manifests itself as an irrational, excessive type of speech, talkativeness.[14] Following the basic format of a *Seelenheilungsschrift*, Plutarch's approach to the problem of talkativeness involves first a *diagnosis* (κρίσις), then a *treatment* (ἄσκησις).

Plutarch's *diagnosis* of talkativeness includes both broad denouncements of the passion and specific examples of its ill effects.[15] With chiastic flair, he characterizes ἀδολεσχία as worst among the passions:

> Now of the other passions and diseases (παθῶν καὶ νοσημάτων) some are dangerous (ἐπικίνδυνα), some detestable (μισητά), some ridiculous (καταγέλαστα); but talkativeness has all these qualities at once (τῇ δ'ἀδολεσχίᾳ πάντα συμβέβηκε); for babblers are derided (χλευάζονται) for telling what everyone knows, they are hated (μισοῦνται) for bearing bad news, they run into danger (κινδυνεύουσι) since they cannot refrain from revealing secrets. (*Garr.* 504 F)[16]

Plutarch supports his rhetoric with anecdotal evidence of the trouble talkativeness brings, such as the destruction and ruin attending revealed secrets.[17] King Seleucus, for example, escaping a disastrous battle incognito, received food from a farmer whose ἀδολεσχία brought death (*Garr.* 508 D-F). The farmer recognized Seleucus and could not restrain himself (οὐ κατέσχεν):

> [O]n taking leave, [he] said, "Farewell, King Seleucus." And Seleucus, stretching out his right hand to him and drawing him towards himself as though to kiss him, gave a sign to one of his companions to cut off the man's head with a sword. (*Garr.* 508 E)

---

[13] Examples of ἐγκράτεια: 505 D–E: τῆς ἐγκρατείας, 506 A–B: ἐγκρατείας (bis), 506 E: ἐγκρατῶς ἔχειν (cf. 511 D: κρατεῖν; 515 A: ἐπικρατεῖ); examples of ἀκρασία: 503 C: τὴν ἀκρασίαν, 503 E: ἀκρατές, 506 F: τῆς ἀκρασίας, 507 E: τὴν σὴν ἀκρασίαν, 508 B: τὴν ἀκρασίαν, 508 F: τῆς ἀκρασίας (cf. 503 C: ἀχαλίνων ... στομάτων; 504 F: μὴ κρατοῦντες). Cf. Jacques Boulogne, "L'intempérence verbale: L'imaginaire de Plutarche dans la thérapie des maladies de l'âme," in *Les passions antiques et médiévales* (ed. Bernard Besnier et al.; Paris: Presses universitaires de France, 2003), 161–69; Smith, "*Enkrateia*: Plutarch on Self-Control," 83–84.
[14] Plutarch understands "passion" in the Middle-Platonic sense of πλεονάζουσα (ἄμετρος) ὁρμή (see above, pp. 65–70); cf. *Garr.* 514 C: τὸ λάλον ... πλεονάζον.
[15] Philo, too, vilifies immoderate speech: e.g., *Somn.* 2.274–75.
[16] Substituting "passions and diseases" for Helmbold's "affections and maladies"; "talkativeness" for "garrulousness."
[17] *Garr.* 508 D: "[S]ecrets, when they escape, destroy and ruin (ἀπολλύουσι καὶ διαφθείρουσι) those who cannot keep them."

116   CHAPTER FOUR

Plutarch frames this as a deadly case of ἀκρασία (508 F), a lack of *verbal* self-control characteristic of everyone possessed of talkativeness. By this and other examples, framed with disparaging rhetoric, Plutarch hopes to accomplish the express purpose of his diagnosis: revealing the "injuries and shame" (τὰς βλάβας καὶ τὰς αἰσχύνας [510 D]) of ἀδολεσχία, *so that* his readers will embrace the practical treatment he offers in the second part of his treatise.[18]

Having made his diagnostic case against talkativeness, Plutarch turns to a course of *treatment* (ἄσκησις), offering specific exercises (ἐθισμοί) designed to rid the moral agent of talkativeness by inculcating verbal self-control (ἐγκράτεια). These exercises work by orchestrating a contest of power between the soul's rational and non-rational parts—in the case of ἀδολεσχία, reason contends against ἐπιθυμία *as it relates to speech*. With each successful exercise, the moral agent's capacity to control this type of desire increases, while the likelihood of desire usurping reason to engender ἀδολεσχία correspondingly decreases. Plutarch offers two basic types of ἐθισμός; the first involves refraining from speech for a period of time:

> In the first place (πρῶτον), then, when questions are asked of neighbors, let him accustom himself to remaining silent (ἐθιζέτω σιωπᾶν) until all have refused a response (μέχρι οὗ πάντες ἀπείπωνται τὴν ἀπόκρισιν). (*Garr.* 511 F)[19]

In other words, the moral agent *waits* to speak and in so doing subjugates and restrains desire's impulse toward the pleasure(s) of speech. Plutarch again commends the exercise of delayed response when he considers how the moral agent ought to deal with direct questions (*Garr.* 512 D–F).[20] Neatly summarizing the thrust of his remarks, he identifies the ultimate *goal* of these exercises as the training of non-rational desire:

---

[18] In *Garr.* 510 D, Plutarch summarizes everything learned from his diagnosis: "Thus, ... we perceive in the case of babblers that they are hated when they wish to be liked, that they cause annoyance when they wish to please, that they are laughed at when they think they are admired, that they spend their money without any gain, that they wrong their friends, help their enemies, and destroy themselves."

[19] Plutarch indirectly labels this abstention an ἄσκημα: after this first example (πρῶτον) he goes on to describe a second (δεύτερον) ἄσκημα in *Garr.* 512 C. He describes this sort of exercise as "mastering the disease by habituation" (*Garr.* 511 F: ἔθει ... κρατῆσαι τοῦ νοσήματος).

[20] N.B. *Garr.* 512 D: ἐθιστέον ἐφιστάναι καὶ ποιεῖν τι διάλειμμα μεταξὺ τῆς ἐρωτήσεως καὶ τῆς ἀποκρίσεως; 512 E: τὸν δὲ βουλόμενον ἐμμελῶς ἀποκρίνασθαι δεῖ ... ἀναμεῖναι.

In any case, this ravenous hunger for talking (πρὸς τοὺς λόγους ὀξύπεινον) must be checked so that it may not seem as though a stream (ῥεῦμα) which has long been pressing hard upon the tongue were being gladly discharged at the instance of the question. Socrates, in fact, used to control his thirst in this manner—he would not allow himself to drink after exercise until he had drawn up and poured out the first bucketful, so that his non-rational part might be trained to await the time dictated by reason (ἐθίζηται τὸν τοῦ λόγου καιρὸν ἀναμένειν τὸ ἄλογον). (*Garr.* 512 F)[21]

A second type of ἐθισμός commended by Plutarch involves not the *delay* of speaking but complete *abstinence* from speaking on certain topics that incite talkativeness because of the excessive pleasure they afford:

> Moreover, just as Socrates used to urge men to be on their guard (φυλάττεσθαι) against those foods which induce us to eat when we are not hungry, and against those liquids which induce us to drink when we are not thirsty, so it is with the babbler as regards subjects for talk (τῶν λόγων): those in which he takes most delight (οἷς ἥδεται μάλιστα) and employs *ad nauseam* he should fear and stoutly resist (ἀντιβαίνειν) when they stream in upon him. (*Garr.* 513 D)[22]

In terms of moral psychology, the danger of especially pleasurable topics lies in their capacity to draw the moral agent into speech for the wrong motive—for *pleasure itself* and not for *good reason*, such as a legitimate *need* to speak.[23] By avoiding such topics, the moral agent develops verbal ἐγκράτεια, since rejecting pleasure as a motivation amounts to a subjugation of ἐπιθυμία on the part of λόγος. So within Plutarch's therapeutic program, *delay* and *avoidance* represent two fundamental techniques of ἄσκησις, both designed to counteract *passion* and develop ἐγκράτεια.

Philo's exposition of the Tenth Commandment exhibits the form and function of a *Seelenheilungsschrift*. First of all, it has as its topic one particular passion, ἐπιθυμία.[24] Second, it essentially divides into the two-part structure characteristic of the genre: a "diagnosis" (κρίσις) and a "treatment" (ἄσκησις). In *Spec.* 4.79–94, Philo considers the horrible nature of desire, offering—like Plutarch—both broad denouncements of the passion and specific examples of its ill effects, especially its dangerous capacity to

---

[21] Substituting "non-rational" for Helmbold's "irrational."
[22] Cf. *Garr.* 514 A: "[H]e that has a greater weakness for one class of subjects than for the other should be on his guard against these subjects and force himself to hold back and withdraw as far as possible from them (ὀφείλει τούτους φυλάττεσθαι καὶ ἀνέχειν ἑαυτὸν ἀπὸ τούτων), since they are always able, because of the pleasure they give (δι'ἡδονήν), to lure him on to dilate upon them."
[23] On the compelling force of pleasurable speech, note also *Garr.* 513 E: τὸ ἡδόμενον ἕλκει τὴν φωνὴν ἐφ'ἑαυτό. On *need* as the proper measure for speech, see *Garr.* 513 A–C.
[24] Not the amoral *emotion* ἐπιθυμία, but the immoral *passion* ἐπιθυμία.

burgeon into ἔρως. In *Spec.* 4.95–130, he considers the proper treatment of desire, casting the Mosaic dietary laws as therapeutic exercises comparable to those prescribed by Plutarch in *De garrulitate*. The Mosaic exercises in Philo's exposition mirror not only the ascetic techniques used in *De garrulitate*—for example, delay and avoidance—but also the overall purpose of Plutarch's "treatment": to cure a passion by cultivating ἐγκράτεια *through* ἄσκησις.

Structure of Philo's Exposition

Philo's exposition of the Tenth Commandment (*Spec.* 4.78b–131) exhibits the following structure, which the commentary essentially follows, using excurses to treat separately the parallel material from *De decalogo*:

I. Introduction (§78b)

II. Diagnosis (Κρίσις) (§§79–94)

    A.   Problem: Every Passion (§79)

        §79 Excursus: Parallel Material in Decal. *142–45*

    B.   Problem: Passionate Desire Burgeoned into Tyrannical Desire (§§80–94)

        i.   Overview of Tyrannical Desire (§§80–83)

            a. Origin (§80a)
            b. Character (§§80b–83): Insatiable, Oppressive, All-Consuming

        §§80 – 83 Excursus: Parallel Material in Decal. *146–50*

        ii.   Tyrannical Desire as "Source of of All Evils" (§§84–91)

            a. Statement of the Claim (§§84–85)
            b. Illustrations (§§86–91)

                1. Mode of Operation
                2. Tyrannical Desire for Money
                3. Tyrannical Desire for Fame
                4. Tyrannical Desire for Power
                5. Tyrannical Desire for Beauty
                6. Tyrannical Desire over the Tongue
                7. Tyrannical Desire over the Belly

        §§84 – 91 Excursus: Parallel Material in Decal. *151–53*

    C.   Location of Ἐπιθυμία (§§92–94)

III. Treatment (Ἄσκησις) (§§95–130)

    A. Overview of Moses' "Paradigmatic Instruction" (§§95–97)

    B. Elements of Moses' "Paradigmatic Instruction" (§§98–125)

        i. First Fruits (§§98–99)

        ii. Clean and Unclean Animals (§§100–118)

            a. Introduction (§§100–102)
            b. Land Animals (§§103–109)
            c. Aquatic Animals (§§110–112)
            d. "Reptiles" (§§113–115)
            e. Birds (§§116–117)
            f. Conclusion (§118)

        iii. Animals Killed by Predators or Natural Causes (§§119–121)

        iv. Blood and Fat (§§122–125)

IV. Conclusion (§§126 – 131)

Translation and Commentary

I. *Introduction (§78b)*

§78b: Introduction

[§78b] Let us move on to the last of the Ten Words, delivered like each of the others in the form of a summary: "You shall not desire."

Philo finally arrives at the Tenth Commandment, after commenting in depth on the other nine in *Spec.* 1.12–*Spec.* 4.78a. He does little more than announce his transition to the last of the "Ten Words," noting only that this Commandment, like the others, has the form of a summary. He provides a basis for the exposition by citing the Tenth Commandment, in an abbreviated version, placing the emphasis on ἐπιθυμία *itself* and not any of its particular objects.[25]

---

[25] On Philo's version of the Tenth Commandment (οὐκ ἐπιθυμήσεις), see above, p. 1.

II. Diagnosis (Κρίσις) (§§79–94)

§79: Problem: Every Passion

[§79] On the one hand,[26] *every* passion[27] is reprehensible, since we are accountable for every unmeasured, "excessive impulse"[28] and for the soul's "irrational and unnatural movement."[29] After all, what do both of these definitions describe if not an unleashing of the emotional part of the soul?[30] So if anyone fails to place limits on the impulses of emotion,[31] fails to bridle, so to speak, his team of unruly horses, he ends up indulging a malignant "passion."[32] And by giving free rein to the team's unruliness, he will careen like an unwitting charioteer into some ditch or chasm, from which he will barely escape—if at all.

---

[26] *On the one hand* (μέν): Philo here compares the passions as a class (πᾶν μὲν πάθος) with one particular passion in §80 (τῶν δὲ παθῶν).

[27] *passion* (πάθος): Philo's use of the terms ἐπίληπτον (*reprehensible*) and ὑπαίτιος (*accountable*) indicates an immoral "passion," not an amoral "emotion" (πάθος).

[28] *every unmeasured, "excessive impulse"* (πᾶσα ἄμετρος καὶ πλεονάζουσα ὁρμή): Philo cites the Stoic definition of "passion" (e.g., DL 7.110: ἔστι δὲ αὐτὸ τὸ πάθος κατὰ Ζήνωνα ... ὁρμὴ πλεονάζουσα) but fundamentally recasts it for Middle-Platonic use by adding the qualifying term ἄμετρος. On Philo's Middle-Platonic concept of passion, see above, pp. 65–70.

[29] *the soul's "irrational and unnatural movement"* (τῆς ψυχῆς ἡ ἄλογος καὶ παρὰ φύσιν κίνησις): Philo cites an alternative Stoic definition of "passion" (e.g., DL 7.110: ἔστι δὲ αὐτὸ τὸ πάθος κατὰ Ζήνωνα ἡ ἄλογος καὶ παρὰ φύσιν ψυχῆς κίνησις), in which ἄλογος clearly denotes a morally problematic "irrational" (vs. "non-rational") movement.

[30] *After all, what do both of these definitions describe if not* (ἑκάτερον γὰρ τούτων <τί> ἐστιν ἕτερον ἤ) *an unleashing of the emotional part of the soul* (παλαιὸν πάθος ἐξηπλωμένον): The addition of τί in PCW seems necessary, since the phrase παλαιὸν πάθος ἐξηπλωμένον further explains, from a Middle-Platonic perspective, the phenomena (τούτων) Philo denotes using Stoic definitions. In the explanatory phrase, πάθος refers to the non-rational part of the soul as seat of emotion(s) (i.e., παθητικὸν μέρος; cf. *Eclog.* 38.5–7: ἄλογον μέρος τῆς ψυχῆς ... ἢ πάθος ἢ παθητικὸν μέρος). So παλαιόν has the sense of "longstanding," indicating an enduring component of the soul activated intermittently (cf. *QE* 1.7 [Gk. Petit]: τὴν ἄρτι φυομένην ἀριστοκρατίαν ἐν ψυχῇ καθελούσης τῆς παλαιᾶς ὀχλοκρατίας, ἣ πρὸς ὀλίγον ἠρεμήσασα πάλιν ἐξ ὑπαρχῆς μετὰ πλείονος δυνάμεως ἀντεπέθετο, where ὀχλοκρατία stands for the Platonic ἐπιθυμητικόν, as in *Resp.* VIII–IX).

[31] *place limits on the impulses of emotion* (μέτρα ταῖς ὁρμαῖς ὁρίζει): Philo undoubtedly has in mind non-rational impulses of the emotional part of the soul (cf. *Opif.* 81: αἱ ἄμετροι τῶν παθῶν ὁρμαί; *Mut.* 173: τὰς τῶν ... παθῶν ὁρμάς)—in other words, discrete impulses of desire etc. requiring the proper "measure" (μέτρον) of reason (cf. *Cherub.* 33: μέτρα ταῖς ἐπιθυμίαις περιθεῖναι).

[32] *indulging a malignant "passion"* (πάθει χρῆται δυσιάτῳ): Philo speaks of the condition *resulting from* a lack of measure: an "emotion" (πάθος) has become a "passion" (πάθος).

To begin his exposition of οὐκ ἐπιθυμήσεις, Philo summarizes the problem posed by *every* passion (πᾶν μὲν πάθος) and not just desire, which he will consider at length beginning in §80 (τῶν δὲ παθῶν ... ἐπιθυμία). In agreement with the Stoics, he notes that passions categorically indicate a moral lapse by using the terms ἐπίληπτον and ὑπαίτιος.[33] But Philo differs radically in his concept of what those passions fundamentally *are*. Reworking a standard Stoic definition, he uses the term ἄμετρος to express the Middle-Platonic notion of passion as a *quantitative* excess of the *non-rational* impulses of emotion.[34] In similar Middle-Platonic fashion, Philo suggests

---

[33] Cf. *Deus* 71: πάνθ'ὅσα δι'ὀργὴν ἢ φόβον ἢ λύπην ἢ ἡδονὴν ἢ τι τῶν ἄλλων παθῶν πράττομεν, ὑπαίτια καὶ ἐπίληπτα ὁμολογουμένως ἐστίν. Philo often uses "reprehensible" (ἐπίληπτος) as an antonym of "praiseworthy" (ἐπαινετός) (e.g., *Post.* 75: πᾶν ὅτι ἂν ἑαυτῷ λαμβάνῃ φαῦλος, πάντως ἐσὶν ἐπίληπτον, ... αἱ τῶν σπουδαίων ἑκούσιοι πράξεις ἐπαινεταὶ πᾶσαι). As he states elsewhere, the deeds of the unjust are reprehensible (ἐπίληπτα), due to lack of measure in their emotions (διά ... τὰς ἀμετρίας τῶν παθῶν)—i.e., due to "passions" (*Spec.* 3.209). In addition, the moral agent stands "accountable" (ὑπαίτιος) not for emotion, but for passion. The moment of moral accountability lies not in the *experience* of desire, distress, pleasure, or fear, but in the *victory* of these emotions over reason, which signals reason's failure to restrict or *measure* their activity properly (cf. Marguerite Harl, "Adam et les deux arbres du paradis (Gen. II–III) ou l'homme milieu entre deux termes (μέσος-μεθόριος) chez Philon d'Alexandrie," *RSR* 50 (1962): 321–88, 341, n. 38: "Ὑπαίτιος est typiquement l'épithète de la γνώμη, volonté, lieu de la responsabilité. On trouve cependant le plus souvent chez Philon l'opposition ὑπαίτιος-ἀνυπαίτιος pour signifier non pas «responsable-irresponsable» mais «coupable-innocent»."

[34] In Philo's view, every instance of passion involves an "unmeasured" (ἄμετρος) impulse, one excessive in *quantity*, not in *quality* as the Stoics believed. The term ἄμετρος, which appears not a single time in *SVF* (see index, s.v.), is patently *not* Stoic, but commentators persist in labeling ἄμετρος καὶ πλεονάζουσα ὁρμή a "Stoic" definition without accounting for the anomaly of ἄμετρος (e.g., Colson, PLCL 8, 57, n. b; Heinemann, PCH 2, 270, ns. 1–2; Mosès, PAPM 25, 246, n. 2; also David Charles Aune, "Mastery of the Passions," 126; Bréhier, *Idées philosophiques et religieuses*, 253, n. 9; Gaca, *Making of Fornication*, 200; Lilla, *Clement of Alexandria*, 92; Pohlenz, *Philon*, 457; Völker, *Fortschritt und Vollendung*, 80; Reydams-Schils, "Stoic and Platonist Psycho-Physiology," 193; Winston, "Philo on the Emotions," 216, n. 16 [cites *Spec.* 4.79 as πλεονάζουσα ὁρμή (omitting ἄμετρος), adducing parallels from *SVF*]; Wolfson, *Philo*, 2:231). The other definition of passion Philo cites (τῆς ψυχῆς ἡ ἄλογος καὶ παρὰ φύσιν κίνησις) must be understood along similar Middle-Platonic lines: An unmeasured impulse entails a movement of the soul inconsistent with the dictates of reason and thus "irrational," although the movement itself is non-rational and not a function of reason (cf. *Didask.* 32.1 [185.26–30]: ἔστι τοίνυν πάθος κίνησις ἄλογος ψυχῆς ... ἄλογος μὲν οὖν εἴρηται κίνησις ὅτι οὐ κρίσεις τὰ πάθη οὐδὲ δόξαι ἀλλὰ τῶν ἀλόγων τῆς ψυχῆς μερῶν κινήσεις· ἐν γὰρ τῷ παθητικῷ τῆς ψυχῆς συνίσταται). Such a movement is also "unnatural," since Nature prescribes the rule of the superior over the inferior, in this case reason over the emotions (cf. *QG* 4.218). Philo's reference to an "unleashing of the emotional part of the soul" appears as a clarification of the Middle-Platonic moral psychology underlying the Stoic terminology he has just used. An unmeasured (excessive) impulse of desire,

that the moral agent avoids passion by *moderating* these non-rational impulses, and he uses the Platonic chariot figure to make his point.[35] In other words, having framed the *problem* of passion as "unmeasured impulse" (ἄμετρος ὁρμή), Philo frames the *solution* as "measured impulse" (μέτρα ταῖς ὁρμαῖς)—only when the charioteer fails, when emotion oversteps the "measure" of reason's directing authority, only *then* does passion arise in the soul (πάθει χρῆται δυσιάτῳ).[36] Finally, he portrays the disaster in store for all who allow passion to arise in their souls, all who allow otherwise useful *emotions* to run wild, usurping the directing authority of reason. This lack of restraint (ἀφηνιασμόν) "wrecks" the soul, as the non-rational "horses" are given free rein (cf. *Leg.* 1.72–73).

By commending moderation at the outset of his exposition, Philo gives an early indication of how he interprets οὐκ ἐπιθυμήσεις. While obviously a prohibition, the Tenth Commandment does not prohibit ἐπιθυμία per se, since Philo recommends the *limitation* of impulse, not its elimination. In other words, the Tenth Commandment prohibits *passionate* desire (πλεονάζουσα [ἄμετρος] ἐπιθυμία), understood as impulse(s) of the *emotion* ἐπιθυμία exceeding the measure set by reason.

§79 Excursus: Parallel Material in Decal. 142–45

In *Decal.* 142, Philo likewise begins his commentary on οὐκ ἐπιθυμήσεις with a μέν ... δέ distinction between πάθη in general (πάντα μὲν γὰρ τὰ ψυχῆς πάθη χαλεπά ... τῶν μὲν ἄλλων) and the *one* πάθος desire (χαλεπώτατον δ'ἐπιθυμία ... μόνη δ'ἐπιθυμία), which he will consider at length beginning in *Decal.* 146. But unlike *Spec.* 4.79, which emphasizes the moral culpability of a failure to moderate the impulses of emotion—in other words, the moral culpability of a "passion"—Philo merely asserts that πάθη are "grievous" (χαλεπά), without condemning them explicitly.[37] In fact, his analysis of

---

distress, fear, or pleasure indicates *not* the sudden genesis of passion as something qualitatively distinct within the soul, but instead the "unleashing" (ἐξαπλόω—in the sense of a "loosening" or removal of restraint) of a preexisting emotional faculty (παλαιὸν πάθος). Elsewhere, Philo allegorically interprets the biblical prescription for "girded loins" (ὀσφῦς περιεζῶσθαι) as an injunction against just this sort of "slackening" (χαλάω) of the emotions (e.g., *Leg.* 3.151–54).

[35] Cf. Mosès, PAPM 25, 246, n. 3. On Philo's chariot figure, see above, pp. 88–93.

[36] In other words, Philo commends *moderation* of emotion (μετριοπάθεια).

[37] Note the absence of *terms* indicating moral culpability (such as ἐπίληπτον and ὑπαίτιος in *Spec.* 4.79). Emotions are "grievous" (χαλεπά) in their capacity to "unnaturally move and jar the soul, preventing its healthy operation (κινοῦντα καὶ σείοντα αὐτὴν παρὰ φύσιν καὶ ὑγιαίνειν οὐκ ἐῶντα)" (*Decal.* 142; my translation). Philo's formal introduction to this section (*Decal.* 142–53), while it certainly characterizes ἐπιθυμία as a threat, avoids the language of moral culpability: "Finally, [Moses] places a prohibition

pleasure (ἡδονή), distress (λύπη), and fear (φόβος) in *Decal.* 143–45 suggests *no* culpability for these πάθη, since they are involuntary (ἀκούσιον).[38] As Philo explains, the perceptions of a present good (ἀγαθόν), an impending ill (κακόν), or a present ill (κακόν) automatically generate the corresponding πάθη.[39] Although his account of the sensations of pleasure, distress, and fear echoes Stoic *terminology*, Philo's account of the mechanics of these πάθη flatly contradicts Stoic *doctrine.*[40] Above all, Stoics maintained the full accountability of the moral agent for *all* passions, which *all* result from voluntary, rational assent (συγκατάθεσις).[41] So Philo's association of πάθη with involuntary responses to external stimuli clearly reflects a different perspective.

Instead of the Middle-Platonic account of *passions* (πάθη) offered in *Spec.* 4.79, Philo offers in *Decal.* 142–45 a Middle-Platonic account of *emotions* (πάθη). Although he reserves a radically *different* sort of account for ἐπιθυμία (*Decal.* 146–50), because he must show why the Decalogue restricts only this emotion, he otherwise reflects standard Middle-Platonic views comparable to *Didaskalikos* 32.1 [185.24–42].[42] For example, both *Decal.*

---

on desiring (τελευταῖον δ'ἐπιθυμεῖν ἀπαγορεύει), knowing that desire (τὴν ἐπιθυμίαν) is crafty and treacherous (νεωτεροποιὸν καὶ ἐπίβουλον)" (my translation). In other words, emotion is a *potential* threat, passion a *realized* threat. The terms νεωτεροποιός and ἐπίβουλος do not appear in Philo's introduction to *passion* in *Spec.* 4.79.

[38] Cf. *Mut.* 241: τῶν δ'ἀκουσίων οὐδὲν ὑπαίτιον (also *Deus* 48). Although Philo states that ἡδονή, λύπη, and φόβος *seem* involuntary (*Decal.* 142: ἀκούσιον εἶναι δοκεῖ), he clearly asserts that they *are* involuntary. By stating in *Decal.* 142 that *only* desire is voluntary (μόνη δ'ἐπιθυμία ... ἔστιν [*is*, not *seems*] ἑκούσιος), he indicates that the others (ἡδονή, λύπη, and φόβος) are not.

[39] *Decal.* 143 (ἡδονή): τοῦ παρόντος καὶ νομισθέντος ἀγαθοῦ φαντασία διεγείρει καὶ διανίστησι τὴν ψυχήν; *Decal.* 144 (λύπη): κακόν, ὅταν ἐκβιασάμενον πληγὴν ἐπενέγκῃ καίριον, συννοίας καὶ κατηφείας εὐθὺς αὐτὴν ἀναπίμπλησιν ἄκουσαν (retaining MS. ἐκβιασάμενον [cf. *Virt. mor.* 449 C: ἐκβιαζομένων]; Colson has εἰσβιασάμενον [see PLCL VII, 78, n. 1]); *Decal.* 145 (φόβος): ὅταν δὲ τὸ κακόν ... πτοίαν καὶ ἀγωνίαν ... προεκπέμπει.

[40] I.e., he does *not* offer a Stoic account of the passions, *pace* Colson (PLCL 7, 612, on §§142–146: "This disquisition on the four passions is thoroughly Stoic in substance ...").

[41] See Inwood, *Ethics and Human Action*, 42–101 [="The Psychology of Action"], e.g., 44: "the power to give or withhold assent ... makes men morally responsible for their actions"; 54: "Man is responsible because of assent"; 72: "Assent . . is vital to the Stoic analysis of action because it is the locus of moral responsibility." The term συγκατάθεσις appears nowhere in *Decal.* 142–46 nor *anywhere* in Philo's analysis of the passions (cf. Pohlenz, *Philon*, 456, n. 1).

[42] *Didask.* 32.1 clearly speaks of "emotion" (πάθος), not "passion" (πάθος), since the Middle-Platonic concept of *passion* appears later in 32.4 [186.14–29], which contrasts "wild" (ἄγρια) and "tame" (ἤμερα) emotions: "'Tame' are such as belong naturally to man (κατὰ φύσιν), being necessary and proper to him (ἀναγκαῖά τε καὶ οἰκεῖα). They remain in this state as long as they preserve moderation (ἕως ἂν σύμμετρα ὑπάρχῃ); if

142–45 and *Didask.* 32.1 speak of emotions as a *movement* within the soul, with the *Didaskalikos* stating explicitly what Philo certainly presumes: that the movement occurs in the soul's *non-rational* part.[43] Both speak of emotions as *involuntary* responses to the perception of an apparent good or ill.[44] Both presume the existence of four cardinal emotions and describe the respective causes of pleasure, distress, and fear in similar terms.[45] Philo's sketch of a Middle-Platonic theory of *emotion* (πάθος) in *Decal.* 142–45 provides a setting for distinguishing ἐπιθυμία from all other *emotions* (πάθη), just as his sketch of a Middle-Platonic theory of *passion* (πάθος) in *Spec.* 4.79 provides a setting for distinguishing ἐπιθυμία from all other *passions* (πάθη). By considering the unique danger of ἐπιθυμία from the standpoint of both *emotion* and *passion*, Philo comprehensively validates the Tenth Commandment's exclusive focus on desire.

§§80 – 83: Overview of Tyrannical Desire

[§80] On the other hand, *among* the passions, none proves as agonizing as passionate desire for any of the false goods people long to possess,[46] because desire of this kind gives birth to grievous and endless

---

they come to exhibit lack of moderation (ἀμετρίας), they become bad (ἡμαρτημένα)" (trans. Dillon).

[43] *Decal.* 142: κινοῦντα καὶ σείοντα; *Didask.* 32.1 [185.26]: κίνησις ἄλογος ψυχῆς; *Didask.* 32.1 [185.27–29]: ἄλογος μὲν οὖν εἴρηται κίνησις ὅτι οὐ κρίσεις τὰ πάθη οὐδὲ δόξαι ἀλλὰ τῶν ἀλόγων τῆς ψυχῆς μερῶν κινήσεις.

[44] Involuntary: *Decal.* 142: τῶν μὲν ἄλλων ... ἀκούσιον; *Didask.* 32.1 [185.31–32]: ἄκουσι γοῦν ἐν ἡμῖν ἐγγίνεται πολλάκις καὶ ἀντιτείνουσιν. Response to perception of good or ill: *Decal.* 143: ἀγαθοῦ φαντασία; *Decal.* 144: κακόν; *Decal.* 145: τὸ κακόν; *Didask.* 32.1 [185.38–39]: πάντα γὰρ [πάθη] συνίσταται ἢ κατὰ ἀγαθοῦ ἔμφασιν ἢ κατὰ κακοῦ.

[45] **ἡδονή**: *Decal.* 143: τοῦ παρόντος καὶ νομισθέντος ἀγαθοῦ φαντασία; *Didask.* 32.1 [185.39–40]: ἀγαθὸν γὰρ ἐὰν μὲν παρεῖναι ὑπολάβωμεν, ἡδόμεθα; **λύπη**: *Decal.* 144: κακόν, ὅταν ἐκβιασάμενον πληγὴν ἐπενέγκῃ καίριον; *Didask.* 32.1 [185.41]: κακὸν γὰρ ἐὰν μὲν παρεῖναι ὑπολάβωμεν, λυπούμεθα; **φόβος**: *Decal.* 145: ὅταν δὲ τὸ κακόν ... μέλλῃ δ'ἀφικνεῖσθαι; *Didask.* 32.1 [185.41–42]: τὸ δὲ μέλλον [κακὸν] φοβούμεθα.

[46] *passionate desire for any of the false goods people long to possess* (ἐπιθυμία τῶν ἀπόντων ὅσα τῷ δοκεῖν ἀγαθῶν, πρὸς ἀλήθειαν οὐκ ὄντων): In light of his introductory remarks on "passion" (§79), Philo must have in mind *passionate* desire (πλεονάζουσα [ἄμετρος] ἐπιθυμία), although he refers to it simply as ἐπιθυμία. He notes two characteristics of the desired objects. First, they do not exist in the physical presence of the moral agent. They are objects of fantasy generated in the mind (cf. *Decal.* 146: ἐπειδὰν δὲ λαβών τις ἔννοιαν ἀγαθοῦ μὴ παρόντος) and therefore objects of *longing* (cf. *Crat.* 420 A: "πόθος" αὖ καλεῖται σημαίνων οὐ τοῦ παρόντος εἶναι ἀλλὰ τοῦ ἄλλοθί που ὄντος καὶ ἀπόντος). Second, they are false goods: *esteemed* as good (valuable) by the masses but not *actually* good (valuable). Philo has in mind a broad range of false goods (ὅσα, *as many as*; cf. *Spec.* 4.82: χρημάτων, δόξης, ἡγεμονιῶν, εὐμορφίας, ἄλλων ἀμυθήτων).

*tyrannical desires.*⁴⁷ Consider the plight of someone subject to tyrannical desire!⁴⁸ Free of restraint and fixed on the thought of a beloved object,⁴⁹ desire stretches and strains the soul farther and farther out into the boundless distance,⁵⁰ as its quarry now and then turns to flee *backwards* derisively. [§81] For when it notices desire trying hard to catch up, it stops for a moment—just long enough to provide a teasing hope of capture—only to pull away out of reach, jeering mercilessly. And so desire, constantly eluded, constantly deprived, struggles in vain,⁵¹ bringing a punishment of Tantalus upon the poor soul. Surely you remember that wretch, who, as the story goes, could never quench his thirst, because the water would instantly recede every time he tried to take a drink. In the same way, whenever he reached for some fruit on the nearby trees, it would all disappear—the loaded branches would suddenly turn barren. [§82] Now, just as those callous, implacable⁵² taskmasters hunger and thirst rack the *body* more painfully than an inquisitor cranking his torture wheel—often to the point of death, unless someone appeases their savagery with food and drink—desire creates even harsher taskmasters for the *soul* by creating a grumbling emptiness within. People forget what they have right in front of them and bring to mind what lies somewhere off in the

---

⁴⁷ *because this sort of desire gives birth to grievous and endless* tyrannical desires (χαλεποὺς καὶ ἀνηνύτους ἔρωτας ἐντίκτουσα): The participial clause explains *why* ἐπιθυμία τῶν ἀπόντων proves so "agonizing" (ἀργαλέον): *because* it gives birth to "tyrannical desires" (ἐπιθυμία ... ἔρωτας ἐντίκτουσα). Mosès also takes the clause as an explanation, although he makes false goods the subject of the participle: "Mais aucune d'entre les passions n'est aussi cruelle que le désir des biens absent, biens d'opinion qui n'en sont pas en réalité: *car* ils engendrent interminablement des caprices tyranniques" (my emphasis). With χαλεπούς and ἀνηνύτους, Philo states in sum the deleterious traits of tyrannical desire expounded in §§80b–83. Such desires are grievous (χαλεπούς) primarily *because* they are endless (ἀ-ηνύτους)—i.e., perpetually unfulfilled (cf. ἀνύω, *to effect, achieve, accomplish*).

⁴⁸ *Consider the plight of someone subject to tyrannical desire!* (γάρ): The translation interprets expansively the explanatory γάρ, which signals Philo's transition to a detailed narration of tyrannical desire's ill effects.

⁴⁹ *Free of restraint and fixed on the thought of a beloved object*: Philo presupposes but does not actually state these conditions. In his view, the appearance of tyrannical desire within the soul requires (1) the utter defeat of reason, resulting from reason's failure to restrain desire effectively, and (2) the involvement of the mind, which—because of reason's defeat—now operates entirely in the service of desire (see above, pp. 71–75).

⁵⁰ *into the boundless distance*: Colson's translation of εἰς τὸ ἄπειρον.

⁵¹ *struggles in vain* (σφαδάζει): Cf. *Praem.* 140: ἔξω δὲ τοῦ σφαδάζειν οὐδὲν ἐργάσασθαι δυνήσονται πᾶσαν ἰσχὺν ἐκτετμημένοι καὶ ἐκνενευρισμένοι.

⁵² *implacable* (ἀπαρηγόρηται): Philo elsewhere uses ἀ-παρηγόρητος to indicate *inconsolable* grief (e.g., *Mos.* 2.245; *Spec.* 2.134). Here he indicates taskmasters incapable of appeasement.

distance, working themselves into a state of frenzied craving and uncontrolled madness.[53] They become just like Tantalus,[54] racked with "hunger" and "thirst," but not for something to fill the void in their *bellies*—they hunger instead for money, fame, power, voluptuous bodies,[55] or any of the countless other things often considered enviable and worthy of great effort.[56] Rest assured that passionate desire, once indulged, will never stop short of this full-blown agony.[57] [§83] Just as what physicians call the "creeping disease" never stays in one place, but moves around and as its name suggests "creeps" through the whole body, spreading and seeping, taking over the different parts of the body one after another, from head to toe, so too *desire* spreads quickly and eventually infects every last part of the soul. Like a fire with plenty of fuel, it keeps burning, once lit, until the flames consume everything.

Having sketched briefly the problem posed by passions *in general,* Philo now considers ἐπιθυμία *in particular.* Any emotion (πάθος) can become a passion (πάθος) when reason fails to set proper limits—and passion, understood in this way as a failure of restraint, typically brings disaster to the soul (§79). Of course, this general rule applies also to ἐπιθυμία, which turns from amoral emotion to destructive passion when it oversteps the measure of reason. But passionate desire (πλεονάζουσα [ἄμετρος] ἐπιθυμία) poses a *unique* problem and deserves *unique* censure, because it fosters the awful menace of tyrannical desire (ἔρως). Philo wants to describe that menace in

---

[53] *working themselves into a state of frenzied craving and uncontrolled madness* ([ἡ ἐπιθυμία] οἶστρον καὶ μανίαν ἀκάθεκτον ἐγκατασκευάσασα): Desire (ἐπιθυμία) is the subject of ἐγκατασκευάσασα, but the creation of οἶστρον καὶ μανίαν within the soul clearly *accompanies* the moral agent's focus on what he or she does not have, to which Philo has just referred (λήθη μὲν τῶν παρόντων, μνήμῃ δὲ τῶν μακρὰν ἀφεστηκότων). In the end, only a slight distinction exists between what *desire* does and what moral agents do *to themselves* through their indulgence of desire.

[54] *They become just like Tantalus*: Philo does not actually mention Tantalus again, but clearly he has just described in §82 the "punishment of Tantalus" (Ταντάλειον τιμωρίαν) mentioned in §81.

[55] *voluptuous bodies* (εὐμορφίας): Literally a reference to excellent (beautiful) form, but "voluptuous bodies" conveys the sense of a physical form arousing desire's pursuit of pleasure.

[56] *things often considered enviable and worthy of great effort* (ὅσα κατὰ τὸν ἀνθρώπινον βίον ζηλωτὰ καὶ περιμάχητα εἶναι δοκεῖ): According to the conventional standards of human life embraced by most people, many things *seem* to possess ultimate value when in fact they do *not* (cf. §80: ὅσα τῷ δοκεῖν ἀγαθῶν, πρὸς ἀλήθειαν οὐκ ὄντων).

[57] Some such thought underlies Philo's introduction of disease and fire imagery in §83, which otherwise seems out of place. If desire oversteps the bounds of reason and remains unchecked, the agony he has just described inevitably results.

detail in order to illustrate just how bad ἐπιθυμία can be, not ἐπιθυμία per se—and certainly not ἐπιθυμία the moderated, useful emotion—but ἐπιθυμία at its full-blown worst, ἐπιθυμία burgeoned into ἔρως. In §§80–83, Philo introduces the topic of tyrannical desire (ἔρως) then begins his "diagnosis" (κρίσις) in earnest by explaining its torturous effect on the soul.

Philo first states the type of passionate desire he has in mind (§80a): a *longing* (ἐπιθυμία τῶν ἀπόντων) after false goods that gives birth to *tyrannical desires* (ἔρωτας ἐντίκτουσα).[58] Here he alludes to the close Platonic association of ἔρως with πόθος—both terms suggest an obsessive desire, but with different emphases.[59] In particular, πόθος involves objects *not* in the subject's physical presence.[60] As Philo explicitly states, the desire is τῶν ἀπόντων, which makes it a *longing*, a *pining*, for something remote and invisible. Since there is by definition nothing to perceive through the senses, the moral agent must *produce* and *hold in mind* an image of the beloved object. And ἔρως, in particular, involves objects deemed "good" and thus worthy of ultimate pursuit. So tyrannical desire, as Philo points out, tragically involves a *mistaken* perception of what is good, compelling the moral agent to pursue fervently *as good* what really is not (ὅσα τῷ δοκεῖν ἀγαθῶν, πρὸς ἀλήθειαν οὐκ ὄντων).[61] In terms of Middle-Platonic moral psychology, this happens when the emotion ἐπιθυμία not only oversteps the bounds of reason to become passionate desire (πλεονάζουσα [ἄμετρος] ἐπιθυμία), but defeats reason entirely, compelling the vanquished moral agent to

---

[58] Cf. *Her.* 269: ὅταν δὲ ἐπιθυμία κρατήσῃ, ἔρως ἐγγίνεται τῶν ἀπόντων. In *Leg.* 870 A, Plato speaks of ἡ ... ἔρωτας μυρίους ἐντίκτουσα δύναμις, clearly related to a sort of desire mentioned earlier in the passage: ἐπιθυμία κρατοῦσα ψυχῆς ἐξηγριωμένης ὑπὸ πόθων (cf. *Resp.* 586 C: ἔρωτας ... ἐντίκτειν).

[59] *Symp.* 197 D: πόθου πατήρ [ἔρως] (cf. *Phaedr.* 250 D). Philo elsewhere makes the association: *Opif.* 5: ἔρωτι καὶ πόθῳ ... κατεσχημένην; *Opif.* 111: ἔρωτι καὶ πόθῳ δαμασθέν; *Opif.* 77: πληχθεὶς ὁ νοῦς ἔρωτα καὶ πόθον ἔσχε (cf. *Congr.* 166; *Somn.* 2.150; *Spec.* 4.161); Ps.-Andr. 231.93 defines πόθος as ἐπιθυμία κατὰ ἔρωτα ἀπόντος. In *Spec.* 4.82, Philo uses other terms closely associated with ἔρως: οἶστρος and μανία (e.g., *Phaedr.* 240 C–D: ὁ ἐραστής ... ὑπ᾽ἀνάγκης τε καὶ οἴστρου ἐλαύνεται; *Phaedr.* 241 A: ἀντ᾽ἔρωτος καὶ μανίας; *Phaedr.* 256 D: τῆς ἐρωτικῆς μανίας).

[60] *Crat.* 420 A: "πόθος" αὖ καλεῖται σημαίνων οὐ τοῦ παρόντος εἶναι ἀλλὰ τοῦ ἄλλοθί που ὄντος καὶ ἀπόντος.

[61] Attachment to false goods reflects entanglement with the sensible world and its system of values, as Philo implies in *Spec.* 4.82: ὅσα κατὰ τὸν ἀνθρώπινον βίον ζηλωτὰ καὶ περιμάχητα εἶναι δοκεῖ; also *Deus* 148: τὸν βασιλέα τῶν φαινομένων ἁπάντων ἀγαθῶν τὸν γήινον Ἐδώμ—ὄντως γὰρ τὰ τῷ δοκεῖν ἀγαθὰ πάντα γήινα (cf. *Resp.* 586 A–C).

embrace *its* false notion of the good—namely, pleasure, which a variety of false goods afford.[62]

Once he identifies tyrannical desire (ἔρως) as his topic, Philo explains its characteristic ill effects, beginning with the tortuous *insatiability* ἔρως creates in the soul (§§80b–82). Philo uses both the image of a maddening, futile chase and the mythical figure of Tantalus to portray vividly the same dreadful experience: fervently, endlessly reaching for something but *never* getting hold of it.[63] While the chase image conveys an *impression* of the experience, Philo's commentary on Tantalus provides a genuine analysis in terms of moral psychology. Hunger and thirst are desires *of the soul* especially linked to *physical* states of "emptiness."[64] As long as the physical emptiness remains, the desirous part of the soul (ἐπιθυμία, i.e., τὸ ἐπιθυμητικόν) remains activated in reflexive pursuit of the *pleasure* of a physical "filling" with food or water.[65] The physical emptiness acts as an inherent trigger, constantly goading the "taskmasters" hunger and thirst, which in turn compel the moral agent to eat and drink. But the goading and compelling disappear when the emptiness disappears. Similarly, tyrannical desire creates something like a physical emptiness, insofar as it creates an inherent trigger for the soul's ἐπιθυμία (i.e., τὸ ἐπιθυμητικόν). Obsessed with a false good, the moral agent continually brings an image of that "good" to mind, and because that "good" promises pleasure, ἐπιθυμία remains in a state of continual arousal in pursuit of that pleasure. Unlike physical hunger, which can end once the physical emptiness is filled, this "hunger" *cannot end*,

---

[62] In *Phaedr.* 237 D–238 C, the term ἔρως applies to one in whom ἐπιθυμία has conquered (esp. *Phaedr.* 238 C: κρατήσασα ἐπιθυμία ... ἔρως ἐκλήθη [cf. *Leg.* 870 A]; N.B. *Her.* 269: ὅταν δὲ ἐπιθυμία κρατήσῃ, ἔρως ἐγγίνεται).

[63] On Tantalus, see *Od.* 11.582–92 (cf. *Her.* 269: διψῇ μὲν γὰρ ἀεί, πιεῖν δὲ ἀδυνατεῖ ταντάλειον τιμωρίαν ὑπομένουσα). N.B. Philo's language of "stretching" and "straining" in *Spec.* 4.81 (ἐπιτείνει γὰρ καὶ ἐπελαύνει); cf. *Post.* 116: κατὰ τὰς τῶν ἐπιθυμιῶν μακρὰς καὶ διωλυγίους ἐκτάσεις ἐλαυνομένη; *Gig.* 18: μηκίστας ἐν ἑαυτοῖς τείνοντες ἐπιθυμίας; *Spec.* 3.44: ἔρως οὐ μετρίως ἐπιτείνεται; *Prob.* 159: πρὸς ἐπιθυμίας ἐλαύνεται (cf. *Phaedr.* 240 D: ὑπ'ἀνάγκης τε καὶ οἴστρου ἐλαύνεται). Elsewhere, Philo associates ἔρως with the "unreachable" (ἀνέφικτος): e.g., *Leg.* 1.75: νοῦς ἀνεφίκτων ἐρῶν; *Conf.* 7: τὸν τῶν ἀνεφίκτων ἔρωτα; *Spec.* 1.44: τῶν ἀνεφίκτων ἔρως.

[64] On the relation of hunger and thirst, as desires *of the soul*, to physical states *of the body*, see *Phileb.* 31 E–35 D (cf. Hackforth, *Plato's Examination of Pleasure*, 61; also 79, n. 4; 112, n. 2.; 140, n. 2).

[65] Of course, reason may or may not authorize the pursuit of food or water, depending on the circumstances. In *Resp.* 439 A–D, Plato considers the case of a thirsty person who simultaneously *desires* a drink but *refuses* to drink, because reason keeps desire in check.

because there is no corresponding physical emptiness to fill.⁶⁶ So the soul under tyrannical desire endures an oppressive, agonizing (ἀργαλέον) fate with no hope of relief.⁶⁷

Next, Philo notes the all-consuming nature of tyrannical desire (§83). If left unchecked, desire eventually spreads throughout the *entire* soul (δι'ὅλης ... τῆς ψυχῆς), just as disease consumes *all* of the body (πᾶσαν τὴν κοινωνίαν τῶν τοῦ σώματος μερῶν) and fire consumes *all* available fuel (πᾶσαν [ὕλην]). These images suit Philo's Middle-Platonic psychology, because they portray desire as a distinct power capable of malignant, independent operation—of spreading its influence from one *part* of the soul to another. Once desire has broken free of reason's restraint, it settles for nothing less than complete domination.⁶⁸ In this way, tyrannical desire represents the terminal stage of desire's unrestrained activity: ἐπιθυμία has "consumed" the rational part of the soul, replacing any proper notion of "the good" with its singular focus on pleasure.

§§80 – 83 Excursus: Parallel Material in Decal. 146–50

In *Decal.* 146–50, Philo provides a detailed account, similar to *Spec.* 4.80–83, of the insatiability and all-consuming nature of *tyrannical desire* (ἔρως), despite preliminary remarks (*Decal.* 142–45) promising an account of how the *emotion* ἐπιθυμία differs from other *emotions*. In §142, Philo had identified ἐπιθυμία alone as "voluntary" (ἑκούσιος) due to its *internal* origin (τὴν ἀρχὴν ἐξ ἡμῶν αὐτῶν λαμβάνει), in this way distinguishing it from the other emotions, which he identified as "involuntary" (ἀκούσιος) due to their *external* origin (θύραθεν ... ἔξωθεν).⁶⁹ Philo then explained in §§143–

---

⁶⁶ Cf. *Agr.* 36: "[E]ven if the receptacles of the belly have been completely filled, desire always empty (τὴν ἀεὶ κενὴν ἐπιθυμίαν) and still swelling and panting goes about looking everywhere to see whether haply there are any leavings that have been overlooked and let pass, that like an all-devouring fire (παμφάγου πυρός) it may pick up this as well" (substituting "desire always empty" for Colson's "taste still empty").
⁶⁷ Cf. *Ebr.* 6: αἴτιον ... ἀπληστίας δὲ ἡ ἀργαλεωτάτη παθῶν ψυχῆς ἐπιθυμία.
⁶⁸ Cf. Pelletier, " Passions à l'assaut de l'âme."
⁶⁹ Taken literally and applied *strictly* to the emotion ἐπιθυμία these remarks hardly make sense in the broader context of Philo's theory of πάθος. Wolfson (*Philo*, 2:232–35) identifies but then rejects potential precedents for this line of thinking in Aristotle's philosophy (e.g., *Eth. nic.* 1111 a 23: τὸ ἑκούσιον δόξειεν ἂν εἶναι οὗ ἡ ἀρχὴ ἐν αὐτῷ), looking instead to Philo's concept of human *free will* to explain the unique ἑκούσιος-ἐπιθυμία connection (*Philo*, 2:234–35). While Philo does have strong convictions regarding human free will (e.g., *Deus* 45–50), they have no direct bearing on his Middle-Platonic theory of emotion. According to that theory—broadly attested in Philo's writings (see above, pp. 56–60)—the emotion ἐπιθυμία cannot qualify as "voluntary," since it operates according to a reflexive, non-rational mechanism. Philo's explicit and unique ascription of voluntariness (ἑκούσιος) to ἐπιθυμία in *Decal.* 142—attested only in

45 how the perceptions of present good, present ill, and prospective ill—all originating *externally*—cause the corresponding emotions of pleasure, distress, and fear to occur involuntarily, a fact signaled grammatically by designating the respective *perceptions* as subjects acting upon the soul.[70] A similar account of ἐπιθυμία in §146—one describing *also desire* as a non-rational emotion activated by a reflexive, non-rational mechanism—would have been in keeping with Philo's Middle-Platonic theory of emotion.[71] But instead he changes the grammatical pattern and designates as the subject of his description the *moral agent* (τις), who does not so much *respond* to a perception as *generate* one by bringing a prospective good to mind (λαβών ... ἔννοιαν ἀγαθοῦ μὴ παρόντος). In this way, Philo superficially validates his claim that ἐπιθυμία differs from other emotions, *insofar as* he has described—at the point in sequence reserved for ἐπιθυμία (ἡδονή, λύπη, φόβος, ἐπιθυμία)—a phenomenon with an internal origin. And since it originates within, this phenomenon counts as voluntary, according to the principle established in §142: *external* (origin) equals *involuntary*, *internal* (origin) equals *voluntary*. But Philo has not in fact described the *emotion* ἐπιθυμία at all—he has described instead its offspring, the tyrant ἔρως, which has in fact a better claim to "voluntariness" because it involves the mind in ways that the non-rational *emotion* ἐπιθυμία does not.[72] Ultimately,

---

this passage—ought to be explained as something *other than* a blatant contradiction of his fundamental Platonic convictions. Philo does *need* to set ἐπιθυμία apart, since he needs to account somehow for the Decalogue's prohibition of only this emotion, so reading the ἑκούσιος-ἐπιθυμία connection as an anomalous, ad hoc formulation makes sense at first consideration (cf. Winston, "Philo on the Emotions," 206–07). But certainly an interpretation of the ἑκούσιος-ἐπιθυμία connection consistent with the philosophical perspective evident elsewhere in Philo's writings is to be preferred—if it exists—and it *does* exist, if the term ἐπιθυμία is read expansively as a reference not to ἐπιθυμία itself but to its *offspring* tyrannical desire (ἔρως).

[70] *Decal.* 143 (ἡδονή): τοῦ παρόντος καὶ νομισθέντος ἀγαθοῦ φαντασία διεγείρει καὶ διανίστησι τὴν ψυχήν; *Decal.* 144 (λύπη): κακόν, ὅταν ἐκβιασάμενον πληγὴν ἐπενέγκῃ καίριον, συννοίας καὶ κατηφείας εὐθὺς αὐτὴν ἀναπίμπλησιν ἄκουσαν (retaining MS. ἐκβιασάμενον [cf. *Virt. mor.* 449 C: ἐκβιαζομένων] instead of Colson's εἰσβιασάμενον [see PLCL VII, 78, n. 1]); *Decal.* 145 (φόβος): ὅταν δὲ τὸ κακόν ... πτοίαν καὶ ἀγωνίαν ... προεκπέμπει. Cf. above, pp. 122–24 [="§79 *Excursus: Parallel Material in* Decal. *142–45*"].

[71] *Leg.* 3.115: ἐπιθυμία, [=] ὄρεξις ἄλογος (cf. above, pp. 33–65, esp. 55, n. 76; also *Didask.* 32.1 [185.38–40]: πάντα γὰρ [πάθη] συνίσταται ἢ κατὰ ἀγαθοῦ ἔμφασιν ἢ κατὰ κακοῦ. Ἀγαθὸν γὰρ ἐὰν μὲν παρεῖναι ὑπολάβωμεν, ἡδόμεθα, ἐὰν δὲ μέλλειν, ἐπιθυμοῦμεν).

[72] See above, pp. 71–79; cf. *Sacr.* 129: διαφέρουσι δὲ ὅτι ἐκείνοις μὲν ἀβούλητος ... δι'ἔργον ἀκούσιον, τούτοις δὲ ... ἑκούσιος δι'ἔρωτα τῶν ἀρίστων. Each of Philo's preliminary descriptions of the other cardinal emotions includes a deliberate *naming* of the emotion (*Decal.* 143: καλεῖται δὲ τουτὶ τὸ πάθος ... ἡδονή; *Decal.* 144: ὄνομα δὲ [καὶ] τούτῳ τῷ πάθει λύπη; *Decal.* 145: φόβος δὲ προσαγορεύεται τὸ πάθος), but he never labels as "ἐπιθυμία" the phenomenon he begins describing in §146, because he does not in

Philo has not demonstrated a real difference in the way ἐπιθυμία functions over against the other *emotions*, but he *has* managed to introduce what he considers the true distinctive of ἐπιθυμία: its capacity to burgeon into tyrannical desire.[73]

Although Philo does not introduce his topic in §146 with the *term* ἔρως (as he does in *Spec.* 4.80 [N.B. ἔρωτας]), he nevertheless speaks of tyrannical desire, as his explicit mention of ἔρως in §151 later confirms.[74] He describes a moral agent who holds in mind a *concept* (ἔννοιαν) of an absent "good" (ἀγαθοῦ μὴ παρόντος) and "reaches" to get it (ὀρέγηται τυχεῖν αὐτοῦ). A setting of the mind on something *deemed* good signals the involvement of ἔρως—in this case, a tyrannical desire aimed at *false* goods and the pleasures they afford.[75] By noting the *absence* of the beloved object (μὴ παρόντος), Philo gives additional, incidental evidence for the involvement of ἔρως, since this sort of longing characterizes πόθος, a phenomenon often coupled with ἔρως.[76] In terms of moral psychology, Philo portrays a beloved "good" set up *in the mind*, toward which ἐπιθυμία (τὸ ἐπιθυμητικόν) reflexively "reaches" (ὀρέγηται) in pursuit of pleasure.[77] In this case, desire has completely defeated the moral agent (N.B. §149: κρατηθεὶς ἐπιθυμίᾳ), imposing its ultimate "good" of *pleasure* upon the rational faculty and creating for the *non*-rational faculty—i.e., ἐπιθυμία—an object of hopeless pursuit. As in *Spec.* 4.80–83, Philo vividly portrays the endless, futile striving to grasp an ever-elusive object.

Instead of elaborating the image of an exasperating, futile chase (mentioned summarily in §146), Philo appeals in §§147–149a to the senses of sight and hearing to illustrate the straining, agonizing, fruitless effort to apprehend the beloved object of tyrannical desire.[78] The eyes, he says

---

fact *describe* ἐπιθυμία. In §149, Philo clearly identifies the experience he has in mind: that of the moral agent "mastered by desire" (κρατηθεὶς ἐπιθυμίᾳ). He has in mind not the *emotion* ἐπιθυμία, or even the *passion* ἐπιθυμία (πλεονάζουσα [ἄμετρος] ἐπιθυμία)—he describes instead reason's utter defeat by ἐπιθυμία, i.e., *tyrannical desire* (ἔρως).

[73] This capacity explains Philo's initial identification (*Decal.* 142) of desire as "most grievous" (χαλεπώτατον) among the emotions.

[74] *Decal.*151: χρημάτων ἔρως ἢ γυναικὸς ἢ δόξης ἢ τινος ἄλλου τῶν ἡδονὴν ἀπεργαζομένων.

[75] Cf. *Spec.* 4.80: ὅσα τῷ δοκεῖν ἀγαθῶν, πρὸς ἀλήθειαν οὐκ ὄντων.

[76] On the link between ἔρως and πόθος, see above, p. 127, n. 59. Philo further alludes to πόθος in the expression ψαῦσαι τοῦ ποθουμένου γλιχόμενος (§146; cf. πόθῳ in §148), an expression containing yet another term associated with ἔρως, γλιχόμενος (cf. *Phaedr.* 248 A: γλιχόμεναι ... τοῦ ἄνω; *Opif.* 166: γλίχεται τυχεῖν ἐραστοῦ). Without question, Philo deploys a predictable cluster of terminology consistent with Plato's characterization of ἔρως.

[77] Cf. Plato's use of ὀρέγεται to describe the yearning of ἐπιθυμία (*Resp.* 439 A).

[78] Philo introduces the analogy in §147: ὅμοιον δέ τι καὶ περὶ τὰς αἰσθήσεις ἔοικε συμβαίνειν.

(§147), are often hard pressed for the "apprehension" (κατάληψις) of some far-off object. Despite their intense and continued effort, they are *unable* to get hold of what they "desire" and exhaust themselves.[79] Likewise, the ears (§148–149a) can be "aroused" (ἀνεγερθέντα)[80] by an indistinct, far-off noise, which produces a "longing" (πόθος) for clarity. The sound, however, *remains* indistinct, provoking an even greater yearning for "apprehension" (τοῦ καταλαβεῖν ἵμερον).[81] These analogies from the realm of sense-perception not only present a novel image of insatiability—they also reflect the Middle-Platonic moral psychology underlying Philo's exposition. By choosing to compare the mechanism of tyrannical desire with the *non-rational* mechanism of sense-perception (αἴσθησις), Philo reaffirms his understanding of ἐπιθυμία as a fundamentally *non-rational* power, which *non-rationally* pursues the "good" (pleasure) set before it in the soul subject to tyrannical desire.[82]

As in *Spec.* 4.81–82, Philo cites the mythical figure Tantalus to illustrate the operation of tyrannical desire (§149b). Although brief, his remarks plainly state the condition of someone consumed by ἔρως, someone "conquered by desire" (κρατηθεὶς ἐπιθυμίᾳ). Desire has reached the height of power, supplanting reason and making its *own* goal of pleasure the goal of the moral agent. In this condition, the moral agent "thirsts" always for what is absent (διψῶν ἀεὶ τῶν ἀπόντων) without ever being "filled" (οὐδέποτε πληροῦται). In fact, there is no *possibility* of being filled, since the appetite aroused by an image of false goods has no *capacity* for fulfillment—it is an "empty" (i.e., "pointless") appetite (κενήν ... τὴν ὄρεξιν).

As in *Spec.* 4.83, Philo compares desire to *disease* and *fire* (§150), both of which spread until they have consumed everything available to them. Again, the imagery reflects Middle-Platonic moral psychology by depicting ἐπιθυμία as a destructive force originating in one *part* of something (body,

---

[79] In Philo's account (§147), note esp. τείνοντες αὐτούς (cf. §146: ἐκτείνων; §149: ἐπιτείνεσθαι; *Spec.* 4.80: ἐπιτείνει); πλέον τῆς δυνάμεως; σφαλέντες; τῷ βιαίῳ καὶ συντόνῳ ... ἀσθενήσαντες.

[80] Philo often uses ἀνεγείρω in connection with the emotions (e.g., *Ebr.* 98, *Fug.* 91), which makes sense in light of the moral psychology of ἔρως: the rational part of the soul, consumed with tyrannical desire, holds in mind an image that continually arouses the *emotion* ἐπιθυμία, creating the maddening experience of insatiability (cf. *Spec.* 1.192: ἐπιθυμίας ἐγείρουσαι; *Spec.* 2.193: ἐγείρει ... ἐπιθυμίας; *Spec.* 4.129: ἐπιθυμίαν ἐγείραντες).

[81] Like πόθος, ἵμερος represents a companion phenomenon of ἔρως (e.g., *Symp.* 197 D: ἱμέρου, πόθου πατήρ [ἔρως] [cf. *Phaedr.* 251 C–E]; *Opif.* 70–71: ἑπόμενος ἔρωτι σοφίας ... γεμισθεὶς ἱμέρου καὶ πόθου; *Somn.* 1.36: ἔρωτες ... ἀκάθεκτοι καὶ λελυττηκότες ἵμεροι.

[82] Cf. Philo's bipartite model of reason over against αἴσθησις (see above, pp. 60–62).

fuel, soul) and spreading to other *parts*.[83] Revealing his Middle-Platonic affinities even further, Philo uses this imagery to reflect the adversarial relationship *between* parts (*between* reason and desire) so fundamental to the Platonic perspective. He notes that the soul will suffer infection "lest philosophical reason hold back the stream of desire" (εἰ μὴ λόγος ὁ κατὰ φιλοσοφίαν ... ῥέουσαν τὴν ἐπιθυμίαν ἐπίσχοι).[84] Here reason acts to *restrain* desire, in order to preclude an overpowering of reason *by* desire. If reason fails to hold back the stream, then desire will have its way, ultimately overrunning the entire soul with the tyranny of ἔρως. Similarly, if the "flame" of desire is granted "freedom" (ἄδεια)[85] and "leisure" (ἐκεχειρία)[86]—in other words, if reason fails to *restrain* desire and instead gives it free rein—then it will eventually spread and destroy everything through the tyranny of ἔρως. Philo deploys the imagery in this way because he understands the importance of ἐγκράτεια: reason must either *impose* its rule over non-rational ἐπιθυμία or in the end *suffer* the rule of desire's tyrannical offspring ἔρως.

§§84 – 91: Tyrannical Desire as "Source of All Evils"

[§84] So great and egregious an evil, then, is desire. In fact, if truth be told, it is the source of all evils. Consider the underlying cause of looting, robbery, and swindling; of flattery and insult; of seduction, adultery, murder—of all wrongdoing involving matters private or public, sacred or secular. Do these flow from any source other than desire? [§85] For this reason, among the passions, only passionate *desire* truly deserves the name "Master Vice," whose one little offspring tyrannical desire has repeatedly filled the world with unspeakable disasters[87]—which, too numerous for all the land to contain, have

---

[83] E.g., Philo describes disease spreading throughout the body and leaving no "part" (μέρος) unaffected (ἀπαθές) (§150).

[84] Cf. *Legat.* 65: τὴν πολλὴν αὐτοῦ ῥύμην τῶν ἐπιθυμιῶν ἐφέξοντα. On "stream of desire," see also *Resp.* 485 D–E; cf. *Crat.* 419 E–420 B.

[85] Cf. esp. *Leg.* 2.91, where Philo associates this same "freedom" (ἄδεια) with the eventual rise of tyranny within the soul (τυράννου τρόπον) (also *Post.* 98; *Congr.* 158).

[86] Cf. Philo's use of ἐκεχειρία in connection with the Sabbath (e.g., *Mos.* 2.22; *Spec.* 2.69).

[87] *among the passions, only passionate desire truly deserves the name "Master Vice," whose one little offspring tyrannical desire ...* (ἀψευδῶς ἂν λεχθὲν ἀρχέκακον πάθος ἐστὶν ἐπιθυμία, ἧς ἓν τὸ βραχύτατον ἔγγονον, ἔρως): Since Philo does not consider the *emotion* ἐπιθυμία to have any intrinsic ill effects, he must have in mind the *passion* ἐπιθυμία (πλεονάζουσα [ἄμετρος] ἐπιθυμία) and its preeminence among other *passions*. By describing it as τὸ βραχύτατον, he identifies ἔρως not as the littlest of many but simply as very little (cf. *Her.* 155: τὸ βραχύτατον ζῷον, ἄνθρωπον) In other words, the genesis of ἔρως in the soul seems slight in comparison with the "unspeakable disasters" (ἀμυθήτων ... συμφορῶν) it eventually creates.

spilled out into the sea. Everywhere the vast watery expanse has been filled with ships of war and all the terrible inventions of war. Charging out to sea, their violence runs its course then crashes back like a tide upon the shores of home. [§86] We can better understand the operation of passionate desire[88] by thinking of it as a venomous creature or lethal poison, both of which cause an overall change for the worse anytime they take hold of someone. What exactly am I saying? Think of tyrannical desire as the fatal "bite" of passionate desire, a terminal "taking hold" akin to a "taking over."[89] [§87] For example, if a tyrannical desire for *money* takes over the soul,[90] it turns people into thieves and pickpockets, larcenists and burglars—it makes them likely to swindle and scam, to accept bribes, to violate sacred trusts, to perform any other similar act of greed. [§88] If a tyrannical desire for *reputation* takes over, it makes people pretentious, arrogant, unsteady and unsettled in character. With eager ears they listen for the pronouncements of other people,[91] becoming at the same time dejected and elated as they hear from the fickle masses, who deal out

---

[88] *the operation of passionate desire* (τοῦ πάθους ἐνέργειαν): Reading ἐνέργειαν with MSS (SM) rather than ἐνάργειαν proposed by Mangey and adopted by Cohn-Wendland. Philo, after all, goes on to explain in §§87–91 the *work* of desire in the soul (cf. *Leg.* 2.101: ὁ ἀποπίπτων τῶν παθῶν καὶ ὑστερίζων τῆς ἐνεργείας αὐτῶν; *Leg.* 3.22: ταῖς τῶν παθῶν ἐνεργείαις).

[89] *Think of tyrannical desire as the fatal "bite" of passionate desire, a terminal "taking hold" akin to a "taking over."* Since the Greek of §86 ends with τί δ'ἐστὶν ὃ λέγω ("What exactly am I saying?"), this sentence attempts to clarify the logic of Philo's venom and poison similes in light of the examples given in §§87–91. He presupposes passionate desire as the condition from which tyrannical desire—the worst, terminal grade of desire—is born. Passionate desire represents a genuine danger to the soul, but it fatally "bites" the soul by burgeoning into tyrannical desire, which consumes the moral agent and thoroughly corrupts the character.

[90] *if a tyrannical desire for* money *takes over the soul* (εἰ πρὸς χρήματα γένοιτο): Philo uses γένοιτο to indicate the "birth" of tyrannical desire (cf. §85: τὸ βραχύτατον ἔγγονον, ἔρως) *relative to* a particular beloved object, in this case χρήματα. He envisions the same phenomenon relative to other objects (δόξα, etc.) in subsequent paragraphs.

[91] *With eager ears they listen for the pronouncements of other people* (φωναῖς τὰ ὦτα πεφρακότας): The phrase φωναῖς τὰ ὦτα πεφρακότας most likely represents a play on words. The verb ἐπιφράσσω with τὰ ὦτα means "to stop one's ears" (see LSJ, s.v.), an idiom attested in Philo (e.g., *Leg.* 2.25; *Migr.* 191). But treating φράσσω as an equivalent of ἐπιφράσσω yields a sense directly opposite to what the context demands: people concerned with reputation clearly do not "stop their ears"—they *want* to know what people are saying about them, and *because* they are listening intently to praise and blame, their mood rises and falls accordingly. Philo plays with the ἐπιφράσσω idiom by substituting φράσσω, which can connote fortification (see LSJ, s.v.; cf. *Prob.* 152). The original effect must have been something like: "Their ears are not *stopped*, they're *propped*—eager to hear what people are saying."

praise and blame by indiscriminate whim—they readily exchange love for hatred, or hatred for love, depending on what they hear, and they do all sorts of other kindred deeds. [§89] If a tyrannical desire for *power* takes over, it makes people contentious, inequitable, tyrannical by nature, cruel at heart. They become enemies of their own homelands, harsh masters of anyone weaker, irreconcilable enemies of their equals in strength, and scheming flatterers of anyone stronger. If a tyrannical desire for *voluptuous bodies*[92] takes over, people become seducers, adulterers, pederasts, devotees of indulgence and lust—they consider the greatest of evils to be the happiest of goods. [§90] Overtaking even the *tongue*, tyrannical desire has stirred up endless troubles, since we know that people are often gripped with a desire to keep quiet when they ought to speak or a desire to speak when they ought to keep quiet—and both receive their just deserts. [§91] And when tyrannical desire seizes the *belly*, it produces hopeless, insatiable gluttons, devotees of a life of ease and dissipation, people who revel in guzzling and gorging, base slaves of strong drink and assorted delicacies,[93] who forage around at parties and banquets like ravenous little dogs. Such people end up with a miserable, accursed life more painful than any death.

Proceeding with his "diagnosis" (κρίσις), Philo turns from the agonizing experience tyrannical desire works in the *individual* (§§80–83) to consider the moral corruption and chaos it works in society *through* the individual (§§84–91). Philo makes one central claim in this section: that all moral and social ills stem from ἐπιθυμία. Such a claim both expands the scope of Philo's programmatic condemnation of desire and justifies the Decalogue's prohibition of just *one* πάθος as an effective means of precluding *all* wrongdoing. Philo undoubtedly has in mind *passionate* desire when he calls ἐπιθυμία the "source of all evils" (ἀπάντων πηγὴ τῶν κακῶν in §84) and "Master Vice" (ἀρχέκακον πάθος in §85), although he means it in a quailfied sense.[94] He indicts passionate desire *insofar as* it gives birth to tyrannical desire (ἔρως), and *tyrannical desire* then does the real work of corrupting character and generating corrupt behavior. As Philo puts it in §85,

---

[92] *voluptuous bodies* (σώματος κάλλος): Literally something like Colson's "bodily beauty," but "voluptuous bodies" conveys the sense of a physical form arousing desire's pursuit of pleasure (cf. above, p. 126, n. 55).
[93] *of strong drink and assorted delicacies* (ἀκράτου καὶ ἰχθύων καὶ ἐδεσμάτων).
[94] Philo makes a similar claim in *Decal.* 173: τὴν τῶν ἀδικημάτων πηγήν, ἐπιθυμίαν, ἀφ'ἧς αἱ παρανομώταται πράξεις.

passionate ἐπιθυμία is the Master Vice, "*whose one little offspring tyrannical desire* (ἔρως) *has repeatedly filled the world with unspeakable disasters.*"

Using a series of concrete examples, Philo goes on to explain in §§86–91 just *how* tyrannical desire does its work. Philo's argument presumes a direct stepwise progression from useful ἐπιθυμία, to passionate ἐπιθυμία, to ἔρως itself, which bears ultimate responsibility for the corruption of character. In other words, unrestrained desire gives birth to ἔρως, whose hegemony in turn transforms the moral agent into an evildoer who stops at nothing in pursuit of the beloved object. To clarify the mechanism of this transformation, Philo compares desire to poison, suggesting that *both* effect an overall change for the worse in whomever they afflict.[95] Poison, for instance, when introduced into the body (by venomous creatures or lethal drugs)—despite its initial localization—eventually transforms the *entire body* from healthy to sick, from living to dead.[96] Similarly, ἐπιθυμία, despite the "localization" of its initial break with reason, eventually burgeons into ἔρως and transforms the *entire soul* from healthy to sick, from virtuous to vicious. And moral agents display different *forms* of corruption depending on which false goods they pursue under tyrannical desire's control: money (χρήματα), reputation (δόξα), power (ἀρχή), or voluptuous bodies (σώματος κάλλος) (§§87–89).[97] In each case, the moral agent's obsessive drive for that *particular* "good" ultimately leads to a distinct profile of reprehensible behaviors detrimental to both self and society. For example, an ἔρως for *money* yields thieves and swindlers (§87); an ἔρως for *reputation* yields pretentious braggarts (§88);[98] an ἔρως for *power* yields ruthless oppressors (§89); an ἔρως for *voluptuous bodies* yields sexual immorality (§89). In this way, Philo traces a huge spectrum of wrongdoing to *one* source, tyrannical desire. To complete this spectrum of wrongdoing, Philo adds to his list of four false goods (§§87–89) two *parts of the body* over which tyrannical desire can reign (§§90–91): the tongue (γλῶττα) and the belly (τὰ περὶ γαστέρα).

---

[95] §86: ὅσων ἂν ... προσάψηται, μεταβολὴν ἀπεργάζεται τὴν πρὸς τὸ χεῖρον.

[96] Philo's reference to τὰ ἰοβόλα ζῷα undoubtedly includes the serpent, equated with "pleasure" (ἡδονή) in his allegorical reading of Gen 3: e.g., *Opif.* 157–60, esp. 157: "Following a probable conjecture one would say that the serpent spoken of is a fit symbol of pleasure (τὸν εἰρημένον ὄφιν ἡδονῆς εἶναι σύμβολον) ... because he carries in his teeth the venom (τὸν ἰὸν ἐπιφέρεται τοῖς ὀδοῦσιν) with which it is his nature to destroy (ἀναιρεῖν) those whom he has bitten." Philo's Middle-Platonic perspective often blurs the distinction between desire (ἐπιθυμία) and pleasure (ἡδονή), because of their close connection: desire reflexively, invariably pursues pleasure as its ultimate aim (see above, p. 39, n. 21). For this reason, the moral agent consumed by ἔρως is a φιλήδονος (see above, pp. 71–75).

[97] Cf. Philo's list in §82: χρημάτων, δόξης, ἡγεμονιῶν, εὐμορφίας.

[98] On ἔρως for δόξα see also Plutarch, *Suav. viv.* 1100 B.

As for the tongue, Philo mentions the reprehensible desire of some either to *keep quiet* what ought to be said or to *say* what ought to be kept quiet (§90).[99] He describes a situation of desire having "reached" the tongue (ἐπὶ γλῶτταν φθάσασα)—that is, desire having extended its influence *even so far* as to overtake the tongue, causing people to act (speak) contrary to reason. Just as the tyranny of ἔρως over people enamored of false goods causes corruption and wrongdoing, the tyranny of ἔρως *over the tongue* causes all sorts of troubles. Philo does not dwell on the immoralities caused by speech and silence, since merely *tracing* them to ἐπιθυμία-turned-ἔρως confirms his central claim that *all* moral and social ills—including these—stem from desire.

Finally, Philo speaks of desire "getting hold of the belly" (ἁψαμένη δὲ τῶν περὶ γαστέρα), which clearly indicates more than just *reasonable* desires for food and drink. He has in mind people overcome by tyrannical desire (ἔρως), who have made the pleasure derived from eating and drinking their ultimate "good." Tyrannical desire has made them "base slaves" (κακοὺς δούλους) of drinks and delicacies, who lead a "miserable and accursed life" (ἀθλίαν καὶ ἐπάρατον ... ζωήν) more "agonizing" (ἀργαλεωτέραν) than any death.[100] As with every case of ἔρως, a particular *object* of affection produces a particular *brand* of immorality: those who adore the pleasures of food and drink become, above all, "gluttons" (γαστριμάργους).[101]

§§84 – 91 Excursus: Parallel Material in Decal. 151–53

In *Decal.* 151–53, Philo likewise indicts desire as the source of countless troubles. He initially asks whether ἔρως for money, women, reputation, or "anything else producing pleasure" becomes the cause of only "small and incidental ills."[102] This rhetorical question functions as the thesis for §§151–53 and reflects convictions about desire crucial to Philo's exposition of the Tenth Commandment: tyrannical desire (ἔρως), which can arise in connec-

---

[99] §90: ἔνιοι γὰρ ἐπιθυμοῦσιν ἢ τὰ λεκτέα σιωπᾶν ἢ τὰ ἡσυχαστέα λέγειν (cf. Plutarch, *De garrulitate*).
[100] Cf. §80: οὐδὲν ἀργαλέον ὡς ἐπιθυμία τῶν ἀπόντων ὅσα τῷ δοκεῖν ἀγαθῶν, πρὸς ἀλήθειαν οὐκ ὄντων, χαλεποὺς καὶ ἀνηνύτους ἔρωτας ἐντίκτουσα.
[101] In *Phaedr.* 238 A–B, Socrates labels ἔρως *as it relates to food* "γαστριμαργία" (περὶ μὲν γὰρ ἐδωδὴν κρατοῦσα τοῦ λόγου τοῦ ἀρίστου καὶ τῶν ἄλλων ἐπιθυμιῶν ἐπιθυμία γαστριμαργία). Philo elsewhere associates γαστριμαργία with an absolute dominance of *desire for food* (e.g., *Agr.* 36).
[102] §151: χρημάτων ἔρως ἢ γυναικὸς ἢ δόξης ἢ τινος ἄλλου τῶν ἡδονὴν ἀπεργαζομένων ἆρά γε μικρῶν καὶ τῶν τυχόντων αἴτιος γίνεται κακῶν.

tion with any number of pleasurable aims, in turn becomes responsible for (αἴτιος γίνεται) great and innumerable ills. In §§152–53, Philo considers warfare in particular, ultimately concluding that "all wars flow from one source: desire (ἐπιθυμία) for money, or reputation, or pleasure."[103] He essentially restates here the thesis of §151, but with less precision, metonymically replacing the *specific* term ἔρως with the generic term ἐπιθυμία, replacing also the carefully worded "things that produce pleasure" (τῶν ἡδονὴν ἀπεργαζομένων) with a generic reference to "pleasure" (ἡδονῆς).

§§92 – 94: Location of Ἐπιθυμία

[§92] This overpowering desire for food and drink explains[104] why those who had not simply "tasted" philosophy but had lavishly "feasted" on its sound doctrines—once they had investigated the nature of the soul and recognized its tripartite structure[105] (reason, spirit, desire)—distributed the various parts as they did. They put reason, which rules the soul, in the most appropriate place, the head, which is the topmost part of the body. The head also serves as headquarters for the senses, which together form a sort of entourage for the soul's "king," the mind. [§93] Next, they determined that spirit must reside in the chest, for two reasons: first, in the chest, spirit wears a breastplate, just like a soldier, and this added protection makes it very difficult to defeat, although certainly not invincible; second, in the chest, dwelling near the mind, spirit receives help from its neighbor, whose wise counsel lulls it into compliance. Finally, they determined that desire must reside in the area around the navel known as

---

[103] §153: πόλεμοι πάντες ἀπὸ μιᾶς πηγῆς ἐρρύησαν, ἐπιθυμίας ἢ χρημάτων ἢ δόξης ἢ ἡδονῆς.

[104] *This overpowering desire for food and drink explains* (ταύτης ἕνεκα τῆς αἰτίας). Philo does not *name* the reason philosophers decided to distribute (ἀπένειμαν) the soul's parts as they did, but ταύτης ... τῆς αἰτίας must refer to something in §91, because §§92–94 bear obvious connections to only that paragraph. Fundamentally, §91 and §§92–94 have in common the association of ἐπιθυμία with the same general region of the body (§91: τῶν περὶ γαστέρα; §93: τὸν περὶ τὸν ὀμφαλὸν καὶ τὸ καλούμενον διάφραγμα χῶρον) and the use of language related to eating (§91: οἰνοφλυγίαις, ὀψοφαγίαις, συμπόσια, τραπέζας; §92: γευσάμενοι, ἑστιαθέντες). Since §91 describes corrupt, compulsive eating and drinking, ταύτης ... τῆς αἰτίας undoubtedly refers to the overpowering desire for food and drink underlying such behavior.

[105] *recognized its tripartite structure* (τριττὸν εἶδος ἐνιδόντες αὐτῆς): PCW rightly emends the τρίτον of MSS to τριττόν (despite the unnecessary PCW αὐτῇ for MSS αὐτῆς). Philo's immediate listing of the three Platonic εἴδη (λόγος, θυμός, and ἐπιθυμία) indeed suggests an original reference to "*threefold* [i.e., tripartite] form" rather than "*third* form" (cf. *Aet.* 86: πυρὸς τριττὸν εἶδος· τὸ μὲν ἄνθραξ, τὸ δὲ φλόξ, τὸ δὲ αὐγή).

the "diaphragm." [§94] Since desire has the least to do with reason, it clearly must reside as far as possible from reason's royal domain—practically at the outskirts. Naturally, the pasture of this most insatiable and licentious of beasts is the area of the body associated with primal drives for food and sex.

Paragraphs 92–94 represent an excursus framed as a review of Platonic doctrine on the physical location of each of the soul's three parts.[106] Just before this excursus (§§86–91), Philo had been describing how ἔρως functions as the source of all wrongdoing, using a series of examples that matched specific false goods pursued under tyrannical desire's hegemony with specific types of moral corruption. His final example (§91) noted the ability of ἐπιθυμία-turned-ἔρως to "seize the belly" and so corrupt the moral agent in matters of eating and drinking. But in §92, Philo no longer considers the mechanism of ἔρως, choosing instead to reflect further on the *association* of ἐπιθυμία with a particular region of the body, which he now refers to as τὸν περὶ τὸν ὀμφαλὸν καὶ τὸ καλούμενον διάφραγμα χῶρον (§93) instead of simply τῶν περὶ γαστέρα (§91). Although Philo retains from §91 an interest in the connection between ἐπιθυμία and "belly," his question has changed from *how* ἐπιθυμία (τὸ ἐπιθυμητικόν) tyrannizes the soul to *how* knowledgeable philosophers determined its location.

Philo's manner of juxtaposing §91 and §§92–94 implies that philosophers connected the ἐπιθυμητικόν with the belly *because* so many people experience an overpowering, tyrannical desire for food and drink. He clearly notes in §§92–94 that these philosophers posited the connection "for this reason" (ταύτης ἕνεκα τῆς αἰτίας), and the placement of the phrase requires the "reason" to be somewhere in §91, most likely in the gluttonous immorality Philo portrays in that paragraph. But when he actually spells out the reason in §94, he says nothing about gluttonous immorality, merely citing the logical necessity that (1) the faculty having "least to do with reason" reside farthest from reason and (2) the "most insatiable and licentious of beasts" (ἐπιθυμία) inhabit the bodily regions associated with food and sex. But Philo does not simply abandon the logic of his transitional phrase in favor of an allusion to Plato's *Timaeus*[107]—he moves his train of thought in an entirely new direction. And, in fact, when viewed in the context of Philo's *entire* exposition, §§92–94 do not so much advance the argument as provide a transition *within* the exposition from the *diagnosis* section (κρίσις) to the *treatment* section (ἄσκησις).

---

[106] On Plato's theory, see *Tim.* 69 C–71 D (cf. Runia, *Philo and the* Timaeus, 301–14).
[107] Cf. *Tim.* 70 D–71 A.

Most importantly, §§92–94 function as a transition containing *new material* crucial to Philo's upcoming argument. Part one of his exposition, designed to expose the shameful character of tyrannical desire, essentially ends with §91. Paragraphs 92–94 sharply *digress* from §91 and, in fact, *all* of Philo's preceding diagnosis (κρίσις). The shift reflects Philo's attempt to deal with a problem in the overarching logical flow of his exposition— namely, nothing in part one of his exposition, up to and including §91, gives Philo a theoretical basis for asserting the preeminence of desires for food and drink over against any other type of desire. In fact, the desire for food and drink appears as only *part* of his list, last among desires for money, reputation, etc.—*all* of which are equally capable of causing moral ruin after burgeoning into their respective versions of ἔρως. Yet in his explanation of the rationale underlying Moses' therapeutic program (§96), Philo will argue that management of "the desire having to do with the belly" (τὴν περὶ γαστέρα πραγματευομένην ἐπιθυμίαν) serves as the paradigmatic model for managing *all* corruptible desires, since that one desire is fundamental, the "eldest" (τὴν πρεσβυτάτην) and "chief" (ἡγεμονίδα) of them all. Paragraphs 92–94 give Philo the theoretical justification for such a claim, because they endorse a Platonic view of the soul, which grants preeminence to desires for food and drink while still tracing all corruptible desires to one part of the soul.

In addition to providing critical new material, §§92–94 also facilitate the transition from part one (esp. §91) to part two (esp. §§95–97) by managing to present ἐπιθυμία in a new light without disrupting a basic continuity of content involving the nexus of desire, food and drink, and the belly. Before §§92–94, Philo presents a decidedly negative view of ἐπιθυμία, limiting his concern almost exclusively to the disastrous tyranny of ἔρως, which begins with ἐπιθυμία overstepping the bounds of reason. But the *treatment* section of Philo's exposition concerns itself with how to *prevent* ἐπιθυμία from overstepping the bounds of reason in the first place. In other words, the topic of part two is not *tyrannical* desire, but the useful *emotion* desire, which a moral agent may indulge without compromising virtue—provided reason stays in control. Philo's theoretical consideration in §§92–94 of the location of ἐπιθυμία within the Platonic tripartite soul shifts the emphasis from desire as raging tyrant to desire as natural endowment, *without* entirely losing sight of its dangerous capacity for misconduct (§94: πάντων ἀπληστότατον καὶ ἀκολαστότατον ... θρεμμάτων). He can then begin in §§95–97 his consideration of how best to manage ἐπιθυμία, particularly ἐπιθυμία for food and drink, which—though prone to excess—forms a natural part of every human life.

III. *Treatment (Ἄσκησις) (§§95–130)*

§§95 – 97: Overview of Moses' "Paradigmatic Instruction"

[§95] Now, the most holy Moses (it seems to me) taking all of this into account, made a special point of prohibiting desire.[108] His goal was to eliminate *passionate* desire,[109] having come to detest it both as a horrible disgrace in itself and as the ultimate *cause* of disgraceful behavior, a virtual siege-engine within the soul, bent on conquest.[110] With the passion eliminated, with desire (in other words) *obeying* reason's commanding authority,[111] all of life becomes filled with peace and order, the best of blessings, resulting in perfect happiness. [§96] And since Moses cherishes brevity and tends to address innumerable cases with just one paradigmatic instruction, he builds a comprehensive program on the chastisement and training of just *one* desire, desire involving the belly,[112] supposing that once the most

---

[108] *made a special point of prohibiting desire* (ἀπεῖπεν ἐν τοῖς μάλιστα τὴν ἐπιθυμίαν): Moses' prohibition of desire works through the cumulative effect of an entire set of dietary laws, which together manage the *emotion* and thus preclude the *passion*.

[109] *His goal was to eliminate* passionate *desire* (ἐκδύσασθαι τὸ πάθος): An infinitive of purpose: the goal of Moses' dietary laws corresponds to the goal of the Tenth Commandment itself—viz., the elimination of the *passion* desire (here "τὸ πάθος" [i.e., πλεονάζουσα (ἄμετρος) ἐπιθυμία]).

[110] *a virtual siege-engine within the soul, bent on conquest* (ὥς τινα τῆς ψυχῆς ἑλέπολιν): A ἑλέπολις was a machine of war, designed for assault (and conquest) of an enemy fortification. By using this term, Philo suggests that ἐπιθυμία seeks to overthrow reason: first by overstepping its dictates (*passionate* desire), then by defeating it entirely (*tyrannical* desire). By "storming the citadel" and taking over the soul, ἐπιθυμία-turned-ἔρως then becomes the *cause* of disgraceful behavior. The independent, hostile agency of ἐπιθυμία conveyed by the metaphor illustrates Philo's Platonic perspective (cf. Pelletier, "Passions à l'assaut de l'âme," esp. 57–58; Abraham Malherbe, "Antisthenes and Odysseus, and Paul at War," *HTR* 76 [1983]: 143–73, esp. 145–47).

[111] *With the passion eliminated, with desire (in other words)* obeying *reason's commanding authority* (ἧς ἀναιρεθείσης ἢ πειθαρχούσης κυβερνήτῃ λογισμῷ): The Greek suggests *two* ways of managing ἐπιθυμία to achieve peace and happiness: abolish it entirely (ἀναιρεθείσης) or (ἤ) make it obedient to reason (πειθαρχούσης ... λογισμῷ), but a translation to that effect overlooks the inherent ambiguity of the term ἐπιθυμία. From Philo's Middle-Platonic perspective, the term can indicate either *passion* or *emotion*. He clearly calls for the elimination of *passionate* desire (ἐκδύσασθαι τὸ πάθος [§95]), which amounts to the *emotion* desire obeying reason. In other words, the ἤ indicates not an *alternative solution* to the problem of desire but an alternative conception of the *same solution*: the elimination of passionate desire—*id est*, the obedience of emotion to reason. (Philo elsewhere uses ἤ to introduce an equivalent, not an alternative: e.g., *Leg.* 3.224: ὁ τῆς ψυχῆς ἡνίοχος ἢ κυβερνήτης ὁ νοῦς.)

[112] *he builds a comprehensive program on the chastisement and training of just* one *desire, desire involving the belly* (μίαν τὴν περὶ γαστέρα πραγματευομένην ἐπιθυμίαν ἄρχεται νουθετεῖν τε

primal and commanding desire has learned to submit to the laws of self-mastery, all other desires will likewise quit resisting the reins of reason.[113] [§97] What then is the instruction at the foundation of Moses' comprehensive program?[114] Naturally, its two fundamental concerns are food and drink, and Moses left neither of these unregulated. Instead, he curtailed their use by means of dietary laws whose observance leads to self-control, and philanthropy, and—most important of all—piety.

Philo begins the "treatment" section (ἄσκησις) of his exposition by summarizing the "diagnosis" section (κρίσις) he has just completed (§§79–94). He ascribes to "the most holy Moses" (ὁ ἱερώτατος Μωυσῆς) an understanding of everything (πάντα) he has just explained about the nature, function, and problematic *malfunction* of ἐπιθυμία. With this insight, *Moses* determined "to eliminate *passionate* desire (ἐκδύσασθαι τὸ πάθος), having come to detest it (μυσαξάμενος) both as a horrible disgrace in itself (ὡς αἴσχιστον) and as the ultimate *cause* of disgraceful behavior (τῶν αἰσχίστων αἴτιον)."[115] Passionate desire, in other words, proves not only reprehensible

---

καὶ παιδεύειν): Philo has just noted Moses' tendency to legislate efficiently using *one* "paradigmatic instruction" (παραδειγματικῇ διδασκαλίᾳ), and he now says more *about* the instruction. Moses "begins" (ἄρχεται) to chastise and train *one* desire, desire involving the belly—but this cannot mean "begin" in the sense of starting with one desire, first in a *series*, then proceeding to chastise and train a number of other desires. Indeed, no desires *other than* desire involving the belly figure in the body of legislation Philo spends the rest of his exposition considering. Instead, Moses "begins" (ἄρχεται) with desire involving the belly in the sense of *laying a foundation*: he builds a comprehensive program for training *all* desires on the foundation of a regimen targeting *one*.

[113] *will likewise quit resisting the reins of reason* (οὐκέθ'ὁμοίως ἀφηνιάσειν): On Philo's use of the Platonic chariot figure (and associated terminology) to portray the management of emotion(s), see above, pp. 88–93.

[114] *What then is the instruction at the foundation of Moses' comprehensive program?* (τίς οὖν ἡ διδασκαλία τῆς ἀρχῆς): Philo's use of ἀρχή here to mean "foundation" echoes his use of ἄρχεται in §96 to mean "laying a foundation" (cf. Colson [PLCL 7, 66, n. a]). Philo elsewhere uses ἀρχή to mean "genus"(Jastram, "Generic Virtue," 28), so τίς οὖν ἡ διδασκαλία τῆς ἀρχῆς could also mean, "What then is the generic instruction?" In other words, Philo now considers the *generic* instruction that—once successfully implemented in terms of desire involving the belly—will apply in a number of secondary *specific* cases. A "generic" instruction could also be considered "foundational."

[115] Cf. *Garr.* 510 C–D: "[W]e get well by the diagnosis and treatment of our ailments (τῶν γὰρ παθῶν κρίσει καὶ ἀσκήσει), but the diagnosis must come first (προτέρα δ'ἡ κρίσις ἐστίν); since no one can become habituated to shun or to eradicate from his soul what does not distress him (οὐδεὶς γὰρ ἐθίζεται φεύγειν καὶ ἀποτρίβεσθαι τῆς ψυχῆς ὃ μὴ δυσχεραίνει), and we only grow distressed with our ailments (δυσχεραίνομεν δὲ τὰ πάθη) when we have perceived, by the exercise of reason, the injuries and shame which

in itself—it also *generates* reprehensible behavior when it overtakes and tyrannizes the soul. For this reason, Moses sought to eliminate the *passion* desire by training the *emotion* to obey the commanding authority of reason (πειθαρχούσης κυβερνήτῃ λογισμῷ)—which calls for the exercise of "self-control" (ἐγκράτεια) on the moral agent's part.[116] As Philo explains in §§96–97, Moses addressed this critical need for self-control through his legislation.

According to §96, Moses ingeniously chose to manage ἐπιθυμία by crafting just one "paradigmatic instruction" (παραδειγματικῇ διδασκαλίᾳ), which—although applied *directly* only to desire involving the belly—applies *ultimately* to every type of desire.[117] Of course, this "instruction" never *explicitly* appears in the Pentateuch—Philo must instead consolidate scattered elements into a meaningful association through a particular line of interpretation. He believes that *as a set* the various precepts governing food and drink reveal, upon careful examination, an ulterior motive on Moses' part: to inculcate self-control relative to *desire involving the belly*, which in turn applies to *all* desire. And because the dietary laws promote the management of ἐπιθυμία, Philo considers them the *specific* laws falling under the *generic* heading οὐκ ἐπιθυμήσεις.

Philo could *not* construe the dietary laws as a single coherent therapeutic program whose benefits extend to all desires—*nor* could he reconcile parts one and two of his exposition—without applying the principle of transference.[118] Otherwise he is left "diagnosing" in part one a problem involving *many* desires (for money, reputation, etc.), while "treating" in part two just *one* sort of desire (for food and drink). But casting the Mosaic dietary laws as a paradigmatic instruction allows Philo effectively to account for *all* of the desires mentioned in part one, since *their* successful management necessarily results from the successful management of desire involving the belly. This approach not only solves a practical problem for Philo—it also makes good sense in light of Middle-Platonic theoretical principles. First, the idea of *predominance* for desire involving the belly—

---

result from them (ὅταν τὰς βλάβας καὶ τὰς αἰσχύνας τὰς ἀπ'αὐτῶν τῷ λόγῳ κατανοήσωμεν)."

[116] The term κυβερνήτης evokes the Platonic chariot figure (cf. *Leg.* 3.224: ὁ τῆς ψυχῆς ἡνίοχος ἢ κυβερνήτης ὁ νοῦς; also *Sacr.* 45), which for Philo serves as a model of ἐγκράτεια in action (cf. §79; on the figure and associated terminology, see above, pp. 88–93).

[117] Philo also treats circumcision as a sort of paradigmatic instruction: it symbolically excises *all* excessive pleasures by targeting one *supreme* pleasure: αἰνιττομένοις περιτομὴν περιττῆς ἐκτομὴν καὶ πλεοναζούσης ἡδονῆς, οὐ μιᾶς, ἀλλὰ διὰ μιᾶς ... καὶ τῶν ἄλλων ἁπασῶν (*Spec.* 1.9); cf. *QG* 3.48.

[118] On the principle of transference, see above, pp. 106–8.

which Philo calls τὴν πρεσβυτάτην καὶ ὡς ἡγεμονίδα [ἐπιθυμίαν]—comes from Plato himself, who highlights desires for food and drink in his discussion of ἐπιθυμία.[119] Second, Philo believes that the successful ability of desire involving the belly "to obey the laws of self-mastery" (τοῖς σωφροσύνης νόμοις πειθαρχεῖν) results in restraint among the other desires (οὐκέθ'ὁμοίως ἀφηνιάσειν, ἀλλὰ σταλήσεσθαι), reasoning that *because* desires for food and drink are most powerful, *their* compliance necessarily engenders compliance among all of the other *less powerful* desires stemming from the ἐπιθυμητικόν.[120] Plutarch presumes a similar transference of the moral agent's capacity to manage desire, although his method first develops restraint in *less* difficult situations then applies it stepwise to progressively *more* difficult situations.[121] Moses offers a more efficient method by reversing the progression, training the most difficult desire *first* and so removing the need to address less demanding calls for self-control posed by less difficult desires.

In §97, Philo briefly explains how Moses' paradigmatic instruction works. Obviously, it deals with food and drink (ἐδωδὴ καὶ πόσις), since *they* are the objects of desire involving the belly. As Philo explains, Moses restricted their use with specific ordinances *whose observance leads to self-control* (ἐπεστόμισε διατάγμασι ... πρὸς ἐγκράτειαν ... ἀγωγοτάτοις).[122] In other words,

---

[119] E.g., *Resp.* 437 D: τούτων δὴ οὕτως ἐχόντων ἐπιθυμιῶν τι φήσομεν εἶναι εἶδος, καὶ ἐναργεστάτας αὐτῶν τούτων ἥν τε δίψαν καλοῦμεν καὶ ἣν πεῖναν; *Leg.* 782 E: ταῦτα δ'ἐστὶν ἐδωδὴ μὲν καὶ πόσις εὐθὺς γενομένοις, ἣν πέρι ἅπασαν πᾶν ζῷον ἔμφυτον ἔρωτα ἔχον.

[120] Philo's language of restraint here—esp. his use of ἀφηνιάσειν and σταλήσεσθαι (στέλλω)—reflects his Middle-Platonic view of passion. For example, in Philo's use of the chariot figure as a model of ἐγκράτεια, the term ἀφηνιάζω (also ἀφηνιασμός) denotes "excess"—namely, the excessive movement responsible for turning an *emotion* into a *passion* (see above, pp. 88–93). By claiming that all other types of ἐπιθυμία will no longer "ἀφηνιάσειν" after successful implementation of Moses' therapeutic dietary program, Philo means that they will become moderate in the Middle-Platonic sense of *measured* or *without excess*. In other words, they will become restrained (σταλήσεσθαι) in the very sense he suggests elsewhere in his writings: esp. *Prov.* 2.70: τὴν ἀμετρίαν (cf. ἀφηνιασμός) τῶν ἐπιθυμιῶν στεῖλαι; also *Virt.* 113: ἐστείλατο τὸ σφοδρὸν (cf. ἀφηνιασμός) αὐτῆς (sc. ἐπιθυμίας); *Det.* 25: στέλλοντες τὸ τῶν ἐπιθυμιῶν μέγεθος (cf. ἀφηνιασμός).

[121] Ingenkamp, *Schriften*, 105, identifies this type of ἐθισμοί ("Übung vom Leichteren zum Schwierigeren") as one of *three* forms of practical ἄσκησις prescribed in *De garrulitate*.

[122] Philo's use of ἐπεστόμισε again evokes the Platonic chariot figure (cf. above, pp. 88–93). Along with ἐγκράτεια, Philo mentions also philanthropy and piety, but these do not figure prominently in his exposition until the end, when he revisits the notion of *piety* (εὐσέβεια) in §§128–131 (on Philo's view of piety, see esp. Gregory E. Sterling, "'The Queen of the Virtues': Piety in Philo of Alexandria," *SPhA* 18 [2006]: 103–23). He mentions them here because in his view *each one* of the Ten Commandments, despite its *specific* purposes, also promotes virtue in general.

Moses designed the dietary laws as *ascetic precepts* to promote ἐγκράτεια among his followers—first with respect to food and drink, but ultimately with respect to every object of desire.[123] Viewed in terms of moral philosophy, Moses' method looks much like the recommendation of *practical exercises* aimed at eliminating a passion (πάθος) through the practice (ἄσκησις) of self-control (ἐγκράτεια). His "ordinances" (διατάγματα) serve the same function as the ἐθισμοί of Plutarch's *Seelenheilungsschriften*. In the case of *De garrulitate*, followers of Plutarch's philosophy will eliminate the passion of talkativeness (ἀδολεσχία) from their lives by developing ἐγκράτεια with respect to speaking, as they engage in behaviors enjoined by his ἐθισμοί. Similarly, followers of *Moses'* philosophy will eliminate the passion of gluttony (γαστριμαργία) from their lives by developing ἐγκράτεια with respect to eating and drinking, as they engage in behaviors enjoined by *his* ἐθισμοί, the dietary laws. But with Moses' ingenious program, as Philo presents it, the elimination of gluttony entails the elimination of *all* passions, which likewise involve excessive *desire* for a certain object (wealth, reputation, etc.). While Plutarch treats passions one at a time, Moses treats passions all at once.

§§98 – 99: *First Fruits*[124]

[§98] For example, Moses commands the people to bring as first fruits some of their grain, wine, oil, livestock, and other goods. They are instructed to designate one portion of these first fruits for sacrifice and another portion for the priests—the former out of gratitude to God for bountiful produce and abundance of goods, the latter out of gratitude for the sacred temple-service, in order that the priests might receive a reward for their performance of holy duties. [§99] He completely forbids anyone to sample these goods or take hold of them *until* the first fruits are duly apportioned—and in so doing he prescribes an exercise in that great boon to all of life, self-control.[125]

---

[123] Here Philo *explicitly* links observance of the dietary laws with the term ἐγκράτεια, but note other *implicit* references to ἐγκράτεια in §§95–97: §95: [ἐπιθυμίας] πειθαρχούσης κυβερνήτῃ λογισμῷ; §96: ἐπιθυμίαν ἄρχεται νουθετεῖν τε καὶ παιδεύειν ... τὰς ἄλλας [ἐπιθυμίας] οὐκέθ'ὁμοίως ἀφηνιάσειν, ἀλλὰ σταλήσεσθαι ... τὴν πρεσβυτάτην καὶ ὡς ἡγεμονίδα [ἐπιθυμίαν] μεμαθηκέναι τοῖς σωφροσύνης νόμοις πειθαρχεῖν.

[124] On the law of first fruits, see, for example, Deut 18:4: καὶ τὰς ἀπαρχὰς τοῦ σίτου σου καὶ τοῦ οἴνου σου καὶ τοῦ ἐλαίου σου καὶ τὴν ἀπαρχὴν τῶν κουρῶν τῶν προβάτων σου δώσεις αὐτῷ.

[125] *and in so doing he prescribes an exercise in that great boon to all of life, self-control* (ἅμα καὶ πρὸς ἄσκησιν τῆς βιωφελεστάτης ἐγκρατείας): Since this command enjoins the *practice*

For the one who learns not to indulge impetuously in the season's harvest[126]—who instead *waits* for the consecration of the first fruits—surely restrains the unruliness of the impulses, quieting passionate desire.[127]

Philo begins his study of Moses' "paradigmatic instruction" with the law of first fruits, which involves food *and* drink. Philo lists "grain, wine, oil, and livestock" as items falling under the commandment's purview. Philo's reference here to "wine" (οἶνος) stands alone in the *treatment* section (ἄσκησις) of his exposition: nowhere else does he cite a law mentioning wine or any other drink.[128] So despite his earlier framing of Moses' instruction as a matter of ἐδωδὴ καὶ πόσις (§97), Philo essentially considers only food. He *mentions* both because he knows that desire involving the belly encompasses both eating and drinking, a fact duly noted in the *diagnosis* section (κρίσις) of his exposition (§91).

Philo explicitly identifies the law of first fruits as an exercise in self-control (πρὸς ἄσκησιν ... ἐγκρατείας). Essentially, the law requires people eager to consume fresh stores of food and drink to *wait* (ἀναμένων) until a

---

(ἄσκησις) of ἐγκράτεια, observance of the command amounts to an *exercise* in self-control.
[126] *For the one who learns not to indulge impetuously in the season's harvest* (ὁ γὰρ ταῖς περιουσίαις, αἷς ἤνεγκαν αἱ τοῦ ἔτους ὧραι, μαθὼν μὴ ἐντρέχειν): Reading μαθών as a *gnomic* aorist supports Philo's interpretation of the first-fruits precept as an exercise in self-control: those who observe the precept are—*in doing so*—effecting the mechanism of ἐγκράτεια in their souls. Cohn emends συντρέχειν (MSS.) to ἐντρέχειν, while acknowledging the *lectio vulgata* ἐπιτρέχειν, which undoubtedly captures the true sense of the passage. The idea of "attacking" (ἐπιτρέχειν) the harvest—i.e., voracious, impetuous indulgence (colloquially, "digging in")—paints a clear contrast to waiting patiently, *and* it accurately characterizes the behavior of a moral agent motivated by *passionate* desire (i.e., lacking ἐγκράτεια).
[127] *surely restrains the unruliness of the impulses, quieting passionate desire* (τὸν ἀφηνιασμὸν τῶν ὁρμῶν ἔοικεν ἀναχαιτίζειν ἐξευμαρίζων τὸ πάθος): Having just identified the law of first fruits as an exercise in self-control (§99: πρὸς ἄσκησιν ... ἐγκρατείας), Philo now explains the mechanism of ἐγκράτεια that he envisions at work in such an exercise. In other words, Philo *interprets* the law of first fruits as an exercise in self-control. *According to Philo's understanding*, those who observe the command "seem" (ἔοικεν)—in doing so—to restrain the unruliness of their impulses and thus quiet "the passion" (τὸ πάθος), which in the context of Philo's exposition refers to passionate *desire* (πλεονάζουσα [ἄμετρος] ἐπιθυμία). By using ἔοικεν, Philo does not express uncertainty about his interpretation, which he considers correct and deeply significant—he only acknowledges that it *is* an interpretation, his own speculation on the deeper significance of the law of first fruits (cf. Philo's use of ὡς ἔοικε[ν] in, for example, *Opif.* 154; *Spec.* 2.141 [also μοι δοκεῖ in *Spec.* 4.95]).
[128] Cf. Colson 67, n. b: "This is the only way in which restraint in drinking is enjoined throughout these sections." But note the reference to *strong drink* (ἀκράτου) in §113.

ceremonial dedication has first taken place. In terms of moral psychology, this involves ἐπιθυμία *aroused* by the pleasurable prospect of consuming a variety of goods but forcibly *restrained* for a time by reason. To indulge the initial impulse to eat and drink, ignoring the law, would be to act strictly on a motive for pleasure, which amounts to indulging an unmeasured, excessive impulse—i.e., indulging *passionate* desire. By waiting until reason authorizes the indulgence, the moral agent effectively eliminates through forcible restraint the *excessiveness* of desire's impulses (τὸν ἀφηνιασμὸν τῶν ὁρμῶν ... ἀναχαιτίζειν),[129] which quiets not desire *per se* but desire in its passionate aspect (ἐξευμαρίζων τὸ πάθος).[130] Philo finds this *delay technique* at work not only here in the law of first fruits but elsewhere in Mosaic legislation, attributing to Moses the technique later prescribed by Plutarch in *De garrulitate*.[131]

§§100 – 102: Introduction to Clean and Unclean Animals[132]

[§100] As for foods not otherwise regulated by the law of first fruits,[133] Moses did not in the least allow members of the sacred commonwealth simply to eat whatever they wanted without restriction. In fact, he strictly prohibited all of the richest, most succulent types of meat—meat that tickles and teases our treacherous foe pleasure—by prohibiting just the right animals from land, sea, and sky. He knew that these meats could produce the characteristic insatiability of tyrannical desire, once they had ensnared the most slavish of the senses, taste.[134] And insatiability represents a practically incurable problem not only for souls but also for bodies, since an

---

[129] Cf. *Spec.* 2.18: τὸν ἀφηνιασμὸν τῶν ἐπιθυμιῶν ἀναχαιτίσαι. Philo's use of ἀφηνιασμόν and ἀναχαιτίζειν again evokes the chariot figure (see above, pp. 88–93).

[130] Cf. *Opif.* 81: ἐξευμαρισθεῖεν αἱ ἄμετροι τῶν παθῶν ὁρμαί.

[131] On the same technique at work in other ascetic precepts, see above, pp. 103–8. For an example of the technique in *De garrulitate*, see *Garr.* 511 F: ἑαυτὸν ἐθιζέτω σιωπᾶν μέχρι οὗ πάντες ἀπείπωνται τὴν ἀπόκρισιν (cf. *Spec.* 4.99: ἀναμένων, ἄχρις ἂν αἱ ἀπαρχαὶ καθοσιωθῶσι).

[132] On laws regarding clean and unclean animals, see esp. Lev 11 (cf. Deut 14:1–21).

[133] *As for foods not otherwise regulated by the law of first fruits* (τὴν τῶν ἄλλων μετουσίαν): Philo moves on to other foods (τῶν ἄλλων) *not* under the purview of the first-fruits regulation (cf. Moïsès 259, n.10: "Ceux qui ne sont pas assujettis à une offrande préalable").

[134] *He knew that these meats could produce the characteristic insatiability of tyrannical desire, once they had ensnared the most slavish of the senses, taste* (εἰδὼς ὅτι τὴν ἀνδραποδωδεστάτην τῶν αἰσθήσεων δελεάσαντα γεῦσιν ἀπληστίαν ἐργάσεται): *Pace* Colson, ἀπληστία here means "insatiability," not "gluttony" (cf. Heinemann: "Unersättlichkeit"; Moïsès: "l'insatiabilité"). And ἀπληστία signals the presence of tyrannical desire (ἔρως) in the soul—in this case, ἔρως in regard to food. On the insatiability of tyrannical desire, see above, pp. 75–77.

insatiable desire for food naturally leads to overeating, which in turn leads to indigestion,[135] a foundation and wellspring of diseases and infirmities. [§101] Now, among land animals, everyone acknowledges the meat of pigs as most delectable, and among sea creatures those that have no scales—in these and other restrictions, self-control was Moses' ultimate concern, and he, if anyone, had the philosophical expertise to train those with natural aptitude in the practice of virtue. He accomplishes this inculcation of self-control by training and drilling people to be sparing and easily satisfied, targeting the removal of extravagance.[136] [§102] Determined to promote neither a life of austerity, like the Lacedaemonian lawgiver, nor of daintiness, like the man who introduced habits of feebleness and luxury to the Ionians and Sybarites—cutting instead a straight path right between the two—Moses relaxed what was too severe in one and tightened what was too lax in the other. As with a musical instrument, he sought to blend the excesses of either end of the scale into a moderate tone, promoting a life of harmony and blameless integrity. So he was not at all haphazard when he drew up his legislation on dietary matters. On the contrary, he took the utmost care in determining foods to be eaten and foods to be avoided.

Philo devotes by far the majority of his discussion of the content of Moses' "paradigmatic instruction" to the legislation governing various species of

---

[135] *since an insatiable desire for food naturally leads to overeating, which in turn leads to indigestion* (ἀπληστία γὰρ τίκτει δυσπεψίαν): The insatiability of tyrannical desire does not give birth to indigestion *directly*—it first causes overeating (cf. *Spec.* 4.91), which then becomes the direct cause of indigestion. Philo undoubtedly considered the sequence too obvious to state explicitly.

[136] *Now, among land animals, everyone acknowledges the meat of pigs as most delectable, and among sea creatures those that have no scales—in these and other restrictions, self-control was Moses' ultimate concern, and he, if anyone, had the philosophical expertise to train those with natural aptitude in the practice of virtue. He accomplishes this inculcation of self-control by training and drilling people to be sparing and easily satisfied, targeting the removal of extravagance* (χερσαίων μὲν οὖν τὸ συῶν γένος ἥδιστον ἀνωμολόγηται παρὰ τοῖς χρωμένοις, ἐνύδρων δὲ τὰ γένη τῶν ἀλεπίδων πρὸς γαρ ἐγκράτειαν, εἰ καί τις ἄλλος, ἱκανὸς ὢν ἀλεῖψαι τοὺς εὐφυῶς ἔχοντας πρὸς ἄσκησιν ἀρετῆς δι'ὀλιγοδείας καὶ εὐκολίας γυμνάζει καὶ συγκροτεῖ, πειρώμενος ἀφελεῖν πολυτέλειαν): The obscure Greek of this passage prompted Cohn to posit a lacuna between ἀλεπίδων and πρὸς γαρ ἐγκράτειαν (he suggests in its place τούτων δὴ χρήσεως ἀνέχειν κελεύει), but positing instead an abrupt transition in thought allows the text to makes sense as it stands. Philo here alludes to the prohibitions of pork and scaleless sea creatures, emphasizing the *pleasure* they afford, because they illustrate Moses' *real* purpose for the dietary laws—viz., the promotion of ἐγκράτεια.

clean (καθαρά) and unclean (ἀκάθαρτα) animals (ζῷα).[137] The designations "clean" and "unclean" of course refer to an animal's legal status as either a *permitted* or *prohibited* food source.[138] So with this new topic Philo abides by his initial framing of Moses' instruction as a matter of "food and drink" (§97: ἐδωδὴ καὶ πόσις)—or, in fact, *only* food—but the issue now becomes *whether or not* the people may eat a certain meal, not *how* or *when*, as with the law of first fruits. In any case, his exegetical task remains the same: to explain how these dietary laws promote ἐγκράτεια in service to the Tenth Commandment's prohibition of passionate desire: οὐκ ἐπιθυμήσεις.

According to Philo, the legislation on clean and unclean animals reflects in general an unwillingness on Moses' part to permit the "unrestricted use" (χρῆσιν ἀδεᾶ) of foods not otherwise regulated by the law of first fruits.[139] In particular, Moses selected for prohibition the "fattest" (εὐσαρκότατα) and "richest" (πιότατα) animals from land, sea, and sky, knowing that they yield the tastiest meats. He did this because he understood the dangerous capacity of delicious foods to "ensnare" (δελεάσαντα) the palate and, in so doing, cause people to eat strictly for the *pleasure* of eating.[140] In terms of moral psychology, eating for pleasure represents a victory of ἐπιθυμία over reason: in particular, the victory of ἐπιθυμία as a *motivating disposition* (whose aim is *pleasure*) over reason as a *motivating disposition* (whose aim is *rational benefit*: survival, good health, etc.). The victory of ἐπιθυμία produces in the soul "insatiability" (ἀπληστία), which in turn causes overeating and leads to indigestion, a "foundation and wellspring of diseases and infirmities" (νοσημάτων καὶ ἀρρωστημάτων ἀρχή τε καὶ πηγή). Philo's incidental remark here on the danger of tasty meat both echoes and corroborates his earlier, extended remarks in §§79–91 on the danger, broadly speaking, of passionate desire. In either case, he envisions a torturous Tantalus fate of *insatiability*—the hallmark of tyrannical desire (ἔρως)—looming as the eventual outcome of ἐπιθυμία gaining the upper hand over reason. And just as he earlier associated the terminal grade of desire with a condition of *soul* generating further *moral* decline (§§86–91), Philo here associates the terminal grade of eating for pleasure with a condition of *body* generating

---

[137] Compare Clean-Unclean Animals (§§100–118) to First Fruits (§§98–99), Dead Animals (§§119–121), and Blood and Fat (§§122–125). On Philo's discussion of clean-unclean animals in §§100–118, see especially Rhodes, "Diet and Desire."
[138] E.g., §113: φησὶν εἶναι πρὸς ἐδωδὴν οὐ καθαρά.
[139] Cf. *Prov.* 2.70: οἷς ἐμέλησε τὴν ἀμετρίαν τῶν ἐπιθυμιῶν στεῖλαι, μὴ ἐπιτρέψασι τὴν χρῆσιν ἀδεᾶ πᾶσι πάντων.
[140] In *Garr.* 514 B, Plutarch speaks in similar terms regarding especially "delicious" (pleasureable) *topics*: δελεαζομένη γὰρ ὑπ'αὐτῶν ἡ ἀδολεσχία.

further *physical* decline.[141] These parallels suggest an attempt on Philo's part to coordinate the "diagnosis" and "treatment" portions of his exposition by using similar terms to frame both *problem* and *solution*. Here, the solution Moses offers amounts to a simple principle: avoiding especially pleasurable meats eliminates the risk of indulging passionate desire, which in turn eliminates the even greater risk of suffering tyrannical desire.[142] But understood in this way, Moses' prohibitions only steer the moral agent away from a *specific*—and thus limited—set of dietary incitements to passionate desire, without addressing the broader concern of cultivating ἐγκράτεια in observance of the *general* prohibition οὐκ ἐπιθυμήσεις. In §§101–102, Philo traces a broader connection between the avoidance of tasty meats and a *lifestyle* of ἐγκράτεια.

He begins by citing two examples, presumably his best, of prohibited animals commonly acknowledged "by those who partake" (παρὰ τοῖς χρωμένοις) as "delicious" (ἥδιστον): pigs and scaleless sea creatures.[143] Philo then immediately deploys the agon motif in order to cast these prohibitions as *exercises* designed by Moses to train moral athletes in the practice of ἐγκράτεια.[144] But how exactly does Moses' training program work? Since Moses prescribed these exercises in an effort to remove *extravagance* (ἀφελεῖν πολυτέλειαν), he evidently considered anything done for pleasure's sake to be an extravagance by definition. No one, in other words, ever *needs* to eat something delicious—one only *needs* to eat. By prohibiting delicacies, Moses in effect trained the people to eat according to their

---

[141] In §100, Philo calls "insatiability" (ἀπληστίαν) a δυσίατον κακὸν ψυχαῖς τε καὶ σώμασιν. Philo described its harm to *souls* at length in the diagnosis portion of his exposition, using images such as the frustrated pursuit and fate of Tantalus (§§80–81). He describes its harm to *bodies* in §100, where he links it to indigestion and subsequent ills.

[142] Earlier (§91) Philo described the suffering of tyrannical desire for food and drink.

[143] Philo's reference to creatures of both land (pigs) and sea (scaleless creatures) proves that he still speaks in general, introductory terms at this point (cf. §100: ὅσα τῶν χερσαίων ἢ ἐνύδρων ἢ πτηνῶν). He does not give an example of a tasty bird (cf. Heinemann PCH 2, 276, n. 2: "Auf die Vögel wird hier nicht eingegangen, da bekanntlich, was Philo §100 allerdings ausser acht lässt, sehr wohlschmeckende Vögel zum Genusse erlaubt sind"). His discussion of each distinct domain of creatures begins in earnest with land animals in §103.

[144] §101: πρὸς γὰρ ἐγκράτειαν ... πρὸς ἄσκησιν ἀρετῆς (i.e., ἐγκρατείας). Note esp. the terms in §101 associated with Moses' training regimen: ἀλεῖψαι (*to anoint with oil* [before gymnastic exercises]), γυμνάζει (*to train*), συγκροτεῖ (*to drill*) (cf. *Spec.* 2.98: τὸ παραπλήσιον μέντοι καὶ τοὺς ἀλείπτας ἔστιν ἰδεῖν δρῶντας ἐπὶ τῶν ἀθλητῶν· ὅταν γὰρ αὐτοὺς συγκροτήσωσιν ἐπαλλήλοις καὶ συνεχέσι γυμνασίαις, πρὶν εἰς ἄκρον καμεῖν, ἀνακτῶνται παρέχοντες ἀνέσεις ... τῶν ἐν ἀθλήσει πόνων). On Philo's agon motif, see above, pp. 98–102.

need—not their *pleasure*—instilling the virtues of "frugality" (ὀλιγοδείας) and "contentment" (εὐκολίας).¹⁴⁵ And the consistent practice of living according to *need* amounts to the consistent practice of ἐγκράτεια, since it represents, in terms of moral psychology, the consistent dominance of *reason*, a motivating disposition seeking the rational benefit of sustenance, over *desire*, a motivating disposition seeking the pleasure of delicious food. In other words, ἐπιθυμία trained to accept the measure set by reason never becomes *passionate*. At the same time, since the challenge of limiting indulgence to reasonable need accompanies *any* expression of ἐπιθυμία (for food, wealth, etc.), the habits of ἐγκράτεια Moses cultivates by prohibiting voluptuous *foods* apply more broadly to *any* situation requiring the moral agent to abstain from extravagant (i.e., unnecessary) pleasures.

According to Philo, the lifestyle of ἐγκράτεια Moses promotes through his legislation on clean and unclean animals strikes a perfect balance between two extreme positions. On the one hand, Moses avoids the overly austere approach (σκληραγωγίαν) of Lycurgus (ὁ Λακεδαιμόνιος νομοθέτης), "loosening" the severity of the Spartan way (τὸ μὲν σφοδρὸν ἐχάλασε).¹⁴⁶ On the other hand, he avoids the overly indulgent (τὸ ἀβροδίαιτον) approach of Sardanapalus—"the man who introduced habits of feebleness and luxury to the Ionians and Sybarites" (ὁ τοῖς Ἴωσι καὶ Συβαρίταις τὰ περὶ θρύψιν καὶ χλιδὴν εἰσηγησάμενος)—"tightening" the laxity of his dissolute way of life (τὸ δ'ἀνειμένον ἐπέτεινε).¹⁴⁷ To convey the harmonious moderation of *Moses'* approach, Philo uses the image of a musical instrument (ἐν ὀργάνῳ μουσικῷ) sounding a beautiful "middle chord" (τῇ μέσῃ) in place of extreme tones.¹⁴⁸ In other words, in terms of Philo's *moral psychology*, moral agents of the Sardanapalus type would eat the delicious foods Moses prohibited, indulging in pleasure for pleasure's sake *because*

---

¹⁴⁵ Philo elsewhere associates such traits (esp. ὀλιγοδεία) with ἐγκράτεια: e.g., *Opif.* 164: ἡ μὲν γὰρ [ἐγκράτεια] εὐτέλειαν καὶ ὀλιγοδεῖαν ... ἀσπάζεται; *QG* 4.172 (Petit): ὁ δὲ σπουδαῖος οὐ πλεονέκτης, ἅτε ὀλιγοδεείας καὶ ἐγκρατείας ἑταῖρος; *Spec.* 1.173: ἐγκράτειαν, ἣ δορυφορεῖται πρὸς εὐτελείας καὶ εὐκολίας καὶ ὀλιγοδείας. (cf. *Mos.* 1.28–29: γαστρί τε γὰρ ἔξω τῶν ἀναγκαίων δασμῶν ... οὐδὲν πλέον ἐχορήγει, ... γενόμενός τε διαφερόντως ἀσκητὴς ὀλιγοδεείας).

¹⁴⁶ Cf. *Contempl.* 69: τήν ... Λακωνικὴν σκληραγωγίαν.

¹⁴⁷ On Sardanapalus, see also §122 (cf. Sandnes, *Belly and Body*, 65–68; Abraham Malherbe, "The Beasts at Ephesus," *JBL* 87 (1968): 71–80, esp. 76–77). The tomb of Sardanapalus supposedly read: ἔσθιε, πῖνε, παῖζε (see Sandness, *Belly and Body*, 66; Malherbe, "Beasts at Ephesus," 76). On the Sybarites, see also *Spec.* 3.43.

¹⁴⁸ *Spec.* 4.102: τὰς ἐφ'ἑκατέρων τῶν ἄκρων ὑπερβολὰς ὡς ἐν ὀργάνῳ μουσικῷ κερασάμενος τῇ μέσῃ (cf. *Mut.* 87; also *Resp.* 443 D–E; Plutarch, *Virt. mor.* 444 E; Ps.-Metop. 121.8–9). On the relevant music theory, see Martin L. West, *Ancient Greek Music* (Oxford: Oxford University Press, 1994), 219–23 (cf. Louis Feldman, "Philo's Views on Music," *JJML* 9 [1986]: 36–54).

desire rules their souls without the restraint or "measure" of reason. Moral agents of either the Lycurgus or Moses type would of course avoid *overly* pleasurable foods, but Philo gives no clear indication of what would otherwise distinguish their respective dietary habits. Presumably, Philo envisions the Spartan approach as determined avoidance of *any* pleasure: food serves only to sustain life, and pleasure—because it contributes nothing to that purpose—has no place in the Spartan diet.[149] Philo seems to envision Moses' approach as less severe, but similarly geared toward eating for sustenance over against pleasure. While strictly opposed to eating *for pleasure's sake*, Moses nevertheless allows for the incidental pleasures accompanying a healthful diet. After all, he prohibits only the most delectable meats, generously allowing the people to enjoy a variety of other meats as they choose.

Plutarch offers similar praise of balanced moderation in *De garrulitate*, though he has in mind ἐπιθυμία affecting the *tongue*, not the stomach.[150] Just as Philo acknowledges three basic approaches to *eating*, Plutarch acknowledges three basic approaches to *answering questions*: "the barely necessary" (τὸ ἀναγκαῖον), "the polite" (τὸ φιλάνθρωπον), and "the superfluous" (τὸ περισσόν).[151] And, like Philo, Plutarch associates the "barely necessary" with Spartan austerity:

> For example, if someone asks, "Is Socrates at home?" one person may reply ... "Not at home" (οὐκ ἔνδον). And if he wishes to adopt the Laconic style (λακωνίζειν), he may omit the "At home" (ἔνδον) and only utter the bare negative (αὐτὴν μόνην ... τὴν ἀπόφασιν). So the Spartans, when Philip wrote to ask if they would receive him into their city, wrote a large "No" on the paper and sent it back. (*Garr.* 513 A)

Plutarch disapproves of the Spartan refusal to speak beyond what absolute necessity requires, just as Moses disapproves of the austere Spartan diet's emphasis on necessity *at the expense* of pleasure. But Plutarch disapproves also of *excessive* indulgence in speech, which involves a failure of "the indulgent and talkative man" (ὁ δὲ περιττὸς καὶ ἀδολέσχης) to tailor his answer to the questioner's need (τῇ χρείᾳ τοῦ πυνθανομένου).[152] In fact, Plutarch identifies the questioner's "need" (χρεία) as the "measure" (μέτρον) of a proper response.[153] Here Plutarch illustrates the same Middle-Platonic concept of ἐπιθυμία attested in Philo's writings, in effect under-

---

[149] Some Spartan dishes notoriously gave *no* pleasure to the palate, esp. "black broth" (μέλας ζωμός), a pork stew (e.g., see Plutarch *Lyc.* 12.6–7).
[150] *Garr.* 513 A–C.
[151] *Garr.* 513 A.
[152] *Garr.* 513 B–C.
[153] *Garr.* 513 C.

standing "passionate" desire as *immoderate* desire (ἄμετρος ἐπιθυμία). In Plutarch's example, a desire to speak becomes *passionate* when it oversteps the reasonable measure (μέτρον) of politely providing needed information and motivates the moral agent to indulge in speaking *for the sake of speaking*, in particular for the *pleasure* of speaking. In Philo's example, a desire to eat becomes passionate (ἄμετρος) when it oversteps the reasonable measure (μέτρον) of providing needed sustenance and motivates the moral agent to indulge in eating *for the sake of eating*, in particular for the *pleasure* of eating.

Taken as a unit, §§100–102 serve as a thesis governing *all* of Philo's subsequent comments on Mosaic law concerning clean and unclean animals. Not only do §§100–102 form a discrete text-unit prefacing the detailed analyses of specific laws, but they also speak in the broad terms of an overarching claim. Philo asserts, in sum, that Moses recognized throughout the animal kingdom (land, sea, and sky) the dangerous incitement to ἐπιθυμία posed by delicious meats, so he obviated the risk by declaring those animals "unclean." By removing the incitement, he sought to lessen the incidence of *passionate desire*, thereby precluding its dangerous burgeoning into *tyrannical desire*. Although, as Philo explains, such prohibitions do *in general* promote a lifestyle of ἐγκράτεια (§§101–102)—so §§100–118 serve Philo's earlier, express purpose of showing how dietary laws *of whatever kind* promote ἐγκράτεια (§§95–97)—his thesis regarding the legislation on clean and unclean animals does *in particular* assert Moses' intention to eliminate passionate desire *by prohibiting delicious meats*. Philo makes the claim *prospectively* in §100, but also *retrospectively* in §118, where he in effect restates it and creates an interpretive frame for §§103–117.[154] In other words, Philo ostensibly draws just *one* fundamental conclusion from his investigation of clean and unclean animals—a conclusion he prompts the *reader* to accept by placing it prominently at both the beginning and end of his work. By composing §§100–118 in this way, Philo inadvertently provides a criterion for assessing his work, since each consideration of a certain animal or type of animal either *does* or *does not* support the overarching thesis. If it does, then Philo reveals consistency in his analysis of clean and unclean animals. If it does *not*, then Philo reveals an inconsistency, which calls for some sort of explanation. In fact, the *in*consistencies in Philo's work help to illustrate his expository agenda.

---

[154] Compare §100 (esp. ὅσα τῶν χερσαίων ἢ ἐνύδρων ἢ πτηνῶν ἐστιν εὐσαρκότατα καὶ πιότατα, γαργαλίζοντα καὶ ἐρεθίζοντα τὴν ἐπίβουλον ἡδονήν, πάντα ἀνὰ κράτος ἀπεῖπεν) and §118 (οὕτως ἐφ'ἑκάστου τῶν τοῦ κόσμου μερῶν, γῆς ὕδατος ἀέρος, γένη παντοίων ζῴων, χερσαῖα καὶ ἔνυδρα καὶ πτηνά, τῆς ἡμετέρας χρήσεως ὑφαιρῶν, καθάπερ ὕλην πυρός, σβέσιν τῆς ἐπιθυμίας ἀπεργάζεται). Rhodes ("Diet and Desire," 133) similarly notes the "inclusio" formed by §§100–102 and §118.

§§103 – 109: Land Animals[155]

[§103] Consider, for example, man-eating beasts.[156] Someone might easily consider it fair for them to endure *from* man the same fate they impose *on* man. But Moses, considering what befits a gentle soul, thinks we should abstain from the enjoyment of such creatures, even though they provide a most suitable and delicious feast. He knew that these animal offenders—even if they *deserve* to suffer in kind[157]— should not suffer at the hands of their victims, lest the human avengers inadvertently become beasts *themselves* by indulging the savage emotion of anger.[158] [§104] In fact, Moses makes so extreme an effort to prevent such behavior as to forbid categorically the eating of *all* carnivorous animals, wishing to restrain preemptively the impulse for revenge against man-eaters.[159] He chose instead the herbivores for gentle livestock, since they are tame by nature and eat only the gentle yield of the earth. Such creatures plot no mischief. [§105] Now, of the herbivores, Moses lists ten approved for eating: the calf, the lamb, the

---

[155] See Lev 11:1–8; Deut 14:3–8.

[156] *Consider, for example, man-eating beasts* (θηρία ὅσα σαρκῶν ἀνθρωπίνων ἅπτεται): Philo opens this section by immediately naming a class of animals whose prohibition illustrates the principle stated in §102: "[Moses] was not at all haphazard when he drew up his legislation on dietary matters. On the contrary, he took the utmost care in determining foods to be eaten and foods to be avoided." Philo lists bears (ἄρκτους), lions (λέοντας), and panthers (παρδάλεις) among the γένη τῶν ἀτιθάσων θηρίων, ἃ σαρκῶν ἀνθρωπείων ἅπτεται (*Mos.* 1.109).

[157] *He knew that these animal offenders—even if they* deserve *to suffer in kind* (καὶ γὰρ εἰ τοῖς διατιθεῖσιν ἁρμόττει τὰ παραπλήσια παθεῖν): Philo begins to explain (γάρ) the (hypothetical) rationale of Moses' prohibition of man-eaters (τοῖς διατιθεῖσιν), whose behavior marks them as "offenders" because it merits, in theory, retaliation (ἁρμόττει τὰ παραπλήσια παθεῖν).

[158] *lest the human avengers inadvertently become beasts* themselves *by indulging the savage emotion of anger* (μὴ λάθωσιν ὑπ'ὀργῆς, ἀγρίου πάθους, θηριωθέντες): Those in danger of "becoming beasts inadvertently" (λάθωσιν ... θηριωθέντες) are human beings who might *avenge* (ἀντιδιατιθέναι) fellow human beings victimized by man-eating animals (cf. ἀντιδιαθεῖναι in *Spec.* 3.85).

[159] *wishing to restrain preemptively the impulse for revenge against man-eaters* (ὥστε μακρόθεν ἀνεῖρξαι βουλόμενος τὴν ἐπὶ τὰ λεχθέντα ὁρμήν): Clearly τὰ λεχθέντα refers to the man-eating animals mentioned at the beginning of §103. But ἐπί in this case does not indicate an impulse "for" these creatures, as in a desire *for* their meat, as Colson suggests: "wishing to restrain by implication the appetite for the food just mentioned." Instead, ἐπί indicates the impulse "against" these creatures, as in a desire *for revenge* sated by slaughtering them for food. Colson himself admits the possibility of this reading when he suggests "tendency to such vindictiveness" as another translation for τὴν ἐπὶ τὰ λεχθέντα ὁρμήν. For μακρόθεν as an indication of *preemptive* (preventative) legislation, see Mosès, 351–52 [="Excursus 1"].

kid, the deer, the gazelle, the roebuck, the wild goat, the white-rumped antelope, the antelope, and the giraffe.[160] Because of his constant devotion to numerical theory, which he acutely understood as being of the greatest possible significance in every matter, Moses legislates nothing great or small without first considering the appropriate number and, as it were, affixing that number to the precepts. And of the numbers following the monad, the decad represents absolute perfection—a most holy and sacred number, as Moses declares. Here he places it on the various types of clean animals as a seal of approval, having decided to grant their use to members of his commonwealth. [§106] He also provides a simple way of authenticating and approving these ten animals, based on a pair of traits they all exhibit: each has split hooves and chews its cud. Animals that exhibit neither of these traits, or only one of them, are in Moses' view unclean. Note that both of these traits are symbols of the most enlightened methods of teaching and learning, which can, when put into practice, lead to the clear discernment of moral excellence from its opposite. [§107] Consider the ruminating animal. After a few bites are taken, the food settles in its gullet. Then after a short while, bringing it up again, the animal works it into a smoother substance, before finally sending it down into the stomach. In the same way, a student takes in through his ears various philosophical doctrines and theories from his teacher. But unable to comprehend immediately and grasp the lesson firmly, he continues to hold onto it, until by bringing it up again over and over in his memory through repeated exercises, which act as a sort of cement for ideas, he imprints it securely onto his soul. [§108] But the firm grasp of ideas, it seems, does no good at all without the added ability of sorting through them and making decisions about which to accept and which to reject. This ability to discriminate appears under the symbol of the split hoof, indicating that there are just two roads in life: one leading to vice and one leading to virtue, and we must turn from one and never leave the other. [§109] So animals whose hooves are either not split at all or split more than once are equally unclean, but for different reasons. The first kind represents the idea that good and evil have one and the same nature—in the sense that one spherical surface has both a concave and a convex aspect, or one road runs both up and down a hill at the same time. The second kind,

---

[160] English equivalents of the clean animals (Deut 14:4–5) are from *A New English Translation of the Septuagint* (eds. Albert Pietersma and Benjamin G. Wright; Oxford: Oxford University Press, 2007).

far from offering no choice at all, deceives the traveler by presenting many different roads in life. With a multitude of options, finding the best and most productive path becomes difficult.

Philo's consideration of land animals begins at §103 and continues through §109, dividing easily into three sections: (1) an explanation of why Moses did not sanction the slaughter of man-eating animals (or *any* carnivores) for food (§§103–104), (2) a listing of the ten "clean" herbivores, with special emphasis on the number ten (§105), and (3) a symbolic interpretation of Moses' criteria for designating a land animal "clean" (§§106–109).[161] Of these, only Philo's discussion of man-eating animals (§§103–104) clearly relates to the issues of ἐπιθυμία, ἐγκράτεια, and ἄσκησις informing his overall exposition of the Tenth Commandment, and even this relation seems forced.[162] First of all, Moses never *explicitly* prohibits man-eating animals—or, for that matter, *any* carnivorous land animals—despite their obvious failure to meet the criteria for clean animals.[163] So Philo's decision to make any comment at all on man-eating animals stems from his own agenda. Second, the case of man-eaters does not, strictly speaking, confirm the thesis Philo has just formulated in §100 about *how* Moses' dietary restrictions promote ἐγκράτεια by prohibiting delicious meats. Yet Philo's

---

[161] Philo gives no formal *introduction* to his discussion of land animals in §§103–109, but his retrospective comment in §110 signals his *completion* of the discussion: τούτους ἐπὶ τῶν χερσαίων τοὺς ὅρους θείς.

[162] For detailed consideration of §§103–104 as Philo's reworking of material from the *Letter of Aristeas*, see Svebakken, "Exegetical Traditions," esp. 101–7.

[163] Svebakken, "Exegetical Traditions," overstates this point (esp. 100, n. 29, and 101: "Casting man-eaters as unclean creatures has no biblical warrant"). Lev 11:27 identifies as unclean (ἀκάθαρτα) πᾶς, ὃς πορεύεται ἐπὶ χειρῶν (i.e., "paws") ἐν πᾶσι τοῖς θηρίοις, ἃ πορεύεται ἐπὶ τέσσαρα, making man-eaters (and other carnivores) unfit for eating. The stipulations of Lev 11:27 *do not*, however, make Philo's focus on a Mosaic prohibition of man-eating animals any less contrived. First, insofar as no man-eater appears on a list of unclean land animals, no *explicit* prohibition of man-eaters technically exists (cf. the explicit *listing*—and thus explicit *prohibition*—of carnivores among species of unclean birds in Lev 11:13-19). In fact, the explicit list of unclean land animals in Lev 11:4-7—camel (κάμηλος), hare (δασύπους), coney (χοιρογρύλλιος), and pig (ὗς)—only highlights the awkwardness of Philo's focus on man-eaters. Second, the undeniably *central* question in judging land animals fit (or not) for eating involves *hooves and rumination*, not the eating (or not) of other animals, let alone human beings (cf. *Spec.* 4.106). Although Lev 11:27 does identify a trait belonging to carnivores (paws), the preceding reiteration of criteria involving hooves and rumination in Lev 11:26 highlights the secondary (derivative) significance of paws as merely one way of failing to meet those criteria. Finally, whether or not Philo ever had Lev 11:27 in mind when speaking of a prohibition of man-eaters, he never appeals to the passage as evidence, and the wording of *Spec.* 4.103 suggests his own acknowledgement that a prohibition of man-eaters does not actually exist: Μωυσῆ δὲ τῆς τούτων ἀπολαύσεως ἀνέχειν <u>δοκεῖ</u>.

explication of the hypothetical prohibition of man-eaters does make it *resemble* the type of restriction—and the accompanying strategy for promoting ἐγκράτεια—that his thesis ascribes to Moses. All of this suggests an effort on Philo's part to find at least *one* other example, in addition to the pig, of a land animal whose delicious meat incites ἐπιθυμία and whose removal from the diet signals a Mosaic attempt to obviate passion.

While man-eating animals, in Philo's estimation, no doubt make "a most suitable and delicious feast" (§103), he evidently does not consider them as *dangerously* delicious as pigs and scaleless sea creatures (§101), because he explains their prohibition on different—albeit analogous—grounds. Because these animals kill and eat human beings, retributive justice warrants their *being* killed and eaten in return.[164] Moses, however, recognized a great moral danger whenever victims take the place of dispassionate agents of justice in executing a sentence, since victims easily succumb to their own *desire* for revenge—succumb, in other words, to the emotion of *anger* (ὀργή).[165] If the followers of Moses were, for example, allowed to eat lions, they might do so not from a *reasonable* desire to nourish their bodies (or even from a *reasonable* desire to punish an offense) but from a *passionate* desire to avenge those who have fallen prey to lions. As Philo puts it, they might unwittingly "become beasts" (θηριωθέντες), overtaken by the "savage

---

[164] §103: δίκαιον εἶναι τὰ αὐτὰ πρὸς ἀνθρώπων πάσχειν οἷς διατίθησι ... καὶ γὰρ εἰ τοῖς διατιθεῖσιν ἁρμόττει τὰ παραπλήσια παθεῖν.

[165] Philo's consideration of ὀργή (*anger*, also *wrath*) in an exposition of οὐκ ἐπιθυμήσεις makes sense in light of Aristotle's consideration of ὀργή in *Rhetoric* 1378a30–1378b10, where he defines it as an *appetite* (ὄρεξις) for *retribution* (τιμωρία) (cf. Ps.-Andr. 231.81: Ὀργή ... ἐστιν ἐπιθυμία τιμωρίας τοῦ ἠδικηκέναι δοκοῦντος; also William V. Harris, *Restraining Rage: The Ideology of Anger Control in Classical Antiquity* [Cambridge, Mass.: Harvard University Press, 2001], 61: "All or most of the many definitions of *orgē* which later writers offer are more or less simplified versions of the one in Aristotle's *Rhetoric* ..."). Just as Philo's Middle-Platonic moral psychology does not consider the emotion of desire objectionable *in itself*, Philo's concern here does not involve the desire for retribution (anger) *in itself*, but only the danger of such desire becoming *excessive* (passionate) due to the personal involvement of the agent of justice (cf. Plutarch's Middle-Platonic discussion of delivering punishment on the basis of reason, not passion, in *Cohib. ira* 459 A–460 C). Philo elsewhere characterizes ὀργή as a beneficial "weapon of defense" (ἀμυντήριον ὅπλον) created to help human beings (*Leg.* 2.8); cf. *Leg.* 2.9, where Philo's allegorical interpretation equates τὰ θηρία of Gen 2:19 with τὰ πάθη τῆς ψυχῆς, which God created as "helpers" (Philo tempers—but does not entirely reject—this positive image in *Leg.* 2.10–11). Note also Philo's references to *righteous* ὀργή (e.g., *Fug.* 90, *Mos.* 1.302) and *God's* ὀργή (e.g., *Somn.* 2.179, *Mos.* 1.6), which argue against the idea of anger being objectionable *in itself* (see, however, P. W. van der Horst, "Philo and the Problem of God's Emotions," in *Philon d'Alexandrie*, 171–78).

emotion of anger" (ὑπ'ὀργῆς, ἀγρίου πάθους).[166] So the lion, like the pig, represents a delectable meal, but in a fundamentally different sense. The pig incites ἐπιθυμία by promising abundant pleasure through the sweet taste of delicious meat. The lion incites ἐπιθυμία by promising abundant pleasure, too, but through the sweet taste of *revenge*.[167] Moses, understanding the meat of man-eating animals to be especially pleasurable in this unique sense, recognized the danger and did not allow his followers to consider such animals a source of food. In fact, as Philo goes on to explain in §104, Moses was so eager to protect against the dangerous "impulse" (ὁρμή) to kill and eat *with a vengeance*, that he forbade as a precaution the consumption of any animal that kills and eats other *animals*—let alone human beings.[168] Herbivores, Moses reasoned, never plot mischief against anyone, man or animal (μηδὲν εἰς ἐπιβουλὴν πραγματευόμενα), so no one runs the risk of eating them *with a vengeance*. In other words, no one could ever reasonably perceive *herbivores* as reprehensible aggressors, so no one could ever reasonably harbor a dangerous, potentially overwhelming desire to punish them.

In some respects, Philo's discussion of man-eating land animals, including his remarks on carnivores and herbivores, invites comparison with Eleazar's discussion of clean and unclean birds in the *Letter of Aristeas*.[169] Both discussions highlight the contrasting characteristics of carnivores and herbivores, both label the former "savage" (ἄγριος) and the latter "gentle" (ἥμερος), and both draw attention to correspondingly "savage" (ἄγριος) and "gentle" (ἥμερος) characteristics in human beings.[170] But despite these notable similarities, the two discussions represent radically different understandings of what Moses sought to accomplish through his dietary

---

[166] In *Migr.* 210, Philo speaks of τό ... ὀργῆς πάθος becoming "wild" (ἐξηγριωμένον) and causing beastly behavior (ἐκθηριώσης). He recommends not its *elimination* but its "taming" (ἡμέρωσον) through reduction of *excess* (ἄγαν), thereby reflecting his Middle-Platonic conception of passion as πλεονάζουσα (ἄμετρος) ὁρμή; cf. *Didask.* 32.4 [186.14–24], which defines ἥμερος πάθος as emotion kept within the bounds of moderation (σύμμετρα).

[167] Since ὀργή amounts to an ἐπιθυμία τιμωρίας, it has—like *every* form of ἐπιθυμία—pleasure (ἡδονή) as its ultimate object. On the *pleasure* of retribution, see *Spec.* 3.85 (esp. ἀντεφησθῆναι); cf. Plutarch's description of "gorging oneself" with retribution (τιμωρίας ἐμφορεῖσθαι) for the sake of pleasure (πρὸς ἡδονήν) as "beastlike" (θηριῶδες) (*Cohib. ira* 460 C).

[168] §104: ὥστε μακρόθεν ἀνεῖρξαι βουλόμενος τὴν ἐπὶ τὰ λεχθέντα ὁρμήν.

[169] See Svebakken, "Exegetical Traditions"; also Rhodes, "Diet and Desire," 123–25.

[170] See Svebakken, "Exegetical Traditions," 98–101 [="Common Elements in Philo and Eleazar"], esp. 99–100.

legislation.[171] The *Letter of Aristeas*, on the one hand, believes that the ethical benefit of Moses' legislation on unclean, savage, carnivores and clean, gentle, herbivores comes from a *symbolic* application.[172] The animals exemplify certain noble and ignoble character traits, which Moses either commends or condemns *symbolically* through the designations "clean" and "unclean." To eat or abstain as prescribed does not *in itself* affect the character of the moral agent, who must first correctly discern and then embrace the moral exhortations expressed symbolically through Moses' legislation. Philo, on the other hand, believes that the ethical benefit of the carnivore-herbivore legislation derives from a strictly *literal* application.[173] Man-eating animals do not, in Philo's view, *represent* a reprehensible character trait. They *actually* eat human beings—who might *actually* eat them in return, indulging an *actual* vengeance that overshadows reason. By literally abstaining from the meat of man-eaters, the soul literally avoids an incitement to passion. Similarly, Moses does not prohibit carnivores as a class because they *represent* violence, oppression, or some other vicious trait, but because a person accustomed to eating all sorts of carnivores will have difficulty abstaining from one particular sort, the man-eaters.[174] As for herbivores, both Eleazar

---

[171] *Pace* Rhodes, "Diet and Desire," esp. 125: "[B]oth Philo and Aristeas discern a similar logic operative in the dietary legislation."

[172] *Let. Arist.* 148–49: "By such examples, then, the lawgiver has commended to men of understanding a symbol (σημειοῦσθαι) that they must be just and achieve nothing by violence, nor, confiding in their own strength, must they oppress others. For if it is lawful not even to touch the creatures aforementioned because of their several natures, how must we not in every way guard our characters from degenerating to a similar state"; cf. Svebakken, "Exegetical Traditions," 101–03.

[173] In other words, Philo attributes *no* symbolic significance to Moses' legislation on unclean, savage, carnivores and clean, gentle, herbivores (cf. Svebakken, "Exegetical Traditions," 106–7). Philo obviously *does* engage in symbolic interpretations through much of §§100–118: namely, §§106–109 (criteria for clean land animals), §§110–112 (criteria for clean aquatic animals), §§113–115 (clean and unclean "creeping" animals). But he invariably *announces* his symbolic interpretations: ταυτὶ δὲ τὰ σημεῖα ἀμφότερα σύμβολα (§106), σύμβολα δὲ καὶ ταῦτ'ἐστί (§112), πάλιν αἰνιττόμενος διὰ μὲν ἑρπετῶν (§113), πάλιν διὰ συμβόλων (§114). He makes no such announcement in §§103–105. Heinemann (*Bildung*, 161) acknowledges: "Philon kennt für die Speisegesetze allegorische und wörtliche Begründungen"—and he gives examples of the two approaches (161–66). Under "wörtliche Begründungen," Heinemann mentions first the prohibition of "besonders wohlschmeckende Tiere" (such as pork), recognizing Moses' goal of "zur Selbstbeherrschung anregen" (163). In Heinemann's view, the prohibition of man-eaters involves "wörtliche Begründungen" as well, but he does *not* situate this prohibition within the larger context of promoting self-control in service to the Tenth Commandment.

[174] *Pace* Rhodes, "Diet and Desire," 123: "Philo advances an allegorical argument that explains why no carnivores are among those permitted for food." Unlike Eleazar (*Let. Arist.* 146–149), Philo attributes to Moses no objection to carnivores *per se*, on allegori-

and Philo commend them as "gentle" (ἥμερος) creatures satisfied with the fruit of the earth.[175] But they again differ in regard to the *symbolic* or *literal* significance of such a disposition. For Eleazar, a person who merely follows Moses' instruction to eat only herbivores misses Moses' real purpose, which was to promote the sort of life herbivores *represent*: a life of justice that oppresses no one.[176] For Philo, the person who eats only herbivores—even without reflecting on the *significance* of the rule—fulfills Moses' purpose, which was to safeguard his followers from a passionate desire for revenge by allowing them to eat only harmless creatures.

So despite superficial similarities, Philo's remarks in §§103–104 represent a radical departure from Eleazar's discussion of clean (herbivorous) and unclean (carnivorous) birds in the *Letter of Aristeas*. Eleazar, for his part, understood the dietary laws in terms of moral exhortation. Once properly decoded, obscure regulations about "clean" and "unclean" animals become straightforward ethical maxims—such as, "Be just and achieve nothing by violence" (*Let. Arist.* 148).[177] Although they inform a moral agent's *theoretical* conception of what virtue requires, actual observance of the dietary laws yields no *practical* benefit, no *training* in virtue. In other words, these regulations ultimately involve *learning* (μάθησις), not *practice* (ἄσκησις). Philo, by contrast, understands them in terms of moral psychology, construing them as *practical* exercises designed to eliminate passionate

---

cal, symbolic, or any other grounds. In Philo's view, Moses prohibits *all* carnivores only to increase the likelihood of his followers successfully abstaining from the *one* type of carnivore whose meat endangers the soul—namely, man-eaters (cf. Heinemann, *Bildung*, 164: "Das Verbot anderer Fleischfresser betrachtet Philon als Schutzmaßnahme, um die Begier nach menschenfressenden Tieren zu unterdrücken). In other words, Moses' tacit prohibition of all carnivores *primarily* targets the man-eaters, who grievously offend human beings—for Philo, the behavior of carnivores *as carnivores* has negligible significance. Eleazar, by contrast, understands Moses to have concerned himself *primarily* with the nature of carnivores, whose aggression *happens* (secondarily) to affect human beings in some cases: "But of the winged creatures which are forbidden you will find that they are wild and carnivorous and with their strength oppress the rest and procure their food with injustice at the expense of the tame fowl mentioned above. And not only these, but they also seize lambs and kids, and they do violence to men too (καὶ τοὺς ἀνθρώπους δὲ ἀδικοῦσι), both the dead and the living" (*Let.Arist.* 146).

[175] *Let. Arist.* 145: πάντα ἥμερα; *Let. Arist.* 147: τά ... ἥμερα ζῷα τὰ φυόμενα τῶν ὀσπρίων ἐπὶ γῆς δαπανᾷ; *Spec.* 4.104: ἡμέρους ἀγέλας, ἐπεὶ καὶ τὴν φύσιν ἐστὶ τιθασά, τροφαῖς ἡμέροις αἷς ἀναδίδωσι γῆ χρώμενα.

[176] *Let. Arist.* 147: ἐκ δικαίου τὰ τοῦ βίου κυβερνᾶν ... οὐ καταδυναστεύει πρὸς τὴν ἐπαναίρεσιν τῶν συγγενικῶν. N.B. the analogy in *Let. Arist.* 149 between animal *disposition* (διάθεσις) and human *ways of life* (τρόποι) (cf. *Let. Arist.* 163: κακοποιητικὸς γὰρ ὁ τρόπος).

[177] Cf. esp. Berthelot, "Interprétation symbolique."

desire and promote ἐγκράτεια.¹⁷⁸ Everyone who puts them into *practice* benefits from them, with or without an awareness of the ethical *theory* Moses used to formulate them.¹⁷⁹ In fact, *only* those who put them into practice benefit from them. The relative unimportance of knowledge and understanding stems from the fact that these laws involve the training and management of the soul's non-rational part. In other words, they ultimately involve *practice* (ἄσκησις), not *learning* (μάθησις)—in accordance with Philo's overarching agenda for the exposition. In fact, his interest in construing the dietary laws as matters of ἄσκησις explains his treatment of the criteria involving split hooves and rumination.

After a brief listing of the ten species of clean herbivores (§105), Philo considers the two authenticating "signs" (σημεῖα) common to all ten: split hooves and rumination (§§106–109).¹⁸⁰ Because he ascribes *symbolic* significance to these two traits, Philo's commentary does at this point begin to resemble more closely the *Letter of Aristeas*, which likewise interprets split hooves and rumination symbolically (*Let. Arist.* 150–60). Nevertheless, despite applying the same mode of interpretation to the same dietary regulations, Philo draws *different* conclusions in support of his *different* interpretive agenda. *Philo's* interpretation of split hooves and rumination highlights ἄσκησις, and in this way he relates these regulations to the broader expository agenda of his work, which—along with ἐπιθυμία and ἐγκράτεια—includes ἄσκησις as one of its key elements.¹⁸¹

---

¹⁷⁸ N.B. the terminology of moral psychology in *Spec.* 4.103–04: ὀργῆς, ἀγρίου πάθους ... τὴν ἐπὶ τὰ λεχθέντα ὁρμήν. Such emphases suit the overall purpose(s) of his exposition.

¹⁷⁹ In other words, eliminating man-eaters *from the diet* helps to eliminate passionate desire(s) for revenge *from the soul*—whether or not the moral agent understands *why* it helps.

¹⁸⁰ See Rhodes, "Diet and Desire," 125–27. Philo considers the same "signs" in a similar way in *Agr.* 131–45.

¹⁸¹ In this way, §§106–109 fit sensibly into Philo's exposition, even though he seems to have lost all sight of issues pertinent to the Tenth Commandment—namely, ἐπιθυμία and ἐγκράτεια. Because Colson overlooks the importance of ἄσκησις for Philo's expository agenda, he overlooks the relevance of §§106–109: "In [§§100–105] the prohibition of certain kinds of beasts, fishes, and birds is based on the supposition that they are the most appetizing and to abstain from them encourages self-control. It will be seen that from §106 onwards a totally different line of argument is adopted, viz. that philosophical and moral lessons are intended by the distinctions" (68, n. a); cf. Rhodes, "Diet and Desire," 127: "One cannot help but think that in his discussion of rumination and cloven hooves, Philo has wandered from his initial theme of desire and self-control." Rhodes, however, does *not* miss the relevance of Philo's other symbolic interpretations (§§110–115) to issues of ἐγκράτεια and ἐπιθυμία ("Diet and Desire," 127–31).

Philo highlights ἄσκησις primarily in his remarks on rumination, which both he and Eleazar identify as a symbol of "memory" (μνήμη).[182] But unlike Eleazar—who interprets rumination in terms of the *content* of memory: namely, remembrance *of God*[183]—Philo interprets rumination in terms of the *faculty* of memory itself: in other words, memory as a mode of ἄσκησις that promotes learning by making thoughts *of whatever content* secure in the mind through repetition (§107).[184] This sort of ἄσκησις admittedly does *not* involve the acquisition of ἐγκράτεια through forcible training of a *non-rational power* (ἐπιθυμία), but it *does* involve the moral agent actively engaging certain faculties to achieve certain ends using discrete exercises.[185] So Philo sticks to his agenda in a broad conceptual sense, without construing the eating (or not) of ruminating animals as a *practical* exercise for inculcating ἐγκράτεια.

In §§110–115, Philo likewise does *not* construe the criteria regarding *aquatic animals* and *reptiles* as practical exercises inculcating ἐγκράτεια. Instead, he construes them as symbolic repositories of certain key *principles* of ἐγκράτεια, which—once properly discerned—become secured in the mind through the sort of ἄσκησις described in §107.[186] Here Philo's

---

[182] Philo's particular interest in *memory* comes through in the ordering of his commentary on the two traits: *first* rumination (memory), *then* the split hoof, despite his initial listing of *first* the split hoof, *then* rumination (§106: τό τε διχηλεῖν καὶ τὸ μηρυκᾶσθαι). The Pentateuch mentions *first* the split hoof, *then* rumination (Lev 11:3 [cf. Deut 14:6])—and Eleazar naturally comments on the traits in that order. Philo's reversal suggests a deliberate rearrangement of the material to highlight *memory* (μνήμη).

[183] E.g., *Let. Arist.* 155: μνείᾳ μνησθήσῃ κυρίου (cf. Deut 7:18); *Let. Arist.* 157: πρὸς τὸ διὰ παντὸς μνημονεύειν τοῦ κρατοῦντος θεοῦ καὶ συντηροῦντος; *Let. Arist.* 158: πρὸς τὸ μνείαν ... θεοῦ (cf. *Let. Arist.* 160).

[184] In *Leg.* 3.18, Philo lists τῶν καλῶν μνῆμαι among the μέρη τῆς ἀσκήσεως. On Philo's understanding of the role of μνήμη in the learning process, see *Post.* 148–49 (cf. *Agr.* 131–35).

[185] Memory uses "constant exercises" (συνεχέσι μελέταις) as the "cement of thoughts" (κόλλα νοημάτων) (§107). On the association of μελέτη with ἄσκησις, see, e.g., *Leg.* 3.18: μέρη τῆς ἀσκήσεως ... μελέται; *Sacr.* 85–86: μελέτην καὶ ἄσκησιν αὐτῶν ποιεῖσθαι συνεχῆ ... συνεχὴς γὰρ ἄσκησις ἐπιστήμην πάγιον ἐργάζεται (cf. *Gig.* 26; *Conf.* 110; *Migr.* 31). See also Pierre Hadot, "La philosophie antique: Une éthique ou une pratique?," in *Problèmes de la Morale Antique* (ed. Paul Demont; Amiens: Université de Picardie-Jules Verne, 1993), 7–37, esp. 23–24; and Mosès, 264–65, n. 4: "La μελέτη mémorisante peut être également évoquée à travers l'image de la simple mastication (*Leg.* I, 98) ou à travers le symbole de la manne concassée (*Sacrif.* 86). Ce type d'exercice mental appartient à la plupart des ascèses philosophiques de l'époque."

[186] Cf. §107: τὰ σοφίας δόγματα καὶ θεωρήματα. Philo has in mind *learning* (μάθησις), and the *exercise* of memory that prolongs it (§107: ἐπὶ πλέον ἔχει τὴν μάθησιν). What he de-scribes in general terms as τὰ σοφίας δόγματα καὶ θεωρήματα in §107, becomes *in effect* τὰ ἐγκρατείας δόγματα καὶ θεωρήματα in §§110–115 (e.g., §112: ψυχῆς ἐγκράτειαν ... ποθούσης).

symbolic method closely resembles that of the *Letter of Aristeas*, which likewise extracts ethical *principles* from the dietary laws without concern for their literal observance. For Philo, however, the *theoretical* principles outlined in §§110–115 figure in and ultimately support a very *practical* program of managing ἐπιθυμία.[187]

§§110 – 112: Aquatic Animals[188]

[§110] After establishing these restrictions for land animals, he begins to list aquatic animals that are clean and approved for eating, marking also *these* with two distinguishing characteristics—fins and scales. He rejects and disapproves of any animal exhibiting *neither* or only *one* of them. Now, this requires an accurate explanation. [§111] Creatures lacking *both* or *one* of these traits get dragged along by the current, unable to withstand the force of its movement. But creatures equipped with *both* face the current head-on and repel it. Eager to contend with the opponent, they train themselves with zeal and invincible daring: pushed they push back, chased they turn and charge, hemmed in they clear wide swaths for an easy escape. [§112] Here again we have two *symbols*: the first represents the soul of a lover of pleasure, the second represents the soul enamored of endurance and self-control. For the road to pleasure is downhill all the way—easier than any other. So instead of a path for walking, it ends up being more like a slippery slope. By contrast, the road to self-control is a steep uphill climb—laborious, to be sure, but more beneficial than any other. The road to pleasure whisks us away and compels our descent, bearing us down headlong until at last it flings us off into the lowest depths. But the other road leads upward to heaven, granting immortality to those who do not grow weary, who have the strength to endure its rough and challenging climb.

In his interpretation of criteria for clean land animals, Philo had to reckon with a traditional understanding of the symbolic significance of rumination and split hooves (from the *Letter of Aristeas*), but his interpretation of fins and scales—the criteria for clean *aquatic* animals—seems unprecedented.

---

[187] Philo envisions a close relation between *learning* about ἐγκράτεια through symbolic reflection on some dietary laws (e.g., criteria for aquatic animals and reptiles) and putting ἐγκράτεια into *practice* through actual observance of others (e.g., prohibition of pork). On the relation between learning and practice, see *Somn.* 1.169 (esp. τὸ γὰρ ἀσκήσει ἔγγονον τὸ μαθήσει).

[188] See Lev 11:9–12; Deut 14:9–10.

While he does use the traditional *technique* of correlating animal behavior with human character—just as Eleazar did in the case of carnivorous birds (*Let. Arist.* 145-49)—Philo's *results* seem original and deliberately suited to his expository agenda. He begins with a characterization of the unclean aquatic animal, which lacks fins, or scales, or both. Such a creature, he notes, gets swept away by the current, "unable to withstand the force of its movement" (ἀντέχειν ἀδυνατοῦντα τῇ βίᾳ τῆς φορᾶς) (§111). Since Philo commonly uses the term φορά ("movement") as a synonym for the technical term ὁρμή ("impulse"), his wording here reflects the discourse of moral psychology used elsewhere in his writings.[189] In particular, he portrays the plight of someone mastered by the non-rational impulse(s) of ἐπιθυμία, someone identified explicitly in §112 as the φιλήδονος ψυχή. Consistent with his Middle-Platonic view of the soul, Philo portrays a contest of power within the moral agent whose reason (λόγος) suffers abject defeat, unable (ἀδυνατοῦντα) to withstand the *force* (τῇ βίᾳ) of the dominating non-rational power (ἐπιθυμία). Just as the *current* absolutely directs the movement of a finless, scaleless creature, so ἐπιθυμία-turned-ἔρως absolutely directs the movement of a φιλήδονος ψυχή, as it travels along the easy path to pleasure (ἐφ'ἡδονήν).[190] By contrast, aquatic animals *with* fins and scales stoutly oppose the current (§111). Philo characterizes *their* behavior using the agon motif, portraying the sort of struggle against ἐπιθυμία undertaken by those who acquire ἐγκράτεια through *practice* (ἄσκησις).[191] In his view, these creatures symbolize the soul that yearns for endurance and self-control (καρτερίαν καὶ ἐγκράτειαν ποθούσης [ψυχῆς]).This soul travels a difficult, yet profitable, path, which leads not only to ἐγκράτεια

---

[189] On τῇ βίᾳ τῆς φορᾶς, cf. *Leg.* 1.73: τῇ βίᾳ τῆς ὁρμῆς; *Agr.* 94: ἐπιστομίζειν τῆς πλεοναζούσης τὴν φορὰν ὁρμῆς. On the synonymy of ὁρμή and φορά, note the generic Stoic definition of impulse: λέγουσιν ... ὁρμὴν εἶναι φορὰν ψυχῆς ἐπί τι κατὰ τὸ γένος (*ESE* 9). On Philo's use of φορά in the context of moral psychology, note esp. *Leg.* 3.134: ἵν'οὗτος ἡνιόχου τρόπον ἐπιστομίζῃ τὴν ἐπὶ πλέον [τῶν παθῶν] φοράν; *Leg.* 3.155: ἐπιστομιεῖ γὰρ ὁ λόγος καὶ ἐγχαλινώσει τήν ... φορὰν τοῦ πάθους; *Agr.* 88: τῆς κατὰ ψυχὴν ἀλόγου καὶ ἀμέτρου καὶ ἀπειθοῦς φορᾶς; *Fug.* 91: τὴν τῶν παθῶν ἀνεγείρει φοράν; *Virt.* 14: ὑπὸ τῆς τῶν παθῶν φορᾶς κατακλύζεσθαι. Philo elsewhere equates water (ὕδωρ) with the φορά of the passions (πάθη), e.g. *Leg.* 2.103: ὑπὸ τὸ ὕδωρ τουτέστιν ὑπὸ τὴν φορὰν τῶν παθῶν; *Conf.* 70: "ὑπὸ τὸ ὕδωρ" ... τουτέστιν ὑπὸ τὴν τῶν παθῶν φοράν.

[190] The φιλήδονος ψυχή, mastered by tyrannical desire (ἔρως), orients its life toward the "good" invariably sought by desire, which is pleasure (ἡδονή) (see above, pp. 71-75). In §112, Philo signals the presence of *harmful* ἔρως in the φιλήδονος ψυχή by contrasting it with the soul enamored of endurance and self-control (καρτερίαν καὶ ἐγκράτειαν ποθούσης), whose longing (πόθος) indicates the presence of *beneficial* ἔρως (on the ἔρως-πόθος connection, see above, p. 127, n. 59).

[191] §111: πρὸς τὸν ἀντίπαλον ... γυμνάζεται. Cf. *Spec.* 1.149: ἀντίπαλον δὲ ἐπιθυμίας ἐγκράτεια. For "resisting current," passions, and the agon motif, see esp. *Mut.* 214-15.

but ultimately to heaven (εἰς οὐρανόν) for those strong enough to endure it (§112). By highlighting issues of ἐπιθυμία, ἐγκράτεια, and ἄσκησις, Philo incorporates his interpretation of clean aquatic animals into the larger purpose of his exposition.

§§113 – 115: "Reptiles"[192]

[§113] Moses applies the same idea to reptiles, declaring both creatures with no feet, which wriggle about by sliding on their stomach, and four-legged creatures with many feet unclean for eating—but he is once again hinting at something else. Reptiles with no feet represent people who live for their bellies, who gorge themselves like cormorants, bringing a series of endless tributes to their sovereign ruler, the wretched belly. With strong drink, pastries, seafood, and in general whatever baked treat or tasty relish the exacting culinary arts produce for every sort of dish, these people fan and stoke their boundless and insatiable desires. Reptiles with four legs and many feet represent the miserable slaves of not just *one* passion, desire, but of all passions, which generically are four in number, each having many species. The tyranny of one passion is hard enough—how oppressive and unbearable the tyranny of many! [§114] But among reptiles, Moses designates as "clean" creatures with legs above their feet enabling them to leap up off of the ground. These are the various kinds of grasshoppers, along with the creature known as the "snake fighter." Once again, Moses is using symbols to carefully examine the different habits and dispositions of a rational soul. In this case, we learn that the powerful pull of the body naturally weighs foolish people down, strangling and crushing them as it adds its force to the great sinking mass of mortal existence. [§115] Some happy souls, however, can resist the downward force of that pull with a superior counterforce. Taught by the principles of proper instruction to leap upward from earth and all earthly concerns into the ethereal circuits of heaven, these souls glimpse a vision deemed worthy of envy and struggle by all who forgo half-hearted efforts and attain it through determined resolve.

In his explicit references to the structure of his commentary on clean and unclean animals, Philo acknowledges only *three* major elements—animals of land, sea, and sky—leaving no place in his outline for the reptiles (τὰ

---

[192] See Lev 11:2–23, 41–45. Here "reptiles" in the broad sense of creatures that "creep" (τῶν ἑρπετῶν) (cf. Lat. *repere*).

ἑρπετά) of §§113–115, *except* as part of his discussion of aquatic animals (§§110–112).[193] He obviously does *not* place reptiles in the same *physical* domain, but they do, in his view, share with aquatic creatures the same *symbolic* domain, which justifies their standing together with aquatic creatures under the one rubric. In Philo's view, Moses formulated dietary restrictions for the reptiles using "the same idea" (τῆς δ'αὐτῆς ἰδέας) he had used when formulating restrictions for aquatic creatures (§113).[194] Generally speaking, Moses' "idea" involved the correlation of animal behavior with human character, a correlation noted also by Eleazar in the *Letter of Aristeas* (esp. 145–49). But *specifically*, Moses saw in both aquatic creatures *and* reptiles certain physiological traits indicating ἐγκράτεια: either its abject absence, resulting in φιληδονία, or its salutary presence. By designating creatures either "clean" or "unclean" in accordance with their traits, Moses instructs students of his dietary laws in matters bearing on the Tenth Commandment, either commending the vigorous and successful *management* of ἐπιθυμία associated with ἐγκράτεια or denouncing the bitter *enslavement* to ἐπιθυμία associated with φιληδονία. In the case of aquatic creatures, Moses explores the symbolic significance of fins and scales, while in the case of reptiles, he considers the symbolic significance of *feet.*

Philo subdivides the unclean reptiles into those "with *no* feet" (ἄποδα) and those "with four legs and *many* feet" (τετρασκελῆ καὶ πολύποδα), and both represent souls utterly devoid of ἐγκράτεια (§113).[195] By creatures "with no feet," Philo clearly means *serpents*, which of necessity "wriggle about by sliding on their stomach" (συρμῷ τῆς γαστρὸς ἰλυσπώμενα).[196] Symbolically, serpents represent people who live *for their bellies* (ἐπὶ κοιλίας), specifically for the *pleasure* derived from eating and drinking. Holding pleasure as their ultimate aim, such people embody φιληδονία, the condition of

---

[193] When he finally begins his discussion of birds in §116, Philo claims to have considered only *two* classes of animal (land and aquatic) up to that point, so apparently none of the creatures mentioned in §§113–115 represent a distinct class (§116: ἐπελήλυθως οὖν τῷ λόγῳ τάς τε τῶν χερσαίων καὶ τὰς τῶν ἐνύδρων ζῴων ἰδέας). Elsewhere, Philo plainly states that his discussion of clean and unclean animals involves only three distinct varieties of creature: of *land, sea,* and *sky* (§100: ὅσα τῶν χερσαίων ἢ ἐνύδρων ἢ πτηνῶν; cf. §118).

[194] Cf. §113: πάλιν αἰνιττόμενος διὰ μὲν ἑρπετῶν.

[195] The actual terms Philo uses to classify unclean reptiles do not appear in the biblical prohibition of Lev 11:41–42: καὶ πᾶν ἑρπετόν, ὃ ἕρπει ἐπὶ τῆς γῆς, βδέλυγμα τοῦτο ἔσται ὑμῖν, οὐ βρωθήσεται. ⁴² καὶ πᾶς ὁ πορευόμενος ἐπὶ κοιλίας (cf. ἄποδα) καὶ πᾶς ὁ πορευόμενος ἐπὶ τέσσαρα διὰ παντός (cf. τετρασκελῆ), ὃ πολυπληθεῖ ποσὶν (cf. πολύποδα) ἐν πᾶσιν τοῖς ἑρπετοῖς τοῖς ἕρπουσιν ἐπὶ τῆς γῆς, οὐ φάγεσθε αὐτό, ὅτι βδέλυγμα ὑμῖν ἐστιν. Philo offers a similar interpretation of Lev 11:42 in *Leg.* 3.139.

[196] Cf. Lev 11:42: πᾶς ὁ πορευόμενος ἐπὶ κοιλίας. Cf. the serpent's curse in Gen 3:14: ἐπὶ τῷ στήθει σου καὶ τῇ κοιλίᾳ πορεύσῃ (on which see *Leg.* 3.65, 114–16, 160).

soul indicative of tyrannical desire.[197] Philo further signals the involvement of tyrannical desire through his *description* of those who live "for their bellies," which echoes his earlier description of those consumed by tyrannical desire *affecting the belly* (§91).[198] Instead of *controlling* desire through ἐγκράτεια, such people end up constantly *stimulating* desire, which in their case can never reach satiety because the deposed rational faculty sets no limit.[199] Similarly, creatures "with four legs and *many* feet" represent people who fail categorically to master the soul's non-rational forces through ἐγκράτεια and become instead mastered *by* those forces. In particular, Philo has in mind souls dominated by *all* of the passions (πάθη): not just the four generic passions ("τετρασκελῆ" [ἐπιθυμία, ἡδονή, φόβος, λύπη]), but also their many various species ("πολύποδα"). Philo's symbolical reflection at this point involves *all* passions, not just the *one* passion prohibited by οὐκ ἐπιθυμήσεις. But he does highlight ἐπιθυμία in his description of reptilian souls by comparing their suffering under *many* passions to the miserable slavery and harsh despotism endured under the *one* passion ἐπιθυμία, whose tyranny brings trouble enough.[200] By framing such a comparison, Philo suggests that he has *already* spoken on the nature and effects of tyrannical desire. And indeed he has, in both his symbolic interpretations (§§110–113) *and* the theoretical reflections of the exposition's "diagnosis" portion (esp. §§80–91). Although Philo's remarks on four-legged multipeds do not focus *exclusively* on tyrannical desire, they presume its preeminence within the exposition.

Philo interprets also the *clean* reptiles symbolically (§§114–115), exploring the significance of *their* distinguishing trait: legs above their feet enabling them to leap from the ground (πηδᾶν ἀπὸ τῆς γῆς δύνασθαι).[201] Like their unclean counterparts, these reptiles represent for Philo a certain type of *soul*, which in this case Moses sought to *commend*, not condemn.[202]

---

[197] Cf. *Leg.* 3.159: ὁ μὲν φιλήδονος ἐπὶ κοιλίαν βαδίζει.
[198] Apart from general similarities, note especially the common terminology: γαστέρα (§91) and γαστρός/γαστρί (§113); ἀκορέστους (§91) and ἀκορέστους (§113); ἀκράτου (§91) and ἀκράτου (§113); ἰχθύων (§91) and ἰχθύων (§113); ἐδεσμάτων (§91) and ἐδεσμάτων (§113); ἰλυσπωμένους (§91) and ἰλυσπώμενα (§113). In both passages, Philo compares gluttonous people to other sorts of animals: *dogs* in §91 (τρόπον κυνιδίων) and *cormorants* in §113 (τὸν αἰθυίης τρόπον). For the cormorant (αἴθυια), a voracious bird emblematic of gluttony, see also *Leg.* 3.155, *Det.* 101, and *Contempl.* 55.
[199] §113: ἀναρριπίζουσαι καὶ προσαναφλέγουσαι τὰς ἀπλήστους καὶ ἀκορέστους ἐπιθυμίας.
[200] N.B. §113: τοὺς ... ἑνὸς πάθους, ἐπιθυμίας, ... κακοὺς δούλους ... χαλεπὴ μὲν οὖν καὶ ἡ ἑνὸς δεσποτεία.
[201] Cf. Lev 11:21 : ἃ ἔχει σκέλη ἀνώτερον τῶν ποδῶν αὐτοῦ πηδᾶν ἐν αὐτοῖς ἐπὶ τῆς γῆς.
[202] §114: πάλιν διὰ συμβόλων ἤθη καὶ τρόπους λογικῆς ψυχῆς διερευνώμενος.

In particular, Philo correlates their ability to leap *from* the ground (πηδᾶν ἀπὸ τῆς γῆς) with the ability of souls to "leap" upward from the earth and from all earthly concerns (ἄνω πηδᾶν ... ἀπὸ γῆς καὶ τῶν χαμαιζήλων), which secures for them an invaluable vision of the divine (ἡ θέα ζηλωτὴ καὶ περιμάχητος).[203] Here Philo deploys the agon motif in its distinctively Platonic aspect, casting the practice of ἐγκράτεια as a means of escaping the body's entanglement with the sensible realm.[204] While he does not use the *term* ἐγκράτεια, the *concept* undoubtedly informs his notion of a "leaping" soul that wrestles successfully against the "pull of the body" (ἡ ... τοῦ σώματος ὁλκή) by resisting *with superior strength* (κραταιοτέρᾳ δυνάμει πρὸς τὴν ῥοπὴν τῆς ὁλκῆς ἀντιβιάσασθαι).[205] Also, Philo's specific mention of the "snake fighter" (ὀφιομάχης) suggests an effort on his part to characterize this type of soul as a model of ἐγκράτεια, since he elsewhere interprets the snake fighter in such a way:

---

[203] Philo changes ἐπὶ τῆς γῆς (LXX) to ἀπὸ τῆς γῆς to suit his exegetical purpose. Cf. *Her.* 239: "Conversely Moses gives high approval to those reptiles which can leap upwards (ἄνω δύναται πηδᾶν). Thus he says, 'These shall ye eat of the flying reptiles which go on four legs, which have legs above their feet, so as to leap with them from the earth (ὥστε πηδᾶν ἐν αὐτοῖς ἀπὸ τῆς γῆς).' These are symbols of the souls (ταῦτα δ'ἐστὶ σύμβολα ψυχῶν) which though rooted like reptiles to the earthly body (τῷ γηΐνῳ σώματι) have been purified and have strength to soar on high, exchanging earth for heaven, and corruption for immortality."
[204] On the Platonic aspect of Philo's agon motif, see above, p. 100, n. 60.
[205] On "escaping the body," see *Gig.* 31; *Somn.* 1.43–44. By the term "pull of the body" (ἡ τοῦ σώματος ὁλκή), Philo undoubtedly means the compelling force of primal desires (ἐπιθυμίαι) for pleasure (ἡδονή) closely *associated* with the body yet *residing* in the soul (cf. *Gig.* 33: ταῖς φίλαις καὶ συγγενέσι σώματος ἡδοναῖς; *Gig.* 60: γῆς μὲν οἱ θηρευτικοὶ τῶν σώματος ἡδονῶν ἀπόλαυσίν τε καὶ χρῆσιν ἐπιτηδεύοντες αὐτῶν; *Somn.* 2.13: αἱ σώματος ἡδοναί). In other words, Philo envisions in this passage a moral agent resisting ἐπιθυμία, which amounts to a moral agent exercising ἐγκράτεια (cf. *Somn.* 2.106: σώματος ἡδονήν ... ἀποστρέφηται διὰ πόθον ἐγκρατείας). On Philo and the body, see Pierre Courcelle, "Tradition platonicienne et traditions chrétiennes du corps-prison (*Phédon* 62 b; *Cratyle* 400 c)," *REL* 43 (1965): 406–43, esp. 413–14; Kenneth Fox, "Paul's Attitude toward the Body in Romans 6–8: Compared with Philo of Alexandria" (Ph.D. diss., University of St. Michael's College, 2001), 215–58 [="Philo's Double Attitude toward the Body"]; Josef Groß, *Philons von Alexandreia Anschauungen über die Natur des Menschen* (Inaugural Dissertation, University of Tübingen, 1930), 10–21 [="Der Körper des Menschen"]; Pearce, *Land of the Body*, 81–127 [="Egypt, Land of the Body"]; Runia, *Philo and the Timaeus*, 258–78 [="(M)an's descent into the body"], 321–22; Alexander Sand, *Der Begriff "Fleisch" in den paulinischen Hauptbriefen* (BU 2; Regensburg: Pustet, 1967), 281–84 [="Philo von Alexandrien"]; Eduard Schweizer, "Die hellenistische Komponente im neutestamentlichen σάρξ-Begriff," *ZNW* 48 (1957): 237–53, 246–50 [="Philo"]; David Winston, "Philo and the Rabbis on Sex and the Body," in *The Ancestral Philosophy: Hellenistic Philosophy in Second Temple Judaism: Essays of David Winston* (ed. Gregory Sterling; SPhM 4; BJS 331; Providence: Brown Judaic Studies, 2001), 199–219.

For the snake-fighter is, I think, nothing but a symbolic representation of self-control (συμβολικῶς ἐγκράτεια εἶναί μοι δοκεῖ), waging a fight that never ends and a truceless war against intemperance and pleasure (πρὸς ἀκρασίαν καὶ ἡδονήν). (*Opif.* 164)[206]

So Philo equates the *clean* reptiles with souls possessed of ἐγκράτεια, which prove themselves superior to their unclean counterparts by *rejecting* pleasure instead of embracing it through φιληδονία.

§§116 – 117: Birds[207]

[§116] Having provided a rational account of the nature of land-based and aquatic animals, and having made the most appropriate distinctions among them by the laws he enacted, Moses begins to examine the nature of the last type of creature—the myriad kinds of winged creatures. He rejects a great number of birds, in particular those that prey either on other animals or on human beings. The prohibition includes every carnivorous, every venomous bird, and in general every bird that uses aggressive force of any kind. [§117] But Moses includes ring-doves, pigeons and turtle-doves, and the various types of cranes, geese, and birds of that sort all in one class of tame and gentle creatures. He offers these birds without restriction to anyone who chooses to use them for food.

Philo completes his survey of clean and unclean animals from land, sea, and sky with a short consideration of the legislation governing birds (γένη τῶν πτηνῶν). Philo's brevity contrasts sharply with Eleazar's elaborate interpretation of these same laws in the *Letter of Aristeas*.[208] While Philo does recognize along with Eleazar the Mosaic correlation of "clean" with docility (herbivores) and "unclean" with aggression (carnivores), he does *not* make Eleazar's connection between these behavioral traits and similar character traits. In fact, Philo makes *no* application to the realm of ethics at

---

[206] Cf. *Leg.* 2.105. Philo's symbolic interpretation of the snake fighter resembles Eleazar's method of interpretation but also reveals Philo's unique *appropriation* of that method. Eleazar's method assumes some animal trait reasonably analogous to a human moral trait. Nothing about "fighting snakes," as an animal trait, suggests a comparison with human self-control. The snake-fighter can *only* represent self-control if the "snake" represents pleasure (see Calabi, "Serpente e cavaliere"; Hecht, "Patterns of Exegesis," 111–12; Siegfried, *Philo*, 247), and this identification presumes Philo's *allegory of the soul* (on which see Tobin, *Creation of Man*, 135–76).
[207] See Lev 11:13–19; Deut 14:11–18.
[208] *Let. Arist.* 145–49. On the respective treatments of unclean birds in *Spec.* 4.116–17 and *Let. Arist.* 145–49—and their relation to one another—see esp. Svebakken, "Exegetical Traditions."

all, taking the laws neither *literally* as practical exercises in ἐγκράτεια nor *symbolically* as statements regarding theoretical principles of ἐγκράτεια. Such an omission clearly undermines the purpose of Philo's exposition, which presumes to show how Moses' dietary laws promote the observance of οὐκ ἐπιθυμήσεις by fostering ἐγκράτεια. By citing a set of dietary laws and tracing *no* connection to elements of his overarching expository agenda (ἐπιθυμία, ἐγκράτεια, ἄσκησις), Philo implies that no connection exits.

But Philo earlier proved his creative ability to fabricate connections for the sake of his expository agenda, using a variety of literal and symbolic techniques.[209] So his failure to produce here an interpretation in terms of moral psychology hardly stems from an *inability* to do so—instead it suggests an *unwillingness*. Philo's reluctance makes sense in light of his knowledge of the (for him) traditional interpretation of unclean birds found in the *Letter of Aristeas*.[210] Eleazar's explanation of how Moses ingeniously used obscure regulations about birds to commend justice and condemn violent oppression stands as one of the highlights of Eleazar's apologia for the dietary laws. Eleazar's line of interpretation probably either *was* standard before its inclusion in the *Letter of Aristeas* or *became* standard as a result. In either case, a well-established traditional interpretation of laws governing birds—especially one at odds with his expository agenda—would put Philo in an awkward position as an exegete. According to *Eleazar*, Moses had one clear objective in prohibiting or permitting certain species of birds: the promotion of δικαιοσύνη. But, according to *Philo*, Moses formulated the dietary laws in an effort to promote ἐγκράτεια, *not* δικαιοσύνη. Rather than flatly contradict a venerable traditional interpretation, Philo offers no interpretation at all.[211] As a result, he gives absolutely *no* support to one

---

[209] In fact, the logic of Philo's interpretation of the prohibition of man-eaters (§§103–104), however strained, could just as well apply here to the prohibition of carnivorous birds, since *they too*—as both Philo and Eleazar acknowledge—injure human beings and could therefore incite an inordinate desire for vengeance (§116: ὅσα ... κατ'ἀνθρώπων φονᾷ; *Let. Arist.* 146: τοὺς ἀνθρώπους δὲ ἀδικοῦσι νεκρούς τε καὶ ζῶντας).

[210] On Philo's familiarity with the text of *Let. Arist.* 145–49, see Svebakken, "Exegetical Traditions," 98–101.

[211] Cf. Svebakken, "Exegetical Traditions," esp. 109–10. Philo's reverence for tradition with respect to the *Letter of Aristeas* corroborates the results of Tobin's research in the *Creation of Man*, which notes reverence for tradition with respect to interpretations of Gen 1–3 (e.g., 100: "As was the case with most of the ancient world, previous interpretations were to be prized. Previous interpretations were something to which [Jewish interpreters] felt a responsibility, something which therefore could not be easily or openly rejected." Here Tobin comments in particular on the incorporation by Alexandrian Jewish exegetes of an earlier *Stoic* interpretation of Gen 2:7 into a larger [and later] *Platonic* interpretation of the creation account [idem, 77–101]. But he finds this sort of reverence demonstrated throughout the history of interpretation).

element of his original thesis about the laws of clean and unclean (§§100–102), which states that Moses regulated the consumption of animals from land, sea, *and sky* with a view to eliminating passionate desire. Yet when he summarily concludes his discussion of the laws of clean and unclean, he speaks as if he had made precisely that point.

§118: Conclusion of Clean and Unclean Animals

[§118] In this way, Moses removes from our diet certain animals from every region of the earth—creatures from the land, from the sea, and from the sky—just as one removes fuel from a fire. Thus he extinguishes passionate desire.[212]

In §118, Philo completes the interpretive frame he began in §§100–102, suggesting that Moses crafted his legislation on clean and unclean animals *primarily* to remove incitements to ἐπιθυμία and obviate the risk of passionate desire (πλεονάζουσα [ἄμετρος] ἐπιθυμία). He made the claim explicitly in §100, citing Moses' prohibition of the "fattest" (εὐσαρκότατα) and "richest" (πιότατα) animals from land, sea, and sky—animals with especially *delicious* meats likely to cause the moral agent to eat strictly for the sake of pleasure. Here in §118, Philo uses more general terms to make the same essential point: Moses' strategic prohibition of certain animals from land, sea, and sky amounts to the withdrawal of "fuel from a fire" in order to "extinguish" passionate desire.[213] By framing his entire discussion of the laws governing clean and unclean animals with one specific claim about the *purpose* of those laws, Philo implies that each one of his analyses corroborates—or in theory *should* corroborate—that claim. But only *two* of the animals he considers actually do: pigs and scaleless sea creatures, both of which Philo identifies as especially pleasurable to eat and morally dangerous for that reason. He does manage to fit one other type of prohibited animal, the land carnivores, into his interpretive scheme, but only through a strained notion of man-eaters being "delicious" (§§103–104). Otherwise, he offers strictly symbolic interpretations of the various

---

[212] *Thus he extinguishes passionate desire* (σβέσιν τῆς ἐπιθυμίας ἀπεργάζεται): Mosaic dietary restrictions do nothing to "extinguish" ἐπιθυμία per se, since even those who abstain from prohibited animals repeatedly indulge the amoral, useful emotion ἐπιθυμία when they eat other sorts of food. The ἐπιθυμία Philo has in mind must be *passionate* desire (πλεονάζουσα [ἄμετρος] ἐπιθυμία), which the Mosaic regulations target and eliminate.

[213] Cf. Gemünden, "Culture des Passions," 341. For Philo's use of fire imagery in reference to ἐπιθυμία elsewhere in his exposition of the Tenth Commandment, see *Spec.* 4.83; *Decal.* 150, 173 (cf. *Fug.* 158; *Mos.* 2.58).

clean and unclean species, avoiding any sort of claim about how they actually taste. He discontinues the symbolic mode when he gets to the legislation concerning birds, but instead of interpreting that legislation in light of his claim about delicious fare, he offers no interpretation at all. Philo hardly succeeds in demonstrating a *systematic* tendency on Moses' part to designate delicious animals "unclean" in an effort to combat passionate desire.

But in §§100–118 Philo *does* succeed in promoting the broader expository agenda he brings to *all* of the dietary laws, despite his failure to unite the laws of clean and unclean animals under one interpretive claim. In other words, Philo finds a way of making this subset of the dietary laws speak to issues of ἐπιθυμία, ἐγκράτεια, and ἄσκησις, confirming their essential relation—as species to genus—to the Tenth Commandment's prohibition of desire. In particular, he shows how the Mosaic legislation on clean and unclean species, with almost perfect consistency, addresses the *problem* of πλεονάζουσα (ἄμετρος) ἐπιθυμία by posing the *solution* of ἐγκράτεια *acquired* through ἄσκησις.[214] The prohibitions of pork and scaleless sea creatures of course support *not only* Philo's specific thesis for §§100–118 but *also* his general thesis about the dietary laws overall, since the consistent avoidance of excessive pleasure fosters a lifestyle of ἐγκράτεια, which accepts only rational (moderate) indulgences of ἐπιθυμία. The prohibition of land carnivores promotes ἐγκράτεια through a similar mechanism, even though no one—including Philo—considers the meat of such animals especially tasty. Philo ascribes a symbolic function to all of the other regulations, explaining how the designations "clean" and "unclean" respectively either *commend* ἐγκράτεια and ἄσκησις or *condemn* the excessive indulgence of ἐπιθυμία, quite apart from the palatability of the animals involved.

§§119–121: Animals Killed by Predators or Natural Causes[215]

[§119] In other regulations concerning food, Moses commands the avoidance of dead animals, whether dead by natural causes or savaged by a predator. He prohibits the latter because a human being

---

[214] With two significant exceptions: the laws regarding rumination and split hooves (§§106–109) and the laws governing birds (§§116–117). In the case of rumination, Philo does the best he can, turning the interpretation *toward* his exegetical agenda by highlighting the role of ἄσκησις in connection with μνήμη. In the case of birds, Philo's failure to promote his exegetical agenda likely derives from deference to the interpretive tradition found in the *Letter of Aristeas*.

[215] See, for example, Lev 17:15, 22:8 (cf. Exod 22:30; Lev 11:39–40; Deut 14:21).

should not dine with wild beasts, all but feasting with them on their meal of flesh. He prohibits the former for a couple of likely reasons. First, eating a creature dead by natural causes is harmful and likely to cause disease, since the vital fluid of the creature has died inside the body along with the blood. Second, a creature already claimed by death should be left untouched out of respect for the forces of nature to which it succumbed. [§120] Great hunters, those trained as expert marksmen who down their prey with rarely a miss, boast in their successful exploits, especially when they share some of the catch with the dog handlers and even with the dogs themselves—and they receive praise from most lawgivers among Greeks and barbarians for their character, as men who are not only brave but also generous. But the architect of our sacred commonwealth would surely *condemn* such behavior, having forbidden outright the consumption of animals either dead by natural causes or—as applies in this case—savaged by a predator, for the reasons previously stated. [§121] Suppose, however, one of our commonwealth's athletes of virtue becomes fond of physical training and the hunt,[216] expecting in this way to undergo exercises and preparations for wars and dangerous engagements with his enemies. Whenever he has a successful expedition, he should simply give the catch to his dogs for them to feast on, as a payment or prize for their courage and impeccable service. He himself should never even touch the dead animals, so as to learn in his dealings with non-rational creatures a proper attitude toward human enemies. In particular, he should never do battle with them for unjust gain, which is the business of robbers, but in an effort either to avenge past wrongs or to deal with those he considers imminent.

As part of an overarching thesis for §§100–118, Philo claimed that Moses prohibited animals yielding delicious meats in order to promote ἐγκράτεια, but his discussion in §§119–121 of animals dead from either natural causes

---

[216] *Suppose, however, one of our commonwealth's athletes of virtue becomes fond of physical training and the hunt* (εἰ δέ τις τῶν ἀσκητῶν φιλογυμναστὴς γένοιτο καὶ φιλόθηρος): Philo considers the case of a *moral* athlete (τις τῶν ἀσκητῶν) who becomes enamored of *physical* training and an *actual* sport, the hunt (φιλογυμναστής ... καὶ φιλόθηρος). Both Heinemann and Mosès read the passage in this way: "Wenn aber ein tugendbeflissener Mann auch Freund von Körperübungen und Jagd ist"; "Et si tel athlète de la vertu est aussi un amateur des exercices physiques et de la chasse"). Colson does not identify τις τῶν ἀσκητῶν with a *moral* athlete, "based on the belief that ἀσκητής is not used absolutely in this way" (PLCL 8, 83, n. b). But Philo uses ἀσκητής in precisely this way in *Post.* 154: εἰσὶ δέ τινες τῶν ἀσκητῶν, οἷς τὴν ἐπ'ἀρετὴν ἄγουσαν ὁδὸν τραχεῖαν καὶ δυσάντη καὶ χαλεπὴν νομισθεῖσαν τὸ πρῶτον.

(θνησιμαῖον) or violent attack (θηριάλωτον) clearly requires a different approach.[217] Since these prohibitions *presume* edibility under different circumstances of death, they must involve only the moderately tasty "clean" animals, whose demise from old age, disease, or mauling only makes them less appetizing. Philo can no longer broach the topic of moral psychology, as he did earlier, by analyzing the dietary laws in terms of the *pleasure* (ἡδονή) certain animals afford when eaten. In fact, nothing in his initial explanation of why Moses prohibited the θνησιμαῖον and the θηριάλωτον (§119) speaks *at all* to the issues of ἐπιθυμία, ἐγκράτεια, and ἄσκησις raised elsewhere in his exposition. To *fabricate* a connection between these two prohibitions and his exegetical agenda, Philo uses a convoluted line of legal reasoning to derive *from them* a brand new prohibition—found nowhere in the Pentateuch—which he construes as an exercise in ἐγκράτεια.

Philo contrasts Greek and barbarian lawgivers, who praise the generosity of expert huntsmen who share the catch even with their hounds (σκύλαξι), with Moses, who presumably would find fault with such a practice in light of his prohibition of θνησιμαῖον and θηριάλωτον, particularly the latter. In other words, Moses' prohibition of mauled animals (θηριάλωτον), which Philo characterized in §119 as a prohibition of *sharing* a meal of flesh with animals (συνευωχούμενον ταῖς σαρκοφαγίαις), would also forbid a hunter from *sharing* the catch with his dogs. But Philo still has no clear application to matters of moral psychology, so he poses yet another scenario, which stands at best in a *tertiary* relation to Moses' original prohibition of θηριάλωτον. Suppose, says Philo, someone fond of training becomes an avid hunter (φιλόθηρος), *in order to train for warfare*.[218] Philo suggests that such hunters should not even *touch* their dead quarry (μὴ ψανέτω), but instead should just give the dogs a well-deserved feast. And because he characterizes the hunt as *strictly* a preparation for warfare, Philo can interpret the practice of abstaining from the catch in a brand new way, which does *not* involve the condition of the deceased animal(s) but *does*—at long last—involve the moral condition of the hunter.

By avoiding all contact with the dead quarry, the hunter as moral agent learns through practice with *animal* opponents to battle *human* enemies not for "unjust gain" (διὰ κέρδος ἄδικον), but only for the just causes of

---

[217] Both terms appear, for example, in Lev 17:15: καὶ πᾶσα ψυχή, ἥτις φάγεται θνησιμαῖον ἢ θηριάλωτον ἐν τοῖς αὐτόχθοσιν ἢ ἐν τοῖς προσηλύτοις ... ἀκάθαρτος ἔσται ἕως ἑσπέρας.

[218] §121: μελέτας καὶ προάγωνας ὑπολαμβάνων εἶναι πολέμων καὶ κινδύνων τῶν πρὸς ἐχθρούς. In other words, Philo poses the very specialized case of someone who hunts not in order *to eat*, but in order *to train for war*.

retaliation or preemptive self-defense. Since he has painstakingly managed to cast the law of θηριάλωτον as an exercise in abstaining from κέρδος ἄδικον, Philo has now established its relevance to moral psychology and the management of ἐπιθυμία, though he chooses not to explore that relevance in detail. Elsewhere, however, Philo clearly associates the pursuit of κέρδος ἄδικον with the indulgence of passionate desire, particularly in his interpretation of the law against sowing more than one type of seed in a vineyard.[219] Trying to get more than one crop from one piece of land represents an act of egregious avarice.[220] Whoever makes the attempt incites unjust desires (ἀδίκους ἐπιθυμίας), failing to restrict them within proper limits (μέτροις αὐτὰς μὴ περιορίζων) in the pursuit of "unjust gain" (κέρδος ἄδικον).[221] While seeking gain from *one* crop represents a just and reasonable course of action, seeking gain from *two* crops represents an overstepping of reason's authority on the part of desire. Philo's case of the just warrior suggests a similar sort of excessive desire: while going to war for a just cause represents a *reasonable* course of action, going to war strictly for *gain* represents a triumph of ἐπιθυμία over λόγος, since the violence no longer bears justification on rational grounds.[222] So in Philo's mind, a hunter training for battle who gives his catch to the dogs not only obeys a vague semblance of Moses' prohibition of θηριάλωτον—he also, more importantly, trains himself in going to war with a motive involving reason and necessity, not ἐπιθυμία and pleasure. And by encouraging the dominance of reason over desire, such training promotes ἐγκράτεια.

§§122 – 125: Blood and Fat[223]

[§122] But some Sardanapalus types, greedily extending their ever dainty lack of self-control beyond all bounds and limits, cleverly devise new kinds of pleasure. They prepare meat unfit for any sacrifice by strangling and choking the animals to death. In this way, they entomb the blood, the essence of the soul, within the body—

---

[219] Deut 22:9: οὐ κατασπερεῖς τὸν ἀμπελῶνά σου διάφορον. For Philo's interpretation, see esp. *Spec.* 4.212–18.
[220] *Spec.* 4.212: φιλοχρηματίας ὑπερβαλλούσης ἔργον.
[221] *Spec.* 4.217–18.
[222] Philo suggests in §121 that those who go to war for unjust gain essentially engage in robbery (λωποδυτούντων πράξεις), which is precisely the sort of behavior expected from those taken captive by a tyrannical desire for wealth (§87: εἰ πρὸς χρήματα γένοιτο, κλέπτας ἀποτελεῖ καὶ βαλαντιοτόμους καὶ λωποδύτας).
[223] For the two prohibitions together, note esp. Lev 3:17: πᾶν στέαρ καὶ πᾶν αἷμα οὐκ ἔδεσθε.

blood that should have been liberated and released from the body. They should be content to enjoy the flesh alone, without touching anything akin to the soul. [§123] This explains Moses' decision to legislate elsewhere concerning blood, as he does when he prohibits the consumption of both blood and fat. Blood is prohibited for the reason I mentioned: it is the essence of the soul. I do not mean the intelligent and rational soul, but the soul that operates through the senses—the soul that provides us with the sort of life we share with non-rational animals. But the essence of the other type of soul is divine spirit, especially according to Moses. In his account of the creation of the world, Moses states that God infused the first man and founder of our race with a "breath of life" into his "face," the most commanding part of the body, where the senses are stationed like an entourage for the mind as for a great king. Clearly, what God infused was ethereal spirit, and, if you will, something better than ethereal spirit: an effulgence of the blessed, the triply blessed, Nature. [§124] As for the fat of the animal, Moses prohibits its consumption because it is most succulent. Here again he wants to teach self-control and zeal for an austere life—a life that forgoes what is easiest and convenient and instead endures voluntarily the mental efforts and other labors needed to acquire virtue. [§125] For this reason, the blood and the fat are taken from every sacrificial animal and given as a whole burnt offering, as a sort of first fruits. The blood is poured out onto the altar as a drink offering, while the fat, on account of its richness, is brought instead of oil to fuel the flame of the sacred and holy fire.

Philo now turns to the prohibitions of blood and fat, taking first the prohibition of blood (§§122–123). In the case of unclean animals, Philo cast the dietary laws as exercises in ἐγκράτεια by noting Moses' *implicit* rationale for prohibiting certain species—the pig, for example, tastes delicious and incites ἐπιθυμία, and Moses prohibits it for that reason. In the case of blood, however, Philo must account for a dietary prohibition whose *explicit* rationale has little or nothing to do with ἐπιθυμία, ἐγκράτεια, or ἄσκησις: Moses explicitly forbids blood because of its unique relation to the soul (ψυχή).[224] Yet Philo, despite the contradictory biblical evidence, deliberately frames the topic in terms of moral psychology, characterizing the consumption of blood as one of the decadent *pleasures* (ἡδονάς)

---

[224] Lev 17:10–14 (e.g., v. 11: ἡ γὰρ ψυχὴ πάσης σαρκὸς αἷμα αὐτοῦ ἐστιν).

enjoyed by some "Sardanapalus types" (Σαρδανάπαλλοι).²²⁵ Such people strangle the animals they eat, "entombing" the blood within the body, and so demonstrate an egregious, effeminate lack of self-control.²²⁶ The reprehensible luxury of such a practice lies in its being done strictly *for the sake of pleasure* by those unwilling to content themselves with the reasonable indulgence of eating flesh drained of blood.²²⁷ In this way, Philo effectively frames the prohibition of blood as a deterrent to passionate desire, deploying the same λόγος–ἐπιθυμία dynamic underlying his exposition of the laws of clean and unclean animals. He implies that reason, imposing the proper *measure* (μέτρον) on ἐπιθυμία, only sanctions the eating of meat properly drained of its life force. But someone subject to *passionate desire* (πλεονάζουσα [ἄμετρος] ἐπιθυμία), acting strictly on desire's motivation for *pleasure*, oversteps this reasonable limit in order to enjoy the delectable (but unreasonable) indulgence of blood-infused meat. By avoiding such meat, the moral agent learns by practice (ἄσκησις) to avoid eating *for pleasure's sake*, to operate—in other words—on the basis of a rational motivation and to develop the moderate lifestyle possessed of ἐγκράτεια. Of course, Philo must acknowledge—and he does—that Moses did not have the *pleasures* of blood in mind when he made the prohibition, but rather its *property* of kinship with the soul. But Philo obviously does not *limit* himself to the biblical rationale, because his exposition programmatically seeks to draw some connection between the individual dietary laws and the management of ἐπιθυμία. In Philo's view, followers of Moses, who might *first* avoid the meat of strangled animals because it still contains the essence of life, derive the additional (albeit implicit) benefit of eliminating a dangerously delicious food from their diet.

The Mosaic prohibition of fat, by contrast, perfectly suits Philo's expository agenda, since it corresponds exactly to the prohibition of pork in the way it works.²²⁸ As Philo explained in §100, Moses prohibited animals, like the pig, whose flesh is "most succulent" (πιότατα), knowing that abstinence from delectable fare facilitates proper management of ἐπιθυμία. Echoing these remarks, Philo attributes the prohibition of fat (τὸ στέαρ) to its being "most succulent" (πιότατον), noting that Moses here "again" (πάλιν)—with *this* dietary restriction—offers a lesson in self-control (διδασκαλίαν ἐγκρατείας). By abstaining from fat, the moral agent learns to reject a life

---

²²⁵ On Sardanapalus, see §102.
²²⁶ §122: ἄγχοντες καὶ ἀποπνίγοντες ... τυμβεύοντες τῷ σώματι τὸ αἷμα; cf. Acts 15:29: ἀπέχεσθαι ... αἵματος καὶ πνικτῶν (see A. J. M. Wedderburn, "The 'Apostolic Decree': Tradition and Redaction," *NovT* 35 [1993], 362–89, esp. 366–68).
²²⁷ N.B. §122: σαρκῶν γὰρ αὐτὸ μόνον ἀπολαύειν αὔταρκες ἦν.
²²⁸ Noted also by Heinemann, *Bildung*, 163.

of luxury, which pursues pleasure for pleasure's sake at the prompting of ἐπιθυμία. Of course, the life of ἐγκράτεια, which pursues only *necessities* at the prompting of *reason*, calls for strenuous exercise (ἄσκησις)—a point duly made by Philo through his deployment of the agon motif. In particular, the command to abstain from fat promotes "zeal for an austere life" (ζῆλον αὐστηροῦ βίου), a life that voluntarily forgoes what is easy (τὰ ῥᾷστα) to endure hardships (πόνους), in order to acquire virtue (ἕνεκα κτήσεως ἀρετῆς).[229] In his exposition of criteria for clean aquatic creatures (§112), Philo deployed the same figure in the same way, contrasting the "easy" (ῥᾴστη) road to pleasure with the "toilsome" (ἐπίπονος) road πρὸς ἐγκράτειαν.

§§126 – 131: Conclusion[230]

[§126] Moses rightly condemns some of his contemporaries as gluttons, as those who consider the experience of pleasure to be the pinnacle of happiness. A luxurious life in the city was not enough for them, where the supplies and provisions for all their necessities were inexhaustible. They wanted the same thing in the desolate, trackless wilderness, expecting to find vendors of fish, meat, and every kind of seasonable produce. [§127] When scarcity did come, they joined forces in shouting down, denouncing, and disparaging their leader with shameless audacity. And they did not stop their revolt until they got what they wanted. Their demands were met for two reasons: first, to show that all things are possible for God, who finds a way in the midst of impossible and irresolvable situations; second, to punish the people, who were slaves of their belly and shirkers of holiness. [§128] As the story goes, a great cloud of quail, swept in from over the sea, poured out of the sky at dawn. So thick was this mass of birds that the encampment and the surrounding area—in every direction, as far as a fit man could walk in a day—were overshadowed. In addition, they were flying only a few feet off of the ground, which made them easy to capture. [§129] One would think that the people, struck with amazement by such a marvelous demonstration of power on God's part, would have been satisfied simply with what they saw—that filled

---

[229] Cf. *Det.* 27: οἷς ὑπὲρ κτήσεως ἀρετῆς πόνος διαθλεῖται; *Mut.* 14: τὴν πάλην, ἣν ὑπὲρ κτήσεως ἀρετῆς ὁ ἀσκητὴς ἐπάλαισε.
[230] See Num 11:4–34.

with reverence, and amply *fed* by reverence,[231] they would have abstained from eating any of the meat. Instead, goading their desire to an even greater pitch, they went after what seemed to them the greatest possible good fortune. Raking in the quail with both hands, they packed the folds of their garments. Storing those birds away in their tents, they went back outside to catch others, demonstrating that greedy cravings for more have no limit. Preparing their game in a variety of ways, they gorged themselves insatiably, about to be destroyed—the fools—by their bloat. [§130] And, in fact, they *did* perish before long in a pool of noxious discharges. So in keeping with the passion that destroyed them, that place was named "Tombs of Desire." Clearly, as the story teaches, there is no evil in the soul greater than desire. [§131] For this reason, Moses admirably says in his exhortations, "Let no one do what is pleasing in his own sight." He is saying, in effect, "Let no one indulge his own desire." If a person expects to become truly noble, let him be pleasing to God, the world, Nature, laws, and wise men by rejecting the love of self.

At §126, Philo abruptly turns from his serial treatment of discrete dietary laws to a moralized retelling of God's provision of quail to the Israelites in the wilderness. Philo's narrative ends in §130 with an explicit statement of what the story ultimately teaches: that "there is no greater evil (μεῖζον κακόν) in the soul than desire."[232] This sweeping indictment of ἐπιθυμία clearly resembles the earlier diagnosis (κρίσις) portion of Philo's exposition (§§79–94), which sought above all to illustrate the reprehensible nature and harmful effects of desire, particularly of its most dangerous manifestation, tyrannical desire (ἔρως). Insofar as the material in §§126–130 serves to depict tyrannical desire in a negative light, it too bears analysis as part of Philo's diagnosis, despite its appearing at the *end* of his exposition.

Philo undoubtedly sees *tyrannical desire* as the particular manifestation of ἐπιθυμία at work in the people's clamoring for meat and then gorging

---

[231] *filled with reverence, and amply* fed *by reverence* (γεμισθέντας εὐσεβείας καὶ ταύτῃ τραφέντας): Reading, with Colson and Mosès, καί (MSS) instead of κἂν (PCW).

[232] ἐπιθυμίας, ἧς οὐκ ἔστιν ἐν ψυχῇ ... μεῖζον κακόν. Philo takes the epithet "Tombs of Desire" (Num 11:34: Μνήματα τῆς ἐπιθυμίας) as proof of the story's concern with *passionate* desire (N.B. §130: ὡς καὶ τὸ χωρίον ἀπὸ τοῦ περὶ αὐτοὺς πάθους τὴν ἐπωνυμίαν λαβεῖν). In *Migr.* 155, Philo comments on Num 11:4, interpreting ἐπεθύμησαν ἐπιθυμίαν as a reference to the genus ἐπιθυμία *itself* (αὐτοῦ τοῦ γένους), not any particular *species* of ἐπιθυμία (οὐχ ἑνός τινος τῶν εἰδῶν). In other words, in Philo's view, the story from Numbers speaks to *more* than just desire for food, and for this reason it suits the broader scope of his exposition of οὐκ ἐπιθυμήσεις. On "Tombs of Desire," see also Francis Watson, *Paul and the Hermeneutics of Faith* (London: T&T Clark, 2004), 363–69.

themselves with quail. Specifically, they suffered from tyrannical desire *affecting the belly*, which turned them into "gluttons" (§126: γαστριμάργους), the very effect Philo described as part of the exposition's first and more extensive diagnosis.[233] But despite the stomach's involvement as the physical locus of desire's influence, the real issue—as with *any* instance of tyrannical desire—is the involvement of the rational faculty, in particular its being *usurped* by desire, which results in the moral agent designating pleasure as "the good." As Philo puts it in §126, the people "supposed" (ὑπολαμβάνοντας) that "the experience of pleasure" (τὸ καθηδυπαθεῖν) was the "pinnacle of happiness" (εὐδαιμονικὸν ἐν τοῖς μάλιστα). And because they, under the tyranny of ἐπιθυμία-turned-ἔρως, sought the experience of pleasure *per se*, instead of a rational aim such as the preservation of life, their desire for meat had no limit (μέτρον).[234] They literally ate themselves to death, showcasing the destruction wrought by tyrannical desire.[235] Consistent with the formal aims of a "diagnosis" (κρίσις), Philo not only illustrates the disastrous results of indulging a certain passion (in this case, ἐπιθυμία), but also emphasizes the morally reprehensible nature of such indulgence.[236] In this way, §§126–130 essentially restate the case made in §79–94, but through a *biblical narrative* rather than a *philosophical discourse*. This change in literary vehicle allows Philo to explore for the first time the relation between ἐπιθυμία and *piety*—a relation only hinted at in §97, when he claimed that observance of the dietary laws leads not only to ἐγκράτεια but *also* to εὐσέβεια.[237]

Philo's retelling of Numbers 11:4–34 portrays the states of tyrannical desire and piety as radically incompatible and mutually exclusive. He recognizes two distinct breaches of piety within the story, and both stem from the hegemony of desire within the soul. First, because tyrannical desire compelled Moses' followers to seek pleasure *per se*, they unreasonably craved—and demanded—the luxury of meat in a trackless desert. In Philo's view, this made them "shirkers of holiness" (ἀφηνιαστὰς ὁσιότητος), since the truly pious would have gratefully sated their *necessary desires* for

---

[233] §91: [ἐπιθυμία] ἀψαμένη δὲ τῶν περὶ γαστέρα παρέχεται γαστριμάργους.
[234] §129: αἱ γὰρ ἄγαν πλεονεξίαι μέτρον οὐκ ἔχουσι.
[235] §129: ὑπὸ τῆς πλησμονῆς ἀπόλλυσθαι (cf. §127: ἐπ'ὀλέθρῳ).
[236] §126: μέμφεταί τινας ... ὡς γαστριμάργους; §127: ἀναισχύντῳ θράσει ... τιμωρήσασθαι τοὺς γαστρὸς ἀκράτορας.
[237] §97: διατάγμασι καὶ πρὸς ἐγκράτειαν ... καὶ—τὸ μέγιστον—πρὸς εὐσέβειαν ἀγωγοτάτοις. On Philo's understanding of εὐσέβεια ("piety"), see esp. Sterling, "'Queen of the Virtues,'" (also Wolfson, *Philo*, 2:213–15). Philo often pairs "εὐσέβεια" with "ὁσιότης" (see *Sacr.* 37). The two terms are practically synonymous, insofar as they both denote piety in a general sense (Sterling, "'Queen of the Virtues,'" 113: "Philo used the two terms as virtual synonyms to refer to the human response to and perception of God.").

food with the manna God provided.²³⁸ Second, after God's miraculous provision of quail the people ought to have abstained from eating *any* meat, taking their fill of *piety* instead (γεμισθέντας εὐσεβείας καὶ ταύτῃ τραφέντας). But an obsession with pleasure kept them from properly recognizing both the provision and the power of God—they were unable to see any greater good beyond their own short-sighted indulgence of ἐπιθυμία. In other words, as the story illustrates, those ruled by ἐπιθυμία are unable to count anything or anyone—including God—as more valuable than their own experience of pleasure (ἡδονή), since ἐπιθυμία compels them to accept *its* reflexive aim (ἡδονή) as *their* ultimate good.

Philo concludes his analysis of the quail narrative, and his *entire* exposition of the Tenth Commandment, with a brief reflection on Deut 12:8, which he paraphrases as, "Let no one do what is pleasing in his own sight."²³⁹ To make the passage more directly relevant to both the biblical story (§§126–130) and his overall exposition of οὐκ ἐπιθυμήσεις (§§79–125), he interprets its meaning as, "Let no one indulge his own desire (ἐπιθυμίᾳ)."²⁴⁰ Obviously, such an exhortation applies to the cautionary tale Philo has just retold in §§126–130, since *that* indulgence led unmistakably to a shameful, impious death. But just as the exhortation makes sense in light of Philo's *biblical* "diagnosis" (§§126–130), it makes sense also in light of his earlier *philosophical* "diagnosis" (§§79–94). In fact, since the earlier diagnosis involves a more extensive elaboration of the threats to moral and physical well being posed by ἐπιθυμία, Philo's version of Deut 12:8 pertains at *least* as much to the first (roughly) third of his exposition as it does to the final paragraphs—if not more.

In fact, Philo apparently intends this simple proscription against indulging desire to conclude his *entire* exposition of the Tenth Commandment, not just the diagnosis elements—and it does so in two respects. First, μηδεὶς τῇ ἐπιθυμίᾳ τῇ αὐτοῦ χαριζέσθω reformulates with greater precision the vague prohibition οὐκ ἐπιθυμήσεις, offering the reader a final, more

---

²³⁸ §127: καὶ τοῦ τιμωρήσασθαι τοὺς γαστρὸς ἀκράτορας καὶ ἀφηνιαστὰς ὁσιότητος.
²³⁹ §131: οὐ ποιήσει ἕκαστος τὸ ἀρεστὸν ἐνώπιον αὐτοῦ. Deut 12:8 actually reads: οὐ ποιήσετε πάντα, ἃ ἡμεῖς ποιοῦμεν ὧδε σήμερον, ἕκαστος τὸ ἀρεστὸν ἐνώπιον αὐτοῦ. By opening §131 with διό, Philo makes a logical connection with the preceding narrative, which began in §126. So §§126–131 stand together as the final text unit in Philo's exposition—he announces in §132 the completion of his commentary on laws pertaining to the Tenth Commandment, which in turn signals the end of his entire commentary on the Decalogue: "In these remarks we have discussed the matters relating to desire (τῶν εἰς ἐπιθυμίαν ἀναφερομένων) as adequately as our abilities allow, and thus completed our survey of the ten oracles, and the laws which are dependent on them" (translating ἐπιθυμίαν simply as "desire" instead of Colson's "desire or lust").
²⁴⁰ §131: μηδεὶς τῇ ἐπιθυμίᾳ τῇ αὐτοῦ χαριζέσθω.

definitive encapsulation of what the Tenth Commandment actually prohibits. When Philo speaks elsewhere of "indulging" desire, or other emotions, he has in mind an indulgence *at the expense of reason*—in other words, a "giving in" to emotion that signals the *overpowering of reason* and the moral agent's consequent departure from rational motivation. In *Ios.* 153, for example, Philo explains how for the sake of pleasure (desire's aim) the masses disregard virtue (reason's aim) and instead indulge (χαριζόμενοι) their "unbridled desires," yielding to whatever those desires command.[241] So μηδεὶς τῇ ἐπιθυμίᾳ τῇ αὐτοῦ χαριζέσθω calls not for the *elimination* of desire but for its moderation, for a management of ἐπιθυμία that forbids its indulgence *beyond* the measure set by reason. In other words, Philo takes Moses' exhortation in Deuteronomy as a prohibition of *passionate* desire (πλεονάζουσα [ἄμετρος] ἐπιθυμία), just as he takes οὐκ ἐπιθυμήσεις as a prohibition of passionate desire (πλεονάζουσα [ἄμετρος] ἐπιθυμία). So here at the end of his exposition, Philo appropriately offers a compact summary of what he understands the Tenth Commandment to mean in terms of moral psychology. But Philo adds one final thought on what he understands the Tenth Commandment to mean in terms of the overall orientation of the moral agent's life. To indulge *one's own* desire (τῇ ἐπιθυμίᾳ τῇ αὐτοῦ), Philo suggests, amounts to a reprehensible love of self (φιλαυτία).[242] After all, the subjective experience of pleasure—which ἐπιθυμία invariably seeks—involves only one person, the self. So valuing pleasure above all other concerns, as those tyrannized by desire *must* do, truly represents a self-centered life, since the chief aim necessarily involves *only* the self.[243] Captive to self-interest, the φίλαυτος lacks a proper concern not just for other people, but also for God.[244] In fact, love of self and love of God represent for Philo two radically opposed and incompatible modes

---

[241] *Ios.* 153: ὁ φιλήδονος ἄγονός ἐστι τῶν ἀναγκαιοτάτων, σωφροσύνης, αἰδοῦς, ἐγκρατείας, δικαιοσύνης, ἁπάσης ἀρετῆς· οὐδὲν γὰρ οὕτως ἐχθρὸν ἄλλο ἄλλῳ, ὡς ἀρετῇ ἡδονή, δι'ἣν ἀλογοῦσιν οἱ πολλοὺ ὧν μόνον ἄξιον πεφροντικέναι, ταῖς ἀκαθέκτοις ἐπιθυμίαις χαριζόμενοι καὶ οἷς ἂν προστάττωσιν εἴκοντες (cf. *Leg.* 3.84: μὴ τὰ ἡδέα χαριζόμενος [ψυχῇ]; *Spec.* 4.220: μηδὲν ὀργῇ πρὸ λογισμοῦ χαριζομένη).

[242] N.B. Philo's correlation in §131 of μηδεὶς τῇ ἐπιθυμίᾳ τῇ αὐτοῦ χαριζέσθω and φιλαυτίαν παραιτούμενος. On Philo's concept of φιλαυτία, see esp. Frédéric Deutsch, "La philautie chez Philon d'Alexandrie," in *Philon d'Alexandrie et le langage de la philosophie*, 87–97; also Walter Warnach, "Selbstliebe und Gottesliebe im Denken Philons von Alexandrien," in *Wort Gottes in der Zeit: Festschrift Karl Hermann Schelkle* (ed. Helmut Feld and Josef Nolte; Düsseldorf: Patmos, 1973), 198–214; cf. Pearce, *Land of the Body*, 149–51.

[243] In *Post.* 180, Philo pairs φιλαυτία and φιληδονία, suggesting an equivalence.

[244] Cf. Petit, *QG* N° 10 (*Fragments non identifiés*) (cf. Marcus, PLCL suppl. 2, 236), which begins, οἱ ἑαυτῶν μόνον ἕνεκα πάντα πράττοντες φιλαυτίαν, μέγιστον κακόν, ἐπιτηδεύουσιν.

of life.²⁴⁵ And by drawing this contrast here at the end of his exposition, Philo revisits and substantiates his earlier claim that Moses' dietary laws lead to self-control (ἐγκράτεια), philanthropy (φιλανθρωπία), and—most of all—piety (εὐσέβεια).²⁴⁶ By inculcating ἐγκράτεια, the dietary laws promote observance of the Tenth Commandment, which forbids passionate desire. But by training the moral agent to exercise ἐγκράτεια—in other words, not to indulge ἐπιθυμία—those laws also undermine love of self, allowing instead a life of devotion to God.

---

²⁴⁵ E.g., *Spec.* 1.344: ὑπὸ φιλαυτίας ἐκλαθόμενοι τοῦ πρὸς ἀλήθειαν ὄντος θεοῦ; *Praem.* 12: φιλαυτίαν πρὸ εὐσεβείας ἀσπασάμενοι. Allegorically, Philo identifies Abel as the φιλόθεος δόγμα, while Cain represents the φίλαυτος δόγμα (e.g., *Det.* 32). Cf. Harl, "Deux arbres," 379: "[L]'homme est libre d'opter pour l'un ou l'autre mouvement, pour l'amour de lui-même et ce qui est proche de lui, la φιλαυτία, ou au contraire pour l'attitude proprement religieuse de l'εὐσέβεια."
²⁴⁶ §97: διατάγμασι καὶ πρὸς ἐγκράτειαν καὶ πρὸς φιλανθρωπίαν καὶ—τὸ μέγιστον—πρὸς εὐσέβειαν ἀγωγοτάτοις.

CHAPTER FIVE

SUMMARY AND LINES OF FURTHER RESEARCH

Summary

In the course of a larger, systematic exposition of the Decalogue, Philo offers in *Spec.* 4.78b–131 an extended, detailed exposition of the Tenth Commandment, which he reads—despite its clear *biblical* formulation as a prohibition of desire for the goods of a neighbor—as a prohibition of desire *itself* (οὐκ ἐπιθυμήσεις). Capitalizing on the prominence of ἐπιθυμία in contemporary ethical discourse about the "passions" (πάθη), Philo frames his interpretation of the Tenth Commandment along philosophical lines, explaining the prohibition in light of Middle-Platonic theories of how desire operates within and endangers the human soul. Philo couples this theoretical reflection with a consideration of the Mosaic dietary laws, which in his view fall under the rubric of the Tenth Commandment (as *species* under *genus*) and promote its observance by design. This two-part structure—(1) theoretical reflection on a problem (ἐπιθυμία) and (2) practical consideration of a solution (dietary laws)—signals an effort on Philo's part to frame his philosophical exposition of the Tenth Commandment in an appropriately philosophical way: as a "*Seelenheilungsschrift,*" a type of philosophical literature consisting of (1) the *diagnosis* of a moral problem (κρίσις) and (2) a proposal for practical *treatment* (ἄσκησις). Ultimately, then, Philo offers a philosophical essay on the problem of ἐπιθυμία, although he never loses sight of the biblical warrant for his essay, the simple prohibition οὐκ ἐπιθυμήσεις. In fact, the essential points of Philo's essay on ἐπιθυμία emerge as answers to the two fundamental questions raised by this prohibition:

1. In Philo's view, *what* does the Tenth Commandment prohibit? (All desire? A certain type? What type?)

2. In Philo's view, *how* is the Tenth Commandment observed? (What are the mechanics of its observance? What role do the dietary laws play in its observance?)

The first question deals with Philo's concept of ἐπιθυμία, especially its problematic *malfunction*. The second question deals with Philo's concept of ἐγκράτεια, especially the role played by ἄσκησις in its acquisition.

What, then, does the Tenth Commandment prohibit? From a strictly *verbal* standpoint, οὐκ ἐπιθυμήσεις prohibits any instance of ἐπιθυμία. But the term ἐπιθυμία has a fundamental ambiguity in Philo's Middle-Platonic system of thought, due to the ambiguity of the term πάθος, which refers to either an amoral *emotion* or an immoral *passion*. In other words, the abbreviated Tenth Commandment offers an ambiguous moral imperative in need of interpretation. And Philo clearly does interpret it as a prohibition of *passionate desire*, which—by his own definition—means *excessive* desire (πλεονάζουσα ἐπιθυμία), understood as *immoderate* desire (ἄμετρος ἐπιθυμία). So the Tenth Commandment prohibits any instance of the non-rational emotion desire (ἐπιθυμία) overstepping the *limit* (μέτρον) set by reason (λόγος). In practical terms, the moral agent violates the Tenth Commandment whenever desire's reflexive aim of *pleasure* (ἡδονή) becomes the predominate motivation for human action over against rational considerations such as necessity. By indulging passionate desire in this way, the moral agent not only violates the Tenth Commandment but also risks a much greater ill, tyrannical desire (ἔρως), which Philo sees as the final ruinous outcome of allowing desire to usurp reason. From an initial break with reason's hegemony, ἐπιθυμία proceeds to overtake the entire soul, *including the rational faculty*, which tragically sets desire's aim of *pleasure* as the moral agent's ultimate good. Philo makes such a strong presumption of the eventual progression from passionate to tyrannical desire that his theoretical reflection on the ills of ἐπιθυμία, in part one of his exposition (the "diagnosis"), deals really with the ills of ἔρως. In other words, despite his explicit identification of οὐκ ἐπιθυμήσεις as a prohibition of passionate desire (πλεονάζουσα [ἄμετρος] ἐπιθυμία), Philo sees it ultimately as a *preemptive* prohibition of tyrannical desire (ἔρως).

And *how* is the Tenth Commandment observed? Essentially, obedience to the Tenth Commandment requires the exercise of ἐγκράτεια, since regular enforcement of the dictates of λόγος over against ἐπιθυμία (when the two conflict) both precludes the sort of passionate desire prohibited by the injunction οὐκ ἐπιθυμήσεις and eliminates the risk of tyrannical desire. In other words, the Tenth Commandment's *pro*scription of πλεονάζουσα (ἄμετρος) ἐπιθυμία amounts to a *pre*scription of ἐγκράτεια. Moses understood this, so he devised a way of equipping his followers with ἐγκράτεια by formulating a set of dietary laws that engender ἐγκράτεια through *practice* (ἄσκησις). Primarily, the dietary laws promote ἐγκράτεια through specific practical exercises: *either* the temporary restraint of desire *or* the avoidance of especially pleasurable foods. The first type of exercise orchestrates a subjugation of desire that increases the moral agent's capacity for ἐγκράτεια—

just as weight training builds physical strength and so increases a wrestler's capacity to overthrow an opponent in a contest. The second type of exercise obviates the risk of passionate desire by eliminating *incitements* to passionate desire—but more broadly it promotes a lifestyle of ἐγκράτεια by training the moral agent to act from a motive of *necessity* rather than a motive of *pleasure*, which amounts to the rule of reason over desire. Secondarily, the dietary laws—in particular, certain laws regarding clean and unclean animals—*symbolize* broader ideals and principles of ἐγκράτεια, reinforcing and promoting the goal of Moses' practical regimen. Taken as one comprehensive program, the dietary laws represent a course of "treatment" for the problem of passionate desire "diagnosed" in part one of Philo's exposition, even though they ostensibly deal *only* with the desire for food and drink. This apparent limitation actually reveals to Philo the genius of Moses' plan: due to the preeminence of this *one* type of desire among all others, *its* successful management through ἐγκράτεια necessarily—*a maiore ad minus*—entails successful management of any other type of desire.

Lines of Further Research

A detailed study of Philo's exposition of the Tenth Commandment suggests various lines of further research. Citing one for the respective fields of Philonic studies, Hellenistic Judaism, early Christianity, and Middle Platonism illustrates the range of possibilities.

In order to understand the moral psychology presumed in his exposition of οὐκ ἐπιθυμήσεις, Philo's conception of the soul as a bipartition between rational and non-rational parts received considerable attention. The significance of this basic, bipartite model lies in its ability to accommodate every other model of the soul Philo cites. In other words, Philo does *not* endorse different—even contradictory—models of the soul according to exegetical necessity. He instead endorses *one* model of the soul, which he then cites ad hoc in various equivalent formulations.[1] The idea of Philo's having just *one coherent, overarching model of the soul* should be further tested and either confirmed or discarded. Settling the issue in favor of one model would provide a helpful framework for further research.

Philo's exposition relates also to Hellenistic Judaism broadly, especially the issue of Alexandrian *exegetical traditions*. Philo undoubtedly reworks a

---

[1] Cf. Dillon, *Middle Platonists*, 174–75, on Philo's reference to different soul divisions: "This is not chaotic eclecticism ...; for Philo each of these divisions expresses some aspect of the truth, but the most basic truth remains the division into rational and irrational."

prominent traditional interpretation of clean and unclean winged creatures from the *Letter of Aristeas* to suit his own exegetical agenda. With respect to the animal traits of carnivorous (vs. herbivorous) and wild (vs. tame), Philo turns an originally *symbolic* interpretation promoting *justice* (δικαιοσύνη) into a *literal* interpretation promoting *self-control* (ἐγκράτεια). In general, this reveals something about the communal aspect of biblical exegesis in Alexandria, but it specifically reveals a nexus of text, interpretation, and cultural (especially *philosophical*) milieu worth investigating further.[2] The *Letter of Aristeas* found significance in otherwise obscure dietary laws by correlating its interpretation with current trends in contemporary philosophy, namely Pythagorean philosophy and its symbolic interpretation of dietary laws.[3] Philo correlated his interpretation with *what he knew as* current trends in contemporary philosophy, namely Middle-Platonic philosophy. Both reflect an apologetic aspect of the relation between exegesis and cultural milieu, as they attempt to demonstrate the parity of Mosaic legislation with the highest cultural achievements of their Gentile contemporaries.[4]

In terms of early Christianity, Philo's exposition of the Tenth Commandment relates most directly to the letters of Paul, especially to issues raised in Galatians and Romans about the role and purpose of Mosaic law. Paul's proclamation of Christ involves at some level a marginalization, if not repudiation, of "works of the Law" (e.g., ἔργα νόμου in Gal 2:16), and this effort on Paul's part implies the existence of an opposing viewpoint in which "works of the Law" figure prominently. So properly understanding Paul requires a historically plausible reconstruction of a role for "works of the Law" that accounts for their valorization within first-century Judaism. James Dunn's "new perspective on Paul" correctly rejects anachronistic and theologically loaded notions of ἔργα νόμου, such as "works which *earn*

---

[2] Thomas Tobin investigated this nexus in *The Creation of Man*—i.e., studying different levels of interpretation "involves the analysis of the thought patterns used in the interpretations, and the relationship of those thought patterns to the biblical text and to the philosophical milieu of Alexandria during that period" (9). Philo's interaction with an earlier level of interpretation in the case of *dietary laws* represents precisely the sort of interaction Tobin identifies in the case of the *story of man's creation*. For a detailed consideration of Philo's reworking of the *Letter of Aristeas* as a case study, in light of Tobin's research, see Svebakken, "Exegetical Traditions."
[3] See Berthelot, "Interprétation symbolique."
[4] On the valorization of ἐγκράτεια among Philo's contemporaries as a context for his own emphasis on ἐγκράτεια in regard to the Tenth Commandment (and dietary laws), see Stowers, *Rereading of Romans*, 46–56 [="The Significance of Self-Mastery in Greco-Roman Culture"]; also Niehoff, *Philo on Jewish Identity and Culture*, 75–110 [="Jewish Values: Religion and Self-Restraint"]; cf. Anthony Long, "Philosophical Power."

God's favour, as merit-amassing observances," arguing instead for the notion of cultural "badges" that "mark out the Jews as God's people."[5] The food laws, for example, as "works of the Law," establish an ethnic *identity*—and Paul ultimately disputes the foisting of this *identity* on Gentiles as an addendum to their faith in Christ.[6] Without undermining Dunn's assessment, Philo's view of the food laws nevertheless calls for the consideration of another possibility. Clearly for *some* Jews of the first century, "works of the Law" functioned as *a means to virtue*, in particular the virtue of ἐγκράτεια.[7] Further research into first-century perspectives on the Law *that Paul opposed* should take into account the possibility of ἔργα νόμου representing the sort of exercises Philo describes in his exposition.[8]

Finally, Philo's exposition of the Tenth Commandment brings to light not just a Middle-Platonic *concept* of "passion," but a distinctly Middle-Platonic *definition* of "passion": ἄμετρος καὶ πλεονάζουσα ὁρμή (*Spec.* 4.79). This deliberate revision of the Stoic definition uses ἄμετρος to reinterpret πλεονάζουσα in light of a radically different moral psychology, suggesting not a superficial *eclecticism* within Middle Platonism but a thoughtful effort to appropriate *terminology* without compromising *principles*. Furthermore, Philo provides extensive evidence not only for the definition πλεονάζουσα (ἄμετρος) ὁρμή but also for its consistent *application* in matters of moral psychology in first-century Alexandrian Middle Platonism—for example, in connection with the *Phaedrus* chariot figure. Philo's consistent use of a working Middle-Platonic definition of passion holds significance for further research into the historical development of ethical theory within Middle Platonism.

---

[5] James D. G. Dunn, "The New Perspective on Paul," in *The New Perspective on Paul* (rev. ed.; Grand Rapids: Eerdmans, 2008), 99–120, 111.

[6] On the food laws as identity markers, see Dunn, "New Perspective," 109–10 (cf. 108: "[B]y 'works of the law' Paul intended his readers to think of *particular observances of the law like circumcision and the food laws*" [original emphasis]).

[7] Stowers makes this point in *Romans*, esp. 58–65 [="Judaism as a School for Self-Mastery] (cf. idem, "Paul and Self-Mastery," 531–34). The scope of Stowers work, however, does not allow him to consider in depth either the moral psychology of Philo or precisely *how* the observance of Mosaic law leads to ἐγκράτεια.

[8] Cf. Stowers, *Romans*, 66–74 [="Audience, Opponents, and Self-Mastery in Paul"]; e.g., 67: "Paul's attack on these opponents who taught judaizing practices to gentiles suggests that their appeal may have centered on claims that gentiles could learn self-mastery by association with the Jewish community and by adopting certain practices that were described as methods of self-mastery."

BIBLIOGRAPHY

Primary Sources

Alcinoos, *Enseignement des doctrines de Platon*. Edited by John Whittaker. Translated by Pierre Louis. 2d ed. Paris: Belles Lettres, 2002.
Alcinous: The Handbook of Platonism. Translated with introduction and commentary by John M. Dillon. Oxford: Clarendon, 1993.
Die Apokalypse des Mose: Text, Übersetzung, Kommentar. Edited with translation and commentary by Jan Dochhorn. Texte und Studien zum antiken Judentum 106. Tübingen: Mohr Siebeck, 2005.
Aristeas to Philocrates: Letter of Aristeas. Edited and translated by Moses Hadas. New York: Harper, 1951. Repr., Eugene, Oreg.: Wipf & Stock, 2007.
Aristotle, *Nicomachean Ethics*. Translated by H. Rackham. Rev. ed. Loeb Classical Library. Cambridge: Harvard University Press, 1934.
———. *On the Soul*. Translated by W. S. Hett. Loeb Classical Library. Cambridge: Harvard University Press, 1936.
———. *Art of Rhetoric*. Translated by J. H. Freese. Loeb Classical Library. Cambridge: Harvard University Press, 1926.
Arius Didymus, *Epitome of Stoic Ethics*. Edited and translated by Arthur J. Pomeroy. Texts and Translations 44. Greco-Roman Series 14. Atlanta, Ga.: Society of Biblical Literature, 1999.
Diogenes Laertius, *Lives of Eminent Philosophers*. Translated by R. D. Hicks. 2 vols. Loeb Classical Library. Cambridge: Harvard University Press, 1925.
Eudorus (fragments). In "Raccolta e interpretazione delle testimonianze e dei frammenti del medioplatonico Eudoro di Alessandria: Parte prima: Testo e traduzione delle testimonianze e dei frammenti sicuri." By Claudio Mazzarelli. *Rivista di Filosofia Neo-Scolastica* 77 (1985): 197–209.
Filone di Alessandria, De Decalogo. Edited and translated by Francesca Calabi. Philosophica 24. Pisa: Edizioni ETS, 2005.
Galen, *On the Doctrines of Hippocrates and Plato*. Edited and translated by Phillip De Lacy. 3 vols. 2d ed. Corpus Medicorum Graecorum 5.4.1.2. Berlin: Akademie-Verlag, 1980–84.
Homer, *Odyssey*. Translated by A. T. Murray. Revised by George E. Dimock. 2 vols. Loeb Classical Library. Cambridge: Harvard University Press, 1919.

Long, Anthony A., and David N. Sedley. *The Hellenistic Philosophers*. 2 vols. Cambridge: Cambridge University Press, 1987.
Musonius Rufus, *On Training*. In Cora E. Lutz, *Musonius Rufus: The Roman Socrates*. Yale Classical Studies 10. New Haven: Yale University Press, 1947.
Philo. Translated by F. H. Colson et al. 12 vols. Loeb Classical Library. Cambridge: Harvard University Press, 1929–1962.
Philon D'Alexandrie: Quæstiones: Fragmenta Græca. Edited and translated by Françoise Petit. Les œvres de Philon d'Alexandrie 33. Paris: Cerf, 1978.
Philonis Alexandrini opera quae supersunt. Edited by L. Cohn, P. Wendland, S. Reiter. 6 vols. Berlin: de Gruyter, 1896–1915.
Plato. Translated by Harold North Fowler et al. 12 vols. Loeb Classical Library. Cambridge: Harvard University Press, 1914–1927.
Plutarch, *Moralia*. Translated by F. C. Babbitt et al. 16 vols. Loeb Classical Library. Cambridge: Harvard University Press, 1927–1976.
Pseudopythagorica Ethica: I trattati morali di Archita, Metopo, Teage, Eurifamo. Edited and translated by Bruno Centrone. Elenchos 17. Naples: Bibliopolis, 1990.
Stobaeus, Ioannes. *Anthologii libri duo priores*. 2 vols. Edited by Curt Wachsmuth. Berlin: Weidmann, 1884.
Stoicorum veterum fragmenta. Edited by H. von Arnim. 4 vols. Leipzig: Teubner, 1903–1924.
Timaios of Locri, *On the Nature of the World and the Soul*. Edited and translated by Thomas H. Tobin. Texts and Translations 26. Greco-Roman Religion Series 8. Chico, Calif.: Scholars Press, 1985.

Secondary Sources

Amir, Yehoshua. "Philon und die jüdische Wirklichkeit seiner Zeit." Pages 3–51 in *Die hellenistische Gestalt des Judentums bei Philon von Alexandrien*. Forschungen zum jüdisch-christlichen Dialog 5. Neukirchen-Vluyn: Neukirchener Verlag, 1983.
———. "The Decalogue According to Philo." Pages 121–160 in *The Ten Commandments in History and Tradition*. Edited by Ben-Zion Segal and Gershon Levi. Jerusalem: Magnes Press, 1990.
Annas, Julia. *Hellenistic Philosophy of Mind*. Hellenistic Culture and Society 8. Berkeley: University of California Press, 1992.
———. *Platonic Ethics, Old and New*. Ithaca: Cornell University Press, 1999.
Ash, Rhiannon. "Severed Heads: Individual Portraits and Irrational Forces in Plutarch's *Galba* and *Otho*." Pages 189–214 in *Plutarch and his Intellec-*

tual World: Essays on Plutarch. Edited by Judith Mossman. London: Duckworth, 1997.

Aune, David C. "Mastery of the Passions: Philo, 4 Maccabees and Earliest Christianity." Pages 125–158 in *Hellenization Revisited: Shaping a Christian Response within the Greco-Roman World.* Edited by Wendy E. Helleman. Lanham, Md.: University Press of America, 1994.

Baltes, Matthias. *Timaios Lokros,* Über die Natur des Kosmos und der Seele. Philosophia Antiqua 21. Leiden: Brill, 1972.

Barclay, John M. G. *Jews in the Mediterranean Diaspora: From Alexander to Trajan (323 BCE–117 CE).* Edinburgh: T&T Clark, 1996.

Baudry, Gérard-Henry. "Le péché original chez Philon d'Alexandrie." *Mélanges de science religieuse* 50 (1993): 99–115.

Beardslee, William A. "De Garrulitate (Moralia 502B–515A)." Pages 264–88 in *Plutarch's Ethical Writings and Early Christian Literature.* Edited by Hans Dieter Betz. Studia ad corpus hellenisticum Novi Testamenti 4. Leiden: Brill, 1978.

Becchi, Francesco. "Platonismo medio ed etica Plutarchea." *Prometheus* 7 (1981): 125–145, 263–284.

———. "Plutarco tra Platonismo e Aristotelismo: La Filosofia come ΠΑΙΔΕΙΑ dell'Anima." Pages 25–43 in *Plutarco, Platón y Aristóteles: Actas del V Congreso Internacional de la I.P.S.: Madrid-Cuenca, 4–7 de mayo de 1999.* Edited by Aurelio Peréz Jiménez, José García López, and Rosa M Aguilar. Madrid: Ediciones Clásicas, 1999.

Bentwich, Norman. *Philo-Judaeus of Alexandria.* Philadelphia: Jewish Publication Society of America, 1910.

Berger, Klaus. *Die Gesetzesauslegung Jesu: Ihr historischer Hintergrund im Judentum und im Alten Testament: Teil I: Markus und Parallelen.* Wissenschaftliche Monographien zum Alten und Neuen Testament 40.1. Neukirchen-Vluyn: Neukirchener, 1972.

Berthelot, Katell. "L'interprétation symbolique des lois alimentaires dans la *Lettre d'Aristée:* Une influence pythagoricienne." *Journal of Jewish Studies* 52 (2001): 253–268.

Billings, Thomas H. *The Platonism of Philo Judaeus.* Chicago: University of Chicago Press, 1919. Repr., New York: Garland, 1979.

Birnbaum, Ellen. "Allegorical Interpretation and Jewish Identity among Alexandrian Jewish Writers." Pages 307–29 in *Neotestamentica et Philonica: Studies in Honor of Peder Borgen.* Edited by David E. Aune, Torrey Seland, and Jarl Henning Ulrichsen. Supplements to Novum Testamentum 106. Leiden: Brill, 2003.

———. "Exegetical Building Blocks in Philo's Interpretation of the Patriarchs." Pages 69–92 in *From Judaism to Christianity: Tradition and Transition: A* Festschrift *for Thomas H. Tobin, S.J., on the Occasion of His Sixty-fifth Birthday.* Edited by Patricia Walters. Supplements to Novum Testamentum 136. Leiden: Brill, 2010.

Bonazzi, Mauro. "Eudoro di Alessandria alle origini del platonismo imperiale." Pages 117–160 in *L'eridità platonica: Studi sul platonismo da Arcesilao a Proclo.* Edited by Mauro Bonazzi and Vincenza Celluprica. Elenchos 45. Naples: Bibliopolis, 2005.

———. "Eudorus of Alexandria and Early Imperial Platonism." Pages 365–77 in *Greek and Roman Philosophy 100 BC–200 AD.* Edited by Richard Sorabji and Robert W. Sharples. 2 vols. Bulletin of the Institute of Classical Studies, Supplement 94. London: Institute of Classical Studies, 2007.

———. "Eudorus' Psychology and Stoic Ethics." Pages 109–132 in *Platonic Stoicism–Stoic Platonism: The Dialogue between Platonism and Stoicism in Antiquity.* Edited by Mauro Bonazzi and Christoph Helmig. Ancient and Medieval Philosophy 39. Leuven: Leuven University Press, 2007.

———. "Towards Transcendence: Philo and the Renewal of Platonism in the Early Imperial Age." Pages 233–251 in *Philo of Alexandria and Post-Aristotelian Philosophy.* Edited by Francesca Alesse. Studies in Philo of Alexandria 5. Leiden: Brill, 2008.

———. "Antiochus' Ethics and the Subordination of Stoicism." Pages 33–54 in *The Origins of the Platonic System: Platonisms of the Early Empire and their Philosophical Contexts.* Edited by Mauro Bonazzi and Jan Opsomer. Collection d'études classiques 23. Leuven: Peeters, 2009.

Booth, Peter A. "The Voice of the Serpent: Philo's Epicureanism." Pages 159–172 in *Hellenization Revisited: Shaping a Christian Response within the Greco-Roman World.* Edited by Wendy E. Helleman. Lanham, Md.: University Press of America, 1994.

Borgen, Peder. "Philo of Alexandria." Pages 233–82 in *Jewish Writings of the Second Temple Period: Apocrypha, Pseudepigrapha, Qumran Sectarian Writings, Philo, Josephus.* Edited by Michael E. Stone. Vol. 2 of *The Literature of the Jewish People in the Period of the Second Temple and the Talmud.* Compendia Rerum Iudaicarum ad Novum Testamentum 2. Assen: Van Gorcum, 1984.

———. "Philo of Alexandria." Pages 333–42 in vol. 5 of *The Anchor Bible Dictionary.* Edited by David Noel Freedman. 6 vols. New York: Doubleday, 1992.

———. "Heavenly Ascent in Philo: An Examination of Selected Passages." Pages 246–68 in *The Pseudepigrapha and Early Biblical Interpretation*. Edited by James H. Charlesworth and Craig A. Evans. Journal for the Study of the Pseudepigrapha: Supplement Series 14. Studies in Scripture in Early Judaism and Christianity 2. Sheffield: Journal for the Study of the Old Testament Press, 1993.

———. "Philo of Alexandria—A Systematic Philosopher or an Eclectic Editor?" *Symbolae Osloenses* 71 (1996): 115–34.

———. *Philo of Alexandria: An Exegete for His Time*. Leiden: Brill, 1997.

Borgen, Peder, Kare Fuglseth, and Roald Skarsten. *The Philo Index: A Complete Greek Word Index to the Writings of Philo of Alexandria*. Grand Rapids: Eerdmans, 1999.

Bouffartigue, Jean. "La structure de l'âme chez Philon : Terminologie scolastique et métaphores." Pages 59–75 in *Philon d'Alexandrie et le langage de la philosophie. Actes du colloque international organisé par le Centre d'études sur la philosophie hellénistique et romaine de l'Université de Paris XII–Val de Marne, Créteil, Fontenay, Paris, 26–28 octobre 1995*. Edited by Carlos Lévy. Turnhout: Brepolis, 1998.

Boulogne, Jacques. "L'intempérence verbale: L'imaginaire de Plutarche dans la thérapie des maladies de l'âme." Pages 161–169 in *Les passions antiques et médiévales*. Edited by Bernard Besnier, Pierre-François Moreau, and Laurence Renault. Paris: Presses universitaires de France, 2003.

Bradshaw, David. "The Vision of God in Philo of Alexandria." *American Catholic Philosophical Quarterly* 72 (1998): 483–500.

Brändl, Martin. *Der Agon bei Paulus: Herkunft und Profil paulinischer Agonmetaphorik*. Wissenschaftliche Untersuchungen zum Neuen Testament 222, 2d series. Tübingen: Mohr Siebeck, 2006.

Bréhier, Emile. *Les idées philosophiques et religieuses de Philon d'Alexandrie*. Études de philosophie médiévale 8. 3d edition. Paris: J. Vrin, 1950.

Brenk, Frederick E. "Darkly Beyond the Glass: Middle Platonism and the Vison of the Soul." Pages 39–60 in *Platonism in Late Antiquity*. Edited by Stephen Gersh and Charles Kannengiesser. Christianity and Judaism in Antiquity 8. Notre Dame, Ind.: University of Notre Dame Press, 1992.

Brennan, Tad. "Stoic Moral Psychology." Pages 257–94 in *The Cambridge Companion to the Stoics*. Edited by Brad Inwood. Cambridge: Cambridge University Press, 2003.

Calabi, Francesca. "Il serpente e il cavaliere: Piacere e 'sophrosyne' in Filone di Alessandria." *Annali di scienze religiose* 8 (2003): 199–215.

Classen, Carl Joachim. "Der platonisch-stoische Kanon der Kardinaltugenden bei Philo, Clemens Alexandrinus und Origenes." Pages 68–88 in *Kerygma und Logos: Beiträge zu den geistesgeschichtlichen Beziehungen zwischen Antike und Christentum. Festschrift für Carl Andresen zum 70. Geburtstag.* Edited by Adolf Martin Ritter. Göttingen: Vandenhoeck & Ruprecht, 1979.

Clifford, Hywel. "Moses as Philosopher-Sage in Philo." Pages 151–67 in *Moses in Biblical and Extra-Biblical Traditions.* Edited by Axel Graupner and Michael Wolter. Beihefte zur Zeitschrift für die alttestamentliche Wissenschaft 372. Berlin: de Gruyter, 2007.

Cohen, Naomi. *Philo Judaeus: His Universe of Discourse.* Beiträge zur Erforschung des Alten Testaments und des antiken Judentum 24. Frankfurt am Main: Peter Lang, 1995.

Cohn, Leopold. "Einteilung und Chronologie der Schriften Philos." *Philologus: Supplementband* 7 (1899): 387–436.

Cooper, John M. "Plato's Theory of Human Motivation." Pages 118–37 in *Reason and Emotion: Essays on Ancient Moral Psychology and Ethical Theory.* Princeton: Princeton University Press, 1999. Repr. from *History of Philosophy Quarterly* 1 (1984): 3–21.

———. "Pleasure and Desire in Epicurus." Pages 485–514 in *Reason and Emotion: Essays on Ancient Moral Psychology and Ethical Theory.* Princeton: Princeton University Press, 1999.

———. "Posidonius on Emotions." Pages 449–84 in *Reason and Emotion: Essays on Ancient Moral Psychology and Ethical Theory.* Princeton: Princeton University Press, 1999. Repr. from pages 71–111 in *The Emotions in Hellenistic Philosophy.* Edited by Juha Sihvola and Troels Engberg-Pedersen. New Synthese Historical Library 46. Dordrecht: Kluwer Academic Publishers, 1998.

———. "Reason, Moral Virtue, and Moral Value." Pages 253–80 in *Reason and Emotion: Essays on Ancient Moral Psychology and Ethical Theory.* Princeton: Princeton University Press, 1999. Repr. from pages 81–114 in *Rationality in Greek Thought.* Edited by M. Frede and G. Striker. Oxford: Clarendon, 1996.

———. "Some Remarks on Aristotle's Moral Psychology." Pages 237–52 in *Reason and Emotion: Essays on Ancient Moral Psychology and Ethical Theory.* Princeton: Princeton University Press, 1999. Repr. from *Southern Journal of Philosophy* 27 Supplement (1988): 25–42.

Courcelle, Pierre. "Tradition platonicienne et traditions chrétiennes du corps-prison (*Phédon* 62 b; *Cratyle* 400 c)." *Revue des études latines* 43 (1965): 406–443.

Daniélou, Jean. *Philon D'Alexandrie.* Paris: A. Fayard, 1958.
Daubercies, Pierre. "La vertu chez Philon d'Alexandrie." *Revue théologique de Louvain* 26 (1995): 185–210.
Decharneux, Baudouin. "Interdits sexuels dans l'œuvre de Philon d'Alexandrie dit 'Le Juif.'" Pages 17–31 in *Religion et tabou sexuel.* Edited by Jacques Marx. *Problèmes d'histoire des religions* 1. Bruxelles: Editions de l'Université de Bruxelles, 1990.
Dent, N. J. H. "Varieties of Desire." *Proceedings of the Aristotelian Society Supplementary Volume* 50 (1976): 153–75.
Deutsch, Frédéric. "La philautie chez Philon d'Alexandrie." Pages 87–97 in *Philon d'Alexandrie et le langage de la philosophie. Actes du colloque international organisé par le Centre d'études sur la philosophie hellénistique et romaine de l'Université de Paris XII–Val de Marne, Créteil Fontenay, Paris, 26–28 octobre 1995.* Edited by Carlos Lévy. Turnhout: Brepolis, 1998.
Dierauer, Urs. *Tier und Mensch im Denken der Antike: Studien zur Tierpsychologie, Anthropologie und Ethik.* Studien zur antiken Philosophie 6. Amsterdam: Grüner, 1977.
Dillon, John M. Preface to *Philo of Alexandria:* The Contemplative Life, The Giants, and Selections. Translated with an introduction by David Winston. Classics of Western Spirituality. Mahwah, N.J.: Paulist, 1981.
——. "'Metriopatheia and Apatheia': Some Reflections on a Controversy in Later Greek Ethics." Pages 508–17 in *Essays in Ancient Greek Philosophy II.* Edited by John Anton and Anthony Preus. Albany: SUNY Press, 1983. Repr. *The Golden Chain: Studies in the Development of Platonism and Christianity.* Collected Studies 333. Aldershot, Hampshire; Brookfield, Vt.: Variorum, 1990.
——. "Plotinus, Philo and Origen on the Grades of Virtue." Pages 92–105 in *Platonismus und Christentum: Festschrift für Heinrich Dörrie.* Edited by Horst-Dieter Blume and Friedhelm Mann. Jahrbuch für Antike und Christentum, Ergänzungsband 10. Münster: Aschendorff, 1983.
——. *The Middle Platonists.* Rev. ed. Ithaca: Cornell University Press, 1996.
——. "Philo of Alexandria and Platonist Psychology." Pages 163–169 in *Philon d'Alexandrie.* Edited by Jean-François Pradeau. Études platoniciennes 7. Paris: Belles Lettres, 2010.
Dillon, John, and Abraham Terian. "Philo and the Stoic Doctrine of ΕΥΠΑΘΕΙΑΙ: A Note on *Quaes Gen* 2.57." *Studia Philonica* 4 (1976–77): 17–24.
Dillon, John, and Anthony Long, eds. *The Question of "Eclecticism": Studies in Later Greek Philosophy.* Hellenistic Culture and Society 3. Berkeley: University of California Press, 1988.

Dochhorn, Jan. "Röm 7,7 und das zehnte Gebot: Ein Beitrag zur Schriftauslegung und zur jüdischen Vorgeschichte des Paulus." *Zeitschrift für die neutestamentliche Wissenschaft und die Kunde der älteren Kirche* 100 (2009): 59–77.

Dogniez, Cécile and Marguerite Harl, eds. *Le Pentateuque d'Alexandrie: Text grec et traduction*. Paris: Cerf, 2001.

Dorion, Louis-André. "*Akrasia* et *enkrateia* dans les *Mémorables* de Xénophon." *Dialogue* 42 (2003): 645–72.

Dörrie, Heinrich. "Der Platoniker Eudorus von Alexandreia." *Hermes* 79 (1944): 25–38. Repr., pages 297–309 in *Platonica Minora*. Studia et Testimonia Antiqua 8. München: W. Fink, 1976.

Dressler, Hermigild. *The Usage of Ἀσκέω and Its Cognates in Greek Documents to 100 A.D.* Catholic University of America Patristic Studies 78. Washington: Catholic University of America Press, 1947.

Duff, Tim. *Plutarch's Lives: Exploring Virtue and Vice*. Oxford: Clarendon, 1999.

Dunn, James D. G. "The New Perspective on Paul." Pages 99–120 in *The New Perspective on Paul*. Rev. ed. Grand Rapids: Eerdmans, 2008.

Elsky, Martin, trans. "Erich Auerbach, '*Passio* as Passion' ['*Passio* als Leidenshaft']" *Criticism* 43 (2001): 288–308.

Feldman, Louis H. "Philo's Views on Music." *Journal of Jewish Music and Liturgy* 9 (1986): 36–54.

Feldmeier, Reinhard. "Weise hinter 'eisernen Mauern': Tora und jüdisches Selbstverständnis zwischen Akkulturation und Absonderung im Aristeasbrief." Pages 20–37 in *Die Septuaginta zwischen Judentum und Christentum*. Edited by Martin Hengel and Anna Maria Schwemer. Wissenschaftliche Untersuchungen zum Neuen Testament 72. Tübingen: Mohr, 1994.

Février, James G. *La date, la composition et les sources de la Lettre d'Aristée à Philocrate*. Bibliotheque de l'Ecole des Hautes Etudes 242. Paris: Édouard Champion, 1925.

Fitzgerald, John T. "The Passions and Moral Progress: An Introduction." Pages 1–25 in *Passions and Moral Progress in Greco-Roman Thought*. Edited by John T. Fitzgerald. Routledge Monographs in Classical Studies. New York: Routledge, 2008.

Fitzmyer, Joseph A. *Romans: A New Translation with Introduction and Commentary*. Anchor Bible 33. New York: Doubleday, 1993.

Fox, Kenneth Allan. "Paul's Attitude toward the Body in Romans 6–8: Compared with Philo of Alexandria." Ph.D. diss., University of St. Michael's College, 2001.

Fraade, Steven. "Ascetical Aspects of Ancient Judaism." Pages 253–88 in *Jewish Spirituality: From the Bible through the Middles Ages*. Edited by Arthur Green. World Spirituality: An Encyclopedic History of the Religious Quest 13. New York: Crossroad, 1986.

Frede, Michael. "The Stoic Doctrine of the Affections of the Soul." Pages 93–110 in *The Norms of Nature: Studies in Hellenistic Ethics*. Edited by Malcolm Schofield and Gisela Striker. Cambridge: Cambridge University Press, 1986.

Fuhrmann, François. *Les images de Plutarque*. Paris: Klincksieck, 1964.

Gaca, Kathy L. "Philo's Principles of Sexual Conduct and Their Influence on Christian Platonist Sexual Principles." *Studia Philonica Annual* 8 (1996): 21–39.

———. *The Making of Fornication: Eros, Ethics, and Political Reform in Greek Philosophy and Early Christianity*. Hellenistic Culture and Society 40. Berkeley: University of California Press, 2003.

Geljon, A. C., and David Runia. "An *Index Locorum* to Billings." *Studia Philonica Annual* 7 (1995): 169–85.

Gemünden, Petra von. "La culture des passions à l'époque du Nouveau Testament: Une contribution théologique et psychologique." *Études théologiques et religieuses* 70 (1995): 335–48.

———. "La femme passionnelle et l'homme rationnel? Un chapitre de psychologie historique." *Biblica* 78 (1997): 457–80.

———. "La figure de Jacob à l'époque hellénistico-romaine: L'example de Philon d'Alexandrie." Pages 358–70 in *Jacob: Commentaire à plusieurs voix de Gen 25–36: Mélanges offerts à Albert de Pury*. Edited by Jean-Daniel Macchi and Thomas Römer. Le Monde de la Bible 44. Genève: Labor et Fides, 2001.

———. "Der Affekt der ἐπιθυμία und der νόμος: Affektkontrolle und soziale Identitätsbildung im 4. Makkabäerbuch mit einem Ausblick auf den Römerbrief." Pages 55–74 in *Das Gesetz im frühen Judentum und im Neuen Testament: Festschrift für Christoph Burchard zum 75. Geburtstag*. Edited by Dieter Sänger and Matthias Konradt. Novum Testamentum et Orbis Antiquus / Studien zur Umwelt des Neuen Testaments 57. Göttingen: Vandenhoeck & Ruprecht; Fribourg: Academic Press, 2006.

Geytenbeek, Anton Cornelis van. *Musonius Rufus and Greek Diatribe*. Translated by B. L. Hijmans. Rev. ed. Wijsgerige Teksten en Studies 8. Assen: Van Gorcum, 1963.

Gill, Christopher. *The Structured Self in Hellenistic and Roman Thought*. Oxford: Oxford University Press, 2006.

Glucker, John. *Antiochus and the Late Academy.* Hypomnemata 56. Göttingen: Vandenhoeck & Ruprecht, 1978.

Goodenough, Erwin R. *The Jurisprudence of the Jewish Courts in Egypt.* New Haven: Yale University Press, 1929.

———. "Philo's Exposition of the Law and His *De Vita Mosis.*" *Harvard Theological Review* 26 (1933): 109–125.

Goulet-Cazé, Marie-Odile. *L'ascèse cynique: Un commentaire de Diogène Laërce VI 70–71.* 2d ed. Paris: J. Vrin, 2001.

Grabbe, Lester L. *Etymology in Early Jewish Interpretation: The Hebrew Names in Philo.* Brown Judaic Studies 115. Atlanta: Scholars Press, 1988.

Grant, Robert M. "Dietary Laws among Pythagoreans, Jews, and Christians." *Harvard Theological Review* 73 (1980): 299–310.

Graver, Margaret. "Philo of Alexandria and the Origins of the Stoic ΠΡΟΠΑΘΕΙΑΙ." Pages 197–221 in *Philo of Alexandria and Post-Aristotelian Philosophy.* Edited by Francesca Alesse. Studies in Philo of Alexandria 5. Leiden: Brill, 2008. Repr. from *Phronesis* 44 (1999): 300–325.

Groß, Josef. *Philons von Alexandreia Anschauungen über die Natur des Menschen.* Inaugural Dissertation, University of Tübingen, 1930.

Hackforth, R. *Plato's Examination of Pleasure.* Cambridge: Cambridge University Press, 1945.

Hadas-Lebel, Mireille. *Philon d'Alexandrie: Un penseur en diaspora.* Paris: Fayard, 2003.

Hadot, Pierre. "La philosophie antique: Une éthique ou une pratique?" Pages 7–37 in *Problèmes de la morale antique.* Edited by Paul Demont. Amiens: Université de Picardie-Jules Verne, 1993.

———. "Spiritual Exercises." Pages 81–125 in *Philosophy as a Way of Life: Spiritual Exercises from Socrates to Foucault.* Edited with introduction by Arnold Davidson. Translated by Michael Chase. Oxford: Blackwell, 1995.

Hahm, David E. "The Ethical Doxography of Arius Didymus." *Aufstieg und Niedergang der römischen Welt* 36.4:2935–3055, 3234–3243 [indices]. Part 2, *Principat*, 36.4. Edited by H. Temporini and W. Haase. New York: de Gruyter, 1990.

Halperin, David M. "Platonic *Erôs* and What Men Call Love." *Ancient Philosophy* 5 (1985): 161–204.

———. "Plato and the Metaphysics of Desire." *Proceedings of the Boston Area Colloquium in Ancient Philosophy* 5 (1989): 27–52.

Harl, Marguerite. "Adam et les deux arbres du paradis (Gen. II–III) ou l'homme milieu entre deux termes (μέσος-μεθόριος) chez Philon d'Alexandrie." *Recherches de science religieuse* 50 (1962): 321–388.

Harris, Harold A. "The Foot-Rests in Hippolytus' Chariot." *Classical Review* 18 (1968): 259–260.
——. *Greek Athletics and the Jews.* Trivium: Special Publications 3. Cardiff: University of Wales Press, 1976.
Harris, William V. *Restraining Rage: The Ideology of Anger Control in Classical Antiquity.* Cambridge: Harvard University Press, 2001.
Hayward, C. T. R. "Philo, the Septuagint of Genesis 32:24–32 and the Name 'Israel': Fighting the Passions, Inspiration and the Vision of God." *Journal of Jewish Studies* 51 (2000): 209–26.
Hecht, Richard D. "Preliminary Issues in the Analysis of Philo's *De Specialibus Legibus.*" *Studia Philonica* 5 (1978): 1–56.
——. "Patterns of Exegesis in Philo's Interpretation of Leviticus." *Studia Philonica* 6 (1979–80): 77–155.
Heckel, Theo K. *Der innere Mensch: Die paulinische Verarbeitung eines platonischen Motivs.* Wissenschaftliche Untersuchungen zum Neuen Testament 53, 2d series. Tübingen: J. C. B. Mohr, 1993.
Heil, Christoph. *Die Ablehnung der Speisegebote durch Paulus: Zur Frage nach der Stellung des Apostels zum Gesetz.* Bonner biblische Beiträge 96. Weinheim: Beltz Athenäum, 1994.
Heinemann, Isaak. *Philons griechische und jüdische Bildung: Kulturvergleichende Untersuchungen zu Philons Darstellung der jüdischen Gesetze.* Breslau: Marcus, 1932. Repr., Darmstadt: Wissenschaftliche Buchgesellschaft, 1962.
Hijmans, B. L. *ἌΣΚΗΣΙΣ: Notes on Epictetus' Educational System.* Wijsgerige Teksten en Studies 2. Assen: Von Gorcum, 1959.
Himbaza, Innocent. *Le Décalogue et l'histoire du texte: Etudes des formes textuelles du Décalogue et leurs implications dans l'histoire du texte de l'Ancien Testament.* Orbis biblicus et orientalis 207. Fribourg: Academic Press, 2004.
Horst, P. W. van der. "Philo and the Problem of God's Emotions." Pages 171–178 in *Philon d'Alexandrie.* Edited by Jean-François Pradeau. Études platoniciennes 7. Paris: Belles Lettres, 2010.
Houston, Walter J. "Towards an Integrated Reading of the Dietary Laws of Leviticus." Pages 142–61 in *The Book of Leviticus: Composition and Reception.* Edited by Rolf Rendtorff and Robert A. Kugler. Supplements to Vetus Testamentum 93: Formation and Interpretation of Old Testament Literature 3. Leiden: Brill, 2003.
Ingenkamp, Heinz Gerd. *Plutarchs Schriften über die Heilung der Seele.* Hypomnemata: Untersuchungen zur Antike und zu ihrem Nachleben 34. Göttingen: Vandenhoeck & Ruprecht, 1971.

Inwood, Brad. *Ethics and Human Action in Early Stoicism.* New York: Oxford University Press, 1985.
Jackson, Bernard S. "Liability for Mere Intention in Early Jewish Law." Pages 202–34 in *Essays in Jewish and Comparative Legal History.* Studies in Judaism in Late Antiquity 10. Edited by Jacob Neusner. Leiden: Brill, 1975.
Jastram, Daniel N. "Philo's Concept of Generic Virtue." Ph.D. diss., University of Wisconsin—Madison, 1989.
Jones, C. P. "The Teacher of Plutarch." *Harvard Studies in Classical Philology* 71 (1967): 205–213.
Kahn, Charles H. "Plato's Theory of Desire." *Review of Metaphysics* 41 (1987): 77–103.
Karamanolis, George E. *Plato and Aristotle in Agreement? Platonists on Aristotle from Antiochus to Porphyry.* Oxford Philosophical Monographs. Oxford: Clarendon, 2006.
Kellerman, Ulrich. "Der Dekalog in den Schriften des Frühjudentums: Ein Überblick." Pages 147–226 in *Weisheit, Ethos, und Gebot: Weisheits- und Dekalog-traditionen in der Bibel und im frühen Judentum.* Edited by Henning Graf Reventlow. Biblisch-Theologische Studien 43. Neukirchen-Vluyn: Neukirchener, 2001.
Kittel, G., and G. Friedrich, eds. *Theological Dictionary of the New Testament.* Translated by G. W. Bromiley. 10 vols. Grand Rapids: Eerdmans, 1964–1976.
Klauck, Hans-Josef. *4. Makkabäerbuch. Jüdische Schriften aus hellenistisch-römischer Zeit* 3.1. Edited by Hermann Lichtenberger et al. Gütersloh: Gerd Mohn, 1989.
Knuuttila, Simo, and Juha Sihvola. "How the Philosophical Analysis of the Emotions was Introduced." Pages 1–19 in *The Emotions in Hellenistic Philosophy.* Edited by Juha Sihvola and Troels Engberg-Pedersen. New Synthese Historical Library 46. Dordrecht: Kluwer Academic Publishers, 1998.
Kuntz, Paul Grimley. "Philo Judaeus: A Decalogue in Balance." Pages 11–26 in *The Ten Commandments in History: Mosaic Paradigms for a Well-Ordered Society.* Edited by Thomas d'Evelyn. Emory University Studies in Law and Religion. Grand Rapids: Eerdmans, 2004.
Le Boulluec, Alain. "La place des concepts philosophiques dans la réflexion de Philon sur le plaisir." Pages 129–52 in *Philon d'Alexandrie et le langage de la philosophie. Actes du colloque international organisé par le Centre d'études sur la philosophie hellénistique et romaine de l'Université de Paris XII–*

Val de Marne, Créteil, Fontenay, Paris, 26–28 octobre 1995. Edited by Carlos Lévy. Turnhout: Brepolis, 1998.

Lebeck, Anne. "The Central Myth of Plato's *Phaedrus*." *Greek, Roman and Byzantine Studies* 13 (1972): 267–90.

Lévy, Carlos. "Le concept de doxa des Stoïciens à Philon d'Alexandrie: Essai d'étude diachronique." Pages 250–84 in *Passions and Perceptions: Studies in Hellenistic Philosophy of Mind*. Edited by Jacques Brunschwig and Martha Nussbaum. Cambridge: Cambridge University Press, 1993.

———. "Philon d'Alexandrie et les passions." Pages 27–41 in *Réceptions antiques: Lecture, transmission, appropriation intellectuelle*. Edited by Lætitia Ciccolini, Charles Guérin, Stéphane Itic, and Sébastien Morlet. Études de littérature ancienne 16. Paris: Éditions Rue d'Ulm, 2006.

———. "Philo's Ethics." Pages 146–71 in *The Cambridge Companion to Philo*. Editedy by Adam Kamesar. Cambridge: Cambridge University Press, 2009.

Lichtenberger, Hermann. *Das Ich Adams und das Ich der Menschheit: Studien zum Menschenbild in Römer 7*. Wissenschaftliche Untersuchungen zum Neuen Testament 164. Tübingen: Mohr Siebeck, 2004.

Lilla, Salvatore. *Clement of Alexandria: A Study in Christian Platonism and Gnosticism*. Oxford Theological Monographs. London: Oxford University Press, 1971.

Lluch Baixauli, Miguel. "El tratado de Filón sobre el Decálogo." *Scripta Theologica* 29 (1997): 415–41.

Loader, William. "The Decalogue." Pages 5–25 in *The Septuagint, Sexuality, and the New Testament: Case Studies on the Impact of the LXX in Philo and the New Testament*. Grand Rapids: Eerdmans, 2004.

Löhr, Hermut. "Speisenfrage und Tora im Judentum des Zweiten Tempels und im entstehenden Christentum." *Zeitschrift für die Neutestamentliche Wissenschaft* 94 (2003): 17–37.

Lohse, Bernard. *Askese und Mönchtum in der Antike und in der alten Kirche*. Religion und Kultur der alten Mittelmeerwelt in Parallelforschungen 1. Munich: R. Oldenbourg, 1969.

Long, Anthony A. "Hellenistic Ethics and Philosophical Power." Pages 138–56 in *Hellenistic History and Culture*. Edited by Peter Green. Hellenistic Culture and Society 9. Berkeley: University of California Press, 1993.

———. "Stoic Psychology." Pages 560–84 in *The Cambridge History of Hellenistic Philosophy*. Edited by Keimpe Algra, Jonathan Barnes, Jaap Mansfeld, and Malcolm Schofield. Cambridge: Cambridge University Press, 1999.

Lorenz, Hendrik. *The Brute Within: Appetitive Desire in Plato and Aristotle.* Oxford Philosophical Monographs. Oxford: Oxford University Press, 2006.

Mack, Burton L. "Philo Judaeus and Exegetical Traditions in Alexandria." *Aufstieg und Niedergang der römischen Welt* 21.1:227–271. Part 2, *Principat,* 21.1. Edited by H. Temporini and W. Haase. New York: de Gruyter, 1984.

Malherbe, Abraham. "The Beasts at Ephesus." *Journal of Biblical Literature* 87 (1968): 71–80.

———. "Antisthenes and Odysseus, and Paul at War." *Harvard Theological Review* 76 (1983): 143–73.

Marcus, Joel. "The Evil Inclination in the Epistle of James." *Catholic Biblical Quarterly* 44 (1982): 606–21.

Martens, John W. *One God, One Law: Philo of Alexandria on the Mosaic and Greco-Roman Law.* Studies in Philo of Alexandria and Mediterranean Antiquity 2. Boston: Brill, 2003.

Méasson, Anita. *Du char ailé de Zeus à l'Arche d'Alliance: Images et mythes platoniciens chez Philon d'Alexandrie.* Paris: Études Augustiniennes, 1987.

Mendelson, Alan. *Philo's Jewish Identity.* Brown Judaic Studies 161. Atlanta: Scholars Press, 1988.

Moravcsik, J. M. E. "Reason and Eros in the 'Ascent'-Passage of the *Symposium.*" Pages 285–302 in *Essays in Ancient Greek Philosophy.* Edited by John P. Anton and George L. Kustas. Albany: State University of New York Press, 1971.

Moreschini, Claudio. "Considerazioni sulla dottrina del pathos nel Medioplatonismo." *Studi filosofici* 8–9 (1985–86): 23–33.

Morris, Jenny. "The Jewish Philosopher Philo." Pages 809–89 in Emil Schürer, *The History of the Jewish People in the Age of Jesus Christ (175 B.C.—A.D. 135): A New English Version Revised and Edited by Geza Vermes, Fergus Millar, and Martin Goodman.* Vol. 3, part 2. Edinburgh: T&T Clark, 1987.

Moss, Jessica. "Pleasure and Illusion in Plato." *Philosophy and Phenomenological Research* 72 (2006): 503–535.

Myre, André. "La loi et le Pentateuque selon Philon d'Alexandrie." *Science et esprit* 25 (1973): 209–25.

———. "La loi de la nature et la loi mosaïque selon Philon d'Alexandrie." *Science et esprit* 28 (1976): 163–81.

Niehoff, Maren R. *Philo on Jewish Identity and Culture.* Texte und Studien zum antiken Judentum 86. Tübingen: Mohr Siebeck, 2001.

———. "Philo's Role as a Platonist in Alexandria." Pages 35–62 in *Philon d'Alexandrie*. Edited by Jean-François Pradeau. Études platoniciennes 7. Paris: Belles Lettres, 2010.

Nikiprowetzky, Valentin. *Le commentaire de l'écriture chez Philon d'Alexandrie: Son caractère et sa portée, observations philologiques*. Arbeiten zur Literatur und Geschichte des hellensitischen Judentums 11. Leiden: Brill, 1977.

North, Helen. *Sophrosyne: Self-knowledge and Self-restraint in Greek Literature*. Cornell Studies in Classical Philology 35. Ithaca: Cornell University Press, 1966.

Nussbaum, Martha. *The Therapy of Desire: Theory and Practice in Hellenistic Ethics*. 3d ed. Princeton: Princeton University Press, 2009.

Opsomer, Jan. "L'âme du monde et l'âme de l'homme chez Plutarque." Pages 33–49 in *Estudios sobre Plutarco: Ideas religiosas: Actas del III Simposio Internacional sobre Plutarco, Oviedo 30 de abril a 2 de mayo de 1992*. Edited by Manuela García Valdés. Madrid: Ediciones Clásicas, 1994.

———. "Plutarch's Platonism Revisited." Pages 163-200 in *L'eridità platonica: Studi sul platonismo da Arcesilao a Proclo*. Edited by Mauro Bonazzi and Vincenza Celluprica. Elenchos 45. Naples: Bibliopolis, 2005.

———. "M. Annius Ammonius, A Philosophical Profile," Pages 123–86 in *The Origins of the Platonic System: Platonisms of the Early Empire and their Philosophical Contexts*. Edited by Mauro Bonazzi and Jan Opsomer. Collection d'études classiques 23. Louvain: Peeters, 2009.

Parente, Fausto. "La *Lettera di Aristea* come fonte per la storia del giudaismo alessandrino durante la prima metà del I secolo a.C.." *Annali della Scuola Normale Superiore di Pisa* 3.2.1–2 (1972): 177–237 (part one), 517–67 (part two).

Pearce, Sarah J. K. *The Land of the Body: Studies in Philo's Representation of Egypt*. Wissenschaftliche Untersuchungen zum Neuen Testament 208. Tübingen: Mohr Siebeck, 2007.

Pelletier, A. "Les passions à l'assaut de l'âme d'après Philon." *Revue des études grecques* 78 (1965): 52–60.

Peters, F. E. *Greek Philosophical Terms: A Historical Lexicon*. New York: New York University Press, 1967.

Pfitzner, Victor C. *Paul and the Agon Motif: Traditional Athletic Imagery in the Pauline Literature*. Supplements to Novum Testamentum 16. Leiden: Brill, 1967

Phillips, Thomas E. "Revisiting Philo: Discussions of Wealth and Poverty in Philo's Ethical Discourse." *Journal for the Study of the New Testament* 83 (2001): 111–21.

Pohlenz, Max. *Philon von Alexandreia. Nachrichten von der Akademie der Wissenschaften in Göttingen* 5. Göttingen: Vandenhoeck & Ruprecht, 1942.

Poliakoff, Michael. "Jacob, Job, and Other Wrestlers: Reception of Greek Athletics by Jews and Christians in Antiquity." *Journal of Sport History* 11 (1984): 48–65.

Poplutz, Uta. *Athlet des Evangeliums: Eine motivgeschichtliche Studie zur Wettkampfmetaphorik bei Paulus.* Herders Biblische Studien 43. Freiburg im Breisgau: Herder, 2004.

Rabbow, Paul. *Seelenfürung: Methodik der Exerzitien in der Antike.* München: Kösel, 1954.

Ranocchia, Graziano. "Moses against the Egyptian: The Anti-Epicurean Polemic in Philo." Pages 75–102 in *Philo of Alexandria and Post-Aristotelian Philosophy.* Edited by Francesca Alesse. Studies in Philo of Alexandria 5. Leiden: Brill, 2008.

Reale, Giovanni. *The Schools of the Imperial Age.* Vol. 4. of *A History of Ancient Philosophy.* Edited and translated by J. R. Catan. Albany: State University of New York Press, 1990.

Rees, D. A. "Bipartition of the Soul in the Early Academy." *Journal of Hellenic Studies* 77 (1957): 112–118.

Reydams-Schils, Gretchen. "Posidonius and the *Timaeus*: Off to Rhodes and Back to Plato?" *Classical Quarterly* 47 (1997): 455–76.

———. "Philo of Alexandria on Stoic and Platonist Psycho-Physiology: The Socratic Higher Ground." Pages 169–195 in *Philo of Alexandria and Post-Aristotelian Philosophy.* Edited by Francesca Alesse. Studies in Philo of Alexandria 5. Leiden: Brill, 2008. Repr. from *Ancient Philosophy* 22 (2002): 125–47.

Rhodes, James N. "Diet as Morality: Tracing an Exegetical Tradition." M.A. thesis, Catholic University of America, 2000.

———. "Diet and Desire: The Logic of the Dietary Laws according to Philo." *Ephemerides Theologicae Lovanienses* 79 (2003): 122–33.

Rofé, Alexander. "The Tenth Commandment in the Light of Four Deuteronomic Laws." Pages 45–65 in *The Ten Commandments in History and Tradition.* Edited by Ben-Zion Segal and Gershon Levi. Jerusalem: Magnes Press, 1990.

Romilly, Jacqueline de. "Les conflits de l'âme dans le *Phèdre* de Platon." *Wiener Studien* 16 (1982): 100–113.

Runia, David T. *Philo of Alexandria and the* Timaeus *of Plato.* Philosophia Antiqua 44. Leiden: Brill, 1986.

———. "Was Philo a Middle Platonist?" *Studia Philonica Annual* 5 (1993): 112–140.
———. "Why Does Clement Call Philo 'The Pythagorean'?" Pages 54–76 in *Philo and the Church Fathers: A Collection of Papers.* Supplements to Vigiliae Christianae 32. Leiden: Brill, 1995. Repr. from *Vigiliae Christianae* 49 (1995): 1–22.
———. "A Brief History of the Term *Kosmos Noētos* from Plato to Plotinus." Pages 151–171 in *Traditions of Platonism: Essays in Honour of John Dillon.* Edited by John J. Cleary. Aldershot. Ashgate, 1999.
———. "Philon d'Alexandrie devant le Pentateuque." Pages 99–105 in *Le Pentateuque d'Alexandrie: Text grec et traduction.* Edited by Cécile Dogniez and Marguerite Harl. Bible d'Alexandrie. Paris: Cerf, 2001.
———. Review of Kathy L. Gaca, *The Making of Fornication. Studia Philonica Annual* 17 (2004): 237–43.
———. "Etymology as an Allegorical Technique in Philo of Alexandria." *Studia Philonica Annual* 15 (2005): 101–21.
Sand, Alexander. *Der Begriff "Fleisch" in den paulinischen Hauptbriefen.* Biblische Untersuchungen 2. Regensburg: Pustet, 1967.
Sanders, E. P. "Purity, Food and Offerings in the Greek-Speaking Diaspora." Pages 255–308 in *Jewish Law from Jesus to the Mishnah: Five Studies.* London: SCM Press; Philadelphia: Trinity Press International, 1990.
Sandmel, Samuel. "Confrontation of Greek and Jewish Ethics: Philo: *De Decalogo.*" Pages 163–176 in *Judaism and Ethics.* Edited by Daniel J. Silver. New York: Ktav, 1970.
———. "Philo Judaeus: An Introduction to the Man, his Writings, and his Significance." *Aufstieg und Niedergang der römischen Welt* 21.1:3–46. Part 2, *Principat,* 21.1. Edited by H. Temporini and W. Haase. New York: de Gruyter, 1984.
Sandnes, Karl Olav. *Belly and Body in the Pauline Epistles.* Society for New Testament Studies Monograph Series 120. Cambridge: Cambridge University Press, 2002.
Santas, Gerasimos. "Plato's Theory of Eros in the *Symposium.*" Pages 14–57 in *Plato and Freud: Two Theories of Love.* Oxford: Blackwell, 1988.
Satlow, Michael L. "Philo on Human Perfection." *Journal of Theological Studies* 59 (2008): 500–519.
Schibli, Hermann S. "Xenocrates' Daemons and the Irrational Soul." *Classical Quarterly* 43 (1993): 143–67.
Schmidt, Helmut. *Die Anthropologie Philons von Alexandreia.* Würzburg: Konrad Triltsch, 1933.

Schofer, Jonathan Wyn. *The Making of a Sage: A Study in Rabbinic Ethics.* Madison: University of Wisconsin Press, 2005.
Schweizer, Eduard. "Die hellenistische Komponente im neutestamentlichen σάρξ-Begriff." *Zeitschrift für die Neutestamentliche Wissenschaft und die Kunde der älteren Kirche* 48 (1957): 237–53.
Scott, Dominic. "*Erōs*, Philosophy, and Tyranny." Pages 136–153 in *Maieusis: Essays on Ancient Philosophy in Honour of Myles Burnyeat.* Edited by Dominic Scott. Oxford: Oxford University Press, 2007.
Seland, Torrey. "The Moderate Life of the Christian *paroikoi*: A Philonic Reading of 1 Pet 2:11." Pages 241–64 in *Philo und das Neue Testament: Wechselseitige Wahrnehmungen: I. Internationales Symposium zum Corpus Judaeo-Hellenisticum 1.–4. Mai 2003, Eisenach/Jena.* Edited by Roland Deines and Karl-Wilhelm Niebuhr. Wissenschaftliche Untersuchungen zum Neuen Testament 172. Tübingen: Mohr Siebeck, 2004.
Sheridan, Mark. "Jacob and Israel: A Contribution to the History of an Interpretation." Pages 219–41 in *Mysterium Christi: Symbolgegenwart und theologische Bedeutung.* Edited by M. Löhrer and Elmar Salmann. Studia Anselmiana 116. Roma: Pontificio Ateneo S. Anselmo, 1995.
Sherman, Nancy. "The Habituation of Character." Pages 231–60 in *Aristotle's Ethics: Critical Essays.* Edited by Nancy Sherman. Critical Essays on the Classics. Lanham, Md.: Rowman & Littlefield, 1999.
Siegfried, Carl. *Philo von Alexandria als Ausleger des Alten Testament.* Jena: Hermann Dufft, 1875.
Sihvola, Juha. "Emotional Animals: Do Aristotelian Emotions Require Beliefs?" Pages 50–82 in *Psychology and Ethics.* Edited by Lloyd P. Gerson. Vol. 3 of *Aristotle: Critical Assessments.* London: Routledge, 1999.
Smith, Margaret Demaria. "*Enkrateia*: Plutarch on Self-Control and the Politics of Excess." *Ploutarchos*, n.s., 1 (2003/2004): 79–88.
Sorabji, Richard. *Emotion and Peace of Mind: From Stoic Agitation to Christian Temptation: The Gifford Lectures.* Oxford: Oxford University Press, 2000.
Spanneut, Michel. "*Apatheia* ancienne, *apatheia* chrétienne. Ière partie: L'*apatheia* ancienne." *Aufstieg und Niedergang der römischen Welt* 36.7: 4641–4717. Part 2, *Principat*, 36.7. Edited by W. Haase and H. Temporini. New York: de Gruyter, 1994.
Sterling, Gregory E. "'The School of Sacred Laws': The Social Setting of Philo's Treatises." *Vigiliae Christianae* 53 (1999): 148–64.
———. "'The Queen of the Virtues': Piety in Philo of Alexandria." *Studia Philonica Annual* 18 (2006): 103–23.
Stowers, Stanley K. *A Rereading of Romans: Justice, Jews, and Gentiles.* New Haven: Yale University Press, 1994.

---. "Paul and Self-Mastery." Pages 524–50 in *Paul in the Greco-Roman World: A Handbook*. Edited by J. Paul Sampley. Harrisburg, Pa.: Trinity Press International, 2003.

Svebakken, Hans. "Exegetical Traditions in Alexandria: Philo's Reworking of the *Letter of Aristeas* 145–149 as a Case Study." Pages 93–112 in *From Judaism to Christianity: Tradition and Transition: A* Festschrift *for Thomas H. Tobin, S.J., on the Occasion of His Sixty-fifth Birthday*. Edited by Patricia Walters. Supplements to Novum Testamentum 136. Leiden: Brill, 2010.

Terian, Abraham. "Some Stock Arguments for the Magnanimity of the Law in Hellenistic Jewish Apologetics." *Jewish Law Association Studies* 1 (1985): 141–49.

Termini, Cristina. "Taxonomy of Biblical Laws and φιλοτεχνία in Philo of Alexandria: A Comparison with Josephus and Cicero." *Studia Philonica Annual* 16 (2004): 1–29.

---. "The Historical Part of the Pentateuch According to Philo of Alexandria: Biography, Genealogy, and the Philosophical Meaning of the Patriarchal Lives." Pages 265–95 in *History and Identity: How Israel's Later Authors Viewed Its Earlier History*. Edited by Núria Calduch-Benages and Jan Liesen. Deuterocanonical and Cognate Literature Yearbook 2006. Berlin: de Gruyter, 2006.

---. "Philo's Thought within the Context of Middle Judaism." Pages 95–123 in *The Cambridge Companion to Philo*. Edited by Adam Kamesar. Cambridge: Cambridge University Press, 2009.

Thesleff, Holger. "Notes on Eros in Middle Platonism." *Arctos* 28 (1994): 115–28.

Tobin, Thomas H. *The Creation of Man: Philo and the History of Interpretation*. Catholic Biblical Quarterly Monograph Series 14. Washington: Catholic Biblical Association of America, 1983.

---. *Paul's Rhetoric in Its Contexts: The Argument of Romans*. Peabody, Mass.: Hendrickson, 2004.

Tramontano, Raffaele. *La Lettera di Aristea a Filocrate: Introduzione, testa, versione e commento*. Naples: Ufficio succursale della civiltà cattolica, 1931.

Valantasis, Richard. "Musonius Rufus and Roman Ascetical Theory." *Greek, Roman, and Byzantine Studies* 40 (1999): 207–31.

Van Hoof, Lieve. *Plutarch's Practical Ethics: The Social Dynamics of Philosophy*. Oxford: Oxford University Press, 2010.

Vander Waerdt, P. A. "The Peripatetic Interpretation of Plato's Tripartite Psychology." *Greek, Roman and Byzantine Studies* 26 (1985): 283–302.

———. "Peripatetic Soul-Division, Posidonius, and Middle Platonic Moral Psychology." *Greek, Roman and Byzantine Studies* 26 (1985): 373–94.

Vian, Giovanni Maria. "Purità e culto nell'esegesi giudaico-ellenistica." *Annali di storia dell'esegesi* 13 (1996): 67–84.

Völker, Walther. *Fortschritt und Vollendung bei Philo von Alexandrien: Eine Studie zur Geschichte der Frömmigkeit.* Texte und Untersuchungen zur Geschichte der altchristlichen Literatur 49.1. Leipzig: J. C. Hinrich, 1938.

Warnach, Walter. "Selbstliebe und Gottesliebe im Denken Philons von Alexandrien." Pages 198–214 in *Wort Gottes in der Zeit: Festschrift Karl Hermann Schelkle zum 65.Geburtstag dargebracht von Kollegen, Freunden, Schülern.* Edited by Helmut Feld and Josef Nolte. Düsseldorf: Patmos, 1973.

Wasserman, Emma. *The Death of the Soul in Romans 7: Sin, Death, and the Law in Light of Hellenistic Moral Psychology.* Wissenschaftliche Untersuchungen zum Neuen Testament 256. Tübingen: Mohr Siebeck, 2008.

Watson, Francis. *Paul and the Hermeneutics of Faith.* London: T&T Clark, 2004.

Weber, Reinhard. *Das "Gesetz" bei Philon von Alexandrien und Flavius Josephus: Studien zum Verständnis und zur Funktion der Thora bei den beiden Hauptzeugen des hellenistischen Judentums.* Arbeiten zur Religion und Geschichte des Urchristentums 11. Edited by Gerd Lüdemann. Frankfurt am Main: Lang, 2001.

Wedderburn, A. J. M. "The 'Apostolic Decree': Tradition and Redaction." *Novum Testamentum* 35 (1993): 362–89.

Wendland, Paul. "Philo und die kynisch-stoische Diatribe." Pages 1–75 in *Beiträge zur Geschichte der griechischen Philosophie und Religion.* Berlin: Georg Reimer, 1895.

West, Martin L. *Ancient Greek Music.* Oxford: Oxford University Press, 1994.

Whitchurch, Irl Goldwin. *The Philosophical Bases of Asceticism in the Platonic Writings and in Pre-Platonic Tradition.* Cornell Studies in Philosophy 14. New York: Longmans, Green & Co., 1923.

Whittaker, John. "Platonic Philosophy in the Early Centuries of the Empire." *Aufstieg und Niedergang der römischen Welt* 36.1: 81–123. Part 2, *Principat*, 36.1. Edited by W. Haase and H. Temporini. New York: de Gruyter, 1987.

———. "The Terminology of the Rational Soul in the Writings of Philo of Alexandria." *Studia Philonica Annual* 8 (1996): 1–20.

Williamson, Ronald. *Jews in the Hellenistic World: Philo.* Cambridge Commentaries on Writings of the Jewish and Christian World, 200 BC to AD 200 1.2. Cambridge: Cambridge University Press, 1989.

Winston, David. Introduction to *Philo of Alexandria:* The Contemplative Life, The Giants, *and Selections.* Translated with an introduction by David Winston. Classics of Western Spirituality. Mahwah, N.J.: Paulist, 1981.

———. "Philo's Ethical Theory." *Aufstieg und Niedergang der römischen Welt* 21.1:372–416. Part 2, *Principat,* 21.1. Edited by H. Temporini and W. Haase. New York: de Gruyter, 1984.

———. "Philo and the Rabbis on Sex and the Body." Pages 199–219 in *The Ancestral Philosophy: Hellenistic Philosophy in Second Temple Judaism: Essays of David Winston.* Edited by Gregory E. Sterling. Studia Philonica Monographs 4. Brown Judaic Studies 331. Providence: Brown Judaic Studies, 2001.

———. "Philo of Alexandria on the Rational and Irrational Emotions." Pages 201–220 in *Passions and Moral Progress in Greco-Roman Thought.* Edited by John T. Fitzgerald. Routledge Monographs in Classical Studies. New York: Routledge, 2008.

Wolfson, Harry Austryn. *Philo: Foundations of Religious Philosophy in Judaism, Christianity, and Islam.* 2 vols. 2d rev. print.; Structure and Growth of Philosophic Systems from Plato to Spinoza 2. Cambridge: Harvard University Press, 1948.

Ziesler, J. A. "The Role of the Tenth Commandment in Romans 7." *Journal for the Study of the New Testament* 33 (1988): 41–56.

Zeller, Dieter. *Charis bei Philon und Paulus.* Stuttgarter Bibelstudien 142. Stuttgart: Verlag Katholisches Bibelwerk, 1990.

INDICES

1. *Hebrew Bible / Old Testament*

Genesis
1-3   28n.93, 170n.211
2:7   170n.211
2:8   58n.84
2:19   59n.89, 157n.165
3   136n.96
3:13   74n.138
3:14   57n.81, 166n.196
4:22   76, 79n.156
25:26   99n.57
32:22-32   99
32:25   99n.57
32:26   99n.57, 102n.67

Exodus
12:11   102n.68
20:1-17   1n.2
20:13-15   8n.30
20:16   8n.30
20:17   1, 1n.1, 8n.28, 21n.69
22:30   172n.215
23:10-11   104
23:19   14
23:25b   96, 96n.49

Leviticus
3:17   175n.223
11   147n.132
11:1-8   110n.1, 154n.155
11:2-23   165n.192
11:3   161n.182
11:4-7   156n.163
11:9-12   163n.188
11:13-19   110n.1, 156n.163, 169n.207
11:21   167n.201
11:26   156n.163
11:27   156n.163
11:29   110n.1
11:39-40   172n.215
11:41-42   166n.195
11:41-45   165n.192
11:42   166n.195, 166n.196
16:29-31   104
17:10-14   176n.224
17:11   176n.224
17:15   172n.215, 174n.217
19:19   105n.76, 106
22:8   172n.215
25:2-7   104

Numbers
11:4   179n.232
11:4-34   178n.230, 178-83
11:34   179n.232
29:7-11   104

Deuteronomy
5:1-21   1n.2
5:17-19   8n.30
5:20   8n.30
5:21   1n.1, 8n.28, 21n.69
7:18   162n.183
10:4   1n.2
12:8   181n.239, 181-82
14:1-21   147n.132
14:3-8   154n.155
14:4-5   155n.160
14:6   161n.182
14:9-10   163n.188
14:11-18   169n.207
14:21   172n.215
18:4   14, 145n.124
21:10-14   104
21:18-21   3n.10
22:9   105n.76, 106, 175n.219

2. Old Testament Pseudepigrapha

Apoc. Mos. (*Apocalypse of Moses*)		148-49	159n.72
19.3	12n.38	149	160n.176
		150-60	110n.1, 161
Let. Arist. (*Letter of Aristeas*)		155	162n.183
139	112n.5	157	162n.183
142	112n.5	158	162n.183
144	111n.2, 112n.5	160	162n.183
144-69	110n.1	163	160n.176
145	160n.175	163-67	110n.1
145-49	110n.1, 111-12, 163, 166, 169n.208, 170n.210	169	111n.2
		4 Macc (4 Maccabees)	
146	111, 160n.174, 170n.209	Entire text	12, 104n.74
		2:4	12n.37
146-49	159n.74	2:4-6	12n.36
147	111, 112, 160n.175, 160n.176	2:5	12n.37
		2:6	12n.37
148	111n.2, 112, 160		

3. New Testament

Acts		Galatians	
15:29	177n.226	Entire text	187
		2:16	187
Romans			
Entire text	187	James	
7:7	12n.37	1:14-15	12n.38
7:7-25	12n.36		
13:9	9n.30, 12n.37		

4. Philonic Works

Abr. (*De Abrahamo*)		*Aet.* (*De aeternitate mundi*)	
Entire text	3	86	138n.105
3-4	3n.7		
29	65n.110	*Agr.* (*De agricultura*)	
29-30	63	26-66	84
96	52n.65	29	84n.7
52	15n.45, 98-99, 107n.83	30	84n.8
		30-34	63n.106
52-54	99n.56	36	129n.66, 137n.101
103	86n.16	37	82n.2
160	64n.109	41	55n.76
236	59n.86	45-46	72n.128
236-39	61n.96	46	78
242	72n.128, 78n.153	48	94n.43
256	101	58	92n.36
257	101n.64, 102n.66		

212 INDICES

Agr. (*De agricultura*) continued
63	84n.9
70	68n.120, 91
72-73	89n.26
78	57n.81, 93n.39
88	164n.189
93	90n.29
94	92, 164n.189
131-35	162n.184
131-45	161n.180

Anim. (*De animalibus*)
77-100	38n.16

Cher. (*De cherubim*)
33	106n.79

Conf. (*De confusione linguarum*)
7	128n.63
21	41n.29, 51n.60, 72n.127
45-50	79n.157
70	164n.189
110	162n.185
111	51n.59
117	70n.123, 77n.151
164	72n.128

Congr. (*De congressu eruditionis gratia*)
21	58n.83, 61n.94
26	51
31	102
46	98n.52
51	100n.60
81	59
81-82	59n.87
106	60n.91
120	5n.17, 6n.20, 24n.77
158	133n.85
166	127n.59

Contempl. (*De vita contemplativa*)
11-12	71n.126
34	81n.1
37	42n.35, 60n.90
55	76n.146, 167n.198
69	151n.146

Decal. (*De decalogo*)
Entire text	3, 3n.7, 4n.12, 5n.15, 6-8, 8.n25, 8n.26, 10, 15n.46, 118
1	3n.10
1–*Spec.* 4.132	4, 4n.11
2-17	6n.21
18-19	4-5
20-31	6n.21
32-35	5n.14, 6n.21
36	1n.2
36-43	6n.21
50-51	8n.29
50-153	6, 9
121	8n.29
123	53n.66
142	1n.4, 14n.42, 20n.65, 122n.37, 123n.38, 124n.43, 124n.44, 129, 129n.69, 130, 131n.73
142-45	**122-24**, 129, 130n.70
142-46	14n.41, 123n.40, 123n.41
142-53	1n.4, 8, 9, 15, 20, 32
143	123n.39, 124n.44, 124n.45, 130n.70, 130n.72
143-45	123
144	123n.39, 124n.44, 124n.45, 130n.70, 130n.72
145	123n.39, 124n.44, 124n.45, 130n.70, 130n.72
146	24n.78, 124n.46
146-50	123, **129-33**
148	28n.95
150	171n.213
151	2n.4, 27n.87, 74, 131n.74
151-53	79n.154, **137-38**
152-53	27n.87
154	1n.2, 5n.15
154-75	6
157	6n.18
168	5n.16, 6n.18
168-69	25n.81
170	6n.18
171	6n.18
173	1n.4, 12n.38, 107n.82, 135n.94, 171n.213
173-74	1n.4, 9, 15, 20, 20n.65, 32
174	6n.18
175	5n.17

INDICES

Det. (Quod deterius potiori insidiari soleat)
5	55n.76
25	144n.120
27	178n.229
32	183n.245
53	62n.98
65	101n.63
82	54
95	94n.42, 96n.48
101	167n.198
102	65n.111
102-03	63n.107
113	53n.66, 96n.48
168	63n.103, 63n.105

Deus (Quod Deus sit immutabilis)
41	54n.72, 54n.75
45-50	129n.69
48	123n.38
71	121n.33
148	127n.61
149	56n.78

Ebr. (De ebrietate)
6	76n.146, 129n.67
14-95	3n.10
21	28n.95
82	100n.60
98	55n.76, 132n.80
99-103	60n.91
111	55n.76
131	95n.47
206	76n.146
214	53n.66, 60n.90
221	82n.2

Fug. (De fuga et inventione)
24	84n.8
90	157n.165
91	60n.91, 132n.80, 164n.189
158	171n.213
164	28n.95

Gig. (De gigantibus)
Entire text	11
18	128n.63
26	162n.185
31	76n.144, 168n.205
33	168n.205
35	53n.66
44	71n.126
60	168n.205

Her. (Quis rerum divinarum heres sit)
64	51n.60, 51n.61
70	77n.148
75	61n.97
109	65n.110
111	61n.97
132	51n.59
155	133n.87
167	6n.20, 24n.77, 51n.59
168	8n.29
173	1n.4, 6n.20, 24n.77
209	61n.97, 86n.16
232	63n.103
239	168n.203
245	69, 69n.122
253	14n.44, 100n.59, 104n.74
269	73n.132, 75, 127n.58, 128n.62, 128n.63
269-70	47n.52

Hypoth. (Hypothetica)
7.11	102n.69
7.15-19	104n.75

Ios. (De Iosepho)
Entire text	3
1	3n.7, 99n.55
40	73n.132
70	53n.68, 74n.134
153	182, 182n.241

Leg. 1-3 (Legum allegoriae I, II, III)
1.11	63n.103
1.24	61n.95
1.30	54n.72, 54n.75
1.57	98n.52
1.70	85-86
1.70-71	42n.35, 88n.20
1.70-72	41n.29, 51n.60
1.72	84n.8, 89n.26
1.72-73	122
1.73	164n.189
1.75	128n.63
1.86	42n.35, 60n.90, 87n.19, 88n.20, 95
1.103	60n.91
1.105-07	72n.129
2.1-8	58n.84
2.2	51n.59, 58n.84
2.5	58n.84
2.6	58, 58n.84, 61n.96

Leg. 1-3 (*Legum allegoriae*) continued

2.8	58n.84, 59, 157n.165
2.9	59n.89, 157n.165
2.10-11	59n.89, 157n.165
2.16	96n.48
2.23	54n.72, 54n.75
2.25	134n.91
2.28	102n.68
2.50	58n.83, 61n.96
2.77	70n.123
2.90	73n.133
2.90-91	73n.132
2.91	72n.128, 133n.85
2.99	89n.26
2.101	134n.88
2.102	6n.19
2.103	164n.189
2.104	91n.33
2.105	169n.206
2.107	53n.68
3.18	14n.44, 100n.59, 101n.62, 104n.74, 162n.184, 162n.185
3.22	134n.88
3.37-38	73n.133
3.39	76n.144
3.50	61n.95
3.59-64	74n.138
3.65	166n.196
3.79-80	78n.153
3.80	72n.128
3.84	182n.241
3.93	99n.57, 101n.61
3.111	70n.123
3.114	57n.81
3.114-16	57, 166n.196
3.115	41n.29, 51n.60, 51-52, 52n.63, 93n.39, 130n.71
3.116	51n.61, 52, 57, 57n.83, 93n.39
3.118	92n.35
3.118-37	93
3.123	43n.38, 53n.69, 93n.39
3.124	41n.29
3.127	93n.39
3.128-29	93n.38
3.130	53n.69
3.131	93n.38
3.132	101n.63
3.134	93, 164n.189
3.138	52
3.139	166n.195
3.147	42n.35, 60n.90, 95n.47
3.149	76
3.151-54	122n.34
3.153-54	102n.68
3.154	96n.50
3.155	164n.189, 167n.198
3.159	166n.197
3.160	166n.196
3.185	55n.76
3.190	99n.57, 101n.61
3.193	90n.27
3.212	73n.133
3.222	84n.8
3.222-24	90n.28
3.223	90n.29
3.224	62n.99, 90n.28, 141n.111, 143n.116

Legat. (*Legatio ad Gaium*)

65	133n.84
162	70n.123

Migr. (*De migratione Abrahami*)

18	70n.125
21	70n.123, 70n.125
25-26	57n.80
31	162n.185
66	51n.61
66 ff.	51n.60
67	51n.60, 53n.69, 53n.71, 89n.26
89-93	12n.35, 112n.5
155	24n.76, 179n.232
191	134n.91
210	53n.69, 158n.166
213	61n.95
214	100n.60

Mos. 1-2 (*De vita Mosis* I, II)

Entire text	3n.8
1.6	157n.165
1.25	91n.33
1.25-26	55-56, 103n.72
1.28	97n.50
1.28-29	151n.145
1.76	99n.55
1.109	154n.156
1.160-61	96
1.161	86n.16, 96n.48
1.191	42n.35
1.302	157n.165
2.10	103n.71
2.22	133n.86
2.23-24	104n.75

2.46	3n.7	117	79
2.46-47	2n.5, 3n.7	148-49	162n.184
2.47	2n.5	154	173n.216
2.58	171n.213	157	71n.126
2.245	125n.52	180	182n.243

Mut. (*De mutatione nominum*)

12	99n.55		
14	178n.229		
85	101n.62		
87	151n.148		
111	63n.103		
143	70n.125		
173	120n.31		
214-15	164n.191		
241	123n.38		

Praem. (*De praemiis et poenis*)

Entire text	3n.8
1	2n.5, 3n.7
2	4n.11
2-3	3n.8
12	183n.245
36-40	100n.60
47	102
48	102
59	51, 51n.60, 84n.8
71	52n.65
84	71n.126
88	59n.89
100	102n.69
104	53n.71
140	125n.51
153-56	104n.75
154	105

Opif. (*De opificio mundi*)

Entire text	2
5	28n.95, 127n.59
70-71	132n.81
73	38n.16, 86n.16
77	127n.59
79	53n.68
81	120n.31, 147n.130
83-86	84n.8
88	90, 91
111	127n.59
117	63n.103
151-52	28
152	28, 28n.95
154	146n.127
157-60	136n.96
158	96n.48
164	87, 151n.145, 168-69
166	131n.76

Prob. (*Quod omnis probus liber sit*)

45	72n.128
152	134n.91
159	128n.63

Prov. 2 (*De providentia* II)

2.58	90n.30
2.70	70n.123, 144n.120, 149n.139

QE 1-2 (*Quaestiones et solutiones in Exodum* I, II)

Frag. 24	68n.120
1.7	120n.30
2.18	96

Plant. (*De plantatione*)

43	59n.89
105	70n.123

Post. (*De posteritate Caini*)

26	52n.62
42	82n.2
71	52n.65
75	121n.33
78	101n.63
98	133n.85
112	77n.149
112-15	77n.149
113	77n.148
116	53n.67, 77, 77n.148, 128n.63
116-17	79n.155

QG 1-4 (*Quaestiones et solutiones in Genesim* I, II, III, IV)

Frag. 10	182n.244
1.55	55n.76
2.57	70n.122
2.59	57n.80
2.68	94n.44
3.48	97, 143n.117
4.163	101n.61
4.172	151n.145
4.216	51n.61
4.218	84n.8, 121n.34

Sacr. (*De sacrificiis Abelis et Caini*)
17	101n.61
32	114n.12
37	180n.237
45	143n.116
46	37-38
47	54n.75
85-86	162n.185
104-05	61-62
104-06	84n.7
129	130n.72

Sobr. (*De sobrietate*)
24	73n.133
65	101n.61

Somn. 1-2 (*De somniis* I, II)
1.28	58n.83
1.36	132n.81
1.43-44	168n.205
1.46	100n.60
1.169	163n.187
2.13	168n.205
2.48	96n.48
2.106	168n.205
2.150	127n.59
2.151-52	84-85
2.179	157n.165
2.267	65n.110
2.274-75	115n.15
2.276	69n.122

Spec. 1-4 (*De specialibus legibus* I, II, III, IV)
Entire text	3, 4n.12, 6n.19, 6-8, 7n.24, 8n.25, 8n.26, 10
1.1	1n.2, 6n.20
1.1-4.132	3
1.9	143n.117
1.44	128n.63
1.66	51n.59
1.101	55n.76
1.146-50	51n.60
1.148	64n.109, 65n.110
1.149	87, 164n.191
1.173	81n.1, 151n.145
1.175	81n.1
1.186-88	104n.75
1.192	106n.80, 132n.80
1.192-93	104n.75
1.193	55n.76, 92n.36, 106
1.201	51n.59
1.206ff.	51n.60
1.260	38n.16
1.333	51n.59
1.343	70n.124
1.344	183n.245
2.18	92, 147n.129
2.29-31	3n.10
2.39	6n.19
2.69	133n.86
2.86-109	104n.75
2.87	105n.76
2.87-88	105n.76
2.88	105n.76
2.89	38n.16, 61n.95
2.98	150n.144
2.134	125n.52
2.135	92n.37
2.141	146n.127
2.142	56n.79
2.163	107n.82
2.189	5n.14
2.195	104n.75
2.193	106n.80, 132n.80
2.193-203	104n.75
2.195	104n.75, 107, 108
2.223	6n.19
2.232	3n.10
2.242	6n.19
3.7	1n.2, 7n.23
3.7-8	30n.100
3.9-10	30, 30n.100
3.23	73n.133
3.43	151n.147
3.44	128n.63
3.79	56n.79
3.85	154n.158, 158n.167
3.99	55n.75
3.125	6n.20
3.129	55n.76
3.209	70n.125, 121n.33
4.1	6n.18
4.5	105n.77
4.7	78
4.10	51n.60
4.41	8n.30
4.78	1n.4, 5n.16, 20n.65
4.78b	24n.77, **119**
4.78b-94	10
4.78b-131	1n.4, 8, 10, 15, 15n.46, 20, 32, 118, 184
4.79	13n.38, 14n.41, 14n.42, 19n.61, 68, 68n.120, 70, 91, **120-22**, 122n.37, 123, 124, 188
4.79-94	117, 179-81

4.79-125	181	4.101	14n.43, 30n.102, 30n.103, 150n.144
4.79-135	10n.34		
4.80	24, 121, 126n.56, 131, 131n.75, 132n.79, 137n.100	4.102	151n.148
		4.103	156n.163, 157n.164
		4.103-04	160n.178, 170n.209, 171
4.80-81	75n.141		
4.80-83	**124-29**, 131	4.103-09	**154-63**
4.81	128n.63	4.104	107n.82, 158n.168, 160n.175
4.81-82	132		
4.82	25, 25n.80, 27, 42n.35, 124n.46, 127n.59, 127n.61, 136n.97	4.106	156n.163, 159n.173, 161n.182
		4.106-09	161n.181, 172n.214
		4.107	162n.186
4.83	132, 171n.213	4.110-12	**163-65**
4.84	27-28	4.111	164n.191
4.84-85	12n.38	4.112	14n.43, 159n.173, 162n.186, 164n.190, 178
4.84-91	**133-37**		
4.85	20n.65, 26-27, 27n.87, 79	4.113	159n.173, 166n.194, 167n.198, 167n.199, 167n.200
4.86-91	9n.32, 25n.79		
4.87	18n.58, 23n.71, 175n.222		
4.87-96	20n.65	4.113-15	**165-69**
4.88	25n.80	4.114	159n.173, 167n.202
4.89	25n.80, 25n.81	4.116	166n.193, 170n.209
4.90	65n.111, 114n.12, 137n.99	4.116-17	**169-71**, 172n.214
		4.118	31, **171-72**, 153n.154
4.91	148n.135, 167n.198, 180n.233		
		4.119-21	**172-75**
4.92	26n.84, 41n.29, 51n.60	4.119-31	30n.101
		4.121	174n.218, 175n.222
4.92-94	14n.42, 20n.66, 26, 26n.82, 26n.83, **138-41**	4.122	177n.226, 177n.227
		4.122-25	**175-78**
		4.123	61n.95
4.93	2n.4, 51n.60	4.124	14n.43
4.93-94	26	4.126	180n.236
4.95	145n.123, 146n.127	4.126-31	**178-83**
4.95-97	**141-45**	4.127	180n.235, 180n.236, 181n.238
4.95-130	118		
4.95-131	10	4.129	105n.77, 132n.80, 180n.234, 180n.235
4.96	24n.78, 29-30, 145n.123		
		4.130	179n.232
4.96-97	42n.35	4.131	181n.239, 181n.240, 182n.242
4.96-131	29-31		
4.97	14n.43, 180n.237, 183n.246	4.132	6n.18, 7
		4.132-34	3n.9
4.98-99	**145-47**	4.133-238	3, 4n.11
4.99	14n.43, 14n.44, 147n.131	4.133-35	4n.11
		4.161	127n.59
4.100	30, 153n.154, 166n.193, 177	4.179	103n.71
		4.208-18	105n.76
4.100-02	**147-53**, 171	4.212	175n.220
4.100-18	20n.65, 30, 30n.101, 110, 172, 173	4.212-18	104n.75, 105n.76, 175n.219
		4.215-18	105n.76

218   INDICES

Spec. 1-4 (*De specialibus legibus*)
  continued
  4.216   105n.76
  4.217   70, 106n.79
  4.217-18   175n.221
  4.218   106-07
  4.220   182n.241

Virt. (*De virtutibus*)
  Entire text   3, 4n.11
  13   51n.60, 90n.29
  14   164n.189

100   105n.77
110   104n.75
110-15   104n.75
113   92n.37, 106,
                   106n.81, 144n.120
114   104n.75
130   42n.35
136   53n.66
160   38n.16
180   86n.16
195   60n.91, 70n.125

5. Ancient Authors (Except Philo)

ALCINOUS
Didask. (*Didaskalikos*)
  Entire text   37, 41n.30
  1.2   71n.126
  5.2   47n.51
  16.2   61n.94
  17.4   47n.51
  23   39n.22
  24   39n.19
  24.4   98n.53, 107n.83
  28.4   99n.56, 107n.83
  29.1   85n.12
  29.2   43n.39
  30.3   98n.53, 107n.83
  30.5   71n.125
  30.5-6   71n.125
  32.1   14n.42, 58n.84,
                   121n.34, 123n.42,
                   123-24, 124n.43,
                   124n.44, 124n.45,
                   130n.71
  32.2   69n.121
  32.4   48n.55, 59n.89,
                   123n.42, 158n.166
  34.3   72n.127

ARISTOTLE
De an. (*De anima*)
  414b2   42n.32
  414b5-6   39n.21, 43n.37,
                   52n.64

Eth. eud. (*Ethica eudemia*)
  1223b11-14   17n.53

Eth. nic. (*Ethica nicomachea*)
  VII   72n.130
  1102a29-30   40
  1103a17-18   107n.83

1106a29-33   68n.118
1111a23   129n.69
1119b6-8   43n.37, 52n.64
1147b25-26   42n.35
1147b25-29   42n.35

Rhet. (*Rhetorica*)
  1378a30-b10   157n.165

ARIUS DIDYMUS (APUD STOBAEUS)
Eclog. (*Eclogae Physicae et Ethicae*)
  37.18-38.1   98n.53
  37.18-38.15   35, 35n.5
  38.3-4   40n.25
  38.5-6   40n.25, 83n.6
  38.5-7   47n.51, 120n.30
  38.6-7   48n.55
  38.8   43
  38.10-14   44n.43
  38.12-13   40n.25
  38.14-15   35, 35n.5, 47
  42.13-23   45n.44
  42.23   66n.115
  44.3-6   66n.115
  86.17-88.7   45n.46
  117.11-12   44n.43

ESE (*Epitome of Stoic Ethics*)
  9   44n.41, 56n.78,
                   164n.189
  10   14n.42, 48n.53,
                   66n.112
  10b   44n.42

DIOGENES LAERTIUS
Lives of Eminent Philosophers
  5.18   99n.56
  7.110   14n.42, 66n.112,
                   120n.28, 120n.29

7.111	57n.83	237D-238C	71n.126, 128n.62
7.113	52n.63	238A	39n.21, 71n.126
7.114	44n.42	238A-B	137n.101
		238B	71n.126

EPICURUS
Letter to Menoeceus
21B (LS)	73n.133	238C	71n.126, 128n.62
		240C-D	127n.59
		240D	128n.63
		241A	127n.59

EUDORUS
Author	33-37, 66-67	245B-257B	71n.126
1.4-10	45n.44	246A	89n.24
1.10	66n.115	246A-B	88
1.23-24	66n.115	248A	131n.76
		250D	127n.59
		251C-E	77n.148, 132n.81

EUSEBIUS
Hist. eccl. (*Historia ecclesiastica*)
2.18.5	6n.19	253D-254E	40n.26
		253D-256D	88
		256D	127n.59

GALEN
PHP (*De placitis Hippocratis et Platonis*)

Phileb. (*Philebus*)
		31E-35D	128n.64
IV 2.2-3	52n.63	52C	71n.125
IV 2.8	14n.42		
IV 2.39-42	73n.130	*Resp.* (*Respublica*)	
IV 4.13-15	37	VIII-IX	72n.129, 73n.131, 120n.30
V 5.8	39n.21		
V 5.28	47n.49	IX	72n.127
V 7.1-33	39n.19	390B	82n.2
VI 1.5-23	9n.33	430D-432A	82n.2
		430E	85n.11

HOMER
Od. (*Odyssey*)
		430E-431A	83
11.582-92	75n.142, 128n.63	431A	83
12.168	86	432A	85n.11
		436A-B	42n.35
		436B	38n.19

MUSONIUS RUFUS
Troph.^{B} (Περὶ τροφῆς^B)
		437D	23n.72, 42n.35, 144n.119
116.9-11	95n.46		
118.6-7	95n.46	439A	131n.77
		439A-D	38n.19, 128n.65
		439A-E	23n.72

PLATO
Crat. (*Cratylus*)
		439B	42n.32
419E-420B	133n.84	439D	20n.66, 39n.20, 39n.21
420A	124n.46, 127n.60		
		439E-440A	42n.34
Leg. (*Leges*)		440A	42n.34
626E	83n.3	441A	40n.26, 41n.29
782E	42n.35, 144n.119	443D-E	151n.148
870A	127n.58, 128n.62	485D-E	133n.84
		486D	71n.125
		518E	107n.83
Phaed. (*Phaedo*)		545C	71n.126
66C	27n.87	548C-550B	43n.38
81B	42n.35	549A	43n.38
		558C-E	42n.35
Phaedr. (*Phaedrus*)		558C-559D	95n.47
237D	72n.127	558D-E	60n.90

220 INDICES

Resp. (*Respublica*) continued
559A-D	42n.35
572C-576B	71n.126
572E	71n.127
573B	71n.126, 71n.127
573D	71n.126, 71n.127
573E	71n.127
574E	71n.126
574E-575A	78
575A	71n.126, 71n.127
575B	23n.71
577E	71n.126
578A	76n.143
580D	42n.32
580D-E	38n.18
580E	23n.71, 42n.35
581A-B	25n.80
586A-C	127n.61
586C	127n.58
588B-D	84n.7
588B-591A	39n.22

Symp. (*Symposium*)
197D	127n.59, 132n.81
205D	27n.87, 74n.137, 75n.139
206A	74n.137, 75n.139
210A-212C	71n.126
211C	77n.148

Tim. (*Timaeus*)
27C-92C	36
42A-B	61n.94
69C-71D	139n.106
70D	42n.35
70D-E	20n.66, 39n.22
70D-71A	26n.83, 139n.107
71D	39n.20

Plutarch

An. corp. (*Animine an corporis affectiones sint peiores*)
501D	67n.115

An. procr. (*De animae procreatione in Timaeo*)
Entire text	36n.13
1013B	36n.11
1019E	36n.11
1020C	36n.11

Cohib. ira (*De cohibenda ira*)
Entire text	37n.13, 43n.38, 113n.7
459A-460C	157.165
460C	158n.167

Curios. (*De curiositate*)
Entire text	37n.13, 113n.7

De laude (*De laude ipsius*)
Entire text	37n.13, 113n.7

Garr. (*De garrulitate*)
Entire text	37n.13, 113n.7, 113-18, 137n.99, 144n.121, 145, 147, 152
502E	114
503C	115n.13
503E	115n.13
504E	114n.12
504F	115, 115n.13
505D-E	115n.13
506A-B	115n.13
506E	115n.13
506F	115n.13
507E	115n.13
508B	115n.13
508D	115n.17
508D-F	115
508E	115
508F	115n.13, 116
510C	98n.53
510C-D	107n.83, 113, 142n.115
510D	116, 116n.18
511D	115n.13
511F	116, 116n.19, 147n.131
512C	116.19
512D	116n.20
512D-F	116
512E	116n.20
512F	117
513A	152, 152n.151
513A-C	117n.23, 152n.150
513B-C	152n.152
513C	152n.153
513D	117
513E	117n.23
514A	117n.22
514B	149n.40
514C	115n.14
515A	115n.13

Lyc. (*Lycurgus*)
12.6-7	152n.149

INDICES

Stoic. rep. (*De Stoicorum repugnantiis*)
1057A   55n.76

Suav. viv. (*Non posse suaviter vivi secundum Epicurum*)
1100A-D   74n.134
1100B   136n.98

Virt. mor. (*De virtute morali*)
Entire text   36n.13, 47n.51
440D   48n.55
441C   47n.51, 69n.121
442A   39n.19, 47n.51, 83n.6
443B   47n.51
443C   48n.55
443D   48n.56
444B   68n.120, 70n.125
444B-C   67n.115, 68n.119
444C   48n.56, 68n.119, 70n.125
444C-D   60n.91
444E   151n.148
445A   48n.56
445B-C   87
445B-D   89n.21
445B-446C   73n.130
445B-446E   86n.15
446D-E   86
446F-447A   48n.53
446F-447C   47n.51
447C   40n.22
448D   47n.51
448F   70n.122
449A   70n.122
449A-C   47n.50
449B   70n.122
449C   123n.39, 130n.70
450D-E   83n.3
450E-F   43n.39, 45n.44
450E-451B   68n.119
451C   48n.55

Vit. pud. (*De vitioso pudore*)

Entire text   37n.13, 113n.7

POSIDONIUS
Author   46n.49, 57n.80, 57n.82, 88n.21
Fragment(s)   47n.49

PS.-ANDRONICUS
On Passions
231.81   157n.165
231.93   127n.59

PS.-ARCHYTAS
On Moral Education
41.16   48n.56

PS.-ARISTOTLE
Magna moralia
Entire text   41, 44n.40

PS.-METOPUS
On Virtue
Entire text   36
117.9-10   43n.39
117.12-14   45n.44
117.16-18   83
117.21-22   88n.20
118.1-5   41n.30
118.9-13   85n.12
119.8   48n.55
120.24   48n.56
121.7   48n.55
121.8-9   151n.148
121.10-12   48n.55

PS.-THEAGES
On Virtue
193.13-14   43n.39

PS.-TIMAEUS
On the Nature of the World and the Soul
Entire text   35-36
46   40, 41n.30
71   45n.44, 47, 48n.55
72   47n.52, 48n.56, 70n.123
73   48n.55
73-74   66n.115
82   40n.24, 41n.30, 43n.38, 86n.14

6. Modern Authors

Amir, Yehoshua	4n.11, 4n.12, 5n.14, 16n.47, 18n.59
Annas, Julia	40n.22, 45n.46, 73n.131, 84n.7
Ash, Rhiannon	89n.21
Aune, David C.	10n.33, 104n.74, 121n.34
Baltes, Matthias	35n.6, 35n.7, 47n.52, 48n.55, 67n.115
Barclay, John M. G.	11n.35
Baudry, Gérard-Henry	61n.92
Beardslee, William A.	114n.11
Becchi, Francesco	67n.115, 68n.118
Bentwich, Norman	31n.105
Berger, Klaus	16n.47
Berthelot, Katell	12n.35, 110n.1, 111n.3, 160n.177, 187n.3
Billings, Thomas H.	13n.40, 50n.58, 88n.21
Birnbaum, Ellen	15n.45, 98n.54, 99n.57, 112n.5
Bonazzi, Mauro	33n.1, 34n.1, 34n.2, 45n.44, 66n.115, 67n.116, 67n.117, 70n.122
Booth, Peter A.	29n.96
Borgen, Peder	2n.5, 2n.6, 3n.7, 3n.9, 4n.11, 4n.12, 7n.22, 8n.25, 12n.36, 31n.105, 53n.70, 71n.126
Bouffartigue, Jean	41n.29, 51n.58, 60n.92
Boulogne, Jacques	115n.13
Bradshaw, David	100n.60
Brändl, Martin	100n.58
Bréhier, Emile	10n.34, 58n.84, 95n.46, 100n.60, 104n.74, 121n.34
Brenk, Frederick E.	100n.60
Brennan, Tad	44n.40
Calabi, Francesca	5n.13, 15n.46, 29n.96, 169n.206
Centrone, Bruno	36n.8, 36n.9, 36n.10
Classen, Carl Joachim	85n.12
Clifford, Hywel	103n.72
Cohen, Naomi	7n.22
Cohn, Leopold	2n.5, 3n.7, 10n.34, 77n.149, 105n.78, 146n.126, 148n.136

Colson, F. H.	2n.5, 3n.10, 5n.13, 5n.15, 7n.23, 10n.34, 15n.46, 17n.56, 24n.76, 27n.87, 51n.61, 54n.75, 56n.77, 57n.82, 59n.89, 60n.90, 72n.128, 77n.148, 85n.10, 101n.65, 102n.68, 102n.70, 103n.72, 107n.82, 121n.34, 123n.39, 123n.40, 125n.50, 129n.66, 130n.70, 135n.92, 142n.114, 146n.128, 147n.134, 154n.159, 161n.181, 173n.216, 179n.231, 181n.239
Cooper, John M.	25n.80, 38n.17, 38n.18, 39n.20, 39n.21, 42n.32, 42n.33, 42n.34, 43n.36, 47n.49, 57n.80, 73n.133, 75n.140, 94n.41
Courcelle, Pierre	168n.205
Daniélou, Jean	36n.12
Daubercies, Pierre	85n.12
Decharneux, Baudouin	25n.81
Dent, N. J. H.	39n.20
Deutsch, Frédéric	182n.242
Dierauer, Urs	39n.22
Dillon, John M.	10n.33, 13n.40, 19n.62, 33n.1, 34n.1, 36n.11, 36n.12, 37n.14, 48n.56, 49n.57, 50n.58, 67n.116, 67n.118, 70n.122, 71n.125, 93n.38, 99n.56, 124n.42, 186n.1
Dochhorn, Jan	12n.38
Dogniez, Cécile	1n.3
Dorion, Louis-André	81n.1
Dörrie, Heinrich	34n.1, 34n.2
Dressler, Hermigild	15n.45, 98n.53
Duff, Tim	43n.38, 74n.134
Dunn, James D. G.	188, 188n.5, 188n.6
Elsky, Martin	9n.33
Feldman, Louis H.	151n.148
Feldmeier, Reinhard	112n.5
Février, James G.	111n.1
Fitzgerald, John T.	101n.63
Fitzmyer, Joseph A.	12n.36
Fox, Kenneth Allan	168n.205
Fraade, Steven	104n.74

Frede, Michael	9n.33, 48n.54, 66n.114
Fuglseth, Kåre	53n.70
Fuhrmann, François	89n.21
Gaca, Kathy L.	20-31, 94n.45, 121n.34
Geljon, A. C.	13n.40
Gemünden, Petra von	10n.33, 13n.39, 60n.91, 61n.92, 99n.57, 171n.213
Geytenbeek, A. C. van	95n.46, 98n.53
Gill, Christopher	60n.91
Glucker, John	36n.12
Goodenough, Erwin R.	3n.8, 16n.47
Goulet-Cazé, M.-O.	98n.53
Grabbe, Lester L.	76n.147, 100n.60
Grant, Robert M.	12n.35
Graver, Margaret	10n.33, 55n.76, 70n.122
Gross, Josef	168n.205
Hackforth, R.	42n.35, 128n.64
Hadas, Moses	110n.1, 111n.1, 111n.4, 112n.5
Hadas-Lebel, Mireille	11n.35, 31n.105
Hadot, Pierre	14n.44, 104n.74, 162n.185
Hahm, David E.	35n.3, 35n.4
Halperin, David M.	27n.87, 39n.21, 71n.126, 74n.135, 76n.143
Harl, Marguerite	1n.3, 121n.33, 183n.245
Harris, Harold A.	90n.30, 99n.57
Harris, William V.	157n.165
Hayward, C. T. R.	99n.57, 104n.74
Hecht, Richard D.	2n.5, 4n.12, 7n.22, 11n.35, 31n.105, 111n.1, 169n.206
Heckel, Theo K.	84n.7
Heil, Christoph	11n.35
Heinemann, Isaak	3n.10, 8n.25, 12n.35, 15n.46, 30n.103, 31n.105, 121n.34, 147n.134, 150n.143, 159n.173, 159n.174, 173n.216, 177n.228
Hijmans, B. L.	98n.53
Himbaza, Innocent	1n.1
Horst, P. W. van der	157n.165
Houston, Walter J.	12n.35, 16n.47, 31n.105
Ingenkamp, H. G.	37n.13, 113, 113n.7, 113n.8, 114n.11, 144n.121

Inwood, Brad	14n.42, 34n.2, 44n.40, 44n.41, 45n.45, 45n.46, 46n.47, 46n.48, 47n.52, 54n.72, 54n.73, 55n.76, 56n.78, 62n.100, 62n.101, 66n.113, 68n.119, 89n.26, 123n.41
Jackson, Bernard S.	16n.49
Jastram, Daniel N.	4n.12, 6n.20, 142n.114
Jones, C. P.	36n.12
Kahn, Charles H.	25n.80, 38n.18, 75n.140
Karamanolis, George	41n.28
Kellerman, Ulrich	4n.12, 16n.47
Klauck, Hans-Josef	12n.36
Knuuttila, Simo	9n.33
Kuntz, Paul G.	4n.12
Le Boulluec, Alain	29n.96, 58n.84, 59n.87
Lebeck, Anne	89n.22
Lévy, Carlos	10n.33, 57n.82, 59n.87, 60n.91, 63n.106
Lichtenberger, H.	16n.47
Lilla, Salvatore	10n.33, 47n.51, 48n.56, 58n.84, 60n.91, 85n.12, 88n.21, 93n.38, 99n.56, 121n.34
Lluch Baixauli, Miguel	4n.12, 16n.47
Loader, William	16n.47
Löhr, Hermut	11n.35
Lohse, Bernard	104n.74
Long, Anthony A.	19n.62, 46n.47, 54n.74, 62n.100, 81n.1, 82n.2, 187n.4
Lorenz, Hendrik	38n.18, 39n.19, 39n.20, 39n.21, 75n.140, 94n.41
Mack, Burton L	111n.1
Malherbe, Abraham	141n.110, 151n.147
Marcus, Joel	16n.49
Martens, John W	103n.71
Méasson, Anita	16n.47, 27n.86, 53n.69, 88n.21, 89n.21, 89n.24, 89n.25, 90n.28, 91n.32
Mendelson, Alan	12n.35, 31n.105
Moravcsik, J. M. E.	74n.136
Moreschini, Claudio	48n.56
Morris, Jenny	2n.6, 3n.7, 4n.11, 7n.24

Mosès, André	8n.26, 15n.46, 24n.76, 121n.34, 122n.35, 125n.47, 147n.133, 147n.134, 154n.159, 162n.185, 173n.216, 179n.231
Moss, Jessica	74n.138
Myre, André	4n.12, 103n.71
Niehoff, Maren R	14n.43, 31n.105, 34n.1, 81n.1, 94n.45, 95n.46, 187n.4
Nikiprowetzky, Valentin	1n.3, 3n.7, 5n.13, 15n.46
North, Helen	72n.130, 85n.11, 85n.12
Nussbaum, Martha	9n.33
Opsomer, Jan	36n.12, 36n.13, 68n.120, 89n.21
Parente, Fausto	110n.1, 112n.5
Pearce, Sarah J. K.	100n.60, 168n.205, 182n.242
Pelletier, A.	78n.153, 129n.68, 141n.110
Peters, F. E.	9n.33
Pfitzner, Victor C.	100n.58
Phillips, Thomas E.	16n.47
Pohlenz, Max	10n.33, 55n.76, 57n.80, 58n.84, 62n.102, 121n.34, 123n.41
Poliakoff, Michael	99n.57
Poplutz, Uta	100n.58
Rabbow, Paul	103n.73, 113n.8
Ranocchia, Graziano	29n.96, 73n.133
Reale, Giovanni	34n.2
Rees, D. A.	40n.26, 83n.5
Reydams-Schils, G.	50n.58, 121n.34
Rhodes, James N.	12n.35, 31n.105, 111n.1, 149n.137, 153n.154, 158n.169, 158n.171, 159n.174, 161n.180, 161n.181
Rofé, Alexander	16n.47
Romilly, Jacqueline de	89n.23
Runia, David T.	1n.3, 10n.33, 13n.40, 21n.67, 26n.83, 36n.9, 50n.58, 60n.92, 61n.97, 77n.147, 139n.106, 168n.205
Sand, Alexander	168n.205

Sanders, E. P.	11n.35
Sandmel, Samuel	3n.10, 4n.12
Sandnes, Karl Olav	31n.105, 50n.58, 151n.147
Santas, Gerasimos	74n.137
Satlow, Michael L.	103n.71
Schibli, Hermann S.	50n.58, 61n.93
Schmidt, Helmut	10n.33, 25n.80, 29n.96, 47n.52, 50n.58, 51n.58, 52n.63, 53n.68, 54n.71, 57n.80, 58n.84, 64n.108
Schofer, Jonathan Wyn	16n.49
Schweizer, Eduard	168n.205
Scott, Dominic	71n.126
Seland, Torrey	16n.47
Sheridan, Mark	99n.57, 104n.74
Sherman, Nancy	107n.83
Siegfried, Carl	59n.89, 104n.74, 169n.206
Sihvola, Juha	9n.33, 59n.85
Skarsten, Roald	53n.70
Smith, Margaret D.	87n.18, 115n.13
Sorabji, Richard	60n.91
Spanneut, Michel	10n.33, 60n.91
Sterling, Gregory E.	111n.1, 144n.122, 180n.237
Stowers, Stanley K.	13n.39, 14n.43, 16n.47, 17n.51, 81n.1, 187n.4, 188n.7, 188n.8
Svebakken, Hans	111n.1, 113n.6, 156n.162, 156n.163, 158n.169, 158n.170, 159n.172, 159n.173, 169n.208, 170n.210, 170n.211, 187n.2
Terian, Abraham	12n.35, 70n.122
Termini, Cristina	3n.7, 4n.12, 5n.15, 6n.20, 7n.22, 7n.23, 12n.35, 31n.105
Thesleff, Holger	71n.126
Tobin, Thomas H.	13n.39, 16n.47, 35n.6, 35n.7, 40n.24, 61n.92, 66n.115, 111n.1, 169n.206, 170n.211, 187n.2
Tramontano, Raffaele	111n.1
Valantasis, Richard	98n.53
Van Hoof, Lieve	114n.11
Vander Waerdt, P. A.	25n.80, 35n.5, 40n.26, 41n.27, 41n.28, 41n.29, 41n.30, 41n.31, 45n.43, 88n.21, 89n.21
Vian, Giovanni Maria	12n.35, 31n.105, 111n.1

Völker, Walther	10n.33, 100n.60, 104n.74, 121n.34
Warnach, Walter	182n.242
Wasserman, Emma	13n.39, 16n.47, 72n.129
Watson, Francis	179n.232
Weber, Reinhard	5n.14
Wedderburn, A. J. M.	177n.226
Wendland, Paul	95n.46
West, Martin L.	151n.148
Whitchurch, Irl G.	100n.60
Whittaker, John	34n.2, 37n.14, 40n.23, 41n.29, 69n.121, 71n.125, 72n.127
Williamson, Ronald	15n.46, 24n.76, 59n.88, 60n.91
Winston, David	10n.33, 19n.62, 29n.96, 50n.58, 57n.82, 60n.91, 104n.74, 121n.34, 130n.69, 168n.205
Wolfson, Harry A.	14n.43, 16-19, 24n.76, 31, 55n.75, 70n.122, 103n.71, 121n.34, 129n.69, 180n.237
Ziesler, J. A.	13n.38
Zeller, Dieter	71n.126

Lightning Source UK Ltd.
Milton Keynes UK
UKOW041917080513

210397UK00001B/198/P

9 781589 836181